AN INTRODUCTION TO THE INTERN
LAW OF ARMED CONFLICTS

This book provides a modern and basic introduction to a branch of international law constantly gaining in importance in international life, namely international humanitarian law (the law of armed conflict). It is constructed in a way suitable for self-study. The subject matters are discussed in self-contained chapters, allowing each to be studied independently of the others. Among the subject matters discussed are: the relationship between *jus ad bellum* and *jus in bello*; the historical evolution of international humanitarian law; the basic principles and sources of international humanitarian law; Martens clause; international and non-international armed conflicts; material, spatial, personal and temporal scope of the application of international humanitarian law; special agreements under international humanitarian law; the role of the International Committee of the Red Cross; targeting; objects specifically protected against attack; prohibited weapons; perfidy; reprisals; assistance of the wounded and sick; definition of combatants; protection of prisoners of war; protection of civilians; occupied territories; protective emblems; sea warfare; neutrality; and the implementation of international humanitarian law.

An Introduction to the International Law of Armed Conflicts

Robert Kolb and Richard Hyde

·H A R T·
PUBLISHING

OXFORD—PORTLAND OREGON
2008

Published in North America (US and Canada) by
Hart Publishing
c/o International Specialized Book Services
920 NE 58th Avenue, Suite 300
Portland, OR 97213-3786
USA
Tel: +1 503 287 3093 or toll-free: (1) 800 944 6190
Fax: +1 503 280 8832
E-mail: orders@isbs.com
Website: http://www.isbs.com

Hart Publishing, 16C Worcester Place, Oxford, OX1 2JW
Telephone: +44 (0)1865 517530 Fax: +44 (0)1865 510710
E-mail: mail@hartpub.co.uk
Website: http://www.hartpub.co.uk

British Library Cataloguing in Publication Data
Data Available

ISBN: 978-1-84113-799-5

Typeset by Forewords, Oxford
Printed and bound in Great Britain by
TJ International Ltd, Padstow, Cornwall

PREFACE

This book began life as a training course written for the Swiss Military by Robert Kolb. It should be noted that the course was initially conceived for use as a training aid for mid-level officers, of a number of different nationalities, and for this reason the chapters are simply written and self-contained. Richard Hyde became involved when this text was evolving into a book, and applied references and polish to the initial text. At this time some material was added to reflect the rapid development of the law under the impetus of new treaties and the jurisprudence of international and domestic courts. The book reflects the state of the law as of Easter 2008. The book can be treated as a whole, providing a wide ranging introduction to the Law of Armed Conflict, or dipped into and out of as desired. A wide-ranging bibliography, prepared with the assistance of Andreas Frutig, is provided for those who wish to explore particular areas in greater depth. It should be noted that although the book was initially written with military professionals in mind it should not be thought that the readership is thus restricted. The authors have attempted to make this text as accessible and readable as possible, in the hope that all readers with an interest in this important, now more than ever, area of law find this book useful. Of course, this book could not have been written without the help of a large number of people, to whom warm appreciation is extended, in particular Section 155 of the Swiss Army (Law of Armed Conflicts Section) with its head, as he then was, Col. Peter Hostettler, Catriona McCollam, Professor Robert Cryer of the University of Birmingham, Professor Olympia Bekou of the University of Nottingham and all the kind people at Hart Publishing, in particular Richard Hart, Mel Hamill and Rachel Turner. Obviously, all errors remain the responsibility of the authors.

Robert Kolb
Richard Hyde
July 2008

CONTENTS

TABLE OF CASES, DECISIONS, OPINIONS

TABLE OF TREATIES AND INTERNATIONAL INSTRUMENTS

INTERNATIONAL TREATIES AND CONVENTIONS

INTERNATIONAL CHARTERS, COVENANTS AND STATUTES

PART I

INTRODUCTION

THE LAW OF ARMED CONFLICT AS A BRANCH OF PUBLIC INTERNATIONAL LAW

Learning objectives: To understand the concept of public international law (PIL) and its relationship with the law of armed conflict (LOAC).

1. Since time immemorial, humans have divided themselves into innumerable groups, variously known as, amongst others, tribes, collectivities and states. Each of these groups gave themselves, more or less independently from each other, a certain form of public organisation. Thus, some groups were loosely organised as non-sedentary assemblages of family clans. Others were strictly militarily groupings, with a strong hierarchical element. Others became settled on a certain territory and developed forms of monarchy, republicanism or federalism. Over centuries, these groups have tended to evolve, and the current stage of this evolution is the modern state, with its complex relationship between legislative, executive and judicial branches. The groups that were not conquered or subjugated by another group retained their sovereignty and remained in a condition of relative independence from each other. These groups are not subject to any higher entity with the right to decide policy to be applied within their territory.

2. Since the beginnings of their existence, all groups and public collectivities have engaged in relations with one another. These relations can be categorised as either relations of peace or relations of war. Contact between groups was unavoidable. One of the first forms of contact was belligerent: the groups came to struggle for control over a certain territory or resources, or over the primacy of their own gods when compared with foreign ones. War is perhaps the most ancient form of inter-group relationship. However, soon peaceful relations also came into play. Embassies were exchanged; agreements were concluded in order to protect commercial exchanges or to enable the extradition of fugitives; the erection of common installations such as irrigation aqueducts was organised. With the passing of time, the peaceful relations between states developed considerably, mirroring the increase in their general interdependence and the increase in globalisation. Thus, today, there is hardly any question which is not regulated by some rules of conduct agreed between different states. It is not only traditional inter-state questions, such as war, diplomacy, treaties and the peaceful settlement of disputes that are matters of international regulation, but also subjects such as labour, human rights, crimes,

intellectual property, protection of the environment, financial policy and immigration. At the same time, belligerent relationships have not been erased from the face of the earth. States still use force in their dealings with foreign entities and this use of force, whether legal or illegal, legitimate or illegitimate, needs some regulation.

3. We have seen that the various groups that comprise humanity have not remained isolated from one another. They engage in relations, ranging from hostile to cooperative. All human relations need some form of regulation. Humanity cannot live in anarchy; without some form of shared expectations, proper relations are impossible. One could thus say, '*ubi societas, ibi regula*'; where there is society, there must be rules; without rules, there is no social compact of any kind. The common feature shared by any 'regulation' is that it sets out rules of behaviour. A rule tells you that in a given set of circumstances, you may or must do this and/or that, or that in these circumstances you may or must not do this and/or that. Hence, the expression *pacta sunt servanda* or 'treaties must be observed' embodies a rule.[1] Why? Because the expression tells you that, as long as certain circumstances exist, for example if there is no duress, something, in this case the execution of the agreement, ought to be done. This is the core of any rule. Regulation can take different forms, since rules can be of different natures.

4. A rule can express a moral, religious, social, political or any other form of imperative or counsel. Thus, the rule 'I should behave as socially expected when I am invited somewhere' is an imperative expression of the behaviour I should engage in when interacting with my hosts and other guests, and also an indication of what I should do if I want to be invited again. For if I bring no present where it is expected, or put my feet on the table where that is considered unsuitable, it is certain that I will not to be invited again. The rule that we have considered so far appears to us as a moral and a social rule. However, human groups also use another form of rules to encapsulate their relations: legal rules. These rules characteristically regulate matters concerning the external dealings of subjects, rather than internal morality; they concentrate on matters important for a proper functioning of society which cannot simply be left to the personal judgement of any single member of the society, so-called socially relevant matters of importance; and they are obligatory on the persons concerned. In other words, legal norms are compulsory. The last element is the most well known. Law is binding on its subjects; it is compulsory; its rules are coercive.

Whether a matter is regulated only by moral or social rules, or also by legal rules, depends on the choices of a particular society at a given time. Homosexual relations were for a long time only the object of moral and religious rules; only later did they become the object of legal rules, originally rules of prohibition and criminal sanction, and today rules of family law.

5. We have seen that any society has rules, and that among these rules there will be legal rules. In the world of today, there are innumerable societies: the family, the football club, the county, the trade union, the Church, and so on. However, only

---

[1] Vienna Convention on the Law of Treaties (adopted 22 May 1969, entered into force 27 January 1980) 1155 UNTS 331 Art 26.

two large and important societies are of interest to us here: first, the society of individuals organised in the form of a state, which will be examined in this paragraph; and secondly, the society of states, which will be examined in the paragraph below. These are the two greatest and most inclusive societies. First, there is the state: it binds together all the people linked by a common nationality, and to a large extent all of the other people present on a territory, in a form of social compact. To this end, the state is organised by a series of legal rules. These rules can be found in the constitution, statutes, regulations of the public administration and case law of judicial tribunals. These legal norms are mainly concerned with the regulation of mutual dealings among the private citizens and corporations situated on the territory of the state: marriage, labour contracts, investment, wrongful acts, and so on. They will also regulate the relationship between private persons and the public organs of the state, as well as the relationships between the public organs themselves. Here one may mention tax law, which governs the relations between private individuals and the state, or the separation of powers between the various organs of the state, which governs the relationship between state organs.

6. However, relationships do not stop at the boundary of the state. States have relations among themselves; they conclude treaties in order to regulate their action in a given field, for example the treatment they will accord to foreign investment. The law of one state alone cannot pretend to regulate these dealings. To be sure, each state could claim that its internal law should apply to the investment. However, how would it be possible to choose one of the two concurrent municipal laws without compromising the equality of the two states, without subjugating one to the other? Here, a common law which is external to both states and which applies equally to them, being superior to the internal law of each of them, is needed. This common law, which regulates the relations between states and is independent from the internal legal order of each of them, is called public international law (PIL).

7. We must now understand the definitions which are given to PIL. One of these definitions is that PIL is that body of law which is composed for its greater part of the principles and rules of conduct which states (and some other subjects) feel themselves bound to observe, and therefore, do commonly observe in their relations with each other.[2] Why is the term 'some other subjects' included? Another definition makes this point clearer:

> International law is the body of rules which are legally binding on states in their intercourse with each other. These rules are primarily those which govern the relations of states, but states are not the only subjects of international law. International organizations and, to some extent, also individuals may be subjects of rights conferred and duties imposed by international law.[3]

The rules of international law that envisage individuals as subjects are mainly those pertaining to human rights law and to international criminal law. International law grants the individual some fundamental rights, but also subjects him or her to some fundamental duties, the transgression of which can be criminally sanctioned. To

---

[2] I Shearer, *Starke's International Law*, 11th edn (Oxford, OUP, 1994) 3.
[3] R Jennings and A Watts (eds), *Oppenheim's International Law Volume 1: Peace*, 9th edn (Harlow, Longman, 1992) 4.

international organisations and individuals one can add subjects such as insurgents, the International Committee of the Red Cross (ICRC) and the Holy See, all of which participate to international law transactions, albeit that their participation is limited to a particular sector. Hence, PIL regulates not only the relations between states, but also the dealings of some other subjects, such as international organisations.[4]

8. 'Public international law' must be distinguished from 'private international law'. We have seen that the internal law of the state is mainly responsible for the regulation of relationships between individuals. Of course, these relationships do not stop at the boundary of states; they straddle across such boundaries. For example, there are today millions of marriages between citizens of different states. The question then arises as to which law should be applicable to such a mixed nationality marriage. Is it the law of the husband's state of origin or that of the wife's state of origin? Should the marriage and the family arising from it be subjected to the law of the husband or the bride, to the law of the place of celebration of the marriage or to the law of the habitual residence of the couple? This collision of different internal laws will be solved by the application of particular rules. These rules indicate which internal law shall apply to what cases and when a particular internal law will have preference. The point here is not to subject these dealings to a common superior law, such as PIL; it is rather to decide which municipal law applies. This is the proper object of private international law rules. Private international law is a province of the internal law of each state which indicates which law, foreign or domestic, shall apply in a given set of circumstances, where some dealing involving foreign elements is at stake: transnational contracts, transnational company mergers, transnational inheritance, or transnational marriage are examples of situations where some consideration of private international law is necessary. Obviously, if questions of private international law are regulated by treaties between states, a public international law element is introduced into the question: the treaty itself will be regulated by public international law, and questions regarding its conclusion or modification must be dealt with by considering the applicable PIL norms, but its content will remain one of private international law.

9. What are the main provinces of public international law? In other words: what is public international law composed of? As we have seen, PIL can be used to regulate any matter of common interest among states: it can regulate the recognition of marriages or of intellectual property patents, as it can regulate the status of the moon or other celestial bodies. There is thus no point in trying to define PIL from the point of view of its possible content: it can encompass any question and its possible content is limitless. The line between what is left to the states, the so-called domestic jurisdiction, and what is regulated by international law is substantially open-ended and varies over time. However, there are some core areas that PIL has always, to some extent, regulated, because these areas of common concern can only

---

[4] See, eg: Vienna Convention on the Law of Treaties between States and International Organizations or between International Organizations (adopted 21 March 1986, not yet in force) UN Doc A/CONF.129/15 available at <http://untreaty.un.org/ilc/texts/instruments/english/conventions/1_2_1986.pdf> accessed 14 May 2008.

be regulated at that level of a common law binding all of the states. What are these core matters that must be regulated by PIL? One may list the following:

a) *The sources of the law*, that is, the recognised means through which PIL may be created and modified.[5]

b) *The subjects of the law*, that is, the persons and entities to which the legal order grants rights and on which it imposes duties. For example, PIL applies to states, international organisations, insurgents, and so on. Each of these subjects must be defined and its rights and duties examined.

c) *The relationship between municipal and international law*. We have seen that all of the states possess an internal legal order, and that states in their mutual dealings obey PIL rules. The relationship between these two legal orders, the municipal and the international, must be defined. For example, in cases of contradiction between a rule of internal law and a rule of international law, which one should prevail?

d) *International responsibility*. The question here concerns the consequences of wrongful acts by the subjects of the law. What happens if a state breaches a rule of PIL? The law of state responsibility responds to that question.[6]

e) *Peaceful settlement of disputes*. In every relationship between human beings or entities, there will at some stage emerge some disputes or differences of opinion. These may need to be solved if they hamper the normal and friendly relationship between the members of a society. The law relating to the peaceful settlement of disputes regulates the means and methods of solving disputes.

f) *The regime applicable to common spaces*, namely the high seas, Antarctica, the Arctic and outer space. There are some spaces which are not subjected to the sovereignty of a single state. These spaces are common to all states. Thus, it falls to the common law applicable between the states, namely PIL, to define their precise status and to set out the rules governing activities in these common spaces.[7]

g) *Diplomacy*. This is the oldest means of intercourse between states. It is regulated by international law rules.[8]

h) *The law of warfare or the LOAC*. If armed conflict breaks out, be it legally or illegally, legitimately or illegitimately, some rules must be applicable in order to regulate the relationship between the states engaged in hostility. For example, some regulation is needed in order to provide for armistices and truces; in order to protect and facilitate the exchange of prisoners; in order to ban certain weapons and means of warfare considered to be far too

---

[5] Statute of the International Court of Justice (adopted 26 June 1945, entered into force 24 October 1945) 15 UNCIO 355 Art 38(1).

[6] ILC Articles on Responsibility of States for Internationally Wrongful Acts UNGA Res 56/83 (12 December 2001) UN Doc A/RES/56/83, available at: <http://untreaty.un.org/ilc/texts/instruments/english/draft%20articles/9_6_2001.pdf> (last accessed 24th May 2008).

[7] See, eg: United Nations Convention on the Law of the Sea (adopted 10 December 1982, entered into force 16 November 1994) 1833 UNTS 3 and the Treaty on Principles Governing the Activities of States in the Exploration and Use of Outer Space, Including the Moon and Other Celestial Bodies (adopted 25 January 1967, entered into force 10 October 1967) 610 UNTS 205.

[8] See, eg: Vienna Convention on Diplomatic Relations (adopted 18 April 1961, entered into force 24 April 1964) 500 UNTS 95.

destructive to be permitted; and in order to protect the rights of the states that do not participate in the war.

10. We thus see that PIL covers questions relating to peacetime and questions relating to war. The title of the classical book by Hugo Grotius, the celebrated Dutch jurist, *De jure belli ac pacis* or 'Of the law of war and of the law of peace',[9] first published in 1625, shows this indissoluble link, which permeates the body of PIL. The LOAC is thus a branch of PIL. More precisely, it is that branch which regulates the conduct of warfare, the protection of persons and of goods and the conditions of the states not participating in a war, known as neutrals. This branch of the law is set in motion every time the peace breaks down and hostilities take place.

Comprehension check:

a) What is PIL? What are its main provinces?
b) How does PIL differ from the internal law of a state?
c) What is the difference between PIL and private international law?
d) To which legal order does the LOAC belong to? Why?

Answers: (these are just typical answers).

a) PIL regulates the legal relations between states and some other subjects. Alternatively: PIL is the legal order which regulates those relationships among states and some other subjects. The main provinces of PIL are sources, subjects, relationship of PIL to municipal law, responsibility, settlement of disputes, rules applicable to common spaces, diplomacy and warfare.
b) PIL is the law regulating the relationships *between* the states, or other subjects, whereas internal law mainly regulates the relationships between individuals and corporations *within* a state.
c) PIL is a legal order regulating inter-state relations, whereas private international law is a part of the internal law of the states deciding which of local or foreign law will apply to an inter-individual relationship that transcends the boundaries of a state. For example, private international law will apply to mixed marriages and will provide the rules by which a decision can be made as to whether Swiss or French law will apply to a Swiss-French mixed marriage.
d) The LOAC is a part of PIL. This is so because the LOAC contains legal norms which regulate the dealings of states when they are at war. The LOAC thus concerns inter-state relations in a particular context. Moreover, it concerns legal inter-state relations, since it posits binding norms. Hence, it is a part of PIL, which is the legal order regulating inter-state relations.

---

[9] H Grotius, *De Jure Belli ac Pacis* (Buffalo, Hein, 1995 [1625]).

2

JUS AD BELLUM: MAIN COMPONENTS

Learning objectives: To understand and briefly describe the law relating to the maintenance of peace.

1. The Latin expression *jus ad bellum* means 'the right to resort to force' or 'the right to wage war'. Who may use force in international relations? In what circumstances may he or she use force? The rules grouped together under the name *jus ad bellum* deal with these questions. To begin, it is helpful to note that in any legal system, the right to resort to force is limited. Not everyone has the right to use force on any occasion he or she sees fit. If this were not true, no peace and no order could be maintained, as anyone would be allowed to influence or intimidate anyone else by physical force. This would be anarchy rather than society. In the municipal law of the states, the use of force has been quite radically monopolised. It is ordinarily only the state which can use force, through its police and military branches.[1] The private individual is required to enforce his or her claims not by force, but by recourse to tribunals, which are made available to him or her by the state.

In international society, there is no single super-state in which to vest such a monopoly on the use of force. There is no 'higher authority' with respect to the states which could have 'expropriated' their power to use force. Rather, there are many states existing in a situation of sovereign equality and, therefore, states are not subjected to an all-embracing higher authority. The right to use force in such an environment remains to a large extent allotted to the states that comprise disorganised international society. Hence, in international law, one may say that the right to use force, or the *jus ad bellum*, is attached to the states. However, the requirements and limitations imposed on the exercise of that right have varied over time.

2. In the period of classical international law, spanning from the 18th to the turn of the twentieth century, international law allowed each state to use force against another state as an unfettered exercise of its discretion. The decision to go to war was thus left to a free choice of every state. There were no limitations on that right, except for the formal procedural rule that war had to be declared.[2] This declaration

---

[1] Although some societies may allow a private citizen to resort to force in self-defence. See, eg: *Beckford v R* [1988] 1 AC 130 (PC), 144.

[2] Codified in Hague Convention (III) relative to the Opening of Hostilities (adopted 18 October 1907, entered into force 26 January 1910) (1907) 205 CTS 264 Art 1.

of war was important for the third states: it signalled to them that a formal war was being fought and put them on notice that they must act to claim their rights of neutrality.[3] Hence, during this period international law granted an unlimited right to resort to war, an unlimited *jus ad bellum*.

At the end of the 19th, and particularly at the beginning of the 20th, centuries, wars became increasingly destructive. Nationalism transformed war in an affair of state survival, and accompanying the fight for the state was a battle for the survival of a unique culture represented by a people whose existence as a coherent whole could be historically established. Consequently, all forces and all people of the state were called upon to contribute to the war effort. The potential extent of the war increased dramatically. Moreover, modern technology developed means of destruction of previously unheard proportions: for example, mustard gas, means of aviation that were able to bomb whole towns situated many miles behind the front lines and modern missiles.[4] For this reason, efforts were made to put in place stricter controls on the use of such devastating force. Thus, in this period states attempted to use international law to place fresh limitations on the resort to war through treaties adopted by a large majority of states. In these treaties the states committed themselves to a more restrictive *jus ad bellum*.

3. One of the first treaties that attempted to limit the *jus ad bellum* of states was the Covenant of the League of Nations.[5] In Articles 10–16, the Covenant required states to exhaust a procedure aimed at the peaceful settlement of disputes before resorting to war. In certain cases, resort to war was absolutely prohibited. However, the Covenant did not prohibit all recourses to force. It only attempted to limit the *jus ad bellum* of states, but it did not 'expropriate' the right to resort to force. A further step towards such an 'expropriation' was taken in 1928 by the Kellogg-Briand (or Paris) Pact,[6] to which all but four states adhered. It prohibited war as an instrument of national policy and required disputes to be solved by peaceful means. However, the Pact of Paris was devoid of any mechanism for enforcement. It contained norms, but no machinery to implement them. Of course, these two attempts to outlaw war failed. The reason was not so much the imperfections and timidity of the legal instruments, it was rather the lack of political will of the great powers, Great Britain and France, who failed to back the League of Nations and refused to implement the system of collective security embodied in the texts, and also the absence of the US from the League. The outbreak of World War II illustrated the shortcomings of this system.

4. A new, and much stronger, stance was taken in the Charter of the United Nations.[7] The Charter is a treaty binding on all states party to it. It purports, to a large extent, to prohibit unilateral uses of force by states because of the terrible experiences which that liberty to go to war had imposed on international society,

---

[3] See generally: ch 34 below.

[4] See generally: ch 5 below.

[5] (Adopted 28 June 1919, adopted 1 October 1920) 225 CTS 195.

[6] General Treaty for the Renunciation of War as an Instrument of National Policy (adopted 27 August 1928, entered into force 24 June 1929) 94 LNTS 57 (Kellogg-Briand Pact, or Pact of Paris).

[7] Charter of the United Nations (adopted 26 June 1945, entered into force 24 October 1945) 892 UNTS 119 (UN Charter).

particularly in the two devastating world wars. The main provisions of the Charter concerning the *jus ad bellum* are Articles 2(4) and 39–51.

Article 2(4), which sets out one of the principles of the United Nations, states:

> All members shall refrain in their international relations from the threat or use of force against the territorial integrity or political independence of any state, or in any other manner inconsistent with the Purposes of the United Nations.

This provision thus contains a strict prohibition on any unilateral use of force by single states or by self-proclaimed coalitions of states. This provision is today considered to be part and parcel of customary international law and hence binds all states of the world independent of the conventional nature of the Charter.[8] The use of force is prohibited only with respect to international relations, that is, mainly, in the relations between states. Civil war is not covered: thus, insurrection is not prohibited by the Charter, and neither is it prohibited for a government to use force in order to put down a rebellion taking place on its territory. Article 2(4) covers all uses of military 'force'. This concept is larger than the concept of 'war'. War is a complex question of the legal relationship between states rather than simply being a question of fact. Actual fighting is not essential to the existence of a state of war and there may be wars where no actual fighting takes place: for example, this was the case between some Latin American nations and Germany during World War II. These nations waged war on Germany without having actually fought at all. The essence of war is a subjective element: it is the will to consider oneself at war with another state.[9] This subjective will is traditionally expressed by a declaration of war. Without the will to be in a state of war, expressed explicitly or implicitly, there is no war. Hence, during the 1930s many states resorted to the use of armed force and at the same time expressly disclaimed any intention of being involved in a war. The bombing of Corfu by Italy in 1923 and the invasion of Manchuria by Japan in 1931 are examples of this. Article 2(4) closes this loophole in the pre-World War II prohibitions by ruling out any use of force, whatever its legal qualification, and not only prohibiting the formal resort to war.

Article 51 of the Charter creates an exception to the prohibitive rule found in Article 2(4). It is concerned with self-defence of states. It reads as follows:

> Nothing in the present Charter shall impair the inherent right of individual or collective self-defence if an armed attack occurs against a Member of the United Nations, until the Security Council has taken the measures necessary to maintain international peace and security. Measures taken by Members in the exercise of this right of self-defence shall be immediately reported to the Security Council and shall not in any way affect the authority and responsibility of the Security Council under the present Charter to take at any time such action as it deems necessary in order to maintain or restore international peace and security.

As an exception to Article 2(4), Article 51, in principle, must be narrowly construed. It allows a state that is attacked to defend itself by way of military force and to call upon other states to come to its defence. This right of self-defence continues at least

---

[8] *Military and Paramilitary Activities in and against Nicaragua (Nicaragua v United States of America)* (Merits) [1986] ICJ Rep 14 paras [187]–[190].

[9] See, eg: *Dalmia Cement Ltd v National Bank of Pakistan* (1984) 67 ILR 611.

up until the time that the collective security machinery of the Security Council begins to function and collective security measures are adopted. It may even continue indefinitely in time if the Security Council fails to take appropriate measures. The interpretation of Article 51 has been fraught with problems. These problems have mainly arisen when some states have constantly and abusively attempted to extend the reach of the exception. Thus, the whole question of pre-emptive self-defence, which is much discussed today, is located, as far as the law is concerned, within Article 51 of the Charter.

Finally, there are the powers of the Security Council of the United Nations. Under the Charter law, the Security Council functions as a sort of guardian of international peace and security. The Charter, in Chapter VII,[10] endows the Security Council with the power to take binding measures in order to safeguard international peace and security, or to restore it if it has already been broken. In Chapter VII we find the nucleus of a system of collective security: an organ representing the international community is granted an extraordinary array of powers to employ in order to suppress any uses of force and to repel any aggression. The voting rules in the Security Council, and particularly the right of veto given to the five permanent members of the Council,[11] obviously limit the possibilities of action by the Council to a more than negligible extent. The Council may also act in cases of threat to the peace, and thus pre-emptively. Hence, the scope of its allowed action is not limited to collective security in the narrow sense and may therefore extend beyond a reaction by all members against an aggressor. The role of the Council extends to a collective responsibility for world peace in the broad sense and has been broadened to encompass what are today often called 'human security' issues. Thus, during the 1990s, the Security Council undertook many actions in order, for example, to halt civil wars and the humanitarian catastrophes linked with them, such as in Somalia and Liberia; to restore democratically elected regimes, such as in Haiti; or to build up new national structures, for example in East Timor. The key provision that governs the action of the Council is Article 39 of the Charter, which states:

> The Security Council shall determine the existence of any threat to the peace, breach of the peace, or act of aggression and shall make recommendations, or decide what measures shall be taken in accordance with Articles 41 and 42, to maintain or restore international peace and security.

Articles 41 and 42 set out in a non-exhaustive way the types of measures the Council may take in order to maintain or restore the peace: namely peaceful coercive means, such as embargoes, which are dealt with in Article 41, or military coercive means, such as enforcement by a military force set up under the auspices of the Security Council, which are dealt with by Article 42. We can thus see that the Security Council has a right to use force in the cases contemplated in Article 39, namely threats to the peace, breaches of the peace or acts of aggression. The Council *may* resort to force in these cases, but, obviously, it is under no obligation to do so. Instead, it can either refrain from acting at all, for example because of an exercise of the veto, or decide to use only peaceful sanctions.

---

[10] UN Charter Arts 39–51.
[11] UN Charter Art 27.

5. This short overview has showed that modern international law, in the era of the United Nations Charter, to a large extent limits the right of states to resort not only to war in the narrow sense, but also to force in general. The *jus ad bellum* of states has been limited conspicuously. One may even say that the Charter has created a sort of *jus contra bellum*, a legal regime devised to prevent the use of force and war. Since the nineteenth century, the law has thus shifted to a remarkable extent. Indeed, it has completely reversed itself: where it previously recognised an unlimited right to resort to force, it today requires states not to use force unless some narrowly defined exceptions are met. Thus, permission has been transformed into prohibition. Obviously, we are talking about the legal position. In fact, war and use of force is equally possible today as it was in the nineteenth century. No one can stop a powerful or determined state from resorting to force, just as one cannot stop a powerful or determined criminal from killing or robbing in domestic society, despite the existence of the criminal law. The point that must be stressed is that the legal qualification of these acts has, as far as international law is concerned, drastically changed.

6. We may thus summarise that the expression *jus ad bellum* relates to the question of who is allowed to use force and in what circumstances, and hence can be used to describe the legal rules regulating resort to force by states. A state is allowed to use force if it is attacked and it is exercising its right of self-defence under Article 51 of the UN Charter, or if it is invited to exercise collective self-defence on behalf of a state which has been attacked. A state is also allowed to use force against another state if it acts on behalf of the Security Council, or by way of an authorisation of the Security Council made under Chapter VII of the Charter. Thus, by Resolution 678 of 29 November 1990,[12] the Security Council authorised all Member States to use 'all necessary means' to implement Resolution 660, which required Iraq to withdraw from Kuwait. When the Iraqis failed to comply with Resolution 660 by 15 January 1991, the date on which the ultimatum expired, on 17 January coalition forces commenced military operations under the code name 'Operation Desert Storm.' These coalition states based their action on the authorisation given by the Security Council in Resolution 678 which allowed them to 'use all necessary means'. Hence, one may say that these states possessed the right to use force under the UN Charter; they possessed a *jus ad bellum*.

7. At the end of this chapter, it is useful to mention a possible slight variation in the use of the term *jus ad bellum*.

   a) Sometimes, the term is used to denote a *subjective entitlement* to use force. It is in this sense that we have used the term in the foregoing paragraphs. A state A has the right to use force in circumstance B. It thus has a *jus ad bellum*, a right to use force, in these circumstances. This is a subjective entitlement because we are just considering its personal right to use force in given circumstances.
   b) However, sometimes the term *jus ad bellum* is used to designate the whole *body of norms* regulating the question as regarding the resort to force. Here, we are not dealing with the subjective entitlement of a state in a specific context.

[12] UN Doc S/RES/678.

Rather, we are dealing with the question of the use of force in an objective and general setting, ie in public international law. Hence, one may say that the Charter of the United Nations contains important norms as to the *jus ad bellum*. One may talk of the *jus ad bellum* of the Charter.

The precise sense of the phrase *jus ad bellum*, subjective or objective, has to be found from the context of its use in a particular sentence. It has thus a double sense, as is the case with many words of ordinary language, such as 'football', which may mean either American football or soccer.

Comprehension check:

a)   What does the term *jus ad bellum* mean?

b)   Which are the main provisions relating to the *jus ad bellum* today?

c)   In what sense (subjective or objective) is the term *jus ad bellum* used in the following extracts:

i)   'The *jus ad bellum*, or right to go to war, had been claimed by factually independent powers long before the concept of sovereignty was formulated'.[13]

ii)   'In particular, this volume avoids all questions as to the legality of recourse to the use of inter-state force in accordance with the *jus ad bellum* ...'[14]

Answers:

a)   The term *jus ad bellum* designates the conditions under which a state, or perhaps eventually another subject of public international law, may resort to force in international relations. In a subjective sense it denotes the entitlement of a particular state to use force in a given set of circumstances. In an objective sense it designates the legal norms which set out the conditions of legality of a resort to force.

b)   The main provisions on the use of force are today to be found in the Charter of the United Nations, one of the most important contemporary treaties. The norms regulating the use of force are found essentially in Article 2(4), which prohibits the unilateral use of force by states; Article 51, which allows, by way of exception, the use of force in cases of self-defence; and Chapter VII, Articles 39*ff* of the Charter, which sets out the specific powers of the Security Council in the field of the maintenance of international peace and security.

c)   Statement (1): subjective. It is the entitlement and claim by the individual state which is at stake. Statement (2): objective. It is a reference to the law relating to the use of force.

---

[13] B Simma (ed), *The Charter of the United Nations—A Commentary: Volume I*, 2nd edn (Oxford, OUP, 2002) 72.

[14] Y Dinstein, *The Conduct of Hostilities under the Law of International Armed Conflict* (Cambridge, CUP, 2004) 2.

3

JUS IN BELLO: MAIN COMPONENTS

Learning objectives: To understand and briefly describe the law relating to the conduct of warfare.

1. The Latin expression *jus in bello* means the rules relating to the conduct of warfare. Once hostilities have begun, or a state of war has been constituted by a declaration of war, there is a need for some rules to regulate the relationships that arise as a result of the use of force or the state of hostility. It is necessary to confer binding force to truces; it is necessary to mutually ban some means of warfare because of their excessive destructiveness, for example poisoned weapons; it is necessary to prohibit some means and methods of warfare because of the general disapproval they elicit, for example enlisting children in combat roles and the use of perfidy; it is necessary to protect the victims, or potential victims, of the war, such as military personnel placed *hors de combat* (the wounded and sick or prisoners of war) or the civilian population. War is a social phenomenon, albeit one of conflict; however, it does not take place in a vacuum of legal rules. Even warfare has its constraints and limitations. The rules responsible for regulating and limiting the phenomenon of armed conflict by spelling out the rights and duties of the belligerents and of the third states not participating in the armed conflict are called the law of armed conflict (LOAC). The term international humanitarian law (IHL) is seen today as practically synonymous with the LOAC. We will return to this point below.

2. In a very useful book on the LOAC, the following helpful introduction is given to this body of public international law rules:

> International Humanitarian Law (IHL) can be defined as the branch of international law limiting the use of violence in armed conflicts by: a) sparing those who do not or no longer directly participate in hostilities; b) limiting the violence to the amount necessary to achieve the aim of the conflict, which can be—independently of the causes fought for—only to weaken the military potential of the enemy. This definition leads to the basic principles of IHL:
>
> — the distinction between civilians and combatants;
>
> — the prohibition to attack those *hors de combat*;
>
> — the prohibition to inflict unnecessary suffering;
>
> — the principle of necessity; and

— the principle of proportionality.

This definition however also shows the inherent limits of IHL:

— it does not prohibit the use of violence;

— it can not protect all those affected by an armed conflict;

— it can not prohibit a party to overcome the enemy;

— IHL presupposes that parties to an armed conflict have rational aims.[1]

We will return to all these principles.

3. Throughout your studies you will notice that the law of armed conflict (LOAC) is often denoted by different terms. In the passage quoted above, the authors use the term 'international humanitarian law' (IHL) to refer to the branch of the law that was formerly called the LOAC. In effect, four terms are frequently used in a more or less interchangeable way.

   a) First, there is the oldest term, the law of war or the law of warfare, or the laws of war. An equivalent of these terms would be the often-used neo-Latin expression *jus in bello*, which literally means law in war.

   b) Then the term 'the LOAC' came into common usage. It was brought into existence by the 1949 Geneva Conventions which, in their Common Article 2, use the words 'armed conflict'.[2] This term was introduced by the Conventions with the intention of increasing the number of conflicts covered by the norms regulating state action in this area. The 'state of war', which previously governed the application of law of war norms, does not cover all actual fighting. It rather depends upon the free choice of a state to be at war with another. This subjective will is normally expressed in a formal declaration, such as a declaration of war. Conversely, the term 'armed conflict' encompasses all actual fighting, whether it is formally qualified as war by the concerned states or not. The term 'the LOAC' hence expresses this shift from 'war' to 'armed conflict' in the coverage of the law. The use of the phrase 'the LOAC' makes clear that the rules protecting the victims and limiting the means and methods of fighting are applicable to all situations where hostilities actually take place and does not remain limited to formal and declared wars. Thus, a dangerous and unwelcome gap in the protection of the LOAC norms was filled.

   c) Finally, there is the term international humanitarian law, or IHL. This is the youngest term. It originates from the Red Cross Movement, which first used it to describe the essential content of the modern law of warfare, as expressed in

---

[1] M Sassoli and A Bouvier, *How does Law Protect in War? Cases, Documents and Teaching Materials on Contemporary Practice in International Humanitarian Law: Volume I*, 2nd edn (Geneva, ICRC, 2006) 81–82.

[2] Geneva Convention I for the Amelioration of the Condition of the Wounded and Sick in Armed Forces in the Field (adopted 12 August 1949, entered into force 21 October 1950) 75 UNTS 31; Geneva Convention II for the Amelioration of the Condition of Wounded, Sick and Shipwrecked Members of Armed Forces at Sea (adopted 12 August 1949, entered into force 21 October 1950) 75 UNTS 85; Geneva Convention III relative to the Treatment of Prisoners of War (adopted 12 August 1949, entered into force 21 October 1950) 75 UNTS 135; and Geneva Convention IV Relative to the Protection of Civilian Persons in Time of War (adopted 12 August 1949, entered into force 21 October 1950) 75 UNTS 287, common Art 2.

the Geneva Conventions. The focus of the 1899 and 1907 Hague Conventions had been on the means and methods of warfare conducted by belligerents. The Geneva Conventions shifted focus to the protection of the victims of war, such as wounded and sick military personnel, prisoners of war and civilians. The widespread and ruthless atrocities committed against prisoners and civilians by the Axis powers before and during World War II were the reasons for this shift. Today, IHL is the most frequently used term. It can be taken as synonymous with the term 'the LOAC'. This will be the case in this book. However, one must note that the term IHL can also be taken more narrowly. It can be seen as referring only to that part of the LOAC which aims at the protection of potential victims of the war, whereas some other rules, such as, for example, the rules concerning combat between warships, prizes at sea or neutrality, would be covered only be the term 'the LOAC'.

4. What are the main branches of the LOAC? First, we should note that there are three main provinces to this area of law, although the first two areas are intimately interlinked.

a) The LOAC first regulates, by way of prohibitions, the allowed *means and methods of warfare*. The law in this area does not enumerate what is allowed. As states are sovereign, it is supposed that they are free to use all means of warfare without needing a specific allowance to be given to them.[3] Conversely, the law generally or specifically prohibits certain means and methods which are considered to be excessive. Such prohibited means and methods are of different types: they may relate to weapons, for example poisoned weapons; to actual conduct, for example perfidy; to the use of certain classes of persons as military personnel, for example children; to announcements and declarations, for example refusal of quarter, which involves announcing that no prisoners will be taken and that all those surrendering will be killed. Since this 'means and methods' aspect of the LOAC was codified in part by the 1899 and 1907 Hague Conventions,[4] lawyers often speak of this area of law as 'Hague Law'. This branch of the law spans all theatres of war and mediums of combat: land warfare, sea warfare and air warfare, even if the last is more loosely regulated.

b) Secondly, the LOAC regulates, by way of positive injunctions and negative prohibitions, the *protection of so-called 'protected persons'*, that is the potential or actual victims of armed conflict. These are persons who no longer participate in an armed conflict, or who never did. These persons are wounded and sick combatants, combatants who have laid down their arms, and have therefore been captured and accorded prisoners of war status, and civilians. The law containing norms ensuring their protection is to be found in the four Geneva Conventions. For this reason lawyers often call this branch of the law 'Geneva Law'. This branch of the law also spans over all theatres of war; land, sea and air. Geneva Convention II specifically concerns

---

[3] See also: *The Case of the SS Lotus* (*Turkey v France*) PCIJ Rep Series A No 10.

[4] See especially: Hague Convention (IV) respecting the Laws and Customs of War on Land and its annex: Regulations concerning the Laws and Customs of War on Land (adopted 18 October 1907, entered into force 26 January 1910) (1907) 205 CTS 227.

sea warfare. Air warfare is less precisely regulated, except for air to land hostilities, where the general rules applicable to land warfare are relevant.

c) Thirdly, the LOAC regulates the relationship between belligerent states on the one hand, and states that do not participate in the conflict on the other. Third states which stay aloof from the conflict are called 'neutral states', provided they fulfil certain conditions. The regulation of the mutual rights and duties of belligerent and neutral states is the proper role of the 'law of neutrality', which is a particular branch of the LOAC. It is particularly important for states which have the status of permanent neutrality, such as Switzerland. The main enumerated rules on neutrality are those codified in 1907 by Hague Convention V.[5]

5. All of these great areas of the LOAC contain a set of general principles and many detailed rules. These principles and rules are directed at two questions. First, some concern the *applicability of the law*. Secondly, others relates to *substantive prohibitions, rights, duties, and powers*. In effect, every time we are confronted with a concrete situation, we must first decide if the LOAC applies to it at all.[6] This may not be the case. Thus, in a situation of internal disturbances that do not rise to the level of an armed conflict, the LOAC does not formally apply. Once we have established that the LOAC applies, if it in fact does so, we must turn to the substantive provisions that require a certain course of conduct. Hence, for example, if someone is a lawful combatant, and therefore enjoys the status of a prisoner of war once captured, Geneva Convention III will apply to them, as long as the state detaining them and the state of origin of the prisoner have ratified or acceded to that convention. Because the convention is applicable, there are a series of duties relating to the treatment of the prisoner that will apply: for example, the detaining state will be obliged to treat the prisoner humanely and to give the prisoner proper food and clothing, rules will govern the work performed by the prisoner and the conditions in which the prisoner may be kept, norms will regulate the freedom to receive mail, the discipline of the prisoner, their freedom of worship, the possibility of release in case of grave injury, and so on. The legal reasoning that must be applied when considering any rule of the LOAC thus rests on two steps: (1) first, a decision must be taken on the applicability of the LOAC to the particular situation at stake; (2) secondly, the substantive norms of the LOAC must be applied to the particular situation, if the question of applicability is resolved in the affirmative. We will encounter the most important rules concerning the applicability and substance of the LOAC in the chapters to come.

6. Traditionally, the rules of the LOAC just applied to armed conflicts between states, also known as *international armed conflicts* (IAC). Most conventional law applicable to armed conflicts, constituted in treaties concluded since 1864, contemplated the situation of inter-state war and purported to apply to it exclusively. This is the case for the Hague Conventions of 1899 and 1907 and also applies, almost without exception, to the rules contained in the Geneva Conventions and their

---

[5] Hague Convention V respecting the Rights and Duties of Neutral Powers and Persons in Case of War on Land (adopted 18 October 1907, entered into force 26 January 1910) (1907) 205 CTS 299, and see generally ch 34 below.

[6] See generally: chs 11–15 below.

Additional Protocol I.[7] However, there are some rules, which have increased in number since 1949, which apply to *non-international armed conflicts* (NIAC). These non-international armed conflicts are, roughly speaking, civil wars, where a government fights against rebels on its own territory. The main rules applicable to NIAC are found in Common Article 3 to the Geneva Conventions and in Additional Protocol II.[8] In NIAC, as in IAC, the applicable rules split into questions relating to the means and methods of warfare, the so-called 'Hague Law', and questions relating to the protection of war victims, so-called 'Geneva Law'. The rules of neutrality do not apply to NIAC unless the conflict is internationalised, for example through the involvement of foreign states in the fighting.

7. There are a series of rules that apply to both types of armed conflict, international and internal. This is certainly the case when we examine the main principles, for example the principle of distinction between civilians and military objectives, the prohibition of certain means of warfare and the prohibition of mistreatment of protected person. However, there are also rules which apply exclusively to international armed conflicts. There have always been fewer rules applicable in NIAC than in IAC, as states have always been more sensitive to limits placed on their freedom of action in civil wars. For example, norms relating to the status and treatment of prisoners of war and the rules relating to occupied territories are limited to IAC. Moreover, traditionally a series of prohibitions that were placed on means and methods of warfare, especially those norms that restricted the use of particular arms, were only applicable in IAC. Due to the fact that the normative frameworks applicable in IAC and NIAC are different, the law has traditionally presented a clear distinction between these two types of conflicts. However, in the last decade, under the impulsion of the United Nations Security Council, the International Criminal Tribunal for former Yugoslavia and the International Criminal Tribunal for Rwanda, and the Rome Statute on the International Criminal Court,[9] the two areas of the law have grown considerably closer. That is to say that many rules that formerly applied only in the context of an IAC are now considered to be applicable also in NIAC. It has been held by the ICTY that customary international law has thus evolved, enlarging the number of rules that are applicable to NIAC.[10]

Comprehension check:

a)   How does *jus in bello* distinguish itself from *jus ad bellum*?
b)   What are the main concerns of the LOAC?
c)   The terms 'the LOAC' and 'IHL' are synonymous. Is that statement correct?

---

[7] The exception is, of course, Geneva Conventions I–IV common Art 3.

[8] Protocol Additional to the Geneva Conventions of 12 August 1949, and relating to the Protection of Victims of Non-International Armed Conflicts (adopted 8 June 1977, entered into force 7 December 1978) 1125 UNTS 609.

[9] Rome Statute of the International Criminal Court (adopted 17 July 1998, entered into force 1 July 2002) 2187 UNTS 3.

[10] See especially: *Prosecutor v Tadic* (Decision on the Defence Motion for Interlocutory Appeal on Jurisdiction) IT-49-1-AR72 (2 October 1995) paras [96]–[127], and see generally below ch 32.

Answers:

a) *Jus in bello* concerns the rules relating to the conduct of warfare and the protection of war victims during the armed conflict. Its rules apply once hostilities or warfare has begun. They regulate only the questions arising out of the relationships of belligerence or neutrality. *Jus ad bellum* concerns the legality of the use of force under the law of peace. It does not regulate actual warfare and conduct during belligerency. It regulates the question of who may use force, when and for what ends. There is thus a neat distinction between these two areas.

b) The main areas regulated by the LOAC are the means and methods of warfare, the protection of war victims (the wounded and sick, prisoners and civilians) and neutrality.

c) The statement may be correct, since it can be observed that many ministries of foreign affairs, humanitarian actors, international institutions and legal writers use these two terms in a synonymous way. However, they can also be distinguished, the term IHL first being linked to the protection of war victims and eventually to the prohibited means and methods of warfare, the term 'the LOAC' being larger and additionally concerning matters such as sea warfare, prize law and neutrality.

4

THE SEPARATION BETWEEN *JUS AD BELLUM* AND *JUS IN BELLO* IN MODERN INTERNATIONAL LAW: EQUALITY OF THE BELLIGERENTS AND JUST WAR

Learning objectives: To learn about the relationship between *jus ad bellum* and *jus in bello* and to understand why questions of the lawfulness of the use of force are separated from questions of the obligations of the parties during armed conflict in modern International Law.

1. The *jus ad bellum* relates to the legality of a use of force in international relations. *Jus ad bellum* attempts to define when and by whom force may be used. Conversely, *jus in bello* deals with the conduct of the belligerents during an armed conflict or a belligerent occupation of territory. *Jus in bello* concentrates on indicating what the belligerent parties may or may not do during an armed conflict. From this brief review, we can see that *jus ad bellum* and *jus in bello* are related through their concern with the same material object, but each has a distinct perspective. Both deal with the use of force, but they regulate it in different ways. *Jus ad bellum* is concerned with the legality of the use of force. It attempts to answer the question, when may force be used? Conversely, *jus in bello* is concerned with the behaviour of the belligerent parties during the war. It attempts to answer the question, what should you do or not do when using force? *Jus ad bellum* relates to the justice of a particular use of force, whereas *jus in bello* relates more to the regulation of the use of force during an armed conflict and attempts to put limits on action during warfare.

2. The relationship between *jus ad bellum* and *jus in bello* has varied over time. During the Middle Ages and until the dawn on the modern era in the eighteenth century, the just war doctrine was predominant. This doctrine distinguished between wars dependant upon the perceived justice of the cause the belligerents were fighting for. A number of factors were considered when deciding whether a particular war satisfied the tests for justness. A war was considered just if:

  a) There was a just cause (*justa causa*). Examples of wars conducted with just cause were wars of self-defence, wars with the aim of avenging injuries and punishing wrongs, and wars with the aim of obtaining reparations for a prior illegal act committed by the adverse belligerent.

b) The lawful authority (*auctoritas publica*) sanctioned the war. The decision to fight the war must have been taken by the legitimate sovereign power. This power belongs exclusively to the state.

c) The belligerent had the right intention (*recta intentio*). The intention of the belligerent and the aims of the war had to remain linked to the just cause throughout the period of conflict: the purpose of the conflict had to remain, during the entire period of the conflict, limited to obtaining a proper sanction for the wrong that gave the just cause for war. The actions of the belligerent should not go beyond those necessary to achieve this purpose. Otherwise, the war was vitiated *ex post* and became unjust. By the same token, some rules of warfare had to be respected. The respect shown to these rules could be seen as a method of demonstrating that a belligerent possessed the right intention. Thus, it was forbidden to kill certain protected persons such as women, children, old people and the clergy.

In the medieval international system, the just war doctrine was practical because of the existence of two interconnected organs that were able to determine whether a particular situation was a result of a just cause for war: these organs were the Pope and the Holy Roman Emperor. Hence, in Europe throughout the Middle Ages, the doctrine of just war was dominant. Modern times witnessed the demise of the just war doctrine, as the rise of modern state, the accompanying doctrine of sovereignty and the schism brought about by the religious wars of the seventeenth century meant that many states no longer recognised the authority of either the Pope or the Holy Roman Emperor to pronounce on whether a particular war was just. From this point onwards, the states of medieval Europe were no longer united in a system that culminated in the dual authority of the Emperor and the Pope. Such authority was a prerequisite for the application of a just war doctrine. From the moment that a state purports to have authority to interpret in a sovereign and uncontrollable way whether it has a just cause to engage in a particular war, the doctrine is bound to fail and thus fall into disuse.

The relationship between *jus ad bellum* and *jus in bello* was closest in the heyday of the just war doctrine. This doctrine held that the rights and duties of the belligerents depended on the justice of the cause for which they waged war. Hence, the party possessing a just cause had a wider array of powers given to it under the law of warfare; whereas the state branded as undertaking an unjust war was denied a series of belligerent rights. There was thus inequality between the belligerents according to the justice of their respective causes for war. In other words, the *jus ad bellum* to a large extent influenced the contents of the *jus in bello*. More precisely, the *jus ad bellum* dominated, and subjected to its own categories, the *jus in bello*.

3. In the nineteenth century, international law became indifferent to the causes of war. It considered the right to wage war to be a sovereign entitlement of every state. Each state could thus choose, at any time, to change its relationship with another state from a state of peace to a state of war by a declaration of war. In such an environment, the principle of equality between the belligerents had to prevail. If war is a sovereign and equal right of every state, then the belligerents must be

considered to be governed by equal rights and duties concerning conduct during warfare. The equality of the entitlement to declare the war (*jus ad bellum*) led to the principle of equality of the belligerents during the war (*jus in bello*). This principle of equality of the belligerents, and hence of non-discrimination, was kept alive during the twentieth century and is applicable today. It is true that since the creation of the League of Nations after World War I and the creation of the United Nations after World War II, some doubts have been expressed as to whether the principle of equality does, or should, remain applicable. The *jus ad bellum* is no longer based on the absolute freedom to go to war. On the contrary, the United Nations Charter prohibits the use of force unless it is undertaken in self-defence or on the basis of an authorisation from the UN Security Council, acting under Chapter VII of the UN Charter. The freedom to go to war (*jus ad bellum*) has changed into a law prohibiting the use of force (*jus contra bellum*).[1] As a result, a profound distinction between the aggressor and the aggressed against exists in modern international law.

In this case is it right to treat the aggressed against and the aggressor equally under the law of warfare? Undoubtedly, both parties are not treated equally under public international law: the aggressor will face sanctions for the breach of the norms prohibiting force, and the international community will eventually take enforcement action against aggressor, as they did against Iraq in 1991 at the time of the Gulf War. However, the point here is more limited. It is not suggested that there should be no discrimination at all, since it is obviously the case that there must be one. The point is rather that there should be no discrimination in the application of one particular area of international law, the LOAC or IHL (excepting neutrality). We must now turn to the question of why this should be the case.

4. There are three fundamental reasons for separating the *jus ad bellum* from the *jus in bello*.

   a) *The absence, in most cases, of an objective definition of the 'aggressor'.* The question of which state is the aggressor and which state is acting in self-defence must be determined in each case. The state that first uses force is presumed to be the aggressor under international law.[2] However, it may be difficult to determine in a particular case which state used force first. It may be that the first visible strike of the armed conflict, conducted by the armed forces of one party, follows a series of less visible small frontier incidents that are provoked by the other state. Moreover, the first use of force is not determinative of aggression; it carries only the presumption that the perpetrator is the aggressor. This means that other criteria may also have some relevance to the judgement of whether aggression has been committed, and by whom. The question of which criteria should be taken into account has never been conclusively determined. Now, if the Security Council, acting under Chapter VII of the UN Charter, uses its Article 39 power to set out who is the aggressor, the international community will possess an 'objective' judgement as to who is the aggressor. Article 39 of the Charter reads as follows:

---

[1] See generally: ch 2 above.
[2] UNGA Res 3314 (XXIX) (14 December 1974), expressing customary international law.

> The Security Council shall determine the existence of any threat to the peace, breach of the peace, or act of aggression and shall make recommendations, or decide what measures shall be taken in accordance with Articles 41 and 42, to maintain or restore international peace and security.

Measures taken under Chapter VII are binding on all Member States, according to Articles 39 and 25 of the Charter. The UN Security Council is authorised to determine the existence of aggression by these Charter provisions, and we have called such a determination an 'objective' determination. By this, we do not necessarily mean that the decision is objective in the scientific sense of the word. Whilst the determination is to some extent based on legal criteria, it is undoubtedly first and foremost a political decision. The word 'objective' in this sense rather connotes the idea that it is a collective organ that makes a binding determination of how the situation must be classified, as opposed to the states acting individually in accordance with their own interests. However, it is exceedingly rare for the Security Council to qualify a situation as an act of aggression. Even in the most evident case, the attack of Iraq against Kuwait, the Security Council abstained from qualifying the situation as one of aggression, preferring to qualify it as a 'breach of the peace'. Qualifying an act as a 'breach of the peace' is equivalent to the qualification of the same act as an 'act of aggression' for the purpose of Article 39: either qualification suffices to trigger the consequences that may result. For this reason, the Council generally refrains from engaging with the complex and politically charged concept of aggression, preferring to qualify acts in terms of the more flexible, and less controversial, notions of 'breach of the peace' or 'threat of the peace'. In effect, the Council has only qualified two states as aggressors, South Africa and Southern Rhodesia, both states that were quite isolated within the international community. Hence, we are left with a situation where collective organs, either the Security Council or a court, are extremely reluctant to pass judgement as to whether aggression exists in a particular situation. Consequently, each state will determine for itself whether a particular situation constitutes aggression. In international law, it is generally the case that each state has to determine for itself the extent of its obligations and rights, as well as which facts of international life it will recognise and which it will not. In practice, a state will consider that an act of aggression has taken place if the state using force is ideologically, politically or otherwise opposed to it, and will determine that the use of force is legitimate if it is conducted by a friendly state. If we were to discriminate in the application of the LOAC on such a shaky basis, a chaotic situation would result. As no state would ever consider itself to be the aggressor, no state would accept discrimination against itself, but it would urge that discriminatory treatment be imposed on its opponent; conversely, all the states belonging to the opposed camp would want to impress upon their opponent some discrimination while refusing to countenance any such discrimination against themselves. The stalemate flowing from these positions would render the application of any body of the LOAC practically impossible. To summarise, we see that the application of a doctrine of discrimination supposes the existence of a collective organ that can, and will, 'objectively' qualify the situation as an act of aggression and determine who the aggressor is and who is the aggressed. In the international environment, which is dominated by self-serving self-judgements, a doctrine of discrimination cannot be made operational.

b) *Humanitarian reasons.* If it was considered that there should be collective responsibility of all the citizens and the inhabitants of a state for all the misdeeds of that state's government, we could perhaps identify a reason that the civilians and other protected persons within the state should suffer during the war, in order to compensate for their collective wrongs. However, we do not think on such lines today. Why should 'innocent' civilians or other protected persons, such as injured and ill military personnel, be treated unfavourably simply because they happen, by mere chance, to be a citizen of the state that has been qualified as the aggressor? Why should the life of such an innocent civilian be worth less than the life of a similarly innocent civilian who happens to be a citizen of the state which was attacked? Moreover, in many cases aggression is perpetrated by authoritarian states. In such states, the civilian population seldom has a say in the establishment of the authoritarian regime, or in the policies that are adopted by such a regime. Most often, they will themselves have suffered in a similar manner to the civilian population of the state which is attacked. Iraq is a case in point. Now, if we were to allow discrimination in the application of the LOAC, this would amount to saying that the protected persons, for example civilians, within the wrongdoing state deserve less protection than those within the wronged state. To the extent that the LOAC codifies minimum requirements regarding humane treatment during warfare and the prohibition of means and methods that are regarded as excessively harmful any lowering of the standard on a discriminatory basis would open the floodgates to further human suffering and ultimately barbarity. Massive and indiscriminate bombings, or nuclear bombings, are a case in point. The idea of equality of belligerents without discrimination dependent upon the justice of the causes of war thus also serves to ensure proper humanitarian protection for all protected persons, and to close any possible serious loopholes.

c) *Practical reasons: reciprocity.* There is a final reason for the adoption of the principle of non-discrimination between belligerents with respect to the justice of the causes of war. In order to be practically applied, the LOAC must apply equally to each belligerent. No belligerent will ever accept that it must apply the rules of warfare against its adversary when this adversary is not itself ready to apply them reciprocally. No state could accept such inequality which would place it at great military disadvantage and, further, which is incompatible with its prestige. Hence, the law of war can, in a practical sense, only function under conditions of general reciprocity. If discrimination is introduced, the system collapses: the protections of the LOAC will progressively be abandoned section by section, in a vicious circle that begins with a state refusing to apply particular LOAC protections and ends in reprisals. The minimum protection against barbarity in warfare will thus be lost.

5. What has been said above is neatly summarised by Sassoli and Bouvier, who state:

> For practical, policy, and humanitarian reasons, IHL has however to be the same for both belligerents: the one resorting lawfully to force and the one resorting unlawfully to force. From a practical point of view, the respect of IHL could otherwise not be obtained, as, at least between the belligerents, it is always controversial which belligerent is resorting to force in conformity with the *ius ad bellum* and which violates the *ius contra bellum*. In addition, from a humanitarian point of view, the victims of the conflict on both sides need the same protection, and they are not necessarily responsible for the violation of the *ius ad bellum* committed by 'their' party. IHL has therefore to be respected independently of any argument of *ius ad bellum* and has to be completely distinguished from *ius ad bellum*. Any past, present, and future theory of just war only concerns *ius ad bellum* and cannot justify (but is in fact frequently used to imply) that those fighting a just war have more rights or less obligations under IHL than those fighting an unjust war.[3]

6. The separation of *jus ad bellum* and *jus in bello* thus means that there must be equality of belligerents irrespective of the justice of the respective causes of war. It does not mean, however, that there cannot be other links between the two areas of the law. Nevertheless, such links must not be used to allow the weakening of the equality of belligerents as to the application of IHL. Conversely, there are a number of points of contact between *jus ad bellum* and *jus in bello* outside the equality of belligerents issue. Hence, for example, the rules concerning 'necessity and proportionality', concepts which exist in both branches of the law, may in some cases be related, albeit in a very careful manner. The limitation of self-defence to repelling the armed attacks may influence military planning by limiting the range of military actions that are permissible in that particular context. Obviously, the concrete measures taken during a military action exercising a right of self-defence would still have to conform, separately, to *jus in bello* requirements. Another example of a relationship between *jus ad bellum* and *jus in bello* can be seen by the fact that serious violations of the LOAC rules have been taken by the UN Security Council as justification for some form of military intervention on the *jus ad bellum* plane. One may recall the cases of Somalia, Liberia, Sierra Leone and also, to some extent, Rwanda. To summarise, the separation of *jus ad bellum* and *jus in bello* is not strict and all-encompassing; it is strict only as to one fundamental purpose, that is, the maintenance of the principle of equality and non-discrimination between the belligerents in warfare.

7. At times, states convinced that they are fighting a just war have attempted to mitigate the distinction between *jus ad bellum* and *jus in bello*, and in particular have attempted to limit the principle of equality of belligerents. Great powers are particularly prone to a belief that their cause is right, on the one hand because they tend to go to war more often, and on the other because they tend to develop a doctrine regarding their 'just mission' in the world, justifying their frequent uses of force. They have argued that their 'just cause' should lead to some form of distinction between them and their adversaries regarding the application of the LOAC rules.

---

[3] M Sassoli and A Bouvier, *How does Law Protect in War? Cases, Documents and Teaching Materials on Contemporary Practice in International Humanitarian Law: Volume I*, 2nd edn (Geneva, ICRC, 2006) 103.

Hence, today the United States argues that in the 'war against terrorism' the two sides, the United States on the one hand and the 'terrorists' on the other, should not have the same rights and be subject to the same duties. It is rhetorically argued that it is not possible to put the United States and a band of criminals on the same plane.

However, the dilemma does not really arise in these terms. There is no 'war' against terrorism in the technical sense, as you cannot wage an armed conflict against a shadowy entity without a territorial basis. It is only possible to engage in an armed conflict with the states that harbour the terrorists, that cooperate with them, and so on. A case in point is the Afghan armed conflict in 2001–2002. Practically speaking, the fight against terrorism is to a great extent a question of penal cooperation among states. Very few 'terrorists' are captured during an armed conflict, such as the war in Afghanistan. Hence, the LOAC applies only to this small section of captured 'terrorists'. It would apply, for instance, to combatants captured in Afghanistan, but not to all other persons arrested outside that armed conflict. Moreover, the LOAC allows the criminal prosecution of all persons captured during warfare for common crimes or war crimes they are accused of having committed prior to capture.[4] The LOAC does not immunise prisoners of war against criminal prosecution. Terrorists who are captured thus remain amenable to criminal prosecution even when the LOAC applies. The question thus arises if it is really worthwhile to engage in an attack on the principle of equality of belligerents, with all the consequences this will have in short, medium and long term, in order to merely ensure ideological and psychological advantages rather than truly practical ones, except for certain facilities under municipal law, triggered by the declaration of war. To the extent that, for example, members of the US army are taken prisoner, the question as to the application of Geneva Convention III, relating to prisoners of war, will immediately arise and certainly be pressed. This will be the case even if the US soldiers are detained by combatants accused of belonging to a 'terrorist organisation'.

This example, as with many others, shows that the LOAC is indispensable in situations of armed conflict. The LOAC is designed to ensure that situations of warfare do not escalate to the extremes of total war and maximum barbarity. Claims of inequality trigger a fatal blow on the functioning of the system of the LOAC. Such claims should therefore be resisted, all the more since no tangible military benefit is obtained from them. The LOAC is perfectly moulded to the requirements of the military, since it is designed for warfare.

Comprehension check:

a) What are the main arguments in favour of maintaining the principle of equality among the belligerents?
b) Were the terrorist acts carried out on 11 September 2001 on the territory of the United States acts of war? Was the United States involved in an armed conflict against those who carried out these acts?

---

[4] Geneva Convention III relative to the Treatment of Prisoners of War (adopted 12 August 1949, entered into force 21 October 1950) 75 UNTS 135 Arts 82*ff* and *US v Noriega* (1997) 99 ILR 143, 167–171.

c)   Assess the following statement:
     And were a civilised nation engaged with barbarians, who observed no rules of
     war, the former must also suspend their observance of them, where they no
     longer serve to any purpose ...[5]

Answers:

a)   Refer to paragraph 4 above and review the three reasons: (1) absence of
     objective determination of the aggressor in most cases; (2) humanitarian
     reasons of protection; (3) practical reasons of reciprocity.

b)   To the extent that the terrorists were not acting on behalf of, or as agents for,
     a state, such as Afghanistan, there was no act of war, but a common and
     possibly also an international crime, in particular a crime against humanity.
     The perpetrators of this act could thus be searched for and brought to justice
     using criminal law and the legal assistance obligations that exist between
     states. Hence, the United States was not involved in an armed conflict against
     these people. Practically speaking, this means that the United States could
     treat them as simple criminals and not as legitimate combatants, who would
     enjoy prisoner of war status if arrested. However, to the extent that Afghan-
     istan was held to be an accomplice to the acts of the al-Qaeda group, and war
     was waged on it in self-defence, all groups, and members of such groups, who
     take part in the armed conflict on the side of the Afghan armed forces and
     respect the requirements of legitimate combatancy could claim to be legitimate
     combatants and have a right to prisoner of war status.[6] This does not mean
     that they cannot be prosecuted for acts of terrorism. Culpability for such acts
     must then be ascertained individually for each accused in a fair trial which
     accords with fundamental human rights guarantees. The sentence can then be
     served in a prison, even if some privileges of combatant status, for example
     visits by the ICRC, receipt of parcels and the wearing of any uniform, must be
     granted. The death penalty remains possible if the applicable municipal law
     makes provision for it.

c)   This is a question for discussion. The danger of such constructions is to render
     impossible any application of the LOAC and to confuse distinct legal
     phenomena (*jus ad bellum, jus in bello*) according to personal ideological
     criteria. The net result will probably be more disorder and less humanity, to the
     detriment of all of the actors involved. According to one's own ideological
     positions, other answers may obviously be given. Legally speaking, the IHL
     conventions would have to be applied when their conditions of applicability are
     fulfilled. The argument of reprisals in response to non-application of LOAC
     rules by the opponent party has been limited by the modern law (see chapter
     22).

---

[5] W Bradford, 'Barbarians at the Gates: A Post-September 11th Proposal to Rationalize the Laws of
War' (2004) 73 *Mississippi Law Journal* 639. This quote attempts to justify US policies in the 'war against
terrorism'.

[6] Geneva Convention III Art 4 and see generally ch 25 below.

5

TOTAL WAR AND LIMITED WAR

Learning objectives: (1) To understand one of the main problems the LOAC has encountered in the modern world as compared with the pre-nineteenth century world. (2) To understand the contemporary problems arising from the necessity to protect civilians during armed conflict.

1. In Europe, from the seventeenth to the nineteenth centuries war tended to be a matter for the king rather than a matter of concern to the whole nation. Roughly speaking, up until the times of the French Revolution in 1789, war was conducted by a small cadre of professional soldiers, normally operating on behalf of a king. War was launched as a means of achieving a particular end in foreign policy, and was particularly aimed at the conquest of territories or in order to alter or maintain the balance of power. The effects of these hostilities were, for the most part, limited to the professional fighters. The civilian population was substantially spared. It had hardly anything to do with the conflict. It might suffer from the shortages or epidemics that accompanied warfare, but it was not directly targeted. The civilians could continue their day-to-day life, some miles behind the battlefield, to a large extent in the same manner as they did prior to the war. Moreover, there was no general hostility between the peoples of the belligerent states. The war was not considered to be their affair; but merely the affair of their rulers. The sentiment first coined by Jean-Jacques Rousseau, that the opposing soldiers on the battlefield are enemies only by accident and during the fighting, whereas they are not enemies in their capacities as men, expresses very aptly the pre-nineteenth century world of 'cabinet wars' fought among kings. Rousseau expressed his idea thus:

> War, then, is not a relation between men, but between states; in war individuals are enemies wholly by chance, not as men, not even as citizens, but only as soldiers.[1]

Often, the warring kings themselves remained bound together by familial bonds and continued to meet during the wars. Moreover, the weapons at the disposal of the belligerent armies were relatively limited in their capacity for destruction. The cannon might have been able to create gaps in old fortification walls, and the firearms used could kill an enemy; but these arms cannot be compared with the modern arsenal and its incomparably greater destructiveness. All of these aspects combined to limit the effects of the war. Thus, it can be seen that the wars of the seventeenth to the nineteenth centuries were 'limited wars'. Direct participation was

---

[1] J-J Rousseau, *The Social Contract* (London, Penguin Books, 2004 [1762]) Book I, ch 4, 10.

limited to professional armies of relatively small numbers; they did not drag the whole of the belligerent nation into the war; and they were fought with arms of limited range and destructiveness.

2. These conditions dramatically changed during the nineteenth and the beginning of the twentieth century. Three developments were paramount in this historical shift.

a) *Shift towards nationalism.* First, there was a change in the psychological and ideological environment. The progressive rise in national feeling and of liberal democracy allowed a whole mass of persons to identify themselves with their state and their nation, as well as to participate in public affairs. People were no longer prepared to passively assist in somebody else's war; on the contrary, they sought to actively participate in a war that was considered, to the highest degree, to be theirs, since it is the survival of their state that was at stake. Alongside and in conjunction with this development, states drastically increased the number of members of their armed forces by way of general conscription. Moreover, there was a great development of militias and other volunteer corps, including the *levée en masse*, as well as the rise of resistance movements in occupied territories. These developments blur the old distinction between combatants and civilians. It has become more difficult to ensure proper protection for civilians since they tend to participate in the hostilities and are consequently perceived as potential enemies by the opposing belligerent.

b) *Shift towards modern industrialism.* Secondly, the conditions of production of arms, ammunition and other commodities of all types useful to the war effort of belligerents changed considerably. Essentially, wars are now won through superior industrial production of all of the commodities needed by the huge armies involved in armed conflicts. Industrial production hence becomes paramount. War is as much won in the mines and industrial plants as it is won on the battlefield. Consequently, huge numbers of civilian are, at the direction of the state, employed in such production sites. As the civilians taking part in such industrial production contribute greatly to the war effort of a belligerent the adverse belligerent perceives them as 'quasi-combatants'. A belligerent will try to attack enemy industrial plants in order to destroy their contribution to the war effort of the adverse belligerent. Therefore, civilians will be deliberately targeted. The limitation of warfare to narrowly defined military objectives is rendered more difficult in this new state of affairs.

c) *Shift in technologies.* The twentieth century witnessed extremely rapid and profound developments in the armaments available to belligerents. Long distance artillery, aviation and missiles allow vital centres within enemy territory to be targeted at a great distance. Moreover, the destructiveness of these weapons cannot be compared to the destructiveness of the cannon and firearms of previous centuries. The atomic bomb is the most extreme example of such a new weapon. Finally, the temptation to use the highly destructive weaponry that is now available in order to spread terror, to crush the morale of the adverse state and to spare, by shortening the war, one's own resources and combatants, has considerably increased. The result is that a further brake on the destructiveness of warfare inherent in the institution of war itself has disappeared. The modern weapons tend to destroy objects and persons who are well beyond the limits of the definition of military objectives. Consequently, today the effects of the war have the potential to spread to an unprecedented extent.

3. The three evolutions highlighted above all tend to push against the old concept of a 'limited war', turning it into a 'total war'. The entirety of the enemy territory tends to become a very large military objective, which can and should be attacked with modern destructive arms. The distinction between civilians and military objectives tends to fade away to the extent that all inhabitants of a state take part in the war effort. Civilians are constantly, and increasingly, dragged into the armed conflict. In World War I, only five per cent of the war casualties concerned civilians; in the modern wars in Korea or Indo-China this proportion of civilian casualties was as high as 80 per cent. One therefore understands the statement of an eminent author that:

> [La guerre est devenue un cataclysme] ne laissant après elle que des ruines, où vainqueurs et vaincus, belligérants et neutres, se débattent dans une même faillite et dans une même angoisse.[2]

One may add to the foregoing that the increase in non-international armed conflict since 1945 has dramatically increased the potential for confusion between civilians and military persons. During a civil war, in effect the army of the state fights against civilians who have taken up arms. These civilians are rebels or 'irregular fighters'. They have no right to be granted prisoner of war status. They often use guerrilla tactics and merge into the civilian population. The net effect of this course of events is to weaken the resolve of the armed forces of the state to spare a civilian population that is no longer easily seen as 'outside' the war.

4. It is interesting to examine the excellent description, given by a British author, of the effects of 'total war' during World War II. He described the results of total warfare in the following words:

> Under the stress of the war even Great Britain, notwithstanding a strong tradition of individualism, was forced to become totalitarian. When the national effort reached its maximum the whole population, male and female, within very wide limits of age, was mobilised for the prosecution of the war. Exemption from compulsory war service was only granted if the applicant could prove that he or she was privately engaged upon work of national importance. No person within the age limits had any free choice of occupation, and every individual could be told by the government what kind of work he or she had to do. Whatever the particular order given might be, whether the conscript was told to join the army or to work in a factory, in every case the only test was how that individual might be most usefully employed for the purpose of winning the war.

---

[2] M Bourquin, 'Le problème de la sécurité internationale' (1934) 49 *Recueil des Cours de l'Académie de Droit International* 475. The statement roughly translates as '[War has become a cataclysmic event] which leaves only devastation. Winners and losers, belligerents and neutrals, each suffers the same ruin and the same anguish.'

To this it must be added that many millions of men and women, in addition to those enrolled in the regular forces, were mobilised for a form of active service which was known as 'civil defence'. The main purpose of this organisation was to reduce as far as possible the damage caused by enemy attacks, and it was therefore a form of direct resistance to the enemy's military effort. Millions of men were also enrolled in what was called the 'Home Guard'. These were combatant troops in the strictest sense when they were on duty and in uniform, but they were only on duty for limited hours and for the rest of their time they were employed on their ordinary work. [...]. If so, it follows that every town and every village in the country contained a large number of combatants who could quite lawfully be the objects of direct and deliberate attack at any time. This is quite a different matter from the incidental destruction of civilian life to which I have referred. [...].

What is true of Great Britain is substantially true of all the belligerent countries which took a major part in the recent war. To this we must add that the principle of complete mobilisation which was applied to persons was applied equally to industry and to property. The whole system of production, importation, and distribution was organised under a single control with a view to the prosecution of the war effort, and nothing more than the barest minimum was permitted for the satisfaction of normal civilian requirements.

In short, the traditional distinction between combatants and non-combatants rested upon the fact that in practice it was usually quite easy to draw a line between those who were taking an active part in the war and those who were not. The great change has entirely taken place within living memory. In all the wars previous to 1914 only a small minority of the population was put into uniform and employed by the government for the purpose of fighting the enemy. The great majority were left free to carry on their ordinary occupations in their own way, and usually there was no difficulty in doing this, except in the immediate neighbourhood of the fighting forces. This distinction was sound in principle, and is still valid today, whenever the facts enable it to be drawn. If it cannot today be observed in practice, the responsibility lies with the governments and peoples who have decided, rightly or wrongly, that the modern war cannot be carried on with anything less than the combined effort of the whole nation. We must accept the consequences of our choice. We cannot boast, as we have done, that every man and woman in the country is now mobilised for war service, and at the same time claim for them immunity of non-combatants.[3]

5. The existence of a law governing the conduct of armed conflict is the antithesis and the negation of total war. If there is total war, anything and everything may be attacked in order to further one's own war effort and to destroy the enemy's war effort. If the targeted object contributes to the war, it may be attacked. As we have seen, in a modern society involved in armed conflict few things do not contribute to the war effort. Hence, almost everything could be made the object of attack. However, one of the most fundamental principles of the LOAC is the distinction between civilians and military objectives.[4] If that distinction is abandoned, a huge number of the protective rules of the LOAC are undermined, and the protection afforded to civilians will be crippled. As can be seen, the basic idea put forward by

---

[3] HA Smith, *The Crisis in the Law of Nations* (London, Stevens, 1947) 75–77.
[4] Protocol Additional to the Geneva Conventions of 12 August 1949, and relating to the Protection of Victims of International Armed Conflicts (adopted 8 June 1977, entered into force 7 December 1978) 1125 UNTS 3 Art 48.

the LOAC is that war must always be limited: as to the means used, as to the persons and objects targeted, as to the aim pursued, which can be conveniently stated as overcoming resistance by causing the least possible damage. Hence, we can understand the famous sentence that we find in Article 22 of the 1907 Hague Regulations, which provides that, '[t]he right of belligerents to adopt means of injuring the enemy is not unlimited'.[5] This is a clear rejection of the lawfulness of total war. It is important to bear this refutation in mind when confronted by the many tendencies of the modern world that make it difficult to maintain firmly this stance.

Comprehension check:

> To what extent is it practically possible to maintain the distinction between civilian and military objectives under the modern law of warfare? What conditions are most conducive to strengthening the principle of distinction and what conditions, on the other hand, are likely to weaken the principle of distinction?

Answer:

> This is a question that requires general reflection and it is not possible to give a standard answer. As to the first point, one may mention the fact that all modern military manuals and instructions to armed forces uphold the principle of distinction. Hence, states recognise that the distinction is practicable and just. However, several factors place stress on compliance with this principle, such as, modern economic conditions during warfare, the desire to destroy all the war making potential of the enemy; the fact that civilians tend to participate in the war effort under the idea of 'national' war; the spread of civil wars and guerrilla warfare; the warfare of warlords and criminals in failed and semi-failed states; but also some modern war techniques, such as the choice to fly at quite high altitudes in order to avoid being shot down, with the result of decreasing precision in bombings and hence increased civilian casualties.[6] On the other hand, there is a desire to avoid civilian casualties and the resulting negative publicity. There are also modern precision weapons which allow a more precise targeting, such as laser-guided missiles. The duty for combatants to distinguish themselves from civilians, at least when engaged in military operations, also contributes to a strengthening of the principle. That is why this duty of distinction is so important in the LOAC. Many further aspects could be added to those few proposed in the preceding lines.

---

[5] Regulations concerning the Laws and Customs of War on Land annexed to Hague Convention IV (adopted 18 October 1907, entered into force 26 January 1910) (1907) 205 CTS 227 Art 22.

[6] See, eg: Final Report to the Prosecutor by the Committee Established to Review the NATO Bombing Campaign Against the Federal Republic of Yugoslavia (2000) 39 ILM 1279 para [56].

PART II

THE LAW OF ARMED CONFLICTS

6

HISTORICAL EVOLUTION OF THE LOAC

Learning objectives: To understand the most influential steps in the evolution of the modern LOAC.

1. From antiquity to the Middle Ages the conduct of warfare was harsh and hardly limited by rules. Whilst some sparse rules existed as to warfare, for example the prohibition of poisoned weapons or the respect due to truces and armistices, there were no protected persons; all the goods and persons of the enemy were considered to be the rightful war booty of the victor, who could dispose of them as he or she wished; goods and movable objects could be seized and appropriated; territory was annexed or otherwise subjected; the treatment of persons was entirely in the discretion of the victor. He or she could free them, or kill them, or enslave them for his or her own use or in order to sell them on the slave markets. It should be recalled that warfare was the root of the slave trade in antiquity. No distinction was made, initially, between men and women, between children and elderly people and those of fighting age. With the passage of time, further mitigations were introduced into the law, often under the influence of religion. Hence, in Europe, the Catholic Church attempted to introduce rules about prohibited weapons,[1] the respect of the non-combatants, the immunity of certain places (eg churches)[2] and the immunity of certain days of the week, when no fighting should take place. As a concrete example one could mention the prohibition on killing prisoners of war: the Church attempted to found this limitation on the idea that no Christian could kill another Christian apart from situations of necessity. Obviously, this rule initially applied only within the religious community of Christendom and not towards non-Christians. However, some thinkers soon extended it to non-Christian fighters. The overall trend was that as time passed the regulation of means and methods of warfare and the protection of persons increased.

2. The modern LOAC was conceived in 1859 on the battlefield at Solferino in Northern Italy. On 24 June 1859, a battle took place between the French, Sardinian and Austrian armies. For want of the proper provision of medical assistance, more

---

[1] For example, the ban on the use of crossbows by the Second Lateran Council.
[2] F Bugnion, 'La genèse de la protection juridique des biens culturels en cas de conflit armé' (2004) 854 *International Review of the Red Cross* 313.

than 40,000 victims were left dead or dying on the battlefield or in the churches of nearby towns and villages. Henry Dunant, a businessman from Geneva who witnessed the carnage and lack of proper relief, was struck by the miserable fate of the wounded left on the battlefield and together with local inhabitants he tried to alleviate their suffering. On his return to Geneva, in 1862, Dunant published a short book entitled *A Memory of Solferino*.[3] In this book, Dunant vividly describes events of the Battle of Solferino in a heroic tone, in stark contrast to the compassionate and miserable tone which he adopts when describing the suffering of the wounded and sick. His experience at Solferino led Dunant to formulate two main proposals. First, he invited states, 'to formulate some international principle, sanctioned by a Convention inviolate in character', giving a legal protection to the military wounded in the field.[4] Secondly, he proposed the creation of national societies who were to prepare in peacetime all the material and personnel needed in war to provide help to the wounded and sick and able to sustain the sanitary services of the army.[5] Dunant's proposal had great resonance and met with success all over Europe. The nineteenth century was a century where great enthusiasm could be aroused for humanitarian tasks within a relatively short space of time. A few months after the publication of Dunant's book, a small Committee of five persons was founded in Geneva. Its main task was to find ways to put the proposals made by Dunant into practice. Its driving force was the lawyer Gustave Moynier, who had the analytical and practical skills to reduce the flamboyant ideas of Dunant into a practical proposal. After a long period of lobbying, the Geneva Committee succeeded in persuading the Swiss Government to convene a diplomatic conference in order to negotiate and adopt an international convention based on the proposals of the Committee and Dunant. The Geneva Convention of 1864 for the Amelioration of the Condition of the Wounded in Armies in the Field,[6] adopted at the conference, quite faithfully realises the central proposals made by Dunant in *A Memory of Solferino*. It stipulates a duty to respect, protect and aid wounded and sick military personnel without adverse discrimination based upon nationality.[7] To enable compliance with this article each state party should include within its armed forces a medical service. Moreover, national Red Cross Societies should be created in order to provide supplementary help to such services.[8] Finally, there should be protective emblems to visually distinguish the medical units and personnel serving with such units, in order to facilitate the operation of the immunity from attack granted by the convention.[9] With the 1863 Resolution and the 1864 Convention, the modern LOAC was born.

3. The main evolutionary advances since the birth of the modern LOAC in 1864 have been:

---

[3] HJ Dunant, *A Memory of Solferino* (Geneva, International Committee of the Red Cross, 1986).

[4] *Ibid.*

[5] *Ibid.*

[6] The Geneva Convention for the Amelioration of the Condition of the Wounded in Armies in the Field (adopted 22 August 1864, entered into force 22 June 1865) (1864) 129 CTS 361.

[7] *Ibid*, Art 6.

[8] Resolutions of the Geneva International Conference of 1863, in Schlindler and Toman, 361, Arts 1*ff*.

[9] Geneva Convention 1864 Arts 1, 2 and 7.

a) the constant enlargement of the categories of war victims protected by the LOAC: beginning with the military wounded[10]; then the sick and ship-wrecked[11]; then prisoners of war; then in 1899 civilians in occupied territories[12]; and finally, in 1949, the whole adverse civilian population[13];

b) the constant increase in the activities falling within the scope of the LOAC, and the ever increasing number of functions performed by the International Committee of the Red Cross (ICRC): from providing experts to be sent on to a hospital ship in order to testify to its proper use, to sending humanitarian aid to civilian populations suffering from famine, etc;

c) the extension of situations in which victims are protected: first international and then later non-international armed conflict[14]; later still, accompanying the rise of human rights law, a developing trend towards protecting victims during internal disturbances and tensions, including ICRC visits to prisoners held in these situations.

Consistent with this evolutionary path, there has been a considerable extension of treaty law concerning the LOAC. Throughout the twentieth century a great series of treaties have been concluded with the object of formalising the rights and duties of belligerents and especially the duties of protection owed to certain persons. A discussion of the most relevant treaties is to be found in the chapter on the 'Main Sources of the LOAC'.[15]

4. A seminal event in the history of the LOAC was World War II, the horrors of which led to a remarkable paradigm shift in the assumptions underlying the LOAC. Before that war, the law tended to concentrate on military matters and the codification of the rights and duties attendant upon certain means and methods of warfare, along with administrative duties in occupied territory.[16] The LOAC was mainly—but not exclusively—military law. The horrific violations of the most fundamental individual rights of many persons, civilians both inside and outside occupied territory and prisoners of war, by the Axis Powers during World War II led states to adopt a new way of thinking. Thus, new ground was broken in 1949 with the adoption of the four Geneva Conventions.[17] Against their terrible

---

[10] *Ibid.*

[11] Geneva Additional Articles Relating to the Condition of the Wounded in War (adopted 20 October 1868) (1868–69) 138 CTS 189 and Hague Convention (III) for the adaptation to Maritime Warfare of the Principles of the Geneva Convention of 22 August 1864 (adopted 29 July 1899, entered into force 4 September 1900) (1898–99) 187 CTS 443.

[12] Hague Convention (II) with Respect to the Laws and Customs of War on Land and its annex: Regulations concerning the Laws and Customs of War on Land (adopted 29 July 1899, entered into force 4 September 1900) (1898–99) 187 CTS 429.

[13] Geneva Convention IV Relative to the Protection of Civilian Persons in Time of War (adopted 12 August 1949, entered into force 21 October 1950) 75 UNTS 287 (Geneva Convention IV).

[14] Geneva Convention IV Art 3 and Protocol Additional to the Geneva Conventions of 12 August 1949, and relating to the Protection of Victims of Non-International Armed Conflicts (adopted 8 June 1977, entered into force 7 December 1978) 1125 UNTS 609 (Additional Protocol II).

[15] See generally: ch 8 below.

[16] See, eg: Convention (IV) respecting the Laws and Customs of War on Land and its annex: Regulations concerning the Laws and Customs of War on Land (adopted 18 October 1907, entered into force 26 January 1910) (1907) 205 CTS 227.

[17] Geneva Convention I for the Amelioration of the Condition of the Wounded and Sick in Armed Forces in the Field (adopted 12 August 1949, entered into force 21 October 1950) 75 UNTS 31 (Geneva

backdrop, these Conventions gave a wholly new impetus to an important, but until 1949 substantially ignored, role of the LOAC in protecting from the evils of the war certain persons not taking part in the hostilities. The Geneva Conventions concentrate on the needs of the protected persons, ie the victims of war, namely wounded and sick military personnel,[18] prisoners of war,[19] and, newly, civilians.[20] The protection given to these classes of victims is greatly increased, or, in the case of civilians, newly created, and a number of 'fundamental human rights' provisions are inserted into both Geneva Convention III[21] and, particularly, Geneva Convention IV.[22] This new dimension distinguishes to some extent the old law ('Hague Law') from the new law ('Geneva Law').[23]

Moreover, not only was there an expansion of the classes of persons protected by the Conventions, the degree of protection was increased by the inclusion of very detailed substantive provisions. One may just compare the title on belligerent occupation in the Hague Regulations 1907[24] with that contained in Geneva Convention IV[25] to grasp the full extent of the new spirit. In 1907, one finds sparse rules leaving many loopholes, lacunae and uncertainties; in 1949 one finds a series of long and precisely formulated rules, which came together as part of an attempt to form a coherent and complete system. These substantive provisions are moreover protected against any attempt at derogation by the explicit guarantees contained in Common Articles 6/6/6/7 and 7/7/7/8 of Geneva Conventions I–IV, as well as Article 47 of Geneva Convention IV.[26] These clauses mean both that the belligerents cannot conclude special agreements among themselves lowering the substantive guarantees given to protected persons and that the protected persons themselves are unable to renounce any rights given to them by the Conventions.

5. Within the codified law, that is, within the treaties, two separate currents have become evident and crystallised. The so-called 'Hague Law', centred on the Hague Conventions 1899, which were revised in 1907, came to be identified with provisions relating to limitations or prohibitions of specific means and methods of warfare, covering for example the prohibition of poisoned weapons[27] and the prohibition of treacherous warfare.[28] So-called 'Geneva Law', centred on the Geneva Conventions

---

Convention I); Geneva Convention II for the Amelioration of the Condition of Wounded, Sick and Shipwrecked Members of Armed Forces at Sea (adopted 12 August 1949, entered into force 21 October 1950) 75 UNTS 85 (Geneva Convention II); Geneva Convention III relative to the Treatment of Prisoners of War (adopted 12 August 1949, entered into force 21 October 1950) 75 UNTS 135 (Geneva Convention III); Geneva Convention IV.

[18] Geneva Convention I and Geneva Convention II, *ibid.*
[19] Geneva Convention III.
[20] Geneva Convention IV.
[21] Eg Geneva Convention III Art 13.
[22] Eg Geneva Convention IV Art 27.
[23] On this distinction, see para 5 below.
[24] Regulations concerning the Laws and Customs of War on Land annexed to Hague Convention IV (adopted 18 October 1907, entered into force 26 January 1910) (1907) 205 CTS 227, Arts 42–56.
[25] Geneva Convention IV, Arts 47–78, as well as Arts 13–26, 27–34 and 79–135.
[26] See generally: ch 29 below.
[27] Hague Regulations Art 23(a).
[28] Hague Regulations Art 23(b).

of 1864, 1906,[29] 1929[30] and finally 1949, is mainly concerned with the protection of the actual or potential victims of armed conflicts, ie the non-combatants (civilians) and those who no longer take part in hostilities (wounded and sick military personnel, shipwrecked military personnel and prisoners of war, ie persons *hors de combat*). Thus, the equations are: Hague Law = means and methods of warfare; Geneva Law = protected persons.

These two branches of the law are only relatively autonomous. Whilst it is true that Hague Law concerns the relations between opposing military forces during hostilities, and Geneva Law touches upon the relations of the military forces with protected persons outside the actual hostilities, the distinction is not hard and fast. Often, the Hague Law expresses the active side of the coin (what the military may do) and the Geneva Law the passive side of the same coin (what the protected persons should not suffer). Clearly 'what the military may do' is conditioned by 'what the protected persons should not suffer'. Moreover, for example, restrictions as to how a belligerent may use bombings (means and methods of warfare, an example of Hague Law) have a considerable impact on the protection of the civilian population (who are protected persons and whose treatment is governed by Geneva Law). Hence the difference between the two corpuses of the law is mainly descriptive and pedagogic, and does not entail differences of substance.[31] It may be added that upon the adoption of Additional Protocol I to the Geneva Conventions,[32] the two branches of the law were for all practical purposes merged. Additional Protocol I contains provisions as to protected persons[33] intermingled with provisions as to means and methods of warfare.[34]

Comprehension check:

a) What is 'the modern LOAC'? At what time in history does it start and what are the main lines of its evolution?
b) What is the essential difference between 'Hague Law' and 'Geneva Law'?
c) Is this statement correct: 'Medical aid for wounded and sick military personnel is the primary responsibility of the ICRC'?

Answers:

a) The modern LOAC is the branch of international law which evolved from the middle of the nineteenth century, upon the initiative of Henry Dunant following the battle of Solferino. The main lines of the evolution are an enlargement in the categories of war victims protected by IHL, a constant

---

[29] Geneva Convention for the Amelioration of the Condition of the Wounded and Sick in Armies in the Field (adopted 6 July 1906, entered into force 9 August 1907) (1906) 202 CTS 144.

[30] Geneva Convention for the Amelioration of the Condition of the Wounded and Sick in Armies in the Field (adopted 27 July 1929, entered into force 19 June 1931) 118 LNTS 303; Geneva Convention relative to the Treatment of Prisoners of War (adopted 27 July 1929, entered into force 19 June 1931) 118 LNTS 343.

[31] Legality of the Threat or Use of Nuclear Weapons (Advisory Opinion) [1996] ICJ Rep 226 para [75].

[32] Protocol Additional to the Geneva Conventions of 12 August 1949, and relating to the Protection of Victims of International Armed Conflicts (adopted 8 June 1977, entered into force 7 December 1978) 1125 UNTS 3 (Additional Protocol 1).

[33] *Ibid*, Pt II.

[34] For example *ibid*, Art 35.

increase of activities falling under IHL and an extension of the situations in which victims are protected (for further precision see above, paragraph 3). Moreover, after World War II, the concept of the 'protected person' was introduced into the law with a series of tight and precise provisions in the four Geneva Conventions. Their aim is to guarantee fundamental rights and protections to non-combatant persons.

b) Hague Law is based on limitations and prohibitions of certain means and methods of warfare. It is hence centred on what the military personnel may do during hostilities and in occupied territory. Geneva Law is centred on the protection of non-combatant persons, ie the potential or actual victims of the war. Protected persons are the wounded, sick or shipwrecked military persons, the prisoners of war and the civilians in contact with a 'hostile' power. The distinction is not hard and fast. Hague Law and Geneva Law now merge into one another, although didactically they can be conveniently separated.

c) The statement is not correct. It is first for the sanitary services of the army, then for the national Red Cross Societies, and only residually for the ICRC to provide help. In practice, obviously, all of these organisations tend to cooperate.

7

BASIC PRINCIPLES OF THE LOAC

Learning objectives: To understand the basic principles upon which the detailed rules of the LOAC rest and from which they can be deduced.

1. On the most general level, one may say that all rules of the LOAC exist at an equilibrium point between two fundamental principles, each of which pulls in a different direction. The contents of norms of the LOAC are the result of particular compromises between these two fundamental principles made during the negotiation of treaties, or decisions made by states to adopt particular practices. The two fundamental principles are the principle of humanity on the one hand and the principle of military necessity on the other. If only the principle of humanity was recognised, the LOAC rules that would exist would not be considered practicable by the military branch. Such rules would be worthless in the context of the hostile environment of armed conflict; they would, to some extent, be in direct contradiction with the fact that armed conflict, the subject they seek to regulate, implies destruction, killing and injury. On the other hand, if the principle of military necessity was allowed to dominate the creation of the LOAC norms, the norms created would be unable to mitigate the evils that accompany war. All that seemed, to a belligerent or a commander on the ground, necessary or useful in order to secure victory would be allowed. Hence, each war would tend to become a total war, without limitations on the conduct of the parties. In reality, it must balance the two fundamental principles. It must be appreciated that war possesses a certain nature which cannot be ignored; on the other hand, the cruelty of war must be mitigated and some rules must be instituted with the aim of controlling warfare. Finding the balance between these two considerations is the role of what can loosely be described as the legislator; the states which negotiate and adopt conventions regarding the LOAC, or contribute, through their practice and *opinio juris*, to the formation of customary international law rules that apply to armed conflicts. This approach is aptly recalled in the Preamble of Hague Convention IV, where one reads:

> According to the views of the High Contracting Parties, these provisions [of the present Convention], the wording of which has been inspired by the desire to diminish the evils of war, as far as military requirements permit, are intended to serve as a general rule of conduct for the belligerents in their mutual relations and in their relations with the inhabitants.[1]

[1] Convention (IV) respecting the Laws and Customs of War on Land and its annex: Regulations concerning the Laws and Customs of War on Land (adopted 18 October 1907, entered into force 26 January 1910) (1907) 205 CTS 227.

Thus, embedded in every rule of the LOAC, one finds a balance between the principles of humanity and military necessity.

The *United States Navy Manual on the Law of Naval Warfare*, published in July 1959, restates the aforementioned principles in the following passage:

[The basic principles of the LOAC] are defined as follows:

a. MILITARY NECESSITY. The principle of military necessity permits a belligerent to apply only that degree and kind of regulated force, not otherwise prohibited by the laws of war, required for the partial or complete submission of the enemy with the least possible expenditure of time, life, and physical resources.

b. HUMANITY. The principle of humanity prohibits the employment of any kind or degree of force not necessary for the purpose of the war, ie, for the partial or complete submission of the enemy with the least possible expenditure of time, life, and physical resources.

c. CHIVALRY. The principle of chivalry forbids the resort to dishonorable (treacherous) means, expedients, or conduct.[2]

2. It is important to note that the modern LOAC only allows a belligerent to depart from a norm of the LOAC on the basis of military necessity where, and to the extent that, the specific rule concerned explicitly makes reference to derogation on the basis of military necessity. Military necessity cannot be invoked to derogate from a rule which does not make such allowance. This is the case because the LOAC is already a compromise between the principles of military necessity and humanity. Therefore, military necessity cannot be allowed to subvert the application of protective norms which have already taken the requirements of the military branch into account during the process of their creation. Moreover, if one allows a belligerent to escape from the rules of the LOAC in a case where he or she believes this is militarily necessary, the whole purpose of the law would be thwarted. As was said by the US military tribunal in the *Krupp* case:

[T]o claim that [the laws of war] can be wantonly – at the sole discretion of any one belligerent – disregarded when he considers his own situation to be critical, means nothing more or less than to abrogate the laws and customs of war.[3]

And, further:

It has been held by military tribunals that the plea of military necessity cannot be considered as a defense for the violation of rules which lay down absolute prohibitions (eg the rule prohibiting the killing of prisoners of war) and which provide no exception for those circumstances constituting military necessity.[4]

An example of a provision which makes allowance for military necessity is Article 23(g) of the Hague Regulations, which provides:

---

[2] M Whiteman (ed), *Digest of International Law: Volume 10* (Washington DC, US Department of State, 1968) 300.

[3] *United States v Krupp* (1948) 15 AD 622, 628.

[4] *Ibid.*

It is forbidden ... To destroy or seize the enemy's property, unless such destruction or seizure be imperatively demanded by the necessities of war.[5]

3. Another pair of fundamental principles that govern the LOAC are those that dominate Hague Law and Geneva Law respectively. The detailed rules of the LOAC may be shown to be elaborations of these two general principles, which exist at the apex of the system of the LOAC. These two foundational principles may also form a basis upon which gaps of the law can be filled and particular rules of the LOAC can be interpreted, especially in cases of doubt. These two principles are the following:

a) *Principle of limitation.* This principle is stated classically in Article 22 of the Hague Regulations, and is now restated in Article 35(1) of Additional Protocol I,[6] 'The right of belligerents to adopt means of injuring the enemy is not unlimited'. This principle rejects the idea of total war: not all means that are useful in achieving the end of winning the war are allowed. It makes clear that limitations may be placed on the means and methods of warfare. Hence, for example, certain weapons, such as poisoned weapons,[7] or weapons causing 'unnecessary suffering',[8] are prohibited. This principle dominates the 'Hague Law', and can be seen as the bedrock upon which this branch of the law rests.

b) *Principle of humanity.* This principle, which has already been discussed as an important component in the balancing act that underlies IHL, permeates the whole of the so-called 'Geneva Law'. At base, the principle requires that those who do not take part in the armed conflict, so-called protected persons, should be treated humanely. This principle is most clearly expressed in common Article 3 to Geneva Conventions I-IV[9]; in Articles 12/12/13/27 of Geneva Conventions I-IV; and Article 4 of Additional Protocol II.[10] Moreover, this principle provides the foundation for all of the detailed rules that are contained in the Geneva Conventions, which in effect attempt to apply the requirement of humane treatment to specific contexts and set out the operation of the obligation in more specific terms. The principle of humanity has four specific facets. First, it requires a belligerent to treat protected persons with respect. In this context, respect is a negative concept,

[5] Regulations concerning the Laws and Customs of War on Land annexed to Hague Convention IV (adopted 18 October 1907, entered into force 26 January 1910) (1907) 205 CTS 227 (Hague Regulations) Art 23(g).

[6] Protocol Additional to the Geneva Conventions of 12 August 1949, and relating to the Protection of Victims of International Armed Conflicts (adopted 8 June 1977, entered into force 7 December 1978) 1125 UNTS 3 (Additional Protocol 1) Art 35(1).

[7] Hague Regulations Art 23(a).

[8] Additional Protocol I Art 35(2).

[9] Geneva Convention I for the Amelioration of the Condition of the Wounded and Sick in Armed Forces in the Field (adopted 12 August 1949, entered into force 21 October 1950) 75 UNTS 31 (Geneva Convention I); Geneva Convention II for the Amelioration of the Condition of Wounded, Sick and Shipwrecked Members of Armed Forces at Sea (adopted 12 August 1949, entered into force 21 October 1950) 75 UNTS 85 (Geneva Convention II); Geneva Convention III relative to the Treatment of Prisoners of War (adopted 12 August 1949, entered into force 21 October 1950) 75 UNTS 135 (Geneva Convention III); Geneva Convention IV Relative to the Protection of Civilian Persons in Time of War (adopted 12 August 1949, entered into force 21 October 1950) 75 UNTS 287 (Geneva Convention IV).

[10] Protocol Additional to the Geneva Conventions of 12 August 1949, and relating to the Protection of Victims of Non-International Armed Conflicts (adopted 8 June 1977, entered into force 7 December 1978) 1125 UNTS 609 (Additional Protocol II).

which imposes upon belligerents a duty of abstention. A belligerent should not mistreat, damage, nor threaten protected persons. It must spare them from suffering. The second facet of the principle of humanity is the requirement of protection.[11] This is a positive duty, which requires action on the part of a belligerent. The role of this obligation is to defend protected persons from evils and sufferings brought about by armed conflict, and to make sure that they are not exposed to undue dangers. For example, as soon as possible after their capture, prisoners of war (POWs) must be removed from an area where fighting continues to take place and moved to a secure camp, which, if possible, should be marked with the letters PG or PW in order to assure immunity from attack.[12] Thirdly, the principle of humanity encompasses a principle of equality, which requires that the belligerent must not engage in adverse discrimination against protected persons. The protected persons must not be discriminated against on the basis of irrelevant criteria. Such irrelevant or 'adverse' criteria are, for example, nationality, religious beliefs, political opinions, race, colour, sex, birth and wealth. However, objective criteria, which are linked to a proper and recognised motive, may be used to distinguish between protected persons and may allow belligerents treat protected persons differently. Thus, the more gravely injured should receive aid before the less gravely injured. Moreover, POWs may be treated differently according to their rank, with higher ranking officers enjoying some privileges. Finally, the principle of humanity requires that the belligerent accord humane treatment to protected persons in all circumstances.[13] It is impossible to spell out in abstract what this sub-principle entails in all circumstances. The detailed provisions of the Conventions attempt to concretise the obligation by providing detailed guidance regarding its operation in certain situations. However, it can be said that the obligation of humane treatment basically states that a protected person is a human being and should always be treated as an end and not as a means to an end, and that in all circumstances he or she must be given a chance to live with a minimum of dignity. The protected person may be subjected to treatment and an environment which means that life is difficult, but this treatment must always be humane, appropriate and acceptable.

4. At a greater level of specificity, one can find a series of more concrete and operational principles that permeate the LOAC. One may mention in particular the following:

a) *The principle of distinction.* This principle requires that belligerents distinguish between military objectives and civilian persons or objects at all times, and attack only military objectives. It is one of the fundamental principles that

---

[11] *The Essen Lynching Case, The Trial of Erich Heyer and Six Others Before a British Military Court* (1945) 1 LRTWC 88.

[12] Geneva Convention III relative to the Treatment of Prisoners of War (adopted 12 August 1949, entered into force 21 October 1950) 75 UNTS 135 (Geneva Convention III) Arts 19 and 23.

[13] *Prosecutor v Kordic and Cerkez* (Trial Judgement) IT-95-14/2-T (26 February 2001) para [256].

underlie the LOAC. Whilst this principle is a norm of customary international law,[14] it is conveniently restated in Article 48 of Additional Protocol I:

> In order to ensure respect for and protection of the civilian population and civilian objects, the Parties to the conflict shall at all times distinguish between the civilian population and combatants and between civilian objects and military objectives and accordingly shall direct their operations only against military objectives.

b) *The principle of necessity.* This principle requires that the belligerent only adopts such measures as are necessary to overpower the enemy and to bring about its surrender. This is the proper aim of armed conflict. The aim of the war should not be seen as the destruction of as much of the adverse belligerents property and killing of as many members of the adverse armed forces as possible; rather, the proper aim is to destroy and to kill as few as possible and to cause such damage only to the extent necessary to overpower the enemy. That idea was aptly expressed in the 1868 St Petersburg Declaration,[15] where it is stated:

> That the only legitimate object which States should endeavour to accomplish during war is to weaken the military forces of the enemy; That for this purpose it is sufficient to disable the greatest possible number of men; That this object would be exceeded by the employment of arms which uselessly aggravate the sufferings of disabled men, or render their death inevitable.

Thus, there is a hierarchy of acts allowed: one should capture rather than wound; one should wound rather than kill; one should kill less persons rather than kill more persons, and so on. It is often possible to obtain the same military result by placing the military personnel of the enemy *hors de combat* rather than killing them. In operation, the principle of necessity therefore requires that the least destructive measure that gains the same military advantage should be preferred. This rule is expressed in Article 57(3) of Additional Protocol I:

> When a choice is possible between several military objectives for obtaining a similar military advantage, the objective to be selected shall be that the attack on which may be expected to cause the least danger to civilian lives and to civilian objects.

For example, there are two positions which offer resistance to a progressing armed force and if one position is neutralised the other will not be able to sustain fire alone, therefore allowing the armed forces to continue their progress. In this situation, it is thus sufficient to attack one of the two positions in order to overpower the resistance. One of the positions is located in a piece of cultural property. In such a situation, the other object should be attacked, as this would cause the least destruction. Secondly, this principle of necessity

---

[14] J-M Henckaerts and L Doswald-Beck (eds), *Customary International Humanitarian Law Volume 1: Rules* (Cambridge, CUP, 2005) (hereinafter *ICRC Customary Study*), Rule 1.

[15] St Petersburg Declaration Renouncing the Use, in Time of War, of Explosive Projectiles Under 400 Grammes Weight (signed 11 December 1868, entered into force 11 December 1868) (1868–69) 138 CTS 297.

prohibits the taking of any war measure which does not offer a definite military advantage. Such a measure would play no part in the furtherance of the war aim and would be unnecessary, and is therefore prohibited. To illustrate, let us take the same example as before, but this time no cultural property is involved. However, it remains the case that both of the positions should not be attacked together if the neutralisation of one of the positions alone will suffice to break the resistance. Contrary to the narrow principle of 'military necessity' that we discussed above, the principle of necessity discussed here limits the freedom of belligerents to use the means and methods of warfare of their choice.

c) *The principle of proportionality.* Proportionality is a third fundamental principle of the LOAC. All military measures taken by belligerents must be proportionate to the aim they seek to accomplish. Proportionality, in the LOAC context, means that the military advantage obtained by a particular operation must outweigh the damage caused to civilians and civilian objects by that action. When planning an operation, each belligerent must carefully weigh up the importance of the military advantage, alternative means by which the advantage may be achieved and the expected losses on the part of the civilians. The importance of the military advantage and the civilian losses must be put into some form of balance and weighed up one against the other. Hence, for example, if it appears that an excessive number of civilians may be killed by an attack when compared to the relative importance of the advantage looked for, the attack will be prohibited. In such a case it can be said that this attack would cause disproportionate damage to the civilian population. This principle is well expressed in Article 51(5)(b) of Additional Protocol I, which states:

> [An attack is indiscriminate and hence prohibited if it] may be expected to cause incidental loss of civilian life, injury to civilians, damage to civilian objects, or a combination thereof, which would be excessive in relation to the concrete and direct military advantage anticipated.[16]

These three principles may be applied to particular plans in order to discover whether the LOAC allows or prohibits the proposed actions.

5. Some of the main principles of the LOAC that have been discussed above have been authoritatively restated by the International Court of Justice in the *Nuclear Weapons* Advisory Opinion:

> 77. All this shows that the conduct of military operations is governed by a body of legal prescriptions. This is so because 'the right of belligerents to adopt means of injuring the enemy is not unlimited' as stated in Article 22 of the 1907 Hague Regulations relating to the laws and customs of war on land. The St. Petersburg Declaration had already condemned the use of weapons 'which uselessly aggravate the suffering of disabled men or make their death inevitable'. The aforementioned Regulations relating to the laws and customs of war on land, annexed to the Hague Convention IV of 1907, prohibit the use of 'arms, projectiles, or material calculated to cause unnecessary suffering' (Art 23).

---

[16] See generally: ch 17 below.

78. The cardinal principles contained in the texts constituting the fabric of humanitarian law are the following. The first is aimed at the protection of the civilian population and civilian objects and establishes the distinction between combatants and non-combatants; States must never make civilians the object of attack and must consequently never use weapons that are incapable of distinguishing between civilian and military targets. According to the second principle, it is prohibited to cause unnecessary suffering to combatants: it is accordingly prohibited to use weapons causing them such harm or uselessly aggravating their suffering. In application of that second principle, States do not have unlimited freedom of choice of means in the weapons they use.

The Court would likewise refer, in relation to these principles, to the Martens Clause, which was first included in the Hague Convention II with Respect to the Laws and Customs of War on Land of 1899 and which has proved to be an effective means of addressing the rapid evolution of military technology. A modern version of that clause is to be found in Article 1, paragraph 2, of Additional Protocol I of 1977, which reads as follows:

'In cases not covered by this Protocol or by other international agreements, civilians and combatants remain under the protection and authority of the principles of international law derived from established custom, from the principles of humanity and from the dictates of public conscience.'

In conformity with the aforementioned principles, humanitarian law, at a very early stage, prohibited certain types of weapons either because of their indiscriminate effect on combatants and civilians or because of the unnecessary suffering caused to combatants, that is to say, a harm greater than that unavoidable to achieve legitimate military objectives. If an envisaged use of weapons would not meet the requirements of humanitarian law, a threat to engage in such use would also be contrary to that law.[17]

6. Finally, one may recall the fundamental purposes of the LOAC, which are, to a large extent, reflected in these principles:

a) to prevent 'unnecessary suffering' of combatants and non-combatants alike. Such suffering may be seen as unnecessary in relation to the war aims or in relation to general humanitarian considerations;

b) to avoid an escalation or a spread in the conflict and to prevent the horrors that accompany total warfare; and

c) to protect non-combatants, particularly the civilian population, civilian objects and civilian property and those combatants rendered *hors de combat* by the conflict.

Comprehension check:

a)   What are the main principles of the LOAC?

b)   What main functions do these principles display in the law?

c)   Is the principle of humanity or that of military necessity more important today?

---

[17] *Legality of the Threat or Use of Nuclear Weapons (Advisory Opinion)* [1996] ICJ Rep 226 paras [77]–[78].

Answers:

a)   At the most general level, the LOAC attempts to balance the competing principles of humanity and military necessity. The law-giver mainly performs this work. In the LOAC, the function of the law-giver is embodied in the states concluding LOAC treaties or performing the state practice and *opinio juris* that results in the rules of customary international law. At an intermediate level we find the two fundamental principles of Hague Law and Geneva Law respectively: the principles of limitation and the principle of humanity. Thus, the principle of humanity can be found at two levels: the most general one and the intermediate one. Finally, at a more concrete level, we find such principles as the principles of distinction, necessity and proportionality.

b)   The principles express the main driving forces in, and behind, the law. They serve as a convenient way to summarise the motivating factors that lie behind a series of concrete provisions, whose common sense could elude the casual reader if they were looked at without the benefit of the general principles. Moreover, the principles provide inspiration for states when they shape new rules of the LOAC. States take notice of the general ideas that lie behind the law when they seek to negotiate new rules. Furthermore, the principles may serve as material which interested parties can use to interpret the specific rules. Still further, the principles may fill gaps in the law, especially when there are evolutions in technology which are not yet covered by specific rules. The legality of a new weapon, for example, may be tested against the principle of necessity and proportionality, or against the requirements not to cause unnecessary suffering or inevitable death of the victim, which derive from the principle of necessity.[18]

c)   It is probably impossible to assign pre-eminence to either of these two principles, even if there is today more pressure to respect humanitarian needs. The law of warfare, if it is to function properly, must accommodate these two trends. No absolute pre-eminence of one principle over the other would be appropriate. As to a relative pre-eminence, all times have found a new equilibrium between the two principles in which one has prevailed somewhat over the other in a concrete context. Thus, for example, before World War II, the principle of military necessity seemed to have some pre-eminence; today, the principle of humanity has gained a significant amount of ground and obtained an equilibrium which is more favourable to it.

---

[18] *Ibid*, paras [77]–[78].

8

MAIN SOURCES OF THE LOAC

Learning objectives: To examine the sources of the LOAC, in particular how the law is made and the places where the law may be found.

1. The term 'source of the law' has a specific legal meaning. It is used to refer to law-creating instruments. Actively speaking, the reference 'a source' determines the means of creating the law; passively, it indicates the place where the law may be found. The conclusion of a treaty is a means of creating legal rules, but the treaty is also a place where one can find legal rules. When these two elements are merged, one can see that sources express the criteria under which a rule is accepted as valid in a given legal system. Hence, in national law, a 'statute' or an 'Act of Parliament' is a source of law. Why is this so? Because it expresses a way in which legal rules can be created, but also refers to a place where the content of law can be found. If one wishes to find information about the law of contracts it is possible, in civil law countries, to look up the rules in the code of obligations or other equivalent legislation.

2. The main sources of international law are treaties and custom.[1] Treaties are formal agreements concluded between states and binding upon them if they ratify or accede to them.[2] Customary international law is composed of unwritten rules developed by state practice bearing testimony to a sense of legal obligation felt by the states. What does this mean? Despite the fact that states adopt many different constant and invariable usages, only some of these are legally binding. In order to be constituted a legally binding norm of customary international law, not only must a course of conduct be generally followed by the states that make up international society, but also the motivation of the states to obey such a norm must be based on legal reasons. The states must be convinced that the way in which they act is the legal course of conduct in a particular situation; that it is the law which indicates or compels them to act the way they act. This is expressed in the requirement that customary international law is based on state practice and *opinio juris* (legal opinion). The International Court of Justice expressed the requirement for *opinio juris* for the formation of customary law in the following way in the *North Sea Continental Shelf* cases:

---

[1] Statute of the International Court of Justice (adopted 26 June 1945, entered into force 24 October 1945) 15 UNCIO 335 Art 38(1).

[2] See generally: the definition adopted by the Vienna Convention on the Law of Treaties (adopted 22 May 1969, entered into force 27 January 1980) 1155 UNTS 331 Art 2(1)(a).

> Not only must the acts concerned amount to a settled practice, but they must also be such, or be carried out in such a way, as to be evidence of a belief that this practice is rendered obligatory by the existence of a rule of law requiring it. [...] The States concerned must therefore feel that they are conforming to what amounts to a legal obligation. The frequency, or even habitual character of the acts is not in itself enough. There are many international acts, eg, in the field of ceremonial and protocol, which are performed almost invariably, but which are motivated only by considerations of courtesy, convenience and tradition, and not by any sense of legal duty.[3]

Hence, acts of ceremony or protocol remain usages situated outside the law and do not harden into rules of customary international law. The concrete difference is that a state cannot be compelled to respect rules of courtesy or of protocol, because they are not legally binding upon states; conversely, a state can be compelled to honour the rule of customary international law, because such a rule is binding upon that state. When both elements that are required to form a binding norm—general practice and *opinio juris*—meet, then a rule can be considered as having become one of general customary international law and therefore binding on all states. As an example, one may discuss the rules on diplomatic immunities. For centuries states have granted immunity to the embassies exchanged between them. The reason motivating states to grant such immunities has always considered by the states to be a legal one. The states granted the immunities because they believed, correctly, that international law compelled them to grant such a privilege. Therefore, these immunities were not given for merely moral, practical or other reasons based on expediency. They were based on a legal conviction and hence on customary international law. As far as the LOAC is concerned, state practice can be elicited not only out of actual state conduct, but also, by, for example, looking at the military manuals published by states.[4] In these military manuals, practice and legal opinion tend to merge into each other.

3. Treaty law constitutes a fundamental source of IHL. Since the nineteenth century, states have always attempted to express the rules of warfare to which they were prepared to commit themselves in formal instruments. Because of this, treaty law concerning the LOAC today constitutes an extensive body of IHL rules covering more than 1,000 pages.[5] The desire for the LOAC to be set out in treaty law, and the pre-eminence of the treaty as a method for developing the law in this area, can be explained by a particularly strong need for legal certainty. The LOAC has to be applied in cases of armed conflict, where circumstances of disorganisation and stress are the norm rather than the exception. Moreover, it has to be applied mainly by the military branch. It is impossible to ask military personnel, not necessarily trained in law, to ascertain the rules governing conflict by complex research

---

[3] *North Sea Continental Shelf Cases (Germany v Denmark; Germany v The Netherlands)* [1969] ICJ Rep 3 para [77].

[4] *US v List* (1948) 15 AD 632, 644 and *Prosecutor v Tadic* (Decision on the Defence Motion for Interlocutory Appeal on Jurisdiction) IT-49-1-AR72 (2 October 1995) para [99].

[5] The full text of these treaties may be found on the website of the International Committee of the Red Cross, at <http://www.icrc.org/ihl> accessed 14 May 2008, or in D Schlindler and J Toman (eds), *The laws of armed conflicts: a collection of conventions, resolutions, and other documents*, 4th edn (Leiden, Martinus Nijhoff, 2004).

into the vagaries of state practice and *opinio juris*. On the contrary, the rules to be applied must be readily available. They must also be precisely and clearly formulated. Vague principles are not sufficient. In the situation of warfare, where there is very little time to decide upon what course of action to take, the rules that are to be ·applied must be set out in such a way that it is possible to know what has to be done in each circumstance in a very precise manner. This is why the LOAC conventions must not only contain the applicable rules, but must additionally formulate these rules in a concrete and detailed manner. Treaties have the great advantage of putting the rules that they contain relatively beyond doubt, crystallising them in black and white, ready to be applied by a soldier. Furthermore, treaties tend to fix and legitimise the rules through a broad ratification or accession process. If a significant number of ratifications or accessions are forthcoming, this will open up the possibility to derive customary rules out of the treaty rules.[6] These characteristics of treaties mean that they have been the vehicle of choice for changes in the LOAC since the birth of the discipline after the battle of Solferino.

The main disadvantage of treaty law is that it only binds states that ratify or accede to the instrument.[7] However, the LOAC treaties are among the most universally ratified. The four Geneva Conventions that were drafted and adopted in 1949 have a membership which is almost universal. On the other hand, Additional Protocol I, although binding on a large number of states by the standards of most treaties, has still not been ratified or acceded to by roughly 40 states. This situation creates legal uncertainty, since the Protocol will not be applicable as treaty law during situations of armed conflict between states not parties to it, or may be applicable as between some parties to an armed conflict, but not others. This has the potential to cause uncertainty, which is undesirable during armed conflict for the reasons referred to above.

4. There are a great number of the LOAC treaties, and it would be impossible to list them all here. However, the main treaties that set out the general rules of the LOAC are, in chronological order, the following:

    a) St Petersburg Declaration Renouncing the Use, in Time of War, of Explosive Projectiles under 400 Grammes Weight.[8] Today, this text is important only as a codification of the general principles stated in the preamble, which sets out the legitimate aims of warfare and the principle that limitations exist on the means of warfare that may be adopted.

    b) The 12 Hague Conventions of 1907, in particular Convention IV respecting the Laws and Customs of War on Land with its annexed Regulations concerning the conduct of Land Warfare,[9] and Convention V respecting the Rights and Duties of Neutral Powers and Persons in Case of War on

---

[6] See para 6 below.

[7] Vienna Convention on the Law of Treaties Art 34.

[8] St Petersburg Declaration Renouncing the Use, in Time of War, of Explosive Projectiles Under 400 Grammes Weight (signed 11 December 1868, entered into force 11 December 1868) (1868–69) 138 CTS 297.

[9] Hague Convention (IV) respecting the Laws and Customs of War on Land with Annexed Regulations concerning the Laws and Customs of War (adopted 18 October 1907, entered into force 26 January 1910) (1907) 205 CTS 227.

Land.[10] The Hague Regulations remain applicable today in a wide range of situations, particularly with respect to prohibited means and methods of warfare[11] and the rights and duties of belligerents in occupied territories.[12]

c)   Geneva Conventions I–IV of 1949: Convention I for the Amelioration of the Condition of the Wounded and Sick in Armed Forces in the Field[13]; Convention II for the Amelioration of the Condition of the Wounded, Sick and Shipwrecked Members of Armed Forces at Sea[14]; Convention III relative to the Treatment of Prisoners of War[15]; and Convention IV relative to the Protection of Civilian Persons in Time of War.[16] These Conventions continue to play an important role as the foundational documents for the protections granted to persons affected by armed conflict.

d)   The Hague Convention for the Protection of Cultural Property in the Event of Armed Conflict,[17] with its two Additional Protocols of 1954[18] and 1999.[19]

e)   The Additional Protocols to the Geneva Conventions of 1949: Protocol Additional to the Geneva Conventions of 12 August 1949 relating to the Protection of Victims of International Armed Conflicts[20]; and Protocol Additional to the Geneva Conventions of 12 August 1949 relating to the Protection of Victims of Non-International Armed Conflicts.[21] Protocol I sets out important updates to the Geneva Conventions, developing the rules that they contain concerning the protection of persons, but also updating the law on means and methods of warfare, in particular codifying norms relating to attacks against military objectives and the correlative immunity of civilian objects and persons.[22] Protocol II is the first LOAC treaty dedicated exclusively to non-international armed conflicts (roughly speaking to 'civil wars'). In 2005, a Third Additional Protocol was adopted

---

[10] Hague Convention V respecting the Rights and Duties of Neutral Powers and Persons in Case of War on Land (adopted 18 October 1907, entered into force 26 January 1910) (1907) 205 CTS 299.

[11] Hague Regulations Art 23.

[12] Hague Regulations Arts 42*ff.*

[13] Geneva Convention I for the Amelioration of the Condition of the Wounded and Sick in Armed Forces in the Field (adopted 12 August 1949, entered into force 21 October 1950) 75 UNTS 31.

[14] Geneva Convention II for the Amelioration of the Condition of Wounded, Sick and Shipwrecked Members of Armed Forces at Sea (adopted 12 August 1949, entered into force 21 October 1950) 75 UNTS 85.

[15] Geneva Convention III relative to the Treatment of Prisoners of War (adopted 12 August 1949, entered into force 21 October 1950) 75 UNTS 135.

[16] Geneva Convention IV Relative to the Protection of Civilian Persons in Time of War (adopted 12 August 1949, entered into force 21 October 1950) 75 UNTS 287.

[17] Convention for the Protection of Cultural Property in the Event of Armed Conflict (adopted 14 May 1954, entered into force 7 August 1956) 249 UNTS 240.

[18] Protocol for the Protection of Cultural Property in the Event of Armed Conflict (adopted 14 May 1954, entered into force 7 August 1956) 249 UNTS 358.

[19] Second Protocol to the Hague Convention of 1954 for the Protection of Cultural Property in the Event of Armed Conflict (adopted 26 March 1999, entered into force 9 March 2004) (1999) 38 ILM 769.

[20] Protocol Additional to the Geneva Conventions of 12 August 1949, and relating to the Protection of Victims of International Armed Conflicts (adopted 8 June 1977, entered into force 7 December 1978) 1125 UNTS 3 (Additional Protocol 1).

[21] Protocol Additional to the Geneva Conventions of 12 August 1949, and relating to the Protection of Victims of Non-International Armed Conflicts (adopted 8 June 1977, entered into force 7 December 1978) 1125 UNTS 609 (Additional Protocol II).

[22] Additional Protocol I Arts 48*ff.*

adding a further protective emblem to those that are set out in Geneva Convention I.[23]

f) The Rome Statute on the International Criminal Court.[24] This treaty does not deal directly with the LOAC; instead it is concerned with the repression of international crimes, and is therefore a part of international criminal law. However, as the violation of the LOAC rules constitutes a prominent species international crime, called war crimes, the Statute is also of interest to those concerned with IHL. In particular, Article 8 of the statute, which deals with war crimes in great depth, indirectly touches upon and develops the LOAC.

5. Furthermore, there are a series of specific treaties limiting the production or use of particular weapons or means of warfare. Again, only some prominent examples will be given:

a) Protocol for the Prohibition of the Use in War of Asphyxiating, Poisonous or Other Gases, and of Bacteriological Methods of Warfare.[25]

b) Convention on the Prohibition of Development, Production and Stockpiling of Bacteriological (Biological) and Toxin Weapons and on their Destruction.[26]

c) Convention on the Prohibition of Military or Other Hostile Use of Environmental Modification Techniques.[27]

d) Convention on Prohibitions or Restrictions on the Use of Certain Conventional Weapons Which may be Deemed to be Excessively Injurious or the Have Indiscriminate Effects,[28] with its protocols I–V on non-detectable fragments (Protocol I)[29]; on mines, booby-traps and other devices (Protocol II)[30]; on incendiary weapons (Protocol III)[31]; on blinding laser weapons

---

[23] Protocol additional to the Geneva Conventions of 12 August 1949, and relating to the Adoption of an Additional Distinctive Emblem (adopted 8 December 2005, entered into force 14 January 2007) available at <http://www.icrc.org/ihl.nsf/FULL/615?OpenDocument> accessed 14 May 2008.

[24] Rome Statute of the International Criminal Court (adopted 17 July 1998, entered into force 1 July 2002) 2187 UNTS 3.

[25] Geneva Protocol for the Prohibition of the Use in War of Asphyxiating, Poisonous or Other Gases, and of Bacteriological Methods of Warfare (signed 17 June 1925, entered into force 8 February 1928) 94 LNTS 65.

[26] Convention on the Prohibition of Development, Production and Stockpiling of Bacteriological (Biological) and Toxin Weapons and on Their Destruction (adopted 16 December 1971, entered into force 26 March 1975) 1015 UNTS 164.

[27] Convention on the Prohibition of Military or any Other Hostile use of Environmental Modification Techniques (adopted 10 December 1976, entered into force 5 October 1978) 1108 UNTS 151.

[28] UN Convention on Prohibitions or Restrictions on the Use of Certain Conventional Weapons which may be deemed to be Excessively Injurious or to Have Indiscriminate Effects (adopted 10 October 1980, entered into force 2 December 1983) 1342 UNTS 137.

[29] Protocol I to the UN Convention on Prohibitions or Restrictions on the Use of Certain Conventional Weapons which may be deemed to be Excessively Injurious or to Have Indiscriminate Effects concerning Non-Detectable Fragments (adopted 10 October 1980, entered into force 2 December 1983) 1342 UNTS 137.

[30] Protocol II to the UN Convention on Prohibitions or Restrictions on the Use of Certain Conventional Weapons which may be deemed to be Excessively Injurious or to Have Indiscriminate Effects concerning Prohibitions or Restrictions on the Use of Mines, Booby-traps and Other Devices (adopted 10 October 1980, entered into force 2 December 1983) 1342 UNTS 137; and Amended Protocol to the UN Convention on Prohibitions or Restrictions on the Use of Certain Conventional Weapons which may be deemed to be Excessively Injurious or to Have Indiscriminate Effects concerning the Use of Mines, Booby Traps and Other Devices (adopted 3 May 1996, 3 December 1998) (1996) 35 ILM 1206.

[31] Protocol III to the UN Convention on Prohibitions or Restrictions on the Use of Certain Conventional Weapons which may be deemed to be Excessively Injurious or to Have Indiscriminate Effects

(Protocol IV)[32]; and on the explosive remnants of war (Protocol V).[33] This is the most important modern treaty concerning the restriction of use of weapons. It is an umbrella treaty, which provides a framework under which the prohibition of specific weapons is concretised through the adoption of successive protocols.

  e) Convention on the Prohibition of the Development, Production, Stockpiling and Use of Chemical Weapons and on Their Destruction.[34]

  f) Convention on the Prohibition of the Use, Stockpiling, Production and Transfer of Anti-Personal Mines and on Their Destruction.[35]

6. It is important that the development of conventional law does not obscure the importance of customary international law (CIL) as a source of the LOAC. We have already described the process by which CIL forms through practice and *opinio juris*.[36] Why is customary law still important in the context of the LOAC when there are so many treaty-based rules? Here are some examples of the pivotal role that customary law still plays in the international legal system:

  a) *Custom as a basis of general international law.* As we have seen above, treaties bind only those states that have ratified them after having participated in their negotiation, or which accede to them later without having participated in their elaboration. The effect of the norms contained in the treaties will therefore remain confined to the parties. However, in order to fulfil the role of reducing the harms of warfare the LOAC needs some general rules which are applicable to all states. This will constitute a common denominator and may be seen as the foundation of the LOAC.[37] Otherwise, depending upon the differing ratifications and accessions to treaties, the law might splinter to a point that practical applications would be rendered nugatory. Customary law provides a solution to this problem.[38] Since it is based on the idea of some general practice and legal opinion, it produces general rules of international law, which will bind all the states of the world. Therefore, customary law allows some

concerning Prohibitions or Restrictions on the Use of Incendiary Weapons (adopted 10 October 1980, entered into force 2 December 1983) 1342 UNTS 137.

[32] Protocol IV to the UN Convention on Prohibitions or Restrictions on the Use of Certain Conventional Weapons which may be deemed to be Excessively Injurious or to Have Indiscriminate Effects concerning Blinding Laser Weapons (adopted 13 December 1995, entered into force 30 July 1998) (1996) 35 ILM 1218.

[33] Protocol V on Explosive Remnants of War to the Convention on Prohibitions or Restrictions on the Use of Certain Conventional Weapons which may be deemed to be Excessively Injurious or to have Indiscriminate Effects (adopted 28 November 2003, entered into force 12 November 2006) UN Doc CCW/MSP/2003/2, available at <http://www.icrc.org/ihl.nsf/FULL/610?OpenDocument> accessed 14 May 2008.

[34] Convention on the Prohibition of the Development, Production, Stockpiling and Use of Chemical Weapons and on Their Destruction (adopted 3 September 1992, entered into force 29 April 1997) 1974 UNTS 45.

[35] Convention on the Prohibition of the Use, Stockpiling, Production and Transfer of Anti-Personnel Mines and on their Destruction (adopted 18 September 1997, entered into force 1 March 1999) 2056 UNTS 211.

[36] See para 2 above.

[37] *Military and Paramilitary Activities in and against Nicaragua* (*Nicaragua v United States of America*) (Judgment) [1986] ICJ Rep 14 para [218], referring to Art 3 common to Geneva Conventions I–IV.

[38] See especially: *Judgment of the Nuremburg International Military Tribunal 1946* (1947) 41 *American Journal of International Law* 172.

rules of the LOAC to be applied universally, without regard to the particular treaties that have been ratified or acceded to by the parties to armed conflict. It is possible that norms that originate in treaty law may, over time, become norms of customary international law.[39] Thus, if it is found that some rules expressed in Additional Protocol I have the status of customary law, these rules will place obligations on the states that have not yet ratified that Protocol.[40] Obviously, it is not the treaty rule which will apply; it is a more or less identical rule of customary law that will be applicable. Moreover, customary international law may serve as common denominator, setting out the minimum law applicable to a multi-national enforcement operation where the participating coalition of states have not ratified the same conventions and where, consequently, the law would fracture. In Somalia in 1992, more than 20 states participated in operations, not all having ratified the same conventions. Finally, customary international law may overcome the effect of reservations added by a state to a treaty rule. A state may exclude the application of a particular treaty rule to itself, provided that the rule is not indispensable to the object and purpose of the treaty, by entering a reservation at the time of ratification or accession.[41] Such a reservation only applies to the treaty norm, but it would not apply to the parallel rule in customary international law.[42]

b) *Filling of gaps.* There are areas of the LOAC which traditionally suffer from limited treaty regulation and, hence, from many gaps. For example, the law relating to non-international armed conflicts has always been less densely regulated than the law relating to international armed conflicts. This is the case because states have always been reticent to concede international rights of belligerency through an international convention to the rebels on their territory, who they regarded as criminals. Moreover, if such treaty regulation was in place, states feared that foreign institutions would intervene in what they felt was their internal affair. However, customary international law develops through practice and *opinio juris*, and through a careful survey of these the protections applying in non-international armed conflict can be seen to have been progressively enlarged, without the necessity for the formalisation of these rules in a treaty. Customary law is flexible; it can develop informally. Hence, in the 1990s, through the practice of the UN Security Council and the International Criminal Tribunal for the former Yugoslavia,[43] as well as through the attitude of many states, the applicability of a series of rules of the LOAC has been extended from international to non-international armed conflicts, augmenting the protection of war victims

---

[41] *Continental Shelf Case (Libyan Arab Jamahiriya v Malta)* [1985] ICJ Rep 13 para [27], and *Military and Paramilitary Activities in and against Nicaragua (Nicaragua v United States of America)* (Judgment) [1986] ICJ Rep 14 para [188].

[42] See, eg: *Western Front, Aerial Bombardment and Related Claims—Eritrea's Claims 1, 3, 5, 9–13, 14, 21, 25 & 26 (Ethiopia v Eritrea)* Eritrea-Ethiopia Claims Commission (19 December 2005) at <http://www.pca-cpa.org/upload/files/FINAL%20ER%20FRONT%20CLAIMS.pdf> accessed 14 May 2008 para [113], concerning Additional Protocol I Art 52(2).

[41] Vienna Convention on the Law of Treaties Arts 19 and 21.

[42] See, eg: the customary prohibition of chemical weapons which would displace any reservations that purport to allow their use: *Prosecutor v Tadic*, n 4, paras [119]–[124].

[43] See especially: *Prosecutor v Tadic*, n 4.

in non-international conflicts. This revolution was brought about primarily by way of developments in customary international law.

c) *Guide to interpretation.* Customary international law, and in particular state practice, may serve as a guide to the interpretation of rules of treaty law.[44] Thus, for example, Article 30 of Geneva Convention I provides that medical personnel whose retention is not indispensable to the care of prisoners of their nationality held in the custody of the adverse belligerent shall be returned to the party to the conflict to whom they owe allegiance, 'as soon as a road is open for their return and military requirements permit'.[45] Compliance with this provision has been aligned with the practice of the International Committee of the Red Cross (ICRC) to transfer medical personnel at the same time as the repatriation of seriously wounded and sick prisoners of war takes place.[46]

7. The question now arises as to which substantive rules of the LOAC are not only treaty rules, but also rules of customary international law. This complicated question cannot be definitively solved here, although it will be addressed at points throughout this book. For a more detailed answer, orientation has to be sought from the ICRC Customary Study,[47] which provides a thorough examination of the subject and sets out the norms, outside the universally accepted Geneva Convention of 1949, that can be considered to be part of custom. There is obviously a strong tendency to equalise conventional and customary law. It is difficult to assume that the states codify standards and principles of the LOAC in the major treaties that are different to those they are ready to, and do, apply in practice. Hence, the first rule of thumb to be applied is that most substantive rules of the LOAC are both conventional and customary. Only if a significant proportion of states oppose to a specific conventional rule will the customary status of that rule be doubtful. This is the case in respect of Article 44 of Additional Protocol I, which enlarges the definition of 'lawful combatant' in order to allow those who take part in guerrilla warfare to claim the status of prisoners of war if captured. Here, the United States and a series of Western powers, who feel that the application of this norm would legitimise terrorism, have resisted this new rule. As this resistance has, over the course of time since the negotiation of Additional Protocol I, dwindled to a small number of states it may be possible that even this Article has become customary.

The equation 'substantive rules of conventional law = customary law' has been accepted by the International Court of Justice in the *Nuclear Weapons* advisory opinion, where the court said the following:

> The extensive codification of humanitarian law and the extent of the accession to the resultant treaties, as well as the fact that the denunciation clauses that existed in the codification instruments have never been used, have provided the international community with a corpus of treaty rules the great majority of which had already became

---

[44] Vienna Convention on the Law of Treaties Art 31(3).
[45] Geneva Convention I Art 30.
[46] Provided for in Geneva Convention III Arts 109*ff.*
[47] J-M Henckaerts and L Doswald-Beck (eds), *Customary International Humanitarian Law Volume 1: Rules* (Cambridge, CUP, 2005).

customary and which reflected the most universally recognized humanitarian principles. These rules indicate the normal conduct and behaviour expected of States.[48]

This idea that most of the substantive rules of the LOAC that can found in the conventional law are also part of customary law is buttressed by the *ICRC Customary Study*. That study shows that the great majority of the rules of the Hague and Geneva Conventions, as well as of the Additional Protocols, have now acquired customary status. It also shows that most of the rules on the conduct of hostilities are also applicable as customary rules in non-international armed conflicts, thus considerably expanding the law applicable in those situations.

Comprehension check:

a)   What is customary international law?
b)   What are the main advantages of treaty law and what are the main advantages of customary law in the area of the LOAC?
c)   Where do you find customary rules of the LOAC?

Answers:

a)   Customary international law is formed from legal rules developed by the practice of states, and to some extent by international organs, to which a sense of legal opinion is added. The states must not only engage in conduct with respect to certain situations with some uniformity, continuity and universality; they must moreover be convinced that legal reasons compel or require to them to act as they do. In short, customary law rests on the idea of state practice and *opinio juris*.
b)   The main advantage of treaty law is its certainty and easy availability. The main advantages of customary international law are the flexibility it allows in the development of the law and its general applicability to all states without regard to who has become a party to what treaty.
c)   Due to the fact that the substantive rules of the LOAC are today, mostly, considered to express also customary international law, one convenient starting point in order to find customary rules is the different LOAC treaties. There is a practical, but not a legal, presumption that the substantive rule contained in a treaty expresses also customary law. The question has then to be asked if a particular rule has been contested by a sufficient number of states, so that its customary nature could be called into question. If there is such a significant attack against one rule, it may be impossible to recognise any customary status to it. One may also consult the ICRC Customary Study.

---

[48] *Legality of the Threat or Use of Nuclear Weapons (Advisory Opinion)* [1996] ICJ Rep 226 para [82]. See also PCA, Eritrea/Ethiopia Claims Commission, *Central Front, Ethiopia's Claim 2*, award of 28 April 2004, §§13*ff*; *Eritrea's Claims 2, 4, 6, 7, 8, 22*, award of 28 April 2004, §§21*ff*; *Prisoners of War, Ethiopia's Claim 4*, award of 1 July 2003, §§30–32; *Civilians' Claims, Ethiopia's Claim 5*, award of 17 December 2004, §§22*ff*; *Eritrea's Claims 15, 16, 23, 27–32*, award of 17 December 2004, §§26*ff*; *Western and Eastern Fronts, Ethiopia's Claims 1 and 3*, award of 19 December 2005, §§14*ff*; etc. Available at www.pca-cpa.org.

THE MARTENS CLAUSE

1. In the preamble to the 1899 Hague Convention II[1] and to the 1907 Hague Convention IV[2] one finds a peculiarly styled clause, which is well renowned within the sphere of international law. It has, in its 1907 iteration, the following wording:

> Until a more complete code of the laws of war has been issued, the High Contracting Parties deem it expedient to declare that, in cases not included in the Regulations adopted by them, the inhabitants and the belligerents remain under the protection and the rule of the principles of the law of nations, as they result from the usages established among civilized peoples, from the laws of humanity, and the dictates of public conscience.[3]

This clause has been repeated in the denunciation clauses of the 1949 Geneva Conventions,[4] and has also been recalled in Article 1(2) of Additional Protocol I with the following, somewhat modernised, wording:

> In cases not covered by this Protocol or by other international agreements, civilians and combatants remain under the protection and authority of the principles of international law derived from established custom, from the principles of humanity and from the dictates of public conscience.[5]

2. This clause was initially suggested to the 1899 Hague Peace Conference by the

---

[1] Hague Convention (II) with Respect to the Laws and Customs of War on Land and its annex: Regulations concerning the Laws and Customs of War on Land (adopted 29 July 1899, entered into force 4 September 1900) (1898–99) 187 CTS 429 (Hague Convention II 1899) Preamble.

[2] Hague Convention (IV) respecting the Laws and Customs of War on Land and its annex: Regulations concerning the Laws and Customs of War on Land (adopted 18 October 1907, entered into force 26 January 1910) (1907) 205 CTS 227 (Hague Convention IV 1907) Preamble.

[3] Hague Convention IV 1907 Preamble.

[4] Geneva Convention I for the Amelioration of the Condition of the Wounded and Sick in Armed Forces in the Field (adopted 12 August 1949, entered into force 21 October 1950) 75 UNTS 31 (Geneva Convention I) Art 63; Geneva Convention II for the Amelioration of the Condition of Wounded, Sick and Shipwrecked Members of Armed Forces at Sea (adopted 12 August 1949, entered into force 21 October 1950) 75 UNTS 85 (Geneva Convention II) Art 64; Geneva Convention III relative to the Treatment of Prisoners of War (adopted 12 August 1949, entered into force 21 October 1950) 75 UNTS 135 (Geneva Convention III) Art 142; Geneva Convention IV Relative to the Protection of Civilian Persons in Time of War (adopted 12 August 1949, entered into force 21 October 1950) 75 UNTS 287 (Geneva Convention IV) Art 158.

[5] Protocol Additional to the Geneva Conventions of 12 August 1949, and relating to the Protection of Victims of International Armed Conflicts (adopted 8 June 1977, entered into force 7 December 1978) 1125 UNTS 3 Art 2(1).

Russian delegate, Frederic de Martens, a professor of international law. Its purpose was to strengthen the then emerging LOAC, which was to be partially codified by the Hague Conventions. The delegates at the Hague were well aware of the fact that they had not produced a complete codification of the LOAC and had in fact only put forward relatively few principles and rules, more often than not relating to prohibited means and methods of warfare. At the same time, huge areas of the conduct of armed conflicts remained beyond the scope of treaty-based regulation. In particular, the protection of civilians, in occupied territory and elsewhere, received scant attention at the conference. Conduct in occupied territories was subject to some regulation as a result of the conference, but the rules were few.[6] Moreover, these rules were often formulated in vague terms or with problematic exceptions. They were concerned more with the administrative powers of the occupier than with a precise set of rules aimed at the protection of civilians. Considering that there thus remained important gaps in the emerging LOAC, the delegates unanimously agreed to include in the preamble to Hague Convention II 1899 the so-called Martens clause, requiring the belligerents to behave in a civilised and humane way even if, in a particular instance, no specific rule could be found in the corpus of the codified LOAC. They particularly had in mind situations which arise in occupied territories, where an occupant faces a population which is, or which he or she deems to be, hostile to his or her presence.

3. The clause has thus two main functions, although others may be added. These two main functions are aptly summarised in the ICRC Commentary to the Additional Protocols:

> First, despite the considerable increase in the number of subjects covered by the law of armed conflicts, and despite the detail of its codification, it is not possible for any codification to be complete at any given moment; thus the Martens clause prevents the assumption that anything which is not explicitly prohibited by the relevant treaties is therefore permitted. Secondly, it should be seen as a dynamic factor proclaiming the applicability of the principles mentioned regardless of subsequent developments of types of situation or technology.[7]

We must now examine these two functions in greater detailed.

First, there may be a great temptation, in the midst of wartime constraints, to apply the concept of sovereignty to argue that all conduct not explicitly prohibited by the LOAC remains lawful: what is not prohibited is therefore allowed.[8] Given the existence of important gaps in the LOAC a limitation on this kind of argument performs a useful function. If such a constraint did not exist the gaps in the written law could lead to utterly destructive and inhumane behaviours, provoking thereafter reprisals of the same kind, creating a continuing cycle of inhumanity. The Martens clause requires all belligerents to consider whether proposed conduct, even if not

---

[6] Hague Regulations 1907 Arts 42–56.

[7] ICRC, *Commentary on the Additional Protocols of 8 June 1977 to the Geneva Conventions of 12 August 1949* (Geneva, ICRC, 1987) 38–9.

[8] For the apogee of the approach to International Law, *The Case of the SS Lotus* (*Turkey v France*) PCIJ Rep Series A No 10, 19.

explicitly prohibited, is compatible with the principles of humanity and compassion.[9] Thus, a moral principle is introduced into the law.

Secondly, the Martens clause may serve as a principle perpetuating the humanitarian ideals and the great principles underlying the LOAC regardless of the inevitable changes in conduct of warfare, due to, in particular, the development of new technology.[10] The clause means that the humanitarian aspects of the LOAC cannot be displaced on the basis of an argument premised upon the existence of a 'fundamental change of circumstances'.

To these main functions, other ones could be added. Thus, for example, the Martens clause serves as a basis for interpreting the LOAC in a humanitarian sense.[11] Moreover, it can be seen as a call to apply international human rights law in order to complement the LOAC and eventually to fill in its gaps.[12] Furthermore, it can be read as a reminder that customary international law applies to all armed conflicts, whether or not a particular situation or event is contemplated by treaty law, and whether or not the relevant treaty law binds as such the parties to the conflict.[13] Finally, the command to consider humanity contained in the clause can serve the purpose of stimulating the states which make the LOAC to heed the interests of the potential victims of armed conflict when negotiating new LOAC norms.

4. Whilst its existence is sometimes forgotten, there is today no doubt that the Martens clause is part and parcel of the applicable LOAC. It has not been confined to the usual fate of a preamble, seen just as a policy indication or a wish expressed by the parties, devoid of any specific legal meaning. That the Martens clause is different has already been made clear by the fact that its content has been inserted into specific legal provisions found in the Geneva Conventions and in Additional Protocol I, a clear contrast to its preambular position in Hague Convention IV. Moreover, the clause has been seen as imposing specific positive law obligations on the participants in armed conflict. For example, in the *Krupp* case, the US Military tribunal in Nuremburg declared that:

> The Preamble is much more than a pious declaration. It is a general clause, making the usages established among civilized nations, the laws of humanity and the dictates of public conscience into the legal yardstick to be applied if and when the specific provisions of the Convention and the Regulations annexed to it do not cover specific cases occurring in warfare, or concomitant to warfare.[14]

In addition, the International Court of Justice, in the *Nuclear Weapons* Advisory Opinion, expressed as follows:

> The Court would likewise refer, in relation to these principles [of the LOAC], to the Martens Clause, which was first included in the Hague Convention II with Respect to

---

[9] *Prosecutor v Kupreskic* (Judgment) IT-95-16-T (14 January 2000) para [525].

[10] *Legality of the Threat or Use of Nuclear Weapons (Advisory Opinion)* [1996] ICJ Rep 226 para [78].

[11] *Nuclear Weapons, ibid*, paras [78]–[79] and *Kupreskic*, n 9, para [525].

[12] T Meron, 'The Martens Clause, Principles of Humanity, and Dictates of Public Conscience' (2000) 94 *American Journal of International Law* 78, 88.

[13] Meron, *ibid*, 87–8.

[14] *United States v Krupp* (1948) 15 AD 622.

the Laws and Customs of War on Land of 1899 and which has proved to be an effective means of addressing the rapid evolution of military technology.[15]

One may regret that in practice the Martens clause is not invoked as often as it could and should be.

Comprehension check:

a) In what contexts may the Martens clause serve and to what end?
b) How can it be argued that the clause is part and parcel of the law and not only a non-binding moral principle?

Answers:

a)   The clause can serve in many contexts, always to the end of strengthening IHL. Some examples are the following:
i)   The clause may help to fill in gaps, in particular by precluding the argument that because a behaviour is not explicitly prohibited it must be considered allowed.
ii)   The clause may recall that the main principles of the LOAC, and in particular the principle of humanity, remain paramount notwithstanding important changes in the technical, political or social environment of warfare.
iii) The clause may serve in the interpretation of particular provisions of IHL.
iv)   The clause may be taken as a reminder of the applicability of International Human Rights Law in conjunction with the LOAC, or in order to fill its gaps.
v)   The clause can be taken as a reminder of the applicability of customary international law alongside and contemporaneously to treaty law.
vi)   The clause may also serve as a basis for creating new rules of IHL at a diplomatic conference, when the delegates are inspired by its injunction of humanity. Further roles can be found. The clause is open-ended and can be invoked in many different, and changing, contexts.
b)   One may invoke in particular two grounds: (1) the fact that the clause is now inserted in operational treaty provisions rather than in a preamble; and (2) international jurisprudence has stated that the clause, which has attained customary status, is part of positive (applicable) law, eg in the *Krupp* case or the *Nuclear Weapons* case.

---

[15] Nuclear Weapons, n 10, para [78] and compare Dissenting Judgement of Judge Shahabuddeen, 405–410.

10

INTERNATIONAL AND NON-INTERNATIONAL ARMED CONFLICTS

Learning objectives: To assess the importance of the distinction between international armed conflicts (IACs) and non-international armed conflicts (NAICs) and to evaluate the recent decline in the importance of this division.

1. Until the adoption of the Geneva Conventions in 1949, the LOAC was only designed to regulate wars, or, as they came to be known, international armed conflicts. The most typical form of international armed conflict, and indeed the only type that existed before 1949, was a war between states. State A confronted, and declared war on, State B; other states made a decision to participate in the hostilities on one side and on the other; and, finally, a series of further states remained outside the conflict and claimed the status of neutrals. The conventions that were negotiated and concluded prior to 1949, such as the 14 Hague Conventions adopted in 1907 (14 if one includes those not regulating LOAC questions) or the Geneva Gas Protocol,[1] adopted in 1925, only applied to such inter-state wars. However, there had always been another, albeit unregulated, type of armed conflict: civil wars. In these conflicts, confined to the territory of one state, insurgents rose up against their government and sometimes, depending upon the outcome of battles between the government and insurgents and the relative strengths of the combatants, managed to control a part of the national territory. Prior to 1949, there were no rules within the LOAC that applied to such conflicts. The states refused to draft such rules, feeling that insurrection and rebellion were a purely domestic matter in which no other states should have a say or have the ability to intervene, and that internal armed conflict should not be subject to rules of international law that would constrain their liberty to act. A conflict that had no international dimension was thus considered to fall into the sphere of exclusive national jurisdiction.

2. However, if the conflict had wide ranging effects within the state that persisted for a lengthy period of time, incentives arose to give the rebels some international status. This was true both on the part of the government of the state affected by the

---

[1] Geneva Protocol for the Prohibition of the Use in War of Asphyxiating, Poisonous or Other Gases, and of Bacteriological Methods of Warfare (signed 17 June 1925, entered into force 8 February 1928) 94 LNTS 65.

civil war and for third states. First, the central government that was fighting the rebels often wanted to be released from the international law duty to respond to unlawful acts, with respect to the acts of the rebels in a part of the territory it had no control over. Secondly, foreign governments also had an interest in giving the rebels some international status, since in these circumstances they could apply the rules of neutrality to both belligerents, and be able to treat directly with the rebels, if they controlled a part of the national territory. For example, if some nationals of a foreign state were present in the part of the territory controlled by the rebels, trying to obtain some protection for them through the offices of the central government would have been illusory, since the central government had no control over the areas where these foreign nationals were situated. In this case direct dealings with the rebels could be of greater use. These desires led the law to develop the so-called 'recognition of belligerency'. To the extent that the rebels were recognised as belligerents, they enjoyed all of the rights and duties of belligerency under the LOAC applicable to international armed conflicts. The local government could opt to recognise the belligerency of the rebels at any time, whereas the foreign states could do so only if the rebels controlled a part of the territory and conducted hostilities in a militarily organised and disciplined way, respecting the LOAC. The key point is that recognition of belligerency was a subjective matter: the application of the LOAC depended on a discretionary political act, either by the territorial state or by third states, which they were free to undertake or not to undertake. The application of the LOAC depended on that act; which was by no means automatic. In situations where, for political reasons, no recognition of belligerency took place, the conflict remained unregulated by the rules of the LOAC. After 1949, recognition of belligerency has fallen progressively into oblivion, since the law has changed to accommodate non-international armed conflicts.

3. Humanitarian needs were, and are, no less pressing in internal conflicts than in international ones. Quite on the contrary: the savageness of internal conflicts was often greater than that of inter-state wars. Moreover, the use of some prohibited means and methods of warfare or the commission of outrages on persons *hors de combat* are no less shocking in an internal conflict than in an international one.[2] Therefore, the International Committee of the Red Cross (ICRC) undertook a series of humanitarian initiatives during both the Russian Civil War (1917–1921) and the Spanish Civil War (1936–39). In the Spanish Civil War, the ICRC concluded an agreement with the belligerents including provisions that ensured that as many captured combatants as possible were to be seen as having a status equivalent to prisoners of war, with the attendant rights and protections; that the protective emblems of the Red Cross were to be recognised and protected; that international assistance for civilians would be transported and distributed under the aegis of the ICRC; and that a central information agency would collect all information on prisoners and missing civilians.

This practice was codified in 1949 through the adoption of Common Article 3 to Geneva Conventions I–IV, which sets out, in identical wording in all four Conventions, a set of minimum guarantees to be respected during non-international armed

---

[2] *Prosecutor v Tadic* (Decision on the Defence Motion for Interlocutory Appeal on Jurisdiction) IT-49-1-AR72 (2 October 1995) paras [97] and [119].

conflicts. For the first time, states were prepared for international law to regulate these conflicts. This Article constitutes a sort of 'mini-convention', providing a set of minimum fundamental protections applicable in all situations of armed conflict,[3] and possibly even applicable beyond the sphere of armed conflict. In its most important part, it reads as follows:

> In the case of an armed conflict not of an international character occurring in the territory of one of the High Contracting Parties, each Party to the conflict shall be bound to apply, as a minimum, the following provisions:
>
> (1) Persons taking no active part in the hostilities, including members of the armed forces who have laid down their arms and those placed hors de combat by sickness, wounds, detention, or any other cause, shall in all circumstances be humanely treated, without any adverse distinction founded on race, colour, religion or faith, sex, birth or wealth, or any other similar criteria.
>
> To this end, the following acts are and shall remain prohibited at any time and any place whatsoever with respect to the above-mentioned persons:
>
> (a) violence to life and person, in particular murder of all kinds, mutilation, cruel treatment and torture;
> (b) taking of hostages;
> (c) outrages upon personal dignity, in particular, humiliating and degrading treatment;
> (d) the passing of sentences and the carrying out of executions without previous judgment pronounced by a regularly constituted court, affording all the judicial guarantees which are recognized as indispensable by civilized peoples.
>
> (2) The wounded, sick and shipwrecked shall be collected and cared for.[4]

4. Additional Protocol II to the Geneva Conventions continues the trend towards greater international law regulation of non-international armed conflict. The obligations imposed by Common Article 3 are developed, with the prohibited acts specified in greater detail[5]; the way in which the wounded and sick have to be collected and cared for prescribed[6]; and a series of rules concerning the prohibited means and methods of warfare inserted.[7] Further evidence for this trend is provided by a series of modern conventions that create obligations that, at least partially, apply to all types of armed conflicts, without any distinctions between international and non-international armed conflicts. For example, the Second Protocol to the

---

[3] *Military and Paramilitary Activities in and against Nicaragua (Nicaragua v United States of America)* (Merits) [1986] ICJ Rep 14 para [218].

[4] Geneva Convention I for the Amelioration of the Condition of the Wounded and Sick in Armed Forces in the Field (adopted 12 August 1949, entered into force 21 October 1950) 75 UNTS 31 (Geneva Convention I) Art 3; Geneva Convention II for the Amelioration of the Condition of Wounded, Sick and Shipwrecked Members of Armed Forces at Sea (adopted 12 August 1949, entered into force 21 October 1950) 75 UNTS 85 (Geneva Convention II) Art 3; Geneva Convention III relative to the Treatment of Prisoners of War (adopted 12 August 1949, entered into force 21 October 1950) 75 UNTS 135 (Geneva Convention III) Art 3; Geneva Convention IV Relative to the Protection of Civilian Persons in Time of War (adopted 12 August 1949, entered into force 21 October 1950) 75 UNTS 287 (Geneva Convention IV) Art 3.

[5] Protocol Additional to the Geneva Conventions of 12 August 1949, and relating to the Protection of Victims of Non-International Armed Conflicts (adopted 8 June 1977, entered into force 7 December 1978) 1125 UNTS 609 (Additional Protocol II) Art 4.

[6] Additional Protocol II Arts 9–12.

[7] Additional Protocol II Arts 13*ff*.

Hague Cultural Property Convention, adopted in 1999, applies equally to international and non-international armed conflicts.[8]

5. As a consequence of such developments, a modern law of armed conflicts is emerging. It centres on the notion of 'armed conflict' when considering whether international law norms should be applicable and gives up, at least partially, the old dichotomy between international and internal armed conflicts. This new paradigm has arisen not just from the conventions adopted in the recent past, but also from the practice of UN Security Council,[9] the Statutes of the International Criminal Tribunals[10] and the case law of these tribunals,[11] which have contributed conspicuously towards the development of this modern law. Two evolutions explain the shift from dichotomy to inclusiveness.

First, most modern conflicts are complex blends of internal and international elements. The conflict in the former Yugoslavia during the years 1991–95 is an example of these so-called 'mixed armed conflicts'. In that case, it was extremely difficult to disentangle the different elements in order to apply different sets of legal rules to the internal and international aspects of the conflict. In one valley the conflict might be non-international, whereas in the other, the intervention of foreign troops might render the conflict international. Therefore, why maintain a distinction which is so difficult to apply in situations of modern warfare?

Secondly, the distinctions in legal protections afforded in international and non-international armed conflicts were progressively felt to be unjustified. Why should the civilians in some Bosnian valley have the fully-fledged LOAC protection applicable in international armed conflicts, whereas some other civilians should be much less protected because in the valley in which they happen to live the conflict is only non-international in character? The difference may be fortuitous: if foreign fighters or foreign-controlled fighters participate in hostilities, the conflict may there be international in character and all the rules of the LOAC apply; whereas if such foreign or foreign-controlled fighters do not appear in an area, the conflict there remains non-international and only the rules of the LOAC for non-international conflicts apply. The rules that applied in non-international armed conflict (NIAC) were traditionally much less numerous and much less compelling. Faced with this situation, the Security Council resolutions concerning the conflict in the former Yugoslavia called for respect of IHL in general, without distinguishing as to the type of armed conflict.[12]

The International Tribunal for the former Yugoslavia thereafter has applied many rules of the LOAC that were previously thought to be applicable only in situations of international armed conflicts to situations of internal armed conflict, holding that customary international law has evolved to the point of prohibiting

---

[8] Second Protocol to the Hague Convention of 1954 for the Protection of Cultural Property in the Event of Armed Conflict (adopted 26 March 1999, entered into force 9 March 2004) (1999) 38 ILM 769 Art 22(1).

[9] See, eg: UNSC Res 1234 (9 April 1999) UN Doc/S/Res/1234 para [6], concerning the conflict in the Democratic Republic of Congo.

[10] Statute of the International Criminal Tribunal for the Former Yugoslavia (adopted 25 May 1993) 32 ILM 1192 and Statute of the International Criminal Tribunal for Rwanda (adopted 8 November 1994) 33 ILM 1589.

[11] See especially: *Tadic*, n 2.

[12] See, eg: UNSC Res 771 (13 August 1992) UN Doc S/RES/771 para [1].

behaviour in NAIC that treaty norms previously proscribed only in IAC. Thus, for example, it was held that the use of chemical weapons would be a war crime (a violation of IHL) in internal armed conflicts.[13] A glance at Article 8 of the Rome Statute of the International Criminal Court confirms the movement towards bridging the gap between the two types of conflict, with many of the war crimes applying to both international and non-international armed conflicts.[14]

6. What is the position today? It is not possible to ignore the difference between international and non-international armed conflicts, since the law has not developed to the point of erasing the distinction. A unitary system of law that applies to all armed conflicts is not yet in existence. However, as the *ICRC Customary Study* shows, the merger of the two branches has already progressed impressively.[15] Most of the important rules concerning both the protection of persons and means and methods of warfare today apply to both types of conflict. However, there are still three areas where the difference in the law applying to IAC and NIAC remains more or less marked. In the first two, the difference is conspicuous; in the last it is less strong:

a) The law relating to *occupied territories*. There are no occupied territories in non-international armed conflicts: the rebels do not occupy foreign territory if they exercise exclusive control over it, and the government does not occupy foreign territory if it re-conquers the parts of the national soil previously held by the rebels. Belligerent occupation thus still applies only to inter-state wars.

b) The law relating to *prisoners of war*. Rebels who take up arms against the state do not possess combatant status under the LOAC and thus they possess no combatant immunity. That means that they can be punished for having taken up the arms against their government. Thus, rebels may face criminal prosecution not only for war crimes or other common crimes committed, which is also true for prisoners of war, but equally for having fought at all, which is not the case for prisoners of war. The foregoing does not mean, however, that the government may not decide to grant rebels a status analogous to that of prisoners of war by special agreement. As we have seen, this happened in certain cases during the Spanish Civil War.

c) The law relating to *means and methods of warfare*. The prohibition of certain weapons in many conventions applies in 'all circumstances'. Hence, it may be said that these prohibitions apply during non-international armed conflicts. This is the case, for example, in the Biological Weapons Convention[16] and the Chemical Weapons Convention.[17] In some cases there is an explicit mention of applicability of the conventional norm to NIAC, for example, in the

---

[13] *Tadic*, n 2, para [119].

[14] Rome Statute of the International Criminal Court (adopted 17 July 1998, entered into force 1 July 2002) 2187 UNTS 3 Arts 8(2)(b) and 8(2)(e).

[15] J-M Henckaerts and L Doswald-Beck (eds), *Customary International Humanitarian Law Volume 1: Rules* (Cambridge, CUP, 2005).

[16] Convention on the Prohibition of Development, Production and Stockpiling of Bacteriological (Biological) and Toxin Weapons and on Their Destruction (adopted 16 December 1971, entered into force 26 March 1975) 1015 UNTS 164 Art 1.

[17] Convention on the Prohibition of the Development, Production, Stockpiling and Use of Chemical Weapons and on Their Destruction (adopted 3 September 1992, entered into force 29 April 1997) 1974 UNTS 45 Art 1.

revised Protocol II to the 1980 Conventional Weapons Convention on the Use of Mines, Booby-Traps and Other Devices.[18] However, if one looks into the Rome Statute on the International Criminal Court, Article 8(2)(b), which deals with war crimes in international armed conflicts, it contains some prohibitions on means and methods of warfare, particularly relating to arms and ammunition, that are not reproduced in Article 8(2)(e) which sets out actions that are considered to be war crimes in NIAC.[19] Thus, the prohibition of poisoned weapons is not mentioned in the list of war crimes in non-international armed conflicts, whereas it is listed as a criminal act in international armed conflicts. Judicial practice in cases such as *Tadic* may well be taken to have overcome differences in the state of the law and aligned these prohibitions for the two types of conflict. However, some doubts remain and some potential differences could be found in this area. Perhaps it can be said, in agreement with authors such as Meron, that there is forthwith a presumption that proscribed arms are prohibited in both types of conflict, but this presumption can be reversed by specific evidence.[20] Indeed, it must be added that even for international armed conflicts, the list of prohibited weapons found in Article 8(2)(b) leaves some loopholes with regard to weapons undoubtedly prohibited in the LOAC: thus, poisoned weapons are listed, but chemical and biological weapons are not. Hence, the absence of certain weapons from the list in Article 8(2)(e) may therefore not be determinative with regard to what is allowed and what is prohibited under the LOAC and in the definition of customary international law. However, these absences mean that certain crimes are not within the jurisdiction of the International Criminal Court. Overall, these distinctions do not detract from the tendency towards the alignment of the prohibitions in situations of international and non-international armed conflicts.

Comprehension check:

a)   Why has there traditionally been a difference between the LOAC applicable in international and non-international armed conflicts?
b)   What is the practical legal reason for the distinction between these two types of conflict?
c)   Where do we stand today regarding the difference between international armed conflicts and non-international armed conflicts?

Answers:

a)   States were ready to concede belligerents rights and duties in their fight against other states, since that was inherently an international phenomenon to

---

[18] Amended Protocol to the UN Convention on Prohibitions or Restrictions on the Use of Certain Conventional Weapons which may be deemed to be Excessively Injurious or to Have Indiscriminate Effects concerning the Use of Mines, Booby Traps and Other Devices (adopted 3 May 1996, entered into force 3 December 1998) (1996) 35 ILM 1206 Arts 1(2) and 1(3).

[19] Rome Statute, n 14.

[20] T Meron, 'International Law in the Age of Human Rights' (2003) 301 *Recueil des Cours de l'Académie de Droit International* 161.

be regulated by international law. If the other belligerent should be held to certain duties, if certain rights should be exercised against the opponent party, an international rule had to apply. Conversely, with regard to non-international armed conflicts, the states were not ready to assume any international regulation, since they considered the civil war taking place on their territory as a purely internal matter in which no foreign state or institution should have a say and to which international legal rules should not apply.

b) Traditionally and to a non-negligible extent even today, the applicable rules of the LOAC are not the same. All rules of the LOAC apply to international armed conflicts; a smaller part of these rules apply also to non-international armed conflict. In order to determine which rules apply, the distinction remains important.

c) The exact situation today is not easy to define, as the law in this area is in a period of development. The treaties still have a marked distinction; but customary international law has progressed. Today, all rules concerning the protection of persons may be said to apply in an internal armed conflict, excepting those provisions that are dependant on prisoners of war status and the rules regarding occupied territories. As far as the means and methods of warfare are concerned, all the main rules apply to both types of conflict. However, some doubts remain as to certain arms. According to the *ICRC Customary Study*, prohibited arms must be taken today to be prohibited in all circumstances, in international and internal armed conflict. We are thus moving towards a corpus of the LOAC which will apply to all armed conflicts alike, with clearly demarcated exceptions in some areas, such as prisoners of war and belligerent occupation.

11

APPLICABILITY OF THE LOAC: MATERIAL SCOPE OF APPLICABILITY

Learning objectives: To understand the principles which govern the material scope of applicability of the LOAC.

1. All branches of the law are divided in two parts. Before the substantive rules are applied, the legal order must first determine whether the extant situation is one in which the regulatory norms apply. This species of legal inquiry, which is the first province of any legal question, is devoted to the determination of the applicability of the law to a certain set of situations. Thus, for example, the LOAC is designed to apply only in a time of armed conflict and not in peacetime. This limits its scope of legal applicability. There are four aspects of applicability of legal rules:

a) subject matter applicability, or material scope of applicability, also known as *ratione materiae*, which defines 'situations of armed conflict' in which LOAC is applicable;

b) the personal scope of the applicability of the LOAC, also known as *ratione personae*, which addresses questions of the applicability of the LOAC to state organs, peace-keeping personnel of international organisations, all belligerents that are not a state and all individuals participating in the armed conflict;

c) the spatial scope of applicability of the LOAC, also known as *ratione loci*, which addresses questions of the applicability of the LOAC to the territory of the belligerent states and further spaces where effective fighting takes place, such as the high seas;

d) the temporal scope of applicability of the LOAC, also known as *ratione temporis*, which addresses questions of the continuing applicability of the LOAC during a situation of armed conflict and the cessation of applicability of the LOAC rules at the end of a conflict.

It is now necessary to enter into a more detailed analysis of these four aspects of applicability.

Once it has been determined that the norms of the LOAC are applicable in a particular situation, the substantive rules may be applied. This is the second province of the law. Thus, for example, if Geneva Convention III on prisoners of war is found to be applicable in all of the four dimensions mentioned above, we

may proceed to ask questions regarding the substantive guarantees the convention affords to prisoners of war (POWs), such as the right to be treated humanely, the right not to be required to perform to dangerous work and the right to be provided with adequate food and care.[1]

The concepts of applicability and application of the law are thus performed in a natural sequence. First, one has to ask if a set of rules is applicable in a given context. If the answer is in the negative, the enquiry stops there, and that set of rules is not applicable in the particular circumstances. The lawyer then has to look for other sets of rules that could apply to the given situation. Thus, for example, if the LOAC does not apply because the situation does not yet have the characteristics of an armed conflict, but has remained a local riot, international human rights law may apply. The question of applicability must then to be decided anew for that separate branch of the law. If, conversely, the answer is positive, and the lawyer finds that a set of rules is applicable to a given situation, he or she will proceed to apply the substantive rules. This is the second phase of his or her work.

2. As far as the *material scope of application* is concerned, the applicability of the LOAC essentially turns on the concept of an 'armed conflict' and some minor related concepts. In other words, the applicability of the LOAC depends on the existence of an armed conflict. This is true for international armed conflicts (IACs) as well as non-international armed conflicts (NIACs), even if the definition of 'armed conflict' is not absolutely identical in both branches of the LOAC.

In the context of IAC, the material scope of applicability turns on three distinct legal concepts, all mentioned in the most important provision on the matter, Common Article 2 of the four Geneva Conventions.[2] It is called a 'common article' because it is reproduced with the same wording in all four conventions. The three concepts are: (1) armed conflict; (2) declared war; (3) occupation of a territory without armed resistance. A further situation is added by Article 1(4) of Additional Protocol I,[3] namely 'wars of national liberation'. If the situation on the ground can be considered to represent either an armed conflict, or a declared war, or a military occupation, even without resistance, or a war of national liberation, it can be said to be an IAC. As far as NIACs are concerned, the conditions of applicability differ according to the instruments we are concerned with, whether the applicable norms are contained in the Geneva Conventions or Additional Protocol II.[4] For any NIAC it is necessary to have actual fighting of some intensity and the rebel forces to have

---

[1] Geneva Convention III relative to the Treatment of Prisoners of War (adopted 12 August 1949, entered into force 21 October 1950) 75 UNTS 135 (Geneva Convention III).

[2] Geneva Convention I for the Amelioration of the Condition of the Wounded and Sick in Armed Forces in the Field (adopted 12 August 1949, entered into force 21 October 1950) 75 UNTS 31 (Geneva Convention I) Art 2; Geneva Convention II for the Amelioration of the Condition of Wounded, Sick and Shipwrecked Members of Armed Forces at Sea (adopted 12 August 1949, entered into force 21 October 1950) 75 UNTS 85 (Geneva Convention II) Art 2; Geneva Convention III Art 2; and Geneva Convention IV Relative to the Protection of Civilian Persons in Time of War (adopted 12 August 1949, entered into force 21 October 1950) 75 UNTS 287 (Geneva Convention IV) Art 2.

[3] Protocol Additional to the Geneva Conventions of 12 August 1949, and relating to the Protection of Victims of International Armed Conflicts (adopted 8 June 1977, entered into force 7 December 1978) 1125 UNTS 3 (Additional Protocol 1) Art 1(4).

[4] Protocol Additional to the Geneva Conventions of 12 August 1949, and relating to the Protection of Victims of Non-International Armed Conflicts (adopted 8 June 1977, entered into force 7 December 1978) 1125 UNTS 609 (Additional Protocol II).

some degree of organisation. Moreover, in order for Additional Protocol II to be applicable, there must be some territorial control by the rebel forces. We will examine all of these criteria more in detail in the following paragraphs.

3. Let us turn first to *international armed conflicts*, those armed conflicts between states. Common Articles 2(1) and 2(2) of the Geneva Conventions, which are the primary sources regarding the definition of IAC, read as follows:

> In addition to the provisions which shall be implemented in peacetime,[5] the present Convention shall apply to all cases of declared war or of any other armed conflict which may arise between two or more of the High Contracting Parties, even if the state of war is not recognized by one of them.

> The Convention shall also apply to all cases of partial or total occupation of the territory of a High Contracting Party, even if the said occupation meets with no armed resistance.

Three independent thresholds of applicability can thus be identified. These thresholds apply to the LOAC in general. The general criteria set out in Common Article 2 of the Geneva Conventions have crystallised into rules that govern the applicability of all LOAC rules under IAC, for both customary and conventional law, and do not merely set out criteria defining the scope of application of the Geneva Conventions themselves. Thus, customary international law and all other IHL conventions also apply if one of these three thresholds is met. This is true even for older conventions which expressly declare that they apply in cases of 'war', such as Hague Convention IV.[6] The rules governing the material scope of application contained in the Geneva Conventions modify and supersede the applicability criteria of these older texts. This is expressly stated when we are concerned with the relationship between the Geneva Conventions and the Hague Conventions.[7] For the other conventions concluded prior to 1949, such as the Geneva Gas Protocol, the change is achieved by way of informal modification, customarily accepted by all of the states. By their practice and *opinio juris* the states have agreed to align themselves with the new relevant criteria expressed and accepted by them in the Geneva Conventions. The three thresholds are the following:

a) *Effective armed conflict, even if a state of war is not recognised by one or both parties.* Two points must be made here. First, the essential question is whether there are effective hostilities between two or more states. It is not essential that these hostilities be conceptualised by the involved states as a formal war. The fact that hostilities are taking place is sufficient to trigger the application of the rules of the LOAC. By utilising this standard as the trigger for application, the Geneva Convention closed a problematic loophole in the applicability of the law. In effect, one may argue almost endlessly about the precise definition of war.[8] It seems generally accepted that a state of war rests on the will of the

---

[5] Those provisions which require the dissemination of knowledge regarding IHL, for example, Geneva Convention III Art 127.

[6] Convention (IV) respecting the Laws and Customs of War on Land (adopted 18 October 1907, entered into force 26 January 1910) (1907) 205 CTS 227.

[7] Geneva Convention II Art 58; Geneva Convention III Art 135; Geneva Convention IV Art 154.

[8] See, eg: *Kawasaki Kisen Kabushiki Kaisha of Kobe v Bantham Steamship Co Ltd* [1939] 2 KB 544 and *Navios Corporation v The Ulysses II* (1958) 161 F Supp 932.

participant states to consider themselves at war.[9] Thus, a subjective element dominates the determination of the existence or non-existence of a war. This subjective will to consider oneself at war was normally expressed in a formal war declaration. Hence, a state could always pretend, whilst engaged in hostile action against another state, that it was not making war, but, for example, merely engaging in a police action, in a reprisal or in an act of self-defence. By using such a contention, Italy, when it bombed Corfu in 1923, or Japan, when it attacked Manchuria in 1931, pretended to avoid, among other things, the applicability of the LOAC. The Geneva Conventions now make the law applicable as soon as there are armed hostilities as a simple fact, judged by an objective standard. Thus, unbroken coverage of the LOAC is guaranteed for all those who need its protection in situations of effective armed clashes, irrespective of niceties as to the precise legal qualification of the conflict. Secondly, it must be added that the interpretation of the threshold of an armed conflict is quite liberal and generous, at least as far as IACs are concerned. The LOAC applies as soon as even minor hostilities occur. One injured person or one prisoner is sufficient to trigger the application of the law. In other words, no specific intensity of the conflict is needed; low intensity hostile contacts between states are sufficient to render the LOAC applicable. The reason for this policy choice is that it is clear that the conventional protections should apply every time some protected person is in need of the LOAC guarantees, and every time restriction is needed on particular means and methods of warfare. The necessity for the protection of the LOAC does not depend on the particular intensity of a conflict, but only on the fact of some, even comparatively minor, hostilities.

b) *Declared war*. Article 2 does not rule out declared wars as a trigger to the application of the LOAC. If a party declares war, and thus establishes a state of war with another state, the LOAC applies. Such a declaration of war is extremely rare today. Consideration of the legality of a war is not essential, since the LOAC applies independently from *jus ad bellum* considerations.[10] If the declaration of war is followed by hostilities, which is normally the case, the applicability of the LOAC is thrown back on the first category, that of effective armed conflict. We then no longer need to consider this separate threshold. However, if the declaration of war is not followed by effective hostilities, the LOAC nonetheless applies. Thus, many Latin American states declared war on Germany during World War II, but never effectively fought against it. In such cases, the rules on means and methods of warfare will not apply in a practical sense, simply because there is no fighting. However, other rules, such as the rules protecting enemy civilians on the territory of a belligerent state, will be applicable and must be complied with by the states in their mutual relations.

c) *Occupation of a territory without armed resistance*. This last category is mentioned by Common Article 2(2) of the Geneva Conventions. In some cases, there may be no actual fighting and no declaration of war. However, in

---

[9] *Dalmia Cement Ltd v National Bank of Pakistan* (1984) 67 ILR 611.
[10] See generally: ch 4 above.

such a case a foreign army may occupy a territory and subject the local population to rule by the foreign military forces. This population is in need of the LOAC protections. A case like the one postulated arises if a state decides not to resist an invasion in any way. A case in point is Denmark when invaded by Germany in 1940. In these cases, the Geneva Conventions are at pains to make clear that the LOAC applies, in particular the law concerning belligerent occupation. Conversely, if a territory is occupied after fighting takes place, the LOAC is applicable by virtue of the general category that governs the application of IHL during effective armed conflict.[11] This is the case, for example, in the case of the Israeli occupied territories in the West Bank and Gaza, which were occupied as a result of the war of 1967.

One can easily see that the most important and frequent case for the application of the LOAC is the first one, that of effective armed hostilities. The other two thresholds are meant to close any possible gaps in the system of protection of the LOAC by ensuring that it is applicable in all cases where this is necessary. However, the last two criteria for applicability are of minor importance, since it is rare today to either have a declaration of war unaccompanied by actual fighting or to have territories occupied without any fighting.

To these cases of IAC where the LOAC is applicable, Additional Protocol I adds a further case, which is of only limited relevance today. It is formulated in Article 1(4), which states:

> The situations referred to in the preceding paragraph [recalling the contents of common Article 2 of the Geneva Conventions] include armed conflicts in which peoples are fighting against colonial domination and alien occupation and against racist regimes in the exercise of their rights of self-determination.

At the negotiations that led to the adoption of Additional Protocol, the so-called third world states managed to include, roughly speaking, wars of decolonisation within the definition of IAC advanced by the Protocol. This article made clear that when a colonised people fought against a colonising power in order to obtain independence, the resulting armed conflict should no longer be regarded as a NIAC, but should be considered to be an IAC to which all the rules of the LOAC, including protection for prisoners of war and the rules relating to belligerent occupation, would apply. Today this is substantially obsolete, since decolonisation has been completed.

4. Let us now turn to *non-international armed conflicts*. The main sources of law applicable to such conflicts are Common Article 3 of the Geneva Conventions; Additional Protocol II[12]; customary international law; and some other texts that explicitly apply in NIAC, such as the Second Protocol to the Hague Cultural Property Convention, which applies equally to international and non-international armed conflicts.[13] There is a difference in the scope of application between

---

[11] Geneva Conventions I–IV common Art 2(1).
[12] See n 4.
[13] Second Protocol to the Hague Convention of 1954 for the Protection of Cultural Property in the Event of Armed Conflict (adopted 26 March 1999, entered into force 9 March 2004) (1999) 38 ILM 769 Art 22(1).

Common Article 3, which applies in certain situations, and Additional Protocol II, which applies in a more restricted circle of situations. Customary international law applies under the same conditions as Common Article 3.[14] Specific conventions apply to NIAC when the conditions for applicability that are set out in those instruments are met. Practically, this means that they apply in the same circumstances as Common Article 3 and customary international law, since they do not fix more restrictive criteria. Let us now look to the thresholds of the two main treaty sources, Article 3 and Protocol II.

Common Article 3 of the Geneva Conventions. Common Article 3 to the four Geneva Conventions contains a set of minimum humanitarian obligations which must be respected in all circumstances. The threshold of applicability of this article is thus quite low, since the aim is to ensure that these minimum protections apply in as many cases as possible. At the same time, the threshold is higher than that applicable in situations of international armed conflict. The concern to ensure that there is minimal international intervention in the internal affairs of states has meant that they are only willing to accept international obligations in cases where the armed conflict has gained a certain degree of intensity. Hence, the two main criteria of applicability are the following.[15] They are not set out in the Geneva Conventions, but have been shaped in practice. First, the rebel forces must display a *minimum of organisation*. These forces must appear as an armed force and not simply as a non-coordinated mass of rioters. Hence, the rebels must be militarily organised, for example, possess a responsible command, abide by military discipline and be capable of respecting the rules of the LOAC.[16] Secondly, the armed conflict must present a *minimum of intensity*. This means that we must be confronted with fighting of collective nature causing a non-negligible number of victims. As a rough rule of thumb, hostilities may be considered to have reached the required intensity for the application of NIAC when the police forces of the state are incapable of dealing with the insurrection, and therefore the army has to be mobilised in order to defeat the rebels.[17] In general, it may be said that the interpretation of the two aforementioned criteria has to be quite generous, since the protective aim of Article 3 and the fact that it contemplates minimum guarantees justifies an attempt to ensure that it is applicable in as many cases as possible. Situations remaining beneath the threshold of an armed conflict are called situations of 'internal disturbances and tensions, such as riots, isolated and sporadic acts of violence and other acts of a similar nature',[18] and the LOAC does not apply. All civil wars which have occurred since 1949 were thus covered by Common Article 3, if the states on the territory where the insurrection occurred were bound by the Geneva Conventions, or, if the state was not a party, the guarantees contained in Article 3 applied as a matter of customary international law. Thus, for example, the civil war in Guatemala in 1954 was covered by Common Article 3 as a matter of conventional

---

[14] *Prosecutor v Tadic* (Decision on the Defence Motion for Interlocutory Appeal on Jurisdiction) IT-49-1-AR72 (2 October 1995) para [70].

[15] *Tadic, ibid*, para [70].

[16] *Prosecutor v Limaj, Bala and Musliu* (Trial Judgement) IT-03-66-T (30 November 2005), paras [88]–[89] and [94]–[134].

[17] *Limaj, ibid*, paras [88]–[89] and [135]–[170].

[18] Additional Protocol II Art 1(2).

law, whereas the civil war in Mozambique between 1961 and 1974 was covered by Article 3 as expression of customary international law, since Mozambique did not accede to the Geneva Conventions until 1983.

Additional Protocol II. Additional Protocol II supplements and develops the contents of Common Article 3 by placing more detailed obligations on states and other parties to the LOAC. The scope of application of Additional Protocol II is set out as follows in Article 1:

> This Protocol [...] shall apply to all armed conflicts which are not covered by Article 1 of the Protocol Additional to the Geneva Conventions of 12 August 1949, and relating to the Protection of Victims of International Armed Conflicts (Protocol I) and which take place in the territory of a High Contracting Party between its armed forces and dissident armed forces or other organized armed groups which, under responsible command, exercise such control over a part of its territory as to enable them to carry out sustained and concerted military operations and to implement this Protocol.

One therefore sees that the material scope of application is somewhat restricted when compared to the scope of applicability of Common Article 3. This is true in two respects. First, Additional Protocol II applies only to situations where the rebels control a part of the territory. This condition does not exist under Common Article 3 or customary international law. Secondly, Additional Protocol II applies only to the relations between the state military forces and rebels. It does not cover, according to its wording, fighting which occurs between rebel groups, for example the Revolutionary Armed Forces of Colombia (FARC) and 'Autodefence' paramilitary groups in Colombia. This restriction is again not contained in Common Article 3, which can apply to situations of armed conflict with no governmental involvement. With regard to the necessity for territorial control, the practice of the ICRC has held that a minimum control suffices. This practice governing the interpretation of this criterion has therefore reduced this requirement to little more than what is contained in Common Article 3. The Statute of the International Criminal Court, in Article 8(2)(f), does not follow the restricted wording of Protocol II, thereby further weakening it.[19] The ICC Statute refers only to 'protracted armed conflict between governmental authorities and organised armed groups or between such groups'.[20] Hence, the Rome Statute brushes away both restrictive criteria of Additional Protocol II, which have not stood the test of time. The guarantees of Additional Protocol II apply today, as part of customary international law, under the same conditions as Common Article 3. Therefore, in order to properly reflect the current conditions of applicability, Additional Protocol II would have to be amended to align it to the conditions of application expressed in Common Article 3.

5. In some cases, the rules of the LOAC applicable in international armed conflicts apply to belligerent relations within a non-international armed conflict, or a civil war. Conflicts where this happens are called 'mixed armed conflicts' or 'internationalised non-international armed conflicts'. In such conflicts, there are some

---

[19] Rome Statute of the International Criminal Court (adopted 17 July 1998, entered into force 1 July 2002) 2187 UNTS 3 Art 8(2)(f).
[20] Reflecting the test set out in *Tadic*, n 14, para [70].

belligerent relations which are internal, in particular the fighting between the governmental forces and the rebels, and also some other belligerent relations which are international in character, for example foreign forces fighting on the side of the rebels and against forces of the local government. Such mixed conflicts have been very numerous in the last few decades. The Vietnam War or the wars in the former Yugoslavia are examples. There are four main means by which a civil war can be at least partly internationalised and some of the LOAC applicable only in situations of international armed conflict being applied to it. The first is the most frequent and practically important:

a) *Intervention by foreign armies.* If regular troops of a foreign state or so-called volunteers organised by some foreign state are sent on to the territory torn by a civil war, the conflict is in part internationalised.[21] Furthermore, if no troops are sent, but the foreign state exercises control over the rebels, this may be sufficient to internationalise a non-international armed conflict.[22] In cases of the internationalisation of armed conflicts, not all of the belligerent relationships will be covered by the LOAC of IAC. However, some of them will, whilst others will remain covered by the LOAC of NIAC. Consequently, to some extent the law will be split according to concrete belligerent relationships at stake. The International Court of Justice acknowledged that the protection of the law will splinter in the *Nicaragua* case:

> The conflict between the *contras'* forces and those of the Government of Nicaragua is an armed conflict which is 'not of an international character'. The acts of the *contras* towards the Nicaraguan Government are therefore governed by the law applicable to conflicts of that character; whereas the actions of the United States in and against Nicaragua fall under the legal rules relating to international conflicts.[23]

Let us look into that aspect in somewhat more detail. In fact, four types of relationships can be distinguished. When we hereafter speak of 'foreign state', 'local government' and so on, we will mean the armed forces of each of these actors, which come to clash on the territory where the civil war takes place. Here are the four types of relationship which may be envisaged:

i) Relationship between the local government and the insurgents: the LOAC concerning NIAC is applicable.
ii) Relationship between a foreign state fighting on the side of the local government and the insurgents: the LOAC concerning NIAC is applicable.

---

[21] *Prosecutor v Lubanga* (Decision on the Confirmation of Charges) ICC-01/04-01/06 (29 January 2007) [205]–[226].

[22] The level of control necessary is disputed. Compare *Military and Paramilitary Activities in and against Nicaragua (Nicaragua v United States of America)* (Merits) [1986] ICJ Rep 14 para [115] and *Application of the Convention on the Prevention and Punishment of the Crime of Genocide (Bosnia and Herzegovina v Serbia and Montenegro)* (Merits) (26 February 2007) available at <http://www.icj-cij.org/docket/files/91/13685.pdf> accessed 14 May 2008 paras [399]–[407], which state that 'effective control' of the rebel armed forces by a foreign state is necessary to internationalise a conflict with *Prosecutor v Tadic* (Appeal Judgement) IT-94-1-A (15 July 1999) paras [99]–[145], which decides that mere 'overall control' is sufficient to ensure the applicability of the LOAC concerning IAC.

[23] *Nicaragua, ibid,* para [219].

iii) Relationship between a foreign state intervening on one side and a foreign state intervening on the other side: the LOAC concerning IAC is applicable.

iv) Relationship between a foreign state intervening on the side of the rebels and the local government: the LOAC concerning IAC is applicable.

Thus, a different set of rules will apply during the same conflict to different belligerent relationships, according to who fights against whom. This produces highly complex situations, which do not simplify the task of applying IHL for the combatants on the ground, or those who have to adjudicate on the legality of a particular action after it has taken place. Therefore, very often it will be useful to conclude special agreements according to Common Article 3(3) of the Geneva Conventions.[24] Under such agreements, the belligerents may voluntarily assume some further obligations which will apply regardless of the precise relationship between belligerents. For example, all participants in an internationalised armed conflict may undertake to treat all prisoners that are taken as at least equivalent to prisoners of war, on a basis of reciprocity. Such special agreements are often negotiated under the aegis of the ICRC.

b) *Intervention of an international organisation.* If the United Nations has stationed armed personnel under UN command, the so-called Blue Helmets, in a state and if these personnel are engaged in fighting, as was the case in Congo in 1960, the result will be that the United Nations is to some extent participating in an armed conflict. This conflict may, originally, have been a non-international armed conflict. However, any hostile relations between the UN troops and troops of the local government, if any, will be covered by the LOAC of IAC. It must be stressed that the question of what law is applicable to the relations between UN troops and rebel troops remains controversial. The better view is that the LOAC of IAC applies.

c) *Civil war with successful secession.* If during a civil war a part of the territory manages to secede from its old mother-country, and if this new entity acquires international recognition, such as admission to the United Nations, the belligerent relations it may continue to face with the old mother-country will no longer be the subject of the law of NIAC, but will be governed by the law concerning IAC. If all of the fighting is concentrated between the old state and the new state, the conflict will become completely subjected to the law of IAC. If there is still fighting also on the territory of the old state, the conflict may become mixed.

d) *Recognition of belligerency.* To the extent that the rebels are recognised as belligerents by any state, either the local government or a third state, the relations between the rebels and the recognising state will be in any case governed by the LOAC applicable to IAC. In practice, such recognition of belligerency is no longer proclaimed today. This category therefore almost completely belongs to legal history.

6. Acts of terrorism do not give rise to a specific form of armed conflict. Such acts

---

[24] See generally: ch 15 below.

are prohibited, whether they are committed in peacetime, during situations of internal disturbances and tensions or during an armed conflict. Thus, for example, Article 51(2) of Additional Protocol I explicitly prohibits acts of terrorism in the context of IAC. Article 4(2)(d) of Additional Protocol II does the same for NIAC.[25] In all of these cases, the suppression of such acts is organised by both internal and international criminal law.

However, acts of terrorism can also be the staring point of an armed conflict, as were the 2001 attacks on the World Trade Centre with regard to the war in Afghanistan. If an armed conflict is launched, IHL applies equally to all groups that fight, regardless as to if one of them commits acts of prohibited terrorism. The war against such groups is thus submitted to the same rules as any other armed conflict, being either an IAC or a NIAC. This follows directly from the principle of equality of belligerents that is fundamental to the LOAC. However, this does not mean that a terrorist group will generally possess the lawful combatant privilege. Hence, al-Qaeda terrorists who are tracked and arrested all over the world remain outside the LOAC and are subject only to criminal law. This is so because they are not caught in the context of an armed conflict. To that extent, the often-used term of 'war against terrorism' is confusing and dangerous: it could connote the wrong idea that all terrorists are adverse warriors and would possibly be endowed with combatant immunity, which is not the case. Of course, some members of such organisations could enjoy such a combatant status. Those members of al-Qaeda who were captured in Afghanistan during the war, when fighting alongside the Taliban armed forces, could be entitled to combatant, and hence to prisoners of war, status, if they fulfilled all of the conditions to that end.[26] This in turn does again not mean that they could not be prosecuted for terrorist acts. Prisoners of war can be criminally prosecuted.[27] The main point to be made in the present context is that there is no special 'war against terrorism'. War against such groups and states sustaining them are either IAC or NIAC and the ordinary rules apply to them.

Comprehension check:

a) What is the essential material criterion for deciding if the LOAC applies?
b) Is there a difference in threshold with respect to the criterion of 'armed conflict' for applying the law of international armed conflicts and the law of non-international armed conflicts? If there is a difference, why is there one?
c) What is a 'mixed armed conflict'? What law applies to such a mixed armed conflict?
d) What law applies to internal disturbances and tensions?
e) During a military exercise, armed forces of State A accidentally fire five cannon shots beyond the borders of the state. The cannon bullets fall down on the territory of State B, in a forest.
   Same case, but this time a civilian in State B is wounded.

---

[25] The prohibition on terrorism is customary, *Prosecutor v Galic* (Judgement) IT-98-29-A (30 November 2006) paras [79]–[90].
[26] See generally: ch 25 below.
[27] Geneva Convention III Arts 82*ff* and *US v Noriega* (1997) 99 ILR 143, 167–171.

Same case, but this time a military building containing ammunitions is destroyed by a bullet.
Does the LOAC apply to these situations?

Answers:

a) The essential material criterion is that of the existence of an 'armed conflict'. The LOAC applies formally if an armed conflict is found to exist. Otherwise, it is the international law applicable during peacetime that governs the relations between international actors. As far as international armed conflicts are concerned, we can add to the concept of armed conflict the older concept of war. Moreover, the LOAC for IAC applies also if there is an occupation of foreign territory by an army without any armed resistance. In the case of NIAC, the application of the LOAC turns only upon the existence of an armed conflict. An armed conflict implies that some hostilities are actually taking place.

b) Yes, there is a difference. In the case of IAC there is no requirement of a certain degree of intensity before applying the LOAC. The LOAC applies from the first shot, the first injured person or the first prisoner. As for the criterion of military organisation of the forces, it is implicit in the very concept of IAC, since in such cases state military forces are involved. Conversely, in the case of NIAC, the requirements are that the conflict must be fought by rebels presenting a sufficient degree of military organisation in order to be able to apply the law, and also that the conflict has a minimum level of intensity, judged by number of deaths and duration. This difference is due to the fact that NIAC are felt by the states to be essentially matters falling into their national jurisdiction, and in such cases they do not like to have foreign involvement.

c) A mixed armed conflict is a conflict in which belligerent relationships belonging to non-international armed conflicts take place alongside other belligerent relationships which belong to international armed conflicts. This is the case mainly if foreign military forces are sent on a territory in order to take part in a civil war by sustaining one party to the conflict. The law applicable splits according to the specific relationships at stake. Thus:
In the relationship between the local government and the insurgents: the LOAC concerning NIAC is applicable. In the relationship between a foreign state fighting on the side of the local government and the insurgents: the LOAC concerning NIAC is applicable. In the relationship between a foreign state intervening on one side and a foreign state intervening on the other side: the LOAC concerning IAC is applicable. In the relationship between a foreign state intervening on the side of the rebels and the local government: the LOAC concerning IAC is applicable. Other situations of such mixed conflicts may occur if an international organisation sends troops under its command in a territory, and these troops happen to be entangled in the conflict; or if fighting continues after a successful secession. In these situations too, the law will split according to the concrete belligerent relationships at stake.

d) The law applying to internal disturbances and tensions is in particular the following: (1) the internal, municipal, law of the territorial state; (2) international human rights law; and (3) general customary international law as well as conventional international law, remaining in force for that state. However, the law of NIAC is not formally applicable, unless it is rendered applicable on a voluntary basis by a special agreement as foreseen in Common Article 3(3) of the Geneva Conventions.

e) No, the LOAC does not apply to any of these situations. We have to look at the law of IAC, since an inter-state relation is at stake. However, there are no hostilities, nor war nor occupation of territory, between the armies of two states. Hence, there is no opportunity to apply any of the protections or rules of the LOAC. No rule on the means and methods of warfare can be applied, since the shots were accidental and unique. Neither are there protections of Geneva Law to be applied since there is no contact between the two armies. In variant 2 of the case, it is the ordinary civilian medical services that have to take care of the civilian injured. These incidents thus remain peacetime incidents and the state that accidentally shot these bullets will incur state responsibility for the damage caused.

12

APPLICABILITY OF THE LOAC: PERSONAL SCOPE OF APPLICABILITY

Learning objectives: To understand in what situations the LOAC is applicable.

1. (Repetition, can be skipped by those who have worked through chapter 11). All branches of the law are divided in two parts. Before the substantive rules are applied, the legal order must first determine whether the extant situation is one in which the regulatory norms apply. This species of legal inquiry, which is the first province of any legal question, is devoted to the determination of the applicability of the law to a certain set of situations. Thus, for example, the LOAC is designed to apply only in a time of armed conflict and not in peacetime. This limits its scope of legal applicability. There are four aspects of applicability of legal rules:

a) subject matter applicability, or material scope of applicability, also known as *ratione materiae*, which define 'situations of armed conflict' in which LOAC is applicable;

b) the personal scope of the applicability of the LOAC, also known as *ratione personae*, which addresses questions of the applicability of the LOAC to state organs, peace-keeping personnel of international organisations, all belligerents that are not a state and all individuals participating in the armed conflict;

c) the spatial scope of applicability of the LOAC, also known as *ratione loci*, which addresses questions of the applicability of the LOAC to the territory of the belligerent states and further spaces where effective fighting takes place, such as the high seas;

d) the temporal scope of applicability of the LOAC, also known as *ratione temporis*, which addresses questions of the continuing applicability of the LOAC during a situation of armed conflict and the cessation of applicability of the LOAC rules at the end of a conflict.

It is now necessary to enter into a more detailed analysis of these four aspects of applicability.

Once it has been determined that the norms of the LOAC are applicable in a particular situation, the substantive rules may be applied. This is the second province of the law. Thus, for example, if Geneva Convention III on prisoners of war is found to be applicable in all of the four dimensions mentioned above, we

may proceed to ask questions regarding the substantive guarantees the convention affords to prisoners of war (POWs), such as the right to be treated humanely, the right not to be required to perform to dangerous work and the right to be provided with adequate food and care.[1]

The concepts of applicability and application of the law are thus performed in a natural sequence. First, one has to ask if a set of rules is applicable in a given context. If the answer is in the negative, the enquiry stops there, and that set of rules is not applicable in the particular circumstances. The lawyer then has to look for other sets of rules that could apply to the given situation. Thus, for example, if the LOAC does not apply because the situation does not yet have the characteristics of an armed conflict, but has remained a local riot, international human rights law may apply. The question of applicability must then to be decided anew for that separate branch of the law. If, conversely, the answer is positive, and the lawyer finds that a set of rules is applicable to a given situation, he or she will proceed to apply the substantive rules. This is the second phase of his or her work.

2. As far as the *personal scope of application* is concerned, two aspects can be distinguished. There is the active aspect: who is bound by the LOAC? In addition, there is also the passive aspect: who is protected by the LOAC?

Who is bound by the LOAC?

Different actors are bound by the LOAC.

a) For the LOAC applicable in IAC, the main actors bound are *states* and in particular the armed forces of the state, as an organ of that state. The rules of the LOAC are specifically designed to apply to these forces.

However, to the state there may be added other subjects who are bound by the LOAC. The main criterion in this context is the substantive ability of an entity or a person to participate in an armed conflict by making acts of war. Those who in fact participate in an armed conflict are also covered *ratione personae* by the law that governs armed conflict. In other words, the material participation in the conflict as an actor induces the personal applicability of the LOAC to the entity or person involved. The dominating principle is that of 'effectiveness': effective participation triggers the application of the law. Why? Simply because the LOAC is designed to provide necessary protection and limitation, and this necessity will arise in each case of effective combat. If entities that were in effect participating in the combat, and thus having the ability to wage hostilities, were not covered by the LOAC, important gaps would appear in the protection granted by the law. Therefore, it is sensible that the law applies to all the cases where its protections are, in effect, needed.

b) Hence, an *international organisation* such as the United Nations can be bound by the LOAC if forces under the command of the UN participate in an armed conflict. In a bulletin of 1999 of the UN Secretary General with the title 'Observance by United Nations Forces of International Humanitarian Law', the highest administrative authority of the United Nations acknowledged that the organisation is bound to follow IHL rules.[2]

---

[1] Geneva Convention III relative to the Treatment of Prisoners of War (adopted 12 August 1949, entered into force 21 October 1950) 75 UNTS 135 (Geneva Convention III).

[2] UN Doc ST/SGB/1999/13 (1999) 38 ILM 1656.

c) Moreover, the LOAC applies to different *non-state entities* which participate in combat. These entities can be 'de facto regimes' that are not recognised by states under international law, such as the Republica Srpska, or can simply be belligerent groups who take part in hostilities, either in an IAC or in a NIAC. Generally, such belligerent groups or entities confirm by a unilateral declaration that they assume the obligation to respect the LOAC, or at least some parts of the LOAC. The declaration made by the Polisario Front of Liberation in Western Sahara in 1975 can be quoted as example. Under customary international law, the LOAC is applicable to such groups if they become belligerents. This position is confirmed by an important resolution adopted by the Institute of International Law, the most eminent collective scientific body in international law, in 1999 entitled 'The Application of International Humanitarian Law and Fundamental Human Rights in Armed Conflicts in which Non-State Entities are Parties'.[3] The point made by the institute is that under customary international law the obligation to respect IHL exists for all parties to the conflict, irrespective of their specific legal status one with regard to the other. Thus, Article 2 of that Resolution reads:

> All parties to armed conflicts in which non-State entities are parties, irrespective of their legal status [...] have the obligation to respect international humanitarian law.

Furthermore, Article 5 adds:

> Every State and every non-State entity participating in an armed conflict are legally bound vis-à-vis each other as well as all other members of the international community to respect international humanitarian law in all circumstances.

This reflects the current state of customary international law.

d) Finally, the LOAC applies also to *individuals* having civilian status if they perform hostile acts in the context of the armed conflict; passively, such persons are protected against attack as civilians. Thus, individuals can commit a war crime, which in turn means that they are subject to the LOAC. After World War II, ministers were prosecuted and sentenced.[4] The same is true of industrialists, such as those sentenced in the *Krupp* or *IG Farben Trials* in 1948 by US Military Tribunals.[5] Even ordinary civilians, without a close link to the government, were found liable for acts which violated the LOAC.[6] The Yugoslav and Rwandan Criminal Tribunals have followed this case law.[7]

A specific problem arises in NIAC. In such conflicts, the government usually faces some rebel groups. The military of the state, bound by IHL as a state organ, faces an insurgent group, which has never ratified the international conventions relating to

---

[3] Available at <http://www.idi-iil.org/idiE/resolutionsE/1999_ber_03_en.PDF> accessed 14 May 2008.

[4] *US v Von Weizsäcker and others, 'The Ministries Trial'* (1949) 16 AD 344.

[5] *US v Krauch and Others, 'IG Farben'* (1948) 15 AD 668, 678 and *US v Krupp* (1948) 15 AD 620, 627. See also: *Re Tesch, 'Zyklon B'* (1946) 13 AD 250.

[6] *The Essen Lynching Case, The Trial of Erich Heyer and Six Others Before a British Military Court* (1945) 1 LRTWC 88.

[7] See, eg: *Prosecutor v Akayesu* (Judgement) ICTR-96-4-A (1 June 2001) paras [444]–[445].

warfare. How then can these conventions apply to the insurgents, if they never ratified or acceded to them? First, we must note that the difficulty arises only in relation to the conventions. It does not exist in the context of customary international law, which is automatically applicable without ratification or accession. For the conventions, the legal explanation which has generally been offered is that by the state's ratification or accession the convention becomes binding on all of the territory of the state and consequently on all of the inhabitants of the state. Moreover, the state party assumes, under all of the main LOAC conventions, a duty to disseminate knowledge as to the requirements of the convention not only to its armed forces, but also, if possible, to all the inhabitants of its territory.[8] Thus, in the case of a NIAC, the rebels organising themselves into an armed force will be bound by the convention as the individuals who make up the armed rebel group were individuals on a territory to which the convention applies, by virtue of the state's ratification of, or accession to, that convention.

Who is protected by the LOAC?

As we have seen with the active personal scope of applicability of the LOAC, when we examine the passive personal scope of applicability we see that several categories of person are protected by the LOAC.

a) *Combatants involved in the armed conflict.* Combatants are not formally seen as protected persons, since they can be attacked and possibly killed. However, the LOAC does not altogether ignore them. All of the main prohibitions on means and methods of warfare are at least partly designed to protect combatants against excessive suffering, injuries or inevitable death.[9] Hence the LOAC contains, amongst other prohibitions, a prohibition on the use of poisoned or chemical weapons,[10] a prohibition of orders that no quarter will be given (which means that no prisoners are taken and instead all of the adverse military combatants are killed)[11] and the prohibition of perfidy.[12] All of the restrictions that may be placed on the means and methods of warfare that may be adopted by the belligerent parties are meant, at least in part, to save combatants from certain excessive evils. In this large sense, combatants are also protected persons under the laws of war.

b) *Combatants wounded, sick or shipwrecked, otherwise known as combatants hors de combat.* This is a classical category of protected persons, and was the first that was defined under IHL. The First Geneva Convention, drafted in 1864, made clear that, '[w]ounded or sick combatants, to whatever nation

---

[8] Geneva Convention III Art 127.

[9] St Petersburg Declaration Renouncing the Use, in Time of War, of Explosive Projectiles Under 400 Grammes Weight (signed 11 December 1868, entered into force 11 December 1868) (1868–69) 138 CTS 297 Preamble, para 4.

[10] Regulations concerning the Laws and Customs of War on Land annexed to Hague Convention IV (adopted 18 October 1907, entered into force 26 January 1910) (1907) 205 CTS 227 (Hague Regulations) Art 23(a) and Convention on the Prohibition of the Development, Production, Stockpiling and Use of Chemical Weapons and on Their Destruction (adopted 3 September 1992, entered into force 29 April 1997) 1974 UNTS 45.

[11] Hague Regulations Art 23(d).

[12] Protocol Additional to the Geneva Conventions of 12 August 1949, and relating to the Protection of Victims of International Armed Conflicts (adopted 8 June 1977, entered into force 7 December 1978) 1125 UNTS 3 Art 37.

they may belong, shall be collected and cared for'.[13] In no circumstances should this category of persons be attacked. Today, it is Geneva Conventions I and II that regulate the protections afforded to these categories of persons.[14]

c) *Prisoners of War.* Regular combatants having laid down their arms in order to surrender and those who are captured by enemy armed forces are entitled to prisoner of war status. Once they have this status they are entitled to a series of protections. The matter was first regulated in some provisions of Hague Convention II,[15] negotiated in 1899 and restated in the Regulations annexed to the Hague Convention IV, negotiated in 1907.[16] The relevant law is today expounded in Geneva Convention III relative to the Treatment of Prisoners of War.

d) *Civilians.* 'Enemy civilians' in particular need some protection under the laws of war. Such enemy civilians are essentially persons who find themselves on the territory of a state becoming a belligerent against their home state, or civilians in occupied territories. This protection is particularly necessary because they will be easily perceived as being hostile individuals, dangerous to the security of the belligerent in whose power they find themselves. Up until 1949, there was hardly any protection for such persons. There was only a quite generic title on occupied territories in the 1899 Hague Convention II and later in the 1907 Hague Regulations.[17] Today, the question is regulated in detail in Geneva Convention IV relative to the Protection of Civilian Persons in Time of War.[18]

Recapitulating, we can see that the main protected persons, who may in no circumstances be attacked and who enjoy a series of protections, are those persons who do not participate in the hostilities, including those who previously took part in the fighting, but no longer participate: wounded, sick and shipwrecked combatants; prisoners of war; and civilians.

Comprehension check:

a)   To what extent can it be said that the LOAC applies to 'everybody'?
b)   Are there non-protected persons under the LOAC?
c)   How can an insurgent entity be bound by a convention on the LOAC that it never ratified or acceded to?

---

[13] The Geneva Convention for the Amelioration of the Condition of the Wounded in Armies in the Field (adopted 22 August 1864, entered into force 22 June 1865) (1864) 129 CTS 361 Art 6(1).

[14] Geneva Convention I for the Amelioration of the Condition of the Wounded and Sick in Armed Forces in the Field (adopted 12 August 1949, entered into force 21 October 1950) 75 UNTS 31 (Geneva Convention I); Geneva Convention II for the Amelioration of the Condition of Wounded, Sick and Shipwrecked Members of Armed Forces at Sea (adopted 12 August 1949, entered into force 21 October 1950) 75 UNTS 85 (Geneva Convention II).

[15] Hague Convention (II) with Respect to the Laws and Customs of War on Land and its annex: Regulations concerning the Laws and Customs of War on Land (adopted 29 July 1899, entered into force 4 September 1900) (1898–99) 187 CTS 429.

[16] Hague Regulations, n 10 above Arts 4–20.

[17] Hague Regulations, *ibid*, Arts 42–56.

[18] Geneva Convention IV Relative to the Protection of Civilian Persons in Time of War (adopted 12 August 1949, entered into force 21 October 1950) 75 UNTS 287.

d)   Are terrorists protected persons?

Answers:

a)   The LOAC applies in the first place to all of the state organs concerned with armed conflicts, ie the military branch. However, as international practice and in particular the jurisprudence of war crimes tribunals has shown, all persons or entities who perform acts during an armed conflict that are linked with that armed conflict bring themselves under the control of the LOAC. There is thus no enumerated category of subjects able to be bound by LOAC rules. The criterion is that of effectiveness: he or she who participates in the conflict or he or she who does acts relevant to the LOAC, such as employing prisoners of war in his or her industrial plants, contrary to the conditions set out in Geneva Convention III, is automatically bound by that law. There is no personal limitation; the only relevant considerations are the material acts at stake. In this sense, the LOAC may apply to 'anybody' and hence potentially to 'everybody'.

b)   Persons formally designed as 'protected persons' under the law are only the military personnel *hors de combat* and civilians protected under the LOAC. These persons possess a series of privileges, one of the most important being immunity from attack. Conversely, military personnel in combat are not 'protected persons' in the sense previously discussed. As we have seen, however, a series of limitations imposed on the means and methods of warfare have, at least partially, the aim of protecting the combatants against excessive cruelty. This also can be envisioned as a form of protection. The answer can thus be either that combatants are non-protected persons, or that all persons enjoy some protection, according to the precise concept of 'protected person' one chooses to follow. One point can be added: irregular combatants are also protected persons in the formal sense that once they are caught and detained, either they are considered as civilians and thus come under the protection of Geneva Convention IV, or they are considered as non-civilian irregular fighters, and then they must be treated at least according to the guarantees of Common Article 3 of the Geneva Conventions.

c)   The most plausible legal construction is that the ratification or accession to the convention in question by the state on whose territory the NIAC takes place binds all of the individuals on the territory of that state and hence also the rebels. The US Military Tribunal had expressed thus in the *Flick* case:

It is asserted that international law is a matter wholly outside the work, interests and knowledge of private individuals. The distinction is unsound. International law, as such binds every citizen just as does ordinary municipal law.[19]

Moreover, states, by ratifying or acceding to the conventions, undertake to disseminate the knowledge as to these conventions to the utmost extent throughout their territory.

---

[19] *US v Flick* (1947) 14 AD 266, 269.

d)   Terrorists are not, as such, protected persons. Whether they are or not depends
     on the context. If a purported terrorist (we do normally not know at any early
     stage if he or she really is one) is arrested outside the context of an armed
     conflict, the question does not at all arise under the LOAC. If a person is
     accused of terrorist acts in the context of an armed conflict, the question of
     protection depends on his or her status. Either he or she is a civilian of an
     'adverse' party to the armed conflict, and therefore he or she enjoys protection
     under Geneva Convention IV; or he or she is an adverse combatant, in which
     case he or she enjoys protection under Geneva Convention III; or he or she is an
     irregular combatant, and then, if caught, he or she is at least protected under
     the minimum guarantees set out in Common Article 3 of the four Geneva
     Conventions,[20] which roughly speaking prohibits those holding him or her from
     carrying out any gravely inhuman acts on him or her. In all of these preceding
     cases, the alleged terrorist can be subjected to criminal prosecution and
     sentenced under the laws of war, even to death. The protections under IHL do
     not relate to his or her qualification as 'terrorist'. They just aim to assure some
     degree of protection, since otherwise any belligerent could escape the
     protections in the LOAC simply by labelling all of his or her adversaries as
     'terrorists', which would induce the opposed party to do the same by way of
     reprisals. In such a case, the protection of persons would become illusory and
     the gaps in the Geneva Conventions almost infinite. One may here recall that
     during World War II the Germans conceptualised a whole series of civilians in
     occupied territories as 'terrorists' since they suspected them of taking part in
     resistance movements. Yet there is no doubt that these civilians in the occupied
     territories badly needed some international protection, wholly independently of
     the question if they could be regarded as 'terrorist' under any possible definition
     of this term.

---

[20] *Hamdan v Rumsfeld* (2006) 126 S Ct 2749.

13

APPLICABILITY OF THE LOAC: SPATIAL SCOPE OF APPLICABILITY

Learning objectives: To learn about the spatial scope of applicability of the LOAC.

1. (Repetition; can be skipped by those who have worked through chapter 11). All branches of the law are divided in two parts. Before the substantive rules are applied, the legal order must first determine whether the extant situation is one in which the regulatory norms apply. This species of legal inquiry, which is the first province of any legal question, is devoted to the determination of the applicability of the law to a certain set of situations. Thus, for example, the LOAC is designed to apply only in a time of armed conflict and not in peacetime. This limits its scope of legal applicability. There are four aspects of applicability of legal rules:

a) subject matter applicability, or material scope of applicability, also known as *ratione materiae*, which defines 'situations of armed conflict' in which LOAC is applicable;

b) the personal scope of the applicability of the LOAC, also known as *ratione personae*, which addresses questions of the applicability of the LOAC to state organs, peace-keeping personnel of international organisations, all belligerents that are not a state and all individuals participating in the armed conflict;

c) the spatial scope of applicability of the LOAC, also known as *ratione loci*, which addresses questions of the applicability of the LOAC to the territory of the belligerent states and further spaces where effective fighting takes place, such as the high seas;

d) the temporal scope of applicability of the LOAC, also known as *ratione temporis*, which addresses questions of the continuing applicability of the LOAC during a situation of armed conflict and the cessation of applicability of the LOAC rules at the end of a conflict.

It is now necessary to enter into a more detailed analysis of these four aspects of applicability.

Once it has been determined that the norms of the LOAC are applicable in a particular situation, the substantive rules may be applied. This is the second province of the law. Thus, for example, if Geneva Convention III on prisoners of war is found to be applicable in all of the four dimensions mentioned above, we

may proceed to ask questions regarding the substantive guarantees the convention affords to prisoners of war (POWs), such as the right to be treated humanely, the right not to be required to perform to dangerous work and the right to be provided with adequate food and care.[1]

The concepts of applicability and application of the law are thus performed in a natural sequence. First, one has to ask if a set of rules is applicable in a given context. If the answer is in the negative, the enquiry stops there, and that set of rules is not applicable in the particular circumstances. The lawyer then has to look for other sets of rules that could apply to the given situation. Thus, for example, if the LOAC does not apply because the situation does not yet have the characteristics of an armed conflict, but has remained a local riot, international human rights law may apply. The question of applicability must then to be decided anew for that separate branch of the law. If, conversely, the answer is positive, and the lawyer finds that a set of rules is applicable to a given situation, he or she will proceed to apply the substantive rules. This is the second phase of his or her work.

2. As far as the *spatial scope of application* is concerned, the principle of effectiveness dominates. It means that the LOAC will apply in all areas covered by the state of war, by actual armed conflict or by belligerent occupation. Hence, the LOAC will apply in three types of areas:

   a) It applies to the *territory of the belligerent states*. In this territory the state can exercise the specific rights and duties conferred by the LOAC.
   b) It applies in all *spaces where there are actual hostilities or relationships between belligerents* outside the territory of the belligerents, for example on the high seas.[2] As is well known, the high seas are not subject to the sovereignty of any state.[3] They are a common space in which all states can, for example, freely navigate, fish or perform scientific research.[4] These freedoms are subject to a general duty placed upon states to act with due regard to the equal rights of all other states.[5] Hence, states may perform acts of warfare on the high seas. They can engage in hostilities there; and they are allowed to exercise belligerent rights such as visit and search foreign ships that are suspected of transporting contraband.[6]
   c) It applies to *territories occupied* without the existence of a state of war or actual hostilities.[7]

3. In sum, it can be said that the LOAC is not truly spatially limited. The application of the principle of effectiveness means that the spatial applicability of the LOAC follows the action: everywhere that an act of belligerency, or an act that

---

[1] Geneva Convention III relative to the Treatment of Prisoners of War (adopted 12 August 1949, entered into force 21 October 1950) 75 UNTS 135 (Geneva Convention III).

[2] The High Seas are defined in United Nations Convention on the Law of the Sea (adopted 10 December 1982, entered into force 16 November 1994) 1833 UNTS 3 (UNCLOS) Art 86.

[3] UNCLOS Art 89.

[4] UNCLOS Art 87(1).

[5] UNCLOS Art 87(2).

[6] L Doswald-Beck (ed), *San Remo Manual on International Law Applicable to Armed Conflicts at Sea* (Cambridge, Cambridge University Press, 1995) [10(b)] and generally.

[7] Geneva Convention IV Relative to the Protection of Civilian Persons in Time of War (adopted 12 August 1949, entered into force 21 October 1950) 75 UNTS 287 (Geneva Convention IV) Art 2(2).

engages the protection of the LOAC, is carried out, the LOAC applies. In this sense the reach of the LOAC is universal. To the foregoing general principle, two aspects may be added.

a) *Principle of the unity of territory.* Even in cases of a localised armed conflict, the LOAC applies to the whole territory of the state. Thus, in the *Akayesu* case the International Criminal Tribunal for Rwanda stated that in case of a non-international armed conflict, Article 3 common to the Geneva Conventions applies, 'in the whole territory of the State engaged in the conflict'.[8] That does not mean that the same rules will be practically relevant throughout the territory. Thus, rules as to the means and methods of combat will be applicable only in the areas where actual fighting takes place. Conversely, that does not mean that in areas where there is no actual fighting the LOAC does not apply. In an international armed conflict, measures of internment of enemy civilians may for example be executed in all parts of the territory and the LOAC must apply to these measures in order for the regime to be effective. This is precisely the reason for saying that the armed conflict envelops the whole territory, or that there is a principle of unity of territory with regard to the applicability of the LOAC. The ICTY expressed this in the *Tadic* case:

> Although the Geneva Conventions are silent as to the geographical scope of international 'armed conflict', the provisions suggest that at least some of the provisions of the Conventions apply to the entire territory of the Parties to the conflict, not just to the actual vicinity of the hostilities. Certainly, some of the provisions are clearly bound up with the hostilities and the geographical scope of those provisions should be so limited. Others, particularly those relating to the prisoners of war and civilians, are not so limited.[9]

Finally, one must pay attention to the possibility that the armed conflict may not be of the same type in all parts of the territory. It is possible to have an international armed conflict on some parts of it, whereas on other parts there is only a non-international armed conflict. This depends upon the facts giving rise to the presence of these two types of armed conflicts.

b) *Special areas.* There are some areas with a special status under the LOAC. Geneva Convention I provides for agreed 'hospital zones':

> In time of peace, the High Contracting Parties and, after the outbreak of hostilities, the Parties to the conflict, may establish in their own territory and, if the need arises, in occupied areas, hospital zones and localities so organised as to protect the wounded and sick from the effects of war.[10]

More specifically, temporary refuge zones for civilians, called neutralised zones, are given special status by Geneva Convention IV:

> Any Party to the conflict may, either direct or through a neutral State or some humanitarian organization, propose to the adverse Party to establish, in

---

[8] *Prosecutor v Akayesu* (Trial Judgment) ICTR-96-4-T (2 September 1998) para [635].

[9] *Prosecutor v Tadic* (Decision on the Defence Motion for Interlocutory Appeal on Jurisdiction) IT-49-1-AR72 (2 October 1995) para [68].

[10] Geneva Convention I for the Amelioration of the Condition of the Wounded and Sick in Armed Forces in the Field (adopted 12 August 1949, entered into force 21 October 1950) 75 UNTS 31 Art 23.

regions where fighting is taking place, neutralized zones intended to shelter from the effects of war the following persons, without distinction: a. wounded and sick combatants or non-combatants; b. civilian persons who take no part in hostilities.[11]

The factual difference between the two zones is that neutralised zones are generally nearer the front, more temporary and organised on an ad hoc basis. Zones of both types are immunised from attack. Prior to their inclusion in the Conventions in 1949, such zones had already been created in 1936 and 1937 in Madrid during the Spanish Civil War and in 1937 during the Japanese shelling of Shanghai. Despite being strictly applicable only in international armed conflicts by virtue of the Geneva Conventions, similar temporary refuge zones have been created in situations of non-international armed conflict in the post-1949 period. These zones were established by agreement between the parties, on the instigation of the ICRC, in 1974 in Nicosia and in 1979 in Managua. The LOAC applies to such zones, but a special status of protection is conferred on them.

An example of an area where the opposite effect, a lowering of the protection available under the general LOAC, is intended can be seen in the 'combat zones' that were proclaimed by both sides during the Falklands/Malvinas War and the Iran/Iraq War. In these cases the belligerents announce that they will attack all enemy ships, aeroplanes or other means of transport entering a certain defined area. These zones thus operate as exclusion zones where the risks and perils of entry are borne by those who ignore the warning. In these cases the ordinary LOAC applies, so that automatic attack upon civilian ships would be unlawful, but certain spatial qualifications are imposed by a special regime. However, it must be stated that the legality of such combat zones is controversial.[12]

Comprehension check:

a)   Does the LOAC apply on the moon?
b)   How does the application of the LOAC differ spatially?
c)   Can the LOAC apply in the territory of a state not party to the conflict?

Answers:

a)   The LOAC does not apply, for the moment, to the moon, since there is no regular human presence and no armed conflict there. If, in the future, an armed conflict should take place on the moon, the principle of effectiveness would ensure that the LOAC would apply there.
b)   Not all of the LOAC rules apply equally at all places. Potentially, they all apply at all places; but actually, events may require the application of only some rules in some places, whereas at other places other rules will apply. Thus, on the territory of a state, rules on IAC may apply at some places, whereas rules of NIAC may apply at others. Moreover, rules as to the means and

---

[11] Geneva Convention IV Art 15.
[12] San Remo Manual [105]–[108].

methods of combat will be applied only where actual fighting takes place, whereas on other parts of the territory only rules protective of the civilians may be at stake. Finally, in certain zones special rules may apply because of an IHL provision or a special agreement by the parties. One may think of 'neutralised' or 'hospital' zones.

c) Yes, a particular branch of the LOAC applies to the relations between belligerents and non-belligerents. It is called the law of neutrality. Hence, the rights and duties of neutrality extend to the territory of the neutral states.[13]

[13] See generally: ch 34 below.

14

APPLICABILITY OF THE LOAC: TEMPORAL SCOPE OF APPLICABILITY

Learning objectives: To understand in which situations the LOAC is temporally applicable.

1. (Repetition, can be skipped by those who have worked through chapter 11). All branches of the law are divided in two parts. Before the substantive rules are applied, the legal order must first determine whether the extant situation is one in which the regulatory norms apply. This species of legal inquiry, which is the first province of any legal question, is devoted to the determination of the applicability of the law to a certain set of situations. Thus, for example, the LOAC is designed to apply only in a time of armed conflict and not in peacetime. This limits its scope of legal applicability. There are four aspects of applicability of legal rules:

a) subject matter applicability, or material scope of applicability, also known as *ratione materiae*, which defines 'situations of armed conflict' in which LOAC is applicable;

b) the personal scope of the applicability of the LOAC, also known as *ratione personae*, which addresses questions of the applicability of the LOAC to state organs, peace-keeping personnel of international organisations, all belligerents that are not a state and all individuals participating in the armed conflict;

c) the spatial scope of applicability of the LOAC, also known as *ratione loci*, which addresses questions of the applicability of the LOAC to the territory of the belligerent states and further spaces where effective fighting takes place, such as the high seas;

d) the temporal scope of applicability of the LOAC, also known as *ratione temporis*, which addresses questions of the continuing applicability of the LOAC during a situation of armed conflict and the cessation of applicability of the LOAC rules at the end of a conflict.

It is now necessary to enter into a more detailed analysis of these four aspects of applicability.

Once it has been determined that the norms of the LOAC are applicable in a particular situation, the substantive rules may be applied. This is the second province of the law. Thus, for example, if Geneva Convention III on prisoners of war is found to be applicable in all of the four dimensions mentioned above, we may proceed to ask questions regarding the substantive guarantees the convention affords to prisoners of war (POWs), such as the right to be treated humanely, the right not to be required to perform to dangerous work and the right to be provided with adequate food and care.[1]

The concepts of applicability and application of the law are thus performed in a natural sequence. First, one has to ask if a set of rules is applicable in a given context. If the answer is in the negative, the enquiry stops there, and that set of rules is not applicable in the particular circumstances. The lawyer then has to look for other sets of rules that could apply to the given situation. Thus, for example, if the LOAC does not apply because the situation does not yet have the characteristics of an armed conflict, but has remained a local riot, international human rights law may apply. The question of applicability must then to be decided anew for that separate branch of the law. If, conversely, the answer is positive, and the lawyer finds that a set of rules is applicable to a given situation, he or she will proceed to apply the substantive rules. This is the second phase of his or her work.

2. As far as the *temporal scope of application* is concerned, the objective temporal aspect must be distinguished from the subjective one.

   a) *Objective scope of application.* The LOAC applies during any period of 'armed conflict', as well as to situations of declared war or occupation of foreign territory without resistance.[2] Hence, in order to decide whether a particular situation is within the temporal scope of the LOAC, we must define the moment in time at which an armed conflict, a declared war or an occupation without resistance begins and at which moment they cease.

   b) *Subjective scope of application.* Particular norms found within LOAC conventions only apply once the convention has entered into force for a state. Conversely, as a matter of treaty law, a norm ceases to apply a certain period of time after a state party has denounced the treaty. These aspects are subjective because they concern the power of every state to decide by an act of will to be a party to a convention or to stop being a party to a convention. Therefore, questions concerning subjective scope of application apply only to treaties. The application of customary law does not depend on ratification by a state and it cannot be denounced. Consequently, the applicability of customary rules to every state is automatic, inescapable and does not need to be accepted by ratification or accession.

3. Let us first look to the *beginning of application of the LOAC*, first concerning the objective scope of temporal applicability and then relating to the subjective scope

---

[1] Geneva Convention III relative to the Treatment of Prisoners of War (adopted 12 August 1949, entered into force 21 October 1950) 75 UNTS 135 (Geneva Convention III).

[2] Geneva Convention I for the Amelioration of the Condition of the Wounded and Sick in Armed Forces in the Field (adopted 12 August 1949, entered into force 21 October 1950) 75 UNTS 31 (Geneva Convention I) Art 2; Geneva Convention II for the Amelioration of the Condition of Wounded, Sick and Shipwrecked Members of Armed Forces at Sea (adopted 12 August 1949, entered into force 21 October 1950) 75 UNTS 85 (Geneva Convention II) Art 2; Geneva Convention III Art 2; Geneva Convention IV Relative to the Protection of Civilian Persons in Time of War (adopted 12 August 1949, entered into force 21 October 1950) 75 UNTS 287 (Geneva Convention IV) Art 2.

of applicability. The starting point of application is quite easy to define. The LOAC will apply from the moment of the first hostile act in the armed conflict that puts at stake one of its protections. That means that the LOAC applies as soon as the first protected person is affected by the conflict, the first attack launched, the war declared or the first portion of foreign territory occupied. The rule is here quite simple and easy to apply. Some complications exist, but they must not be overstated. Hence, there may be a question of interpretation as to when the rules on belligerent occupation start to apply: they will apply as soon as the invasion phase is terminated, hostile resistance is broken and the military authority over the foreign territory established[3]; however, the definition of the precise moment in a specific context may cause some difficulties. In practice, real problems have not been experienced when considering whether the LOAC is applicable at a particular point in time, apart from situations where a state creates such difficulties in bad faith in order to evade its international obligations.

As far as the beginning of applicability of a specific convention is concerned, the question is not specific to the LOAC, but should be answered by reference to the general rules of the law of treaties.[4] A treaty will only be applicable to a state if is has ratified or acceded to it. The difference between ratification and accession is that ratification is performed by the states which participated at the negotiation and the adoption of the text, with all of these states being entitled to ratify, whereas accession is done by states that did not participate in the negotiations and in the adoption of the text. Accession is only possible to the extent that the treaty permits accession. The effect of both ratification and accession is the same: it is to declare the will of the state to be definitively bound by the treaty.[5] Moreover, to be applicable to a particular situation, the treaty must be in force. The moment of entry into force depends on provisions of the treaty which concern that question. Most multilateral treaties contain a clause whereby they will enter into force after a certain number of states have ratified, or acceded to, the text.[6] One must look into the final provisions of each convention in order to be informed on such points.[7] Finally, it must be noted that a treaty does not apply retroactively. It will only cover events that take place after its entry into force. Moreover, it will be applicable to a particular state only for events subsequent to the date of its ratification or accession. For events that take place prior to the entry into force of a particular treaty, customary international law, and conventional law that is already in force, applies.

4. Let us now turn to the *end of applicability of the LOAC*. This question is more complex, at least as far as the objective scope of applicability is concerned. The difficulties are well summarised by Sassoli and Bouvior, who note that:

---

[3] Geneva Convention IV Art 2.

[4] See generally: Vienna Convention on the Law of Treaties (adopted 23 May 1969, entered into force 27 January 1980) 1155 VCLT 331.

[5] Vienna Convention on the Law of Treaties Art 11.

[6] See, eg: Convention on the Prohibition of the Development, Production, Stockpiling and Use of Chemical Weapons and on Their Destruction (adopted 3 September 1992, entered into force 29 April 1997) 1974 UNTS 45 Art 21, which states that the convention will enter into force '180 days after the date of the deposit of the 65th instrument of ratification'.

[7] For the Geneva Conventions: Geneva Convention I Art 58; Geneva Convention II Art 57; Geneva Convention III Art 138; and Geneva Convention IV Art 153.

Most frequently, contemporary armed conflicts result in unstable cease-fires, continue at a lower intensity, or are frozen by an armed intervention by outside forces or by the international community. Hostilities or at least acts of violence with serious humanitarian consequences often break out later again. It is however difficult for humanitarian actors to plead with parties, having made declarations ending the conflict, that it in reality continues. The difficulty to define the end of application of IHL also results from the texts, as they use vague terms to define the end of their application, eg, 'general close of military operations' for international armed conflicts and 'end of the armed conflict' for non-international armed conflicts. As for occupied territories, Protocol I has extended the applicability of IHL until the termination of the occupation, while under Convention IV it ended one year after the general close of military operations, except for important provisions applicable as long as the occupying power 'exercises the functions of government'.[8]

5. There are three alternative thresholds for the end of the objective temporal application of the LOAC:

a) *The end of military operations.* Article 6(2) of Geneva Convention IV and Article 3(b) of Additional Protocol I make reference to the concept of 'general close of military operations' in order to pinpoint the end of the period of application of the LOAC.[9] This concept, which codifies customary international law, locates the end of application of the LOAC at the moment of the conclusion of a general and definitive armistice, of a general capitulation by a belligerent, or at the point in time that witnesses any form of *debellatio*, or the complete surrender of the vanquished belligerent to the will of the victor and the assumption of the functions of government in the vanquished country by the victorious state. The main criterion is once more effectiveness: it is not essential that a formal peace treaty be concluded to end the armed conflict and the applicability of the LOAC (for example, there is still no formal peace treaty between Japan and Russia concerning World War II, but of course the LOAC is not applicable in the relations between these states). An effective and final cessation of hostilities, whether set out in writing or merely de facto, is enough to bring the applicability of the LOAC to a close. The moment of effective cessation of hostilities may be difficult to define if hostilities continue on a smaller scale after hostilities have generally ceased: Iraq in the period following the close of major combat operations in May 2003 is a case in point. To the extent that there is still actual fighting, even through co-belligerent states, the applicability of the LOAC for IAC (or for NIAC) will continue. As we shall immediately see, however, not all of the rules of the LOAC will come to an end at the moment that signifies the general close of military operations. It is essentially the application of the rules concerning the means and methods of warfare that will be ended. Conversely, as considered in the section below, the protections that are provided to prisoners of war or interned civilians in,

---

[8] M Sassòli and A Bouvier, *How does Law Protect in War? Cases, Documents and Teaching Materials on Contemporary Practice in International Humanitarian Law: Volume I*, 2nd edn (Geneva, ICRC, 2006) 116–17.

[9] Geneva Convention IV Art 6(2) and Protocol Additional to the Geneva Conventions of 12 August 1949, and relating to the Protection of Victims of International Armed Conflicts (adopted 8 June 1977, entered into force 7 December 1978) 1125 UNTS 3 (Additional Protocol 1) Art 3(b).

for example, the Geneva Conventions,[10] will continue to apply as long as any such persons remain in the captivity of the adverse belligerents. The application of these norms will only end with the final release and repatriation of these persons.

b) *The end of captivity and detention.* Protected persons detained by a belligerent continue to benefit from the protections of the Geneva Conventions up until the time of their final release and, possibly, repatriation.[11] Thus, Article 5(1) of Geneva Convention III reads as follows:

> The present Convention shall apply to the persons referred to in Article 4 from the time they fall into the power of the enemy and until their final release and repatriation.

Release of such persons may by far exceed in time the general close of military operations. In the Pakistani-Indian conflict, it took more than two years to repatriate the prisoners of war; in the case of the Iran-Iraq War, hundreds of prisoners remained in jail for many years after the close of hostilities.[12]

c) *The end of military occupation.* Article 6(3) of Geneva Convention IV limits the temporal applicability of the rules relating to belligerent occupation contained in the Convention to one year after the general close of the military operations:

> In the case of occupied territory, the application of the present Convention shall cease one year after the general close of military operations; however, the Occupying Power shall be bound, for the duration of the occupation, to the extent that such Power exercises the functions of government in such territory, by the provisions of the following Articles of the present Convention: 1 to 12, 27, 29 to 34, 47, 49, 51, 52, 53, 59, 61 to 77, 143.

This is in stark contrast to the provisions of the Hague Regulations that govern occupied territories which apply as long as the occupation lasts in fact. Article 42(1) of those regulations states that, '[t]erritory is considered occupied when it is actually placed under the authority of the hostile army' and this provision can be interpreted as meaning that the territory remains occupied, with the concurrent rights and duties, for as long as it is under the authority of a hostile army.[13] This rule was returned to in order to delimit the temporal applicability of the norms contained in Additional Protocol I. Article 3(b) states:

> [T]he application of the Conventions and of this Protocol shall cease, in the territory of Parties to the conflict, on the general close of military operations and, in the case of occupied territories, on the termination of the occupation,

---

[10] Geneva Convention III and Geneva Convention IV.

[11] Geneva Convention I Art 5; Geneva Convention III Art 5(1); Geneva Convention IV Art 6(4); and Additional Protocol I Art 3(b).

[12] See also: *Prisoners of War—Eritrea's Claim 17 (Eritrea v Ethiopia)* Eritrea-Ethiopia Claims Commission (1 July 2003) at <http://www.pca-cpa.org/upload/files/ER17.pdf> accessed 15 May 2008 paras [143]–[163] and *Civilians Claim—Ethiopia's Claim 5 (Ethiopia v Eritrea)* Eritrea-Ethiopia Claims Commission (17 December 2004) at <http://www.pca-cpa.org/upload/files/ET%20Partial%20Award%20Dec%2004.pdf > accessed 15 May 2008 para [31].

[13] Regulations concerning the Laws and Customs of War on Land annexed to Hague Convention IV (adopted 18 October 1907, entered into force 26 January 1910) (1907) 205 CTS 227 Art 42(1).

except, in either circumstance, for those persons whose final release, repatriation or re-establishment takes place thereafter.[14]

This rule of effectiveness, as codified in The Hague Regulations and Additional Protocol I, corresponds to customary international law: the law of occupation shall continue to apply as long as the occupation itself lasts. Geneva Convention IV departs from this rule and thus complicates the law. The reasons for this departure were mainly historical and were intimately connected with the special status of territories such as Japan and Germany after World War II, where the law of occupation was thought to be quite unable to facilitate the profound reforms envisaged for the institutional structure of these states. What is the state of the law today? For all states that have ratified Additional Protocol I, the traditional rule of effectiveness applies to situations of occupation. For all states that have accepted only the Geneva Conventions, and have not consented to be bound by Additional Protocol I, the result will be the same by virtue of customary law: the Hague Regulations apply as long as the occupation lasts, and the rules of the Geneva Convention IV continue to apply to the extent that they are expressive of customary international law. Virtually all substantive rules of occupation law are now considered to be reflected in customary international law. The limitation of Article 6(3) therefore seems now largely obsolete. [15]

6. Finally, we must consider the subjective end of the application of IHL. The LOAC conventions can be denounced. Usually, a clause is inserted into LOAC treaties allowing any state party to declare that it no longer wishes to be bound by the treaty, and that it does not wish its future actions to be governed by the norms contained within the convention. For the four Geneva Conventions, such a provision can be found in Common Articles 63/62/142/158. However, despite having such a power, in reality no state has ever denounced a LOAC treaty. In effect, there is little to be gained from such an action. First, a state denouncing, for example, the Geneva Conventions would put itself at the margin of civilised society and to denounce would thus be to perform an act that would have a devastating impact on a state's international prestige. Secondly, there is little to be practically obtained from such a denunciation, since all of the important substantive rules contained in the Conventions are also part of customary international law,[16] which the Conventions, even if they did not do so in 1949, now merely codify. Hence, a denunciation would free a state from the obligation to perform the treaty, but that same state would still be bound to perform almost all of the same obligations as if it had continued to be a party to the convention, because of the parallel rules of customary international law. However, despite these practical reasons why it is unlikely that a state party would withdraw from a LOAC Convention, let us now turn to the rules that govern the denunciation of the LOAC treaties.

---

[14] Additional Protocol I Art 3(b).

[15] However, compare *Legal Consequences of the Construction of a Wall in the Occupied Palestinian Territory (Advisory Opinion)* [2004] ICJ Rep 136 para [125].

[16] See, eg: *Prisoners of War—Ethiopia's Claim 4 (Ethiopia v Eritrea)* Eritrea-Ethiopia Claims Commission (1 July 2003) at <http://www.pca-cpa.org/upload/files/ET04.pdf> accessed 15 May 2008 paras [30]–[32].

7. There are some general rules governing denunciation that appear in most IHL conventions. These rules can be considered as common customary international law rules, applicable to the denunciation of all IHL treaties:

a) A denunciation takes effect only one year after its receipt by the depositary of the treaty.[17]

b) A denunciation will not have effects in an armed conflict that has already begun at the time of denunciation:

> [A] denunciation of which notification has been made at a time when the denouncing Power is involved in a conflict shall not take effect until peace has been concluded, and until after operations connected with the release and repatriation of the persons protected by the present Convention have been terminated.[18]

A party may not free itself of its obligations because it considers that it can thus gain an advantage in a conflict that has broken out, as this is the situation where the protections of the LOAC are most needed.

c) A denunciation will have effect only in respect of the denouncing power. The other states parties to the Convention may not take such a denunciation as a signal that they are no longer required to apply the Convention in their reciprocal relations. They will be freed of their conventional obligations only with respect to the denouncing state.[19]

d) Finally, as noted above, a denunciation liberates a state from its conventional obligations, but does not free a state from its obligations under customary international law. The Conventions explicitly recall that point:

> [The denunciation] shall in no way impair the obligations which the Parties to the conflict shall remain bound to fulfil by virtue of the principles of the law of nations, as they result from the usages established among civilised peoples, from the laws of humanity and the dictates of the public conscience.[20]

Comprehension check:

a) When does the LOAC begin to apply?
b) When does it cease to apply?
c) Could the rules of the LOAC still apply 200 years after the end of an armed conflict?
d) Did the terrorist attacks on the twin towers on 11 September 2001 trigger the application of the LOAC rules?

Answers:

a) The LOAC begins to apply with the first hostile act; the temporal application begins when the first protected person is affected by the conflict, the first

---

[17] Convention (IV) respecting the Laws and Customs of War on Land and its annex: Regulations concerning the Laws and Customs of War on Land (adopted 18 October 1907, entered into force 26 January 1910) (1907) 205 CTS 227 Art 8 and Geneva Conventions I–IV common Art 63/62/142/158.

[18] Geneva Conventions I–IV common Art 63(3)/62(3)/142(3)/158(3).

[19] Geneva Conventions I–IV common Art 63(4)/62(4)/142(4)/158(4).

[20] Geneva Conventions I–IV common Art 63(4)/62(4)/142(4)/158(4).

attack is launched, war is declared or the first portion of foreign territory occupied. In short, with the 'first hostile act'.

b) The protection of the LOAC either ends at the general close of military opera-tions, the end of captivity of protected persons or the end of the occupation of foreign territory.[21] These thresholds are alternatives. The application of some rules will cease under one threshold, while others will continue to apply under another threshold: for example, the application of the rules as to means and methods of warfare will end with the close of military operations, whereas rules as to protected persons continue to apply until the release of the last prisoner. The application of Conventions may also cease because of denunciation, but never during an existing armed conflict or occupation: all states parties remain bound by the conventional rules up until the end of that conflict. In practice, states do not denounce IHL Conventions. Even if they did, the states would in any case remain bound by customary international law.

c) It is difficult to imagine any practical situation, but the applicability of the LOAC to such a situation cannot be denied in the absolute. If property has been confiscated under the laws of war and the point has not been settled for 200 years, the applicability of the relevant LOAC rules can remain relevant over such long periods of time. It must be stressed, however, that the example used here is invented.

d) The attack on the twin towers was not an 'act of war' or a trigger for an armed conflict. It did not emanate, apparently, from a state, bound by the LOAC, but from a terrorist group, sustained to some extent by one or more states. As far as the temporal aspect is concerned, if we take the attack as being an act triggering an 'armed conflict', then the LOAC applies from the moment of the attacks. However, such a construction is senseless, since the United States and al-Qaeda are not involved in an armed conflict under the principle of equality of belligerents. The fight against al-Qaeda takes place mostly under the aegis of criminal international cooperation and not under the umbrella of an armed conflict. Some episodes, however, are different: when the US forces fought in Afghanistan against some militias linked apparently to al-Qaeda, there was an armed conflict between both. This armed conflict began not with the attack on the twin towers, but with the first hostile act in Afghanistan. The members of these militias who take part in the fighting on the spot could be regular combatants, if they fulfilled the apposite legal conditions[22] and in these cases they would possess the rights afforded to combatants within the LOAC framework.

---

[21] See para 5 above for explanation.
[22] Geneva Convention III Art 4 and ch 25 below.

15

APPLICABILITY OF THE LOAC BY SPECIAL AGREEMENTS

Learning objectives: To learn how gaps and insufficiencies in the LOAC applicable to a particular armed conflict may be overcome in practice provided the parties to the conflict are willing to cooperate.

1. There are a series of cases where the applicability of the LOAC is doubtful. There are other situations where only a limited number of rules would normally apply, whereas there may be a need for additional protective rules. Thus, for example, the application of certain conventional rules may be hampered by the fact that a state participating in the conflict is not party to a convention. For example, this was the case during World War II, when the Soviet Union had not ratified the 1929 Geneva Convention on prisoners of war. Moreover, there may be gaps in the LOAC. For a long time, codification was confined to specific areas: first, it covered only wounded and sick combatants on land warfare; then these protections were extended to the sea; then protection was extended to combatants in captivity (prisoners of war); then the law started to contain rules on the protection of civilians, originally in a quite limited way, but gradually expanding its scope; then the law extended to NIAC, and so on. However, during all of these expansions, there remained gaps in protection. For example, in the case of a simple non-international armed conflict, there will be gaps in the protection compared to the rules governing IAC, since the rules applying to NIAC are less numerous. Thus, during the Spanish Civil War of 1936–39, the two belligerents, the Madrid Government and the Burgos Junta, agreed to treat certain prisoners as having a status analogous to prisoners of war. One could even imagine cases in which it might be seen by the parties as wise to apply at least certain rules of the LOAC by analogy to a situation of internal disturbance not amounting to an armed conflict. There may also be gaps in the protections offered by the LOAC in IAC. Thus, for example, certain weapons are not clearly prohibited. One may just mention the controversy concerning weapons containing uranium or cluster bombs.[1] If customary international law applies, the answer to the question of whether such weapons are prohibited may be difficult to determine. Similar problems apply across the range of areas covered by customary law. To these cases, one must add that often a state may deny that a situation in which it finds itself amounts to a situation of international

---

[1] Final Report to the Prosecutor by the Committee Established to Review the NATO Bombing Campaign Against the Federal Republic of Yugoslavia (2000) 39 ILM 1279 para [26].

or non-international armed conflict, or a situation of occupation as provided for in the Conventions. As examples, one may mention the Israeli occupied territories or the Western Sahara under Moroccan rule. Finally, as in the former Yugoslavia, an armed conflict may be mixed international and non-international. In cases of a mixed conflict, it may be unclear exactly what law applies to what situation, since there may be a highly complex merging of belligerent activities.

2. All of the situations described above, to which others could be added, have one point in common. The application of the law is rendered difficult or is stymied by a controversy over its applicability or by the insufficient reach of the rules, leaving lacunae. In such cases, a simple, pragmatic, device may overcome the difficulties. If the parties agree, they may conclude a 'special agreement', or many special agreements, in which they explicitly recognise that certain rules do apply, even if they might not have applied as a matter of strict custom or treaty. These agreements may be concluded in written form among the belligerents, but they may also be concluded informally, orally or by actual mutual conduct. Of course, the parties are free to conclude such agreements or are equally free to refuse to conclude them. The Geneva Conventions, in Common Article 2(3), Common Article 3(3) and Common Article 6/6/6/7 encourage the conclusion of such 'special agreements'. However, despite the positive encouragement found in the Conventions, ultimately the parties remain free to accept them or not. If the parties conclude a special agreement, the scope of the LOAC is increased. Apart from the rules that uncontroversially bind the parties *ex lege*, they will additionally be bound by all of the rules contained in the agreement. Such special agreements are practically speaking very important. They pragmatically and easily help to solve many doubts and quarrels on the applicability of rules of the LOAC. They also encourage humanity by allowing fresh protective rules to be added to the corpus of rules applicable to a specific conflict. In academic circles, often too little attention is paid to this aspect of the LOAC. In effect, there are hundreds of these special agreements concluded between belligerents: some are of minor importance, organising only the execution of conventional and undisputed duties; others are of great importance, putting beyond doubt and giving precision to the rules applicable in a particular armed conflict. Examples of such agreements will be given below.

In order to encourage the parties to enter into special agreements and increase the protection of the LOAC rules, the intervention of a third party is normally required. The belligerents themselves are often on too hostile terms to be able to take the initiative and negotiate such special agreements. In practice, it is most often the ICRC that takes the initiative, and in fact most of the special agreements are concluded through its mediation.

3. The Geneva Conventions envision the conclusion of special agreements, formal or informal, in order to extend the reach of their different provisions in three different articles.[2]

Article 2(3), which deals with international armed conflicts, stipulates that the states parties to a conflict who are parties to the Geneva Conventions shall also be bound by the Conventions in relation to a party to the conflict which is not yet a

---

[2] Geneva Conventions I–IV, Common Arts 2(3), 3(3), 6/6/6/7.

party to the Conventions, if the latter accepts and applies the provisions thereof. This means that the application of the Conventions extends to a non-party if that non-party either formally accepts an obligation to apply the Conventions, or conducts itself in accordance with the obligations therein. The aim, motivated by considerations of humanity, is to extend the reach of the Conventions as much as feasible, and to get around the stumbling block of formal requirements. Thus, if the non-party evinces agreement by word or deed, a special agreement is deemed to have been concluded. In such a case the application of the Conventions is obligatory, as Article 2(3) tells us that in such a case that the provisions of the Conventions 'shall' apply.

Article 3(3) formally deals with NIAC, but the special agreements it provides for have also been concluded outside that narrow compass. The drafters of the Geneva Conventions of 1949 were aware that, at that time, only very few rules applied to NIAC. Thus, they inserted a provision encouraging the parties to accept further obligations. In practice, this provision has had a great impact. One only needs to recall the special agreement concluded in 1992 by the belligerents in the former Yugoslavia, whereby they recognised the applicability to their conflict of a series of sources of the LOAC[3]; this agreement became one of the bases for the prosecution for war crimes at the International Criminal Tribunal for the former Yugoslavia (ICTY), its violations being charged as war crimes.[4]

Moreover, there are provisions that directly deal with the conclusion of special agreements.[5] Article 6 common to the Geneva Conventions reads as follows:

> In addition to the agreements expressly provided for in Articles 10, 15, 23, 28, 31, 36, 37 and 52, the High Contracting Parties may conclude other special agreements for all matters concerning which they may deem it suitable to make separate provision. No special agreement shall adversely affect the situation of the wounded and sick, of members of the medical personnel or of chaplains, as defined by the present Convention, nor restrict the rights which it confers upon them.

Many such special agreements have been concluded either under Article 6 or, for parties not yet bound by the Geneva Conventions, under customary international law. Hence, for example, during the civil war of Yemen in 1962, the belligerents undertook the obligation to respect the essential provisions of the Geneva Conventions, including Common Article 3, despite the fact that Yemen had not yet ratified the Geneva Conventions. Moreover, during the Israeli-Arab War of 1973, the belligerents accepted by a special agreement to apply by anticipation the rules on the protection of the civilian population which were, at that point, being elaborated in the negotiations that led to the conclusion of Additional Protocol I, which was not adopted until 1977.

4. What can be said on the legal status of such agreements?

   a) First, it must be noted that they will apply only to the parties that concluded

---

[3] M Sassoli and A Bouvier, *How does Law Protect in War? Cases, Documents and Teaching Materials on Contemporary Practice in International Humanitarian Law*, 2nd edn (Geneva, ICRC, 2006), 1112.

[4] *Prosecutor v Tadic* (Decision on the Defence Motion for Interlocutory Appeal on Jurisdiction) IT-49-1-AR72 (2 October 1995) paras [143]–[144].

[5] Geneva Conventions I–IV Art 6/6/6/7.

them, for the conflict at stake and under the conditions stipulated. Hence, such special agreements do not add rules to the corpus of the LOAC that are binding against third parties which did not participate in the negotiation and adoption of such agreements. They merely allow parties to fill in gaps and weaknesses in the context of a given conflict and situation. The special agreements will cease application at latest with the end of that conflict.

b)   Secondly, such special agreements may have two different aims. On the one hand, they may be purely executory. Agreements of this type will not add new obligations nor will they clarify the law applicable. Rather, they will allow execution of the obligations contained in the LOAC in a particular context. Thus, for example, Articles 109*ff* of Geneva Convention III stipulate that prisoners of war who are seriously wounded or seriously sick shall be repatriated as soon as possible, without having to await the end of the armed conflict. In order to put this provision into effect, these prisoners must be handed over to the adverse belligerent. To that effect, an agreement on the conditions of this transfer will be necessary. On the other hand, special agreements may be constitutive of fresh obligations. That is the type of agreement we have envisaged in the preceding paragraphs of this chapter.

c)   Thirdly, it must be stressed that the law limits the content of such special agreements. They must either be agreements to execute obligations or rights contained in the LOAC (and hence by definition compatible with the LOAC) or agreements which will give additional protections and do not:

> [A]dversely affect the situation of the wounded and sick, of members of the medical personnel or of chaplains, as defined by the present Convention, nor restrict the rights which it confers upon them.[6]

The Geneva Conventions thus allow special agreements that increase the rights or better the position of protected persons, but not those that attempt to restrict or deny LOAC rights to such persons.[7] An example from World War II of an agreement that sought to deny LOAC rights may be recalled here: by agreements between Vichy and Germany, the position of French prisoners of war in Germany was jeopardised, with the prisoners losing their 'prisoners of war' status. They in fact became civil workers in the German industry. By this device, the prisoners lost the protection of the 1929 Geneva Convention on prisoners of war.

Comprehension check:

a)   In what situations in the LOAC can it be useful to conclude 'special agreements'?

b)   What are the disadvantages of such special agreements?

c)   Who should take the initiative in the conclusion of such special agreements?

---

[6] Geneva Conventions I–IV common Art 6/6/6/7.
[7] See generally: ch 29 below.

Answers:

a) There are many situations where a special agreement may perform a useful service. First, agreements may be necessary in order to facilitate the performance of duties flowing from the LOAC or from a particular convention. Secondly, special agreements may be useful to clarify which sources of the law the parties recognise as applying to their conflict, especially if the question is controversial. In particular, it may overcome the difficulties that may arise if one or more belligerents have not ratified or acceded to certain conventions. The special agreement will then affirm the total or partial applicability of these texts. Thirdly, special agreements may increase the protections or prohibitions under the LOAC by assumption of certain supplementary duties or by the filling of gaps. Fourthly, in a NIAC, special agreements may allow the application of a series of rules of IAC, for example on the treatment of captives. Further aspects are mentioned above.

b) The advantages of such special agreements are manifest: they allow overcoming all of the shortcomings which flow from the problems addressed in question 1. However, as always, there may be also some problems with special agreements. The main shortcoming is the fact that with such special agreements the applicable law may fragment and be different according to each particular belligerent relationship. There is no longer one law that applies objectively to all of the parties, but a series of particular laws applying to different parties according to their wishes. However, in practice, this shortcoming does not outweigh the advantages of the special agreements. In the absence of such agreements, many of the protective rules contained in them would not have been applied, at least in fact. That these rules are applied to the particular belligerent relationship prevails over the disadvantage of the non-uniform nature of the applicable rules.

c) Ideally, each belligerent should take the initiative in the conclusion of special agreements in order to clarify the points which remain controversial, or in order to close any gaps manifested in practice. However, in practice, the ICRC is the institution most active in the furthering of such special agreements. Any neutral state in friendly relations with the belligerents could also propose such agreements, but such third states are often unaware of the practical needs on the spot.

16

THE ROLE OF THE INTERNATIONAL COMMITTEE OF THE RED CROSS

Learning objectives: To learn about the functions that are exercised by the International Committee of the Red Cross (ICRC) and its important contribution in the application and development of the LOAC.

1. As has been related previously, the ICRC was conceived in 1859 on the battlefield at Solferino in Northern Italy. On 24 June 1859, a battle took place between the French, Sardinian and Austrian armies. For want of the proper provision of medical assistance, more than 40,000 victims were left dead or dying on the battlefield or in the churches of nearby towns and villages. Henry Dunant, a businessman from Geneva who witnessed the carnage and the lack of proper relief, was struck by the miserable fate of the wounded who were left on the battlefield, and together with local inhabitants he tried to alleviate their suffering. On his return to Geneva in 1862, Dunant published a short book entitled *A Memory of Solferino*.[1] In this book, Dunant vividly describes events of the Battle of Solferino in a heroic tone, in stark contrast to the compassionate and miserable tone which he adopts when describing the suffering of the wounded and sick. Dunant then formulated proposals to improve the situation of the wounded and sick. Among these proposals was the establishment of National Red Cross Societies, which could contribute to the task of caring for the wounded and sick. In order to put into practice these proposals, a committee of five prominent persons from Geneva was formed, composed of Dunant himself, Gustave Moynier, a lawyer, General Guillaume-Henri Dufour, a soldier, and two physicians, Louis Appia and Théodore Maunoir. This initial Committee of the Five soon became the ICRC, or, as it was also called to begin with, the 'Committee of Geneva'. The first action of the ICRC was to request that the Swiss Federal Government convene a diplomatic conference in order to adopt an international convention on the protection of the wounded and sick soldiers. In due course, the Conference of Geneva adopted the first Geneva Convention for the Amelioration of the Condition of the Wounded in Armies in the Field.[2] The legal basis for the action of the ICRC, its mandate and the

---

[1] HJ Dunant, *A Memory of Solferino* (Geneva, International Committee of the Red Cross, 1986).

[2] The Geneva Convention for the Amelioration of the Condition of the Wounded in Armies in the Field (adopted 22 August 1864, entered into force 22 June 1865) (1864) 129 CTS 361.

principles of neutrality and impartiality guiding its action were laid down. In the years following, the ICRC engaged in many humanitarian initiatives aimed at ameliorating the suffering of the wounded and sick, but progressively became involved in the protection of non-injured prisoners of war and finally of civilians. Due to the horrors experienced during armed conflict in the twentieth century, and in particular during the two World Wars, the ICRC has grown. It developed new spheres of activity to an extraordinary extent.

Legally speaking, the ICRC has a hybrid status. It is constituted as an association under Swiss private law and yet it had been entrusted with international rights and duties under treaty law, which makes it an international actor and also a subject of public international law.[3] Being a subject of international law, or possessing international legal personality, which means the same, is just another way to express the concept that an entity has rights and duties defined by international law. This is the case for the ICRC.

2. Article 5 of the Statutes of the International of the Red Cross and the Red Crescent Movement contains a general statement regarding the missions of the ICRC:

Article 5

The International Committee of the Red Cross

1. The International Committee, founded in Geneva in 1863 and formally recognized in the Geneva Conventions and by International Conferences of the Red Cross, is an independent humanitarian organization having a status of its own. It co-opts its members from among Swiss citizens.

2. The role of the International Committee, in accordance with its Statutes, is in particular:

a)   to maintain and disseminate the Fundamental Principles of the Movement, namely humanity, impartiality, neutrality, independence, voluntary service, unity and universality;

b)   to recognize any newly established or reconstituted National Society, which fulfils the conditions for recognition set out in Article 4, and to notify other National Societies of such recognition;

c)   to undertake the tasks incumbent upon it under the Geneva Conventions, to work for the faithful application of international humanitarian law applicable in armed conflicts and to take cognizance of any complaints based on alleged breaches of that law;

d)   to endeavour at all times—as a neutral institution whose humanitarian work is carried out particularly in time of international and other armed conflicts or internal strife—to ensure the protection of and assistance to military and civilian victims of such events and of their direct results;

e)   to ensure the operation of the Central Tracing Agency as provided in the Geneva Conventions;

f)   to contribute, in anticipation of armed conflicts, to the training of medical personnel and the preparation of medical equipment, in cooperation with the National Societies, the military and civilian medical services and other competent authorities;

---

[3] *Prosecutor v Simic* (Decision on the Prosecution Motion under Rule 73 for a Ruling Concerning the Testimony of a Witness) IT-95-9-PT (27 July 1999) para [46] and fn 9.

g)   to work for the understanding and dissemination of knowledge of international humanitarian law applicable in armed conflicts and to prepare any development thereof;

h)   to carry out mandates entrusted to it by the International Conference.

3. The International Committee may take any humanitarian initiative which comes within its role as a specifically neutral and independent institution and intermediary, and may consider any question requiring examination by such an institution.

4. a) It shall maintain close contact with National Societies. In agreement with them, it shall cooperate in matters of common concern, such as their preparation for action in times of armed conflict, respect for and development and ratification of the Geneva Conventions, and the dissemination of the Fundamental Principles and international humanitarian law.

b)   In situations foreseen in paragraph 2 d) of this Article and requiring coordinated assistance from National Societies of other countries, the International Committee, in cooperation with the National Society of the country or countries concerned, shall coordinate such assistance in accordance with the agreements concluded with the Federation.[4]

3. The specific legal bases for the work of the ICRC can be found in different texts.

a)   First, there are *treaty-based activities*: the LOAC Conventions, in particular the Geneva Conventions and their Additional Protocols, entrust several different activities to the ICRC.[5] In international armed conflicts, the general task of the ICRC is to serve as a neutral intermediary between the parties to the conflict and to bring protection and assistance to the actual or potential victims of the armed conflict. An additional conventional task, which is to be exercised at the discretion of the ICRC, is centred on the exercise of the right of 'humanitarian initiative' in order to improve the situation of the protected persons beyond what is foreseen in the conventions. We will return to this power, which straddles the conventional and extra-conventional missions. There are furthermore a series of specific tasks flowing from the general ones. Such tasks include:

i)   the duty to visit and interview without witness prisoners of war and protected civilians, in particular when interned or detained,[6] which has been described as an 'essential part of the regime for protecting prisoners of war (POWs) that has developed in international practice'[7];

---

[4] Adopted by the 25th International Conference of the Red Cross at Geneva in October 1986. Available at <http://www.icrc.org/Web/eng/siteeng0.nsf/htmlall/statutes-movement-220506/$File/Statutes-EN-A5.pdf>, accessed 15 May 2008 ('Statutes of the Red Cross and Red Crescent').

[5] At least insofar as they concern POWs, the right of the ICRC to undertake these activities has acquired customary status, *Prisoners of War—Ethiopia's Claim 4* (*Ethiopia v Eritrea*) Eritrea-Ethiopia Claims Commission (1 July 2003) at <http://www.pca-cpa.org/upload/files/ET04.pdf> accessed 15 May 2008 paras [58]–[62].

[6] Geneva Convention III relative to the Treatment of Prisoners of War (adopted 12 August 1949, entered into force 21 October 1950) 75 UNTS 135 (Geneva Convention III) Art 126; Geneva Convention IV Relative to the Protection of Civilian Persons in Time of War (adopted 12 August 1949, entered into force 21 October 1950) 75 UNTS 287 (Geneva Convention IV) Art 143.

[7] *Ethiopia's Claim 4*, n 5, para [61].

ii) the duty to provide relief to protected civilians, POWs and to the population of occupied territories[8];

iii) the duty to search for missing persons, to trace prisoners of war and civilians, and to forward family messages[9];

iv) the duty to use the good offices of the ICRC to facilitate the creation of hospital and safety zones, as well as neutralised zones[10];

v) the duty to function as a substitute or quasi-substitute for the protecting power when the belligerent parties have not nominated protecting powers—in these circumstances, the ICRC must take the place of a neutral state representing the interest of a belligerent towards the other and entrusted with the task of controlling the application of the LOAC duties in this context[11]; and

vi) a series of other tasks in which time is of the essence, such as, for example, the nomination of neutral members to the Mixed Medical Commissions which have the task of determining whether a prisoner of war fulfils the requirements to be repatriated as being seriously wounded or sick.[12]

In the context of NIAC, Common Article 3 of the Geneva Conventions provides that the ICRC may offer its services to the parties to the conflict, which is a codification of the general and customary right of the ICRC to take the 'humanitarian initiative' where this is necessary or desirable, which has long been recognised and exercised.

b) Secondly, there are *non-treaty based tasks* of the ICRC. The Statutes of the International Red Cross and Red Crescent Movement assign the ICRC the role of guardian of the Conventions.[13] This allows the ICRC to take a position on all questions that surround the life of the Conventions. Hence, for example, the ICRC is concerned with the application of the Conventions. At the inception of any new armed conflict, it sends a memorandum to the states parties to the conflict, reminding them of the obligations under the LOAC which they are bound to apply. During the conflict, the ICRC takes many steps, which are often confidential, in order to ensure that LOAC obligations are properly complied with, reminding the parties of their duties and making constructive proposals for compliance, but also exercising some pressure. Regularly, the ICRC serves as intermediary for the communication of allegations of violations of the LOAC or for the transmission of claims from one party to the other regarding the conduct of the armed conflict: the ICRC will transmit the claim to the other belligerent without commenting

---

[8] Geneva Convention III Arts 73 and 125; Geneva Convention IV Arts 59, 61 and 142.

[9] Geneva Convention III Art 123; Geneva Convention IV Art 140; Protocol Additional to the Geneva Conventions of 12 August 1949, and relating to the Protection of Victims of International Armed Conflicts (adopted 8 June 1977, entered into force 7 December 1978) 1125 UNTS 3 (Additional Protocol 1) Art 33.

[10] Geneva Convention I for the Amelioration of the Condition of the Wounded and Sick in Armed Forces in the Field (adopted 12 August 1949, entered into force 21 October 1950) 75 UNTS 31 (Geneva Convention I) Art 23; Geneva Convention IV Arts 14–15.

[11] Geneva Convention I Art 9; Geneva Convention II for the Amelioration of the Condition of Wounded, Sick and Shipwrecked Members of Armed Forces at Sea (adopted 12 August 1949, entered into force 21 October 1950) 75 UNTS 85 (Geneva Convention II) Art 9; Geneva Convention III Art 9; Geneva Convention IV Art 10.

[12] Geneva Convention III Art 112 and annex II.

[13] Statutes of the Red Cross and Red Crescent, n 4, Art 5.

upon the facts. Sometimes, albeit rarely, the ICRC publicly expresses concern regarding violations of the LOAC in a particular armed conflict, especially if the violations are grave and persistent. It did this for the first time during World War I, but did not do so during World War II. It has also spoken out against violations of the LOAC in Yemen in 1967, when combat gases were used; in the Iran-Iraq War in 1983–84, when chemical weapons and the bombardment of towns with no military value took place; and again during the armed conflict in the former Yugoslavia, for example in 1991 after a mission of the ICRC had been attacked. At the other end of the spectrum, the ICRC contributes to the codification of the LOAC. Thus, the ICRC undertook the essential preparatory work and later led the conferences which adopted the four Geneva Conventions, and in the 1970s the Additional Protocols. The ICRC may also contribute to the creation of customary international law. As an international actor the practice of the ICRC must be taken into account when assessing the state of customary law.[14]

c) Thirdly, the ICRC has tasks which have a *mixed treaty and non-treaty basis*: this is referred to as the 'humanitarian initiative'. This is one of the most practically important tools possessed by the ICRC. It is a right that the ICRC traditionally enjoyed under customary law, and was very often exercised before the right was codified in a convention. Since the nineteenth century, all states, by their practice and *opinio juris*, accepted the fact that humanitarian initiatives could be taken by the ICRC. Moreover, the right of humanitarian initiative has today been codified and placed on a treaty basis.[15] Hence, 'the ICRC may take any humanitarian initiative which comes within its role as a specifically neutral and independent institution'.[16] It is non-treaty based in the sense that the ICRC may use the right of humanitarian initiative to propose any action going beyond the provisions of any Convention if it is designed to improve the situation of protected persons. Thus, using the right of humanitarian initiative, the ICRC may at any time propose that gaps in the effective protection afforded by the conventions be bridged by action of a practical nature. The right of initiative is a general right: it is not limited to the execution of the conventions, but can include attempts to extend the guarantees contained in the LOAC by adding fresh protections. The history of the ICRC can be seen in a certain sense as a history of humanitarian initiatives. Hence, when the ICRC opened an agency centralising and forwarding all information regarding prisoners of war during the Franco-Prussian War in 1870, it acted on the basis of the right of humanitarian initiative. When it performed humanitarian work during the Russian and Spanish Civil War, it did so on the same basis: for example, it successfully placed pressure on the parties to the Spanish Civil War to grant a status equivalent to that of prisoners of war to a

---

[14] *Prosecutor v Tadic* (Decision on the Defence Motion for Interlocutory Appeal on Jurisdiction) IT-49-1-AR72 (2 October 1995) para [109].

[15] Geneva Conventions I–IV common Arts 3 and 9/9/9/10; Additional Protocol I Art 81; Statutes of the Red Cross and Red Crescent, n 4, Art 5(3); Statutes of the International Committee of the Red Cross, available at <http://www.icrc.org/Web/eng/siteeng0.nsf/html/icrc-statutes-080503> accessed 15 May 2008 Art 4(2).

[16] Statutes of the Red Cross and Red Crescent, n 4, Art 5(3).

series of captives. When during World War II the ICRC, in cooperation with the Swedish Red Cross, organised relief action for starving populations in occupied Greece, that action was based on the right of initiative. When, during the siege of Beirut in 1982, the ICRC obtained the permission to undertake some relief actions to which the Israeli armed forces were not bound to consent, but to which they in fact consented, it was again the right of initiative that was the tool of action.

The right of humanitarian initiative is limited to proposals of humanitarian character. This flows from the general scope of competence of the ICRC. Thus, the ICRC is unable to propose political settlements. Moreover, the right of initiative is limited to the expression of proposals. The ICRC cannot impose; it can only propose. The belligerents thus addressed remain free to accept or reject the proposals. It is only after the agreement or acceptance by the belligerent concerned that any action will be undertaken. The point is not only to protect the sovereignty of each belligerent; it is also simply practical. No action by the ICRC on the spot can be performed if there is no cooperation and protection by the territorial state: the ICRC has no means to impose anything, since it has no army and no political mandate.

The right of humanitarian initiative is not only practically very important. It is also essential from the point of view of the changing circumstances inherent in war. Armed conflicts and their environment are constantly changing. Many aspects of future conflicts are unforeseeable. Thus, any codification of the laws of armed conflict tends to be somewhat outdated with respect to the new techniques of armed conflict and the needs that arise in new warfare situations. In this sense, the right of humanitarian initiative attempts to future-proof the LOAC. The right of humanitarian initiative is, in that context, a highly welcome corrective to the detailed rules, because it remains flexible and can face the new needs in a dynamic and convenient manner. Any belligerent should give utmost attention to the proposals of the ICRC, since there is hardly any institution with more expertise on humanitarian matters, and with a better record on neutrality, impartiality and independence.

4. The day-to-day activities of the ICRC are described in brief below[17]:

   a) The main concern of the ICRC is to provide general *protection to persons* in situations of armed conflict. Its mission is to obtain full respect for the letter and spirit of the LOAC or, more generally speaking, for the principle of humanity. It therefore seeks to:

   i)   minimise dangers to which people are exposed;
   ii) prevent and put an end to violations of the law to which persons are subjected;
   iii) draw attention to their rights and make their voices heard; and
   iv) bring assistance to persons in need.

---

[17] For a more detailed exposition of these activities, see especially M Sassoli and A Bouvier, *How does Law Protect in War? Cases, Documents and Teaching Materials on Contemporary Practice in International Humanitarian Law*, 2nd edn (Geneva, ICRC, 2006).

There are different aspects in these activities: first, the ICRC aims to protect civilians. Civilians often endure horrific ordeals in today's armed conflicts: they serve as direct targets, they face massacres, hostage-taking, sexual violence, harassment, expulsion and forced transfer, looting, denial of access to water, food and health care and terror practices. Persons displaced because of an armed conflict have a particular need for assistance. They often end up as refugees or internally displaced persons (IDPs). As part of the civilian population, in international armed conflicts, IDPs are protected under Geneva Convention IV; they benefit from ICRC protection and assistance programs. The primary responsibility for refugees created by armed conflicts rests with the Office of the United Nations High Commissioner for Refugees.

b) Another important branch of the ICRC activities relates to the *protection of detainees*. In international armed conflicts, the Geneva Conventions recognise the right of ICRC delegates to visit prisoners of war and civilians deprived of their liberty, including civilian internees.[18] In NIAC, the ICRC has no right to visit detainees, but may offer to carry out this function under the right of humanitarian initiative. States are then not obliged to accept such visits. However, they often accept in practice. Through these visits, the ICRC aims to:

i) control the proper application of the Geneva Conventions and prevent, by repeated presence, actions by states that would violate these texts;

ii) prevent or put an end to disappearances and summary executions;

iii) restore family links where they have been disrupted and inform the families of detainees of the current status of the family members who are held in foreign captivity; and

iv) improve conditions of detention, when necessary by making proposals to the detaining power.

The visit normally begins with a meeting between the ICRC delegate and the camp commander. Thereafter, the ICRC delegates conduct private interviews with each detainee to the extent that this is possible. If there are too many detainees, the representatives of the detainees and some particular detainees chosen by the delegate from the list of inmates will be interviewed. The delegate will note the detainees' details in order to be able to follow each one of them up to the time of his or her release. The detainees are interviewed without the presence of a representative of the detaining power. They can thus freely complain about ill treatment or other violations of their rights, as well as simply about the problems they face while in detention. A physician accompanies the delegate during the visit. The ICRC asks for access to all detainees; if it is not granted, the visit will not be made. This is the only way of avoiding being misled and issuing a favourable report which then turns out to be a sham. The delegate then visits the whole camp, demanding that all areas be opened for him or her. At the end of his or her visit, the delegate returns to the camp commander and communicates his or her impressions to him or her. He or she transmits the complaints of the prisoners and suggests

---

[18] Geneva Convention III Art 126; and Geneva Convention IV Art 143.

improvements. Finally, the delegate will draw up a report for the ICRC in which he or she will state all of his or her observations in a standardised sequence. These reports are customarily written in a strongly objective tone, the delegate abstaining from any personal and subjective evaluation. The ICRC will repeat visits in order to maintain the pressure on the detaining power to respect the Conventions and to implement the improvements suggested by the delegate. The visits must be announced. A surprise visit will normally not be possible. Whilst there is a certain danger of embellishment when this practice is adopted, the contingencies of war and the considerations of the safety of the delegation do not allow the system of visits to operate in any other way. The private interviews without witnesses and the eyes of the delegate will to some extent be a corrective to this shortcoming. One can thus summarise these visits as follows. The delegate will:

i)   see all detainees falling within the ICRC's mandate and have access to all places where they are held;
ii) interview detainees of the delegate's choice without witnesses;
iii) draw up lists of detainees or receive such lists from the detaining power, which will be verified and completed if information is missing;
iv) repeat visits to detainees of their choice as frequently as they may feel necessary;
v)   restore family links by transmitting personal messages; and
vi) provide urgent material and medical assistance as required.

c) A further important task of the ICRC is to *restore family links*. The ICRC's Central Tracing Agency works to establish familial links in situations of armed conflict. In such situations, thousands of persons are missing because of, for example, flight, displacement or captivity. Individual inquiries into the whereabouts of a certain person are opened. The persons traced are given the opportunity to send and to receive Red Cross messages, in this manner being put in contact with their families. In international armed conflicts, the ICRC's Central Tracing Agency fulfils the task assigned to it under IHL of gathering, processing and passing on information on protected persons, notably prisoners of war and civilian internees. For detainees and their families, receiving news of their loved ones is always of huge importance. Sometimes, it is necessary to issue a travel document in order to allow a person to be repatriated or to leave a belligerent state for a third country, for example, a neutral state where he or she will be interned. Such documents have been issued by the ICRC and recognised by states.

d) Finally, the ICRC undertakes also *preventive action*. It thus contributes to the development and interpretation of IHL. Since its foundation, the ICRC has constantly tried to improve the protection of war victims through the adoption of new rules of the LOAC. When the ICRC can insist on the application of a ratified convention, its position, and consequently that of the victims, is greatly improved with respect to the situation where, in the absence of a specific treaty provision governing the position, all depends on the goodwill of the belligerent. History has shown the truth of this statement over and over again. Moreover, through its advisory services on IHL, the

ICRC strives to convince the state parties to adopt national measures of implementation that will facilitate respect for the rules of IHL. The ICRC also attempts to contribute to the interpretation of IHL. The commentaries to the Conventions edited under its aegis are the classic products of this effort.[19] However, the same can be said of expert meetings, which help to crystallise legal opinion: for example on the applicability of IHL to UN peacekeeping and/or peace-enforcement operations. Finally, respect for IHL depends on the knowledge that armies, insurgents and the population in general have of it. Thus, the Geneva Conventions require states to disseminate the rules of the LOAC as widely as possible during peacetime.[20] This dissemination of rules of IHL is primarily the responsibility of the states parties to the Geneva Conventions, but the ICRC has often taken over this task. It has developed a global approach to dissemination, focusing on the main target groups: armed and security forces, other weapon bearers, political leaders and opinion makers. In order to train the future decision-makers, numerous dissemination programs target the youth, students and their teachers.

5. The practical importance of the work of the ICRC can hardly be overstressed. In any of the hundreds of armed conflicts and, in a less official capacity, situations of internal disturbance, that have torn the world apart since 1863, the ICRC has been present through relief actions, tracing agencies, prisoner's visits, transmission of personal news and parcels and diplomatic *demarches* urging respect for IHL. Thus, for example, around 91 million individual parcels were transmitted to prisoners of war during World War II. These parcels, which were filled with foodstuffs and other necessities, saved the lives of a great many of their recipients; during World War II, a large part of the Greek civilian population, which was living in conditions of starvation, was only able to survive with the help of assistance delivered through the Swedish Red Cross, in cooperation with the ICRC; during the Israeli-Arab war of 1973, delegates of the ICRC crossed the Jordan River on foot in order to transmit personal messages to the other side of the front. The exemplary humanitarian nature of this work speaks for itself, and further exposition is unnecessary.[21]

6. In all of its actions, the ICRC follows certain fundamental principles, which were first formulated in their modern wording at the Vienna Conference of the Red Cross and Crescent Movement in 1965. These principles are now comprehensively set out in the preamble to the Statutes of the Red Cross and Red Crescent Movement. The seven general principles are formulated as follows:

Reaffirms that, in pursuing its mission, the Movement shall be guided by its Fundamental Principles, which are:

Humanity The International Red Cross and Red Crescent Movement, born of a desire

---

[19] See, eg: JS Pictet (ed), *The Geneva Conventions of 12 August 1949: Commentary. Vol 1: Geneva Convention for the Amelioration of the Condition of the Wounded and Sick in Armed Forces in the Field* (Geneva, ICRC, 1952).

[20] Geneva Conventions I–IV common Art 47/48/127/144.

[21] See generally: F Bugnion, *The International Committee of the Red Cross and the Protection of War Victims* (Geneva, ICRC, 2003).

to bring assistance without discrimination to the wounded on the battlefield, endeavours, in its international and national capacity, to prevent and alleviate human suffering wherever it may be found. Its purpose is to protect life and health and to ensure respect for the human being. It promotes mutual understanding, friendship, cooperation and lasting peace amongst all peoples.

Impartiality It makes no discrimination as to nationality, race, religious beliefs, class or political opinions. It endeavours to relieve the suffering of individuals, being guided solely by their needs, and to give priority to the most urgent cases of distress.

Neutrality In order to continue to enjoy the confidence of all, the Movement may not take sides in hostilities or engage at any time in controversies of a political, racial, religious or ideological nature.

Independence The Movement is independent. The National Societies, while auxiliaries in the humanitarian services of their governments and subject to the laws of their respective countries, must always maintain their autonomy so that they may be able at all times to act in accordance with the principles of the Movement.

Voluntary Service It is a voluntary relief movement not prompted in any manner by desire for gain.

Unity There can be only one Red Cross or one Red Crescent Society in any one country. It must be open to all. It must carry on its humanitarian work throughout its territory.

Universality The International Red Cross and Red Crescent Movement, in which all Societies have equal status and share equal responsibilities and duties in helping each other, is worldwide.[22]

The first fundamental principle, the principle of humanity, can be discussed further and set out with greater specificity. It has three essential aspects. First, it covers the *respect* for the human person, in particular the duty not to inflict pain or suffering. Secondly, it concerns the *protection* of the human person, in particular the duties to prevent and alleviate his or her sufferings and to offer shelter and relief. Thirdly, the requirement of *human treatment* obliges consideration of a human being as an end in themselves and not as a means to an end, and thus offering him or her a series of minimal conditions of life consonant with human dignity.

Comprehension check:

a) What are the main tasks of the ICRC?
b) If a specific competence is not given to the ICRC in the Geneva Conventions or the 1977 Additional Protocols, or elsewhere, can we say that the ICRC is deprived of any right of action?
c) Why does the ICRC act confidentially?

Answers:

a) The main tasks of the ICRC are: (1) the protection of persons in an armed conflict, namely wounded and sick soldiers, prisoners of war and civilians; (2)

---

[22] Statutes of the Red Cross and Red Crescent, n 4, preamble.

in particular the protection of detained protected persons, namely through visit programs; (3) in particular also the restoration of family links; (4) the development, interpretation and dissemination of IHL; and (5) the exercise of a series of rights and duties as provided for in the Conventions, for example the nomination of physicians in the Mixed Medical Commissions.[23]

b) The right of action of the ICRC is not limited to the implementation of the Geneva Conventions. Its tasks are either conventional, and when carrying out duties in these cases the ICRC contributes to the implementation of legal texts; or they are extra-conventional, as when the ICRC proposes, for example, a change in the law through the adoption of a new convention; or the actions undertaken by the ICRC are a mixture between conventional and extra-conventional actions, such as the ICRC attempting to improve the situation of the persons protected by suggesting solutions under its right of 'humanitarian initiative'. To the extent that the ICRC remains within the bounds of humanitarian action, which by reason of its statutes it cannot overstep, it can propose any practical improvement or solution to a humanitarian problem arising during an armed conflict. Thus, it can propose relief action to a besieged place, despite the fact that this action that goes beyond what the Conventions allow. Moreover, it should never be forgotten that the reverse is also true: any state to a conflict can profit from the expertise and resources (material, legal or practical) of the ICRC. Thus, the ICRC can be contacted at any time in order to help in a particular situation where war-related humanitarian and practical problems are faced. The ICRC will not refuse to provide help that is within its capabilities and the limits of its mandate.

c) The basic idea of the ICRC is that only by confidentiality can it retain an acceptable level of contact with all belligerents involved in the conflict, so that the parties will continue to allow it to exercise its duties, such as the visits to the prisoners of war or interned civilians. If a state feels that visits will lead to public denunciations, it will be unlikely to allow the visit. The situation of warfare already creates mistrust and difficulties, which are high obstacles to free access to detainees by the ICRC; public accusations would add even higher ones, because the party publicly accused of breaching the LOAC then loses confidence in the ICRC and tends to feel 'betrayed'. However, the ICRC sometimes, when faced with a pattern of grave and constant violations, has resorted to public denunciations. However, these remain exceptional. In weighing up the pros and cons, the ICRC has felt that it can be more effective, and therefore ensure greater protection for civilians, when it acts confidentially. It thus leaves public denunciations to the many non-governmental organisations operating in the area of human rights. Moreover, the knowledge that the ICRC acts confidentially may encourage belligerent states to have recourse to the ICRC if it has matters it wishes to discuss. The guarantee of confidentially may allow the state to find solutions to its problems in a confidential and constructive way.

---

[23] Geneva Convention III Art 112.

17

TARGETING: THE PRINCIPLE OF DISTINCTION BETWEEN CIVILIAN AND MILITARY OBJECTIVES

Learning objectives: To discover the fundamental rule that governs which objects are liable to be attacked and which objects are immune from attack. To learn about how the application of this fundamental rule allows belligerent parties to make targeting decisions during armed conflicts.

1. The fundamental principle in 'Hague Law', the area of the LOAC that governs the means and methods of warfare, is that any belligerent, whether in an IAC or a NIAC, must distinguish between military objectives on the one hand and civilian persons and goods on the other.[1] Only the former may be attacked; civilian objects must not. Underlying this rule is the principle that, even in an armed conflict, the only legitimate military action is that which is aimed at weakening the military potential of the enemy, whereas attacks on those who do not participate in the conflict are prohibited. The concretisation of this principle in the rules of the LOAC means that the doctrine of 'total war' is repudiated: war must be conducted by limited means; it cannot engage in attacks without giving consideration to whether the target actively participates in the armed conflict. This principle is recalled by Article 22 of the Hague Regulations, which reads, '[t]he right of belligerents to adopt means of injuring the enemy is not unlimited'.[2] One of the most important aspects of the principle of limitation elucidated in the Hague Regulations is the duty to distinguish between military and civilian objectives. Hence, attacks on the civilian population in order to lower the morale of the enemy and create a willingness amongst the civilian population to end the war are not allowed, even if some military advantage would be gained by taking such a course. Here, the LOAC clearly repudiates the principle set out by Clausewitz, in his treatise on War, in which he states that war should not be limited for humanitarian reasons since such limits put the belligerent who respects them at a disadvantage when compared to an enemy who, hypothetically, does not respect such limits.[3] On the

---

[1] J-M Henckaerts and L Doswald-Beck (eds), *Customary International Humanitarian Law Volume 1: Rules* (Cambridge, CUP, 2005) Rule 1.

[2] Regulations concerning the Laws and Customs of War on Land annexed to Hague Convention IV (adopted 18 October 1907, entered into force 26 January 1910) (1907) 205 CTS 227 (Hague Regulations) Art 22.

[3] C von Clausewitz, *On War* (Harmondsworth, Penguin, 1968) ch I, para [3].

contrary, the LOAC asks that both belligerents respect some limitations on their ability to wage war and thus tries to establish a scheme by which humanitarian limitations on behaviour may be obeyed reciprocally, by establishing the equilibrium between humanitarian considerations and military necessity.

2. Armed conflict in the twentieth century has placed a heavy strain on the principle of distinction. This makes it more remarkable that the principle has been fiercely maintained. In IAC the rise of national wars, where the majority of the population of a state contributes, in one way or another, to the war effort tends to expose civilians to belligerent attacks. As industrial production has become the major driving force behind victory in armed conflicts, and such industrial production can only be sustained by work on the part of the population, the danger of such civilians being targeted has increased. Moreover, all civilians, even those not employed in producing industrial products essential for the war effort, ensure, through their support for the war, that the society remains in a state of combativeness. Therefore, the possibility that adverse belligerents may attempt to decrease civilian support for the war by direct attacks on civilians will increase. These challenges to the principle of distinction were first witnessed during World War II, and have been problematic in armed conflicts since.

As far as NIAC are concerned, the distinction between combatants and civilians has always been somewhat more difficult, since the rebels recruit from the ranks of the civilian population and often adopt guerrilla methods. Hence, their distinction from civilians is rendered more difficult. For this reason the law requires that the rebels distinguish themselves from the civilians by some distinctive signs. Moreover, recent armed conflicts, such as that in the former Yugoslavia, have shown that when the aim of the conflict is to practice 'ethnic cleansing', the attack on the civilians becomes unavoidable. In such cases civilians rather than combatants will be deliberately targeted. The same is true when warlords or armed bands start or continue a conflict for economic aims—for example, so they can engage in looting of the natural resources of a territory. In these cases civilians will be dragged into the conflict. Despite these shortcomings, the principle of distinction is so fundamental that it may not be pushed aside. To a very large extent, IHL stands or falls on its observance.

3. The principle of distinction contains three facets:

a) the prohibition placed on the targeting or attacking of civilian persons;
b) the prohibition placed on the targeting or attacking of civilian objects; and
c) the prohibition placed on indiscriminate attacks.

Each of these aspects will be examined separately.

THE PROHIBITION PLACED ON THE TARGETING OR ATTACKING OF CIVILIAN PERSONS

4. The source of states' obligation not to attack civilians can be found in Article 25 of the Hague Regulations, which relates to so-called 'undefended towns', and

Articles 48 and 51 of Additional Protocol I.[4] Article 48 of Additional Protocol I reads:

> In order to ensure respect for and protection of the civilian population and civilian objects, the Parties to the conflict shall at all times distinguish between the civilian population and combatants and between civilian objects and military objectives and accordingly shall direct their operations only against military objectives.

Moreover, the International Court of Justice, in the *Nuclear Weapons* Advisory Opinion, expressed itself thus:

> The cardinal principles contained in the texts constituting the fabric of humanitarian law are the following. The first is aimed at the protection of the civilian population and civilian objects and establishes the distinction between combatants and non-combatants; States must never make civilians the object of attack.[5]

5. A civilian may be defined as any person who is not a combatant. Article 50 of Additional Protocol I contains the following negative definition:

> A civilian is any person who does not belong to one of the categories of persons referred to in Article 4 (A) (1), (2), (3) and (6) of the Third Convention and in Article 43 of this Protocol.

The aim of this negative definition is to avoid the likelihood of loopholes arising in the law. If the law defined 'civilians' and 'combatants' separately and did not relate the two definitions to each other, there is a real possibility that a gap could be left, and a person could be seen as neither a civilian nor a combatant, and therefore be left without the protection of the LOAC. The attempt to avoid any such lacuna, and indeed any further uncertainties that operate to the detriment of civilians, is further reinforced by the presumption of civilian status. In cases of doubt, Article 50 of Additional Protocol I makes clear that a person is to be considered a civilian unless the contrary is proven: '[i]n case of doubt whether a person is a civilian, that person shall be considered to be a civilian'. Finally, it must be noted that the presence of isolated combatants amidst a majority civilian population does not alter the civilian character of that population as a whole and thus does not extinguish its immunity from attack.[6] Hence, Article 50(3) of Additional Protocol I reads as follows:

> The presence within the civilian population of individuals who do not come within the definition of civilians does not deprive the population of its civilian character.

There is, however, one exception to these rules of immunity. Civilians who participate directly in the hostilities lose their immunity during the period of that direct participation and also during any period in which they perform acts preparatory to the attack they intend to launch. Article 51(3) of Additional Protocol I declares that:

---

[4] Protocol Additional to the Geneva Conventions of 12 August 1949, and relating to the Protection of Victims of International Armed Conflicts (adopted 8 June 1977, entered into force 7 December 1978) 1125 UNTS 3 (Additional Protocol 1).

[5] *Legality of the Threat or Use of Nuclear Weapons (Advisory Opinion)* [1996] ICJ Rep 226 para [78].

[6] *Prosecutor v Galic* (Appeal Judgement) IT-98-29-A (30 November 2006) paras [135]–[138].

Civilians shall enjoy the protection afforded by this section, unless and for such time as they take a direct part in hostilities.[7]

One will notice that the time-span during which civilians lose their protection is short and restrictively drawn. Immunity is lost only during the period in which they take a 'direct part in hostilities'. Outside this time-span they can be arrested and tried for unlawful acts of warfare performed during the time that they were a combatant. However, they can no longer be targeted. The limited scope of the loss of immunity attempts to prevent abuses by an adverse belligerent. If the loss of immunity was not temporally limited, a belligerent could always declare that such and such civilian had in the past participated in hostile acts and consequently was a legitimate target. Hence, the obligation not to attack civilians could be rendered largely illusory. Such a possibility is not merely fanciful: the arguments made by the Germans during World War II may be recalled. Furthermore, it should be noted that intentional or reckless attacks on civilians are war crimes.[8]

6. One may recall that certain military persons also have immunity from attacks, which at first glance appears to be similar to the immunity possessed by civilians.[9] This type of immunity from attack is, first of all, granted to military persons who have been rendered *hors de combat*. Such personnel are those who have surrendered to the enemy or those that are wounded, sick or shipwrecked.[10] Article 41 of Additional Protocol I reads as follows:

(1) A person who is recognized or who, in the circumstances, should be recognized to be hors de combat shall not be made the object of attack.

(2) A person is hors de combat if:

(a) he is in the power of an adverse Party;
(b) he clearly expresses an intention to surrender; or
(c) he has been rendered unconscious or is otherwise incapacitated by wounds or sickness, and therefore is incapable of defending himself;

provided that in any of these cases he abstains from any hostile act and does not attempt to escape.

Article 42(1) of Additional Protocol I extends a similar protection to personnel parachuting from an aircraft in distress, during their descent. This provision states that, '[n]o person parachuting from an aircraft in distress shall be made the object of

---

[7] See also: *The Public Committee against Torture in Israel v Government of Israel* (Targeted Killings) HCJ 769/02 (13 December 2006) available at <http://elyon1.court.gov.il/Files_ENG/02/690/007/a34/02007690.a34.HTM> accessed 15 May 2008.

[8] Rome Statute of the International Criminal Court (adopted 17 July 1998, entered into force 1 July 2002) 2187 UNTS 3 Arts 8(b)(i) and 8(e)(i), and see also *Prosecutor v Galic*, paras [110]–[140].

[9] Note, however, that this immunity is not given because these military personnel are civilians. They remain military personnel even when *hors de combat*: *Prosecutor v Blaskic* (Appeal Judgement) IT-95-14-A (29 July 2004) para [114] and *Galic, ibid*, fn 437.

[10] See Hague Regulations Art 23(c); Geneva Convention I for the Amelioration of the Condition of the Wounded and Sick in Armed Forces in the Field (adopted 12 August 1949, entered into force 21 October 1950) 75 UNTS 31 Art 12; Geneva Convention II for the Amelioration of the Condition of Wounded, Sick and Shipwrecked Members of Armed Forces at Sea (adopted 12 August 1949, entered into force 21 October 1950) 75 UNTS 85 Art 12; Geneva Convention III relative to the Treatment of Prisoners of War (adopted 12 August 1949, entered into force 21 October 1950) 75 UNTS 135 Arts 13–14; and Additional Protocol I Art 41.

attack during his descent'. Whilst it was controversial at the time of its adoption, this provision is now generally accepted and must be considered to be part of customary international law. Finally, non-combatant army personnel, in particular personnel attached to the medical services and chaplains, must not be made the object of attack. A similar immunity extends to war correspondents embedded with the army.[11]

7. During peacetime, and in particular during times of armed conflict, states must act in such a way to ensure that the rule guaranteeing the immunity of civilians is workable. Hence, states must take all possible steps to ensure that military objectives are spatially separated from areas of civilian populations and must avoid placing military objectives, such as ammunition deposits, in the vicinity of populated areas. Moreover, each state has an obligation not to place civilians in particular positions with the aim of either protecting military objectives from attack or facilitating military operations. Human shields are the most conspicuous example of a violation of this rule. These prohibitions have the objective of sparing civilians from attack. It is clear that even if military objectives are placed in populated zones, or if civilians are deliberately located in the vicinity of military objectives, the opposing belligerent may still attack the military objectives. However, during such attack he or she may incidentally hit the civilians in the surrounding area. Obviously, the attacking belligerent must take the presence of the civilians into account when weighing the proportionality of a planned attack. This does not detract from the fact that, if the attack goes ahead, civilians will be jeopardised; the aim of the rules that require 'separation' is to minimise the damage done to civilians during legitimate attacks. On the other hand, one should note that the obligation to separate civilians from military objectives exists only 'to the maximum extent feasible'. The obligation may not be the same for a small, densely populated, country, such as Switzerland, and a huge country with many uninhabited areas in which to place military objectives. The rule requiring separation can today be found in Article 58 of Protocol I. This Article reads as follows:

Precautions against the effects of attacks

The Parties to the conflict shall, to the maximum extent feasible:

(a) without prejudice to Article 49 of the Fourth Convention, endeavour to remove the civilian population, individual civilians and civilian objects under their control from the vicinity of military objectives;
(b) avoid locating military objectives within or near densely populated areas;
(c) take the other necessary precautions to protect the civilian population, individual civilians and civilian objects under their control against the dangers resulting from military operations.

THE PROHIBITION PLACED ON THE TARGETING OR ATTACKING OF CIVILIAN OBJECTS

8. The source of states' obligation not to attack civilian objects was traditionally

---

[11] UN Security Council Resolution 1738 (23 December 2006) UN Doc S/RES/1738.

found in Article 23(g) of the Hague Regulations, which relates to civilian property, and in Article 25 of the Hague Regulations, which relates to undefended towns. Today, the rule is set out in Article 52(1) of Additional Protocol I in the following terms: '[c]ivilian objects shall not be the object of attack or of reprisals'. Once again, civilian objects are negatively defined: an object is civilian if it is not military. Thus, Article 52(1) of Additional Protocol I reads: '[c]ivilian objects are all objects which are not military objectives as defined in paragraph 2'. Thus, civilian objects are all of those objects that are not military objectives. The reason for this negative formulation is the same as that for negatively defining civilian persons, namely that such a definition ensures that no gaps are left between the two categories. Moreover, one finds the same legal presumption as to the character of an object: in cases of doubt, objects that are normally used for civilian purposes, such as churches, schools or commercial factories, must be presumed not to contribute to military action and hence not to be a military objective. Thus, Article 52(3) of Additional Protocol I reads:

> In case of doubt whether an object which is normally dedicated to civilian purposes, such as a place of worship, a house or other dwelling or a school, is being used to make an effective contribution to military action, it shall be presumed not to be so used.

This presumption is sensible if one wishes to avoid massive civilian damage and constant errors in targeting. Obviously, it may be difficult to prove that an object normally dedicated to civilian use is in fact being used militarily, since that will normally be done in a hidden manner. However, if the presumption of civilian use did not exist, belligerents could target civilian objects on the slightest suspicion. Civilian goods and persons would be likely to suffer heavy losses. At the same time objects that are targeted on the basis of suspicion would often be revealed to have been devoted to civilian purposes. From the points of view of both civilians and belligerents, this would not be an efficient way to wage warfare.

9. It is therefore important to ask what a military objective is. The modern LOAC has abandoned any attempt to provide a list of such objectives, even a non-exhaustive, illustrative one.[12] Today, military objective is defined in a purely relative and relational way. It is therefore important to examine Article 52(2) of Additional Protocol I, which contains the definition of military objectives:

> Attacks shall be limited strictly to military objectives. In so far as objects are concerned, military objectives are limited to those objects which by their nature, location, purpose or use make an effective contribution to military action and whose total or partial destruction, capture or neutralization, in the circumstances ruling at the time, offers a definite military advantage.

A short analysis of this provision elicits some important insights.[13]

---

[12] See, eg: the attempt to provide an exhaustive list of military objectives in the Hague Draft Rules of Air Warfare [1923] *AJIL Supplement* 245 Art 24(2).

[13] This provision reflects customary international law, *Western Front, Aerial Bombardment and Related Claims—Eritrea's Claims 1, 3, 5, 9–13, 14, 21, 25 & 26 (Ethiopia v Eritrea)* Eritrea-Ethiopia Claims Commission (19 December 2005) at <http://www.pca-cpa.org/upload/files/FINAL%20ER%20FRONT%20 CLAIMS.pdf> accessed 15 May 2008 para [113].

10. The definition of military objectives, which may be targeted and attacked, is composed of two cumulative criteria. There are two requirements which must be present at the same time in order to make a good or facility liable to attack: (1) an object must make an *effective contribution* to military action; and (2) the planned attack against this object must, in this particular case, offer a *definite military advantage*. In short, an object must be used militarily and the planned attack must offer a concrete military advantage. By requiring that these two criteria be fulfilled before an object may be attacked the law attempts to restrict the objects liable to be targeted.

a) The object must make an effective *military contribution*. This means that objects which have simply hypothetical or merely 'possible' military uses will not be seen as military objectives.[14] Moreover, only military uses of the object are relevant. If the political, economic, social or psychological importance of the object was used to determine whether the object could be classified as a legitimate military objective, the assessment would become highly speculative and the category of objects that are liable to attack almost boundless, since in modern armed conflicts, almost all objects make some contribution to the continuation of the war effort of a belligerent. The principle of distinction would in this case be rendered largely nugatory.

b) Moreover, an attack that is planned to target a particular object that makes an effective military contribution must result in a *military advantage*. This advantage has to be definite and concrete, not hypothetical, possible or eventual. The advantage anticipated must be a 'military' advantage, and must not be any other type of advantage, such as a political or propaganda gain. A military advantage normally consists of gaining ground or destroying or weakening the enemy's armed forces. The expression 'concrete and direct' was intended to show that the advantage concerned should be substantial and relatively immediate, and that an advantage that is hardly perceptible or which would only appear in the long term should be disregarded.[15] The judgement that must be made here is purely relative and contextual. Why? An object that, when considered in the abstract, serves a military purpose may not be attacked, under the given definition, if a definite military advantage will not be gained by its destruction. Hence, a military aircraft escaping from the combat area towards a third state in order to surrender, where the third state is neutral and having therefore under a LOAC duty to intern that aircraft up until the end of the war, would not be liable to attack. The aircraft will make no further contribution to the war. There is thus no definite military advantage to be gained from attacking it. An obsolete military installation that contains ammunition that is no longer issued to the troops of the adverse belligerent and which therefore does not or cannot

---

[14] The commander who orders the attack must have information in his or her possession which means that it is reasonable to believe that the object makes an effective contribution to military action: *Prosecutor v Galic* (Trial Judgment) IT-98-29-T (5 December 2003) para [51].

[15] However, according to the Ethiopia-Eritrea Claims Commission, 'the term "military advantage" can only properly be understood in the context of the military operations between the Parties taken as a whole, not simply in the context of a specific attack' (*Western Front, Aerial Bombardment and Related Claims*, n 13, para [113]).

serve any further militarily purpose may not be attacked, because such an attack would not result in a definite military advantage. This result could also be achieved by saying that such attacks are not 'necessary' for the achievement of the war aim and are thus prohibited by virtue of the principle of necessity. The crucial point is obviously the specific information available to the attacker: he or she may not know that an aeroplane is attempting to escape, at least at the beginning of the flight, and he or she may not know that an installation is not used for military purposes or cannot be used for such purposes.

11. To the requirement that a belligerent satisfy the two principles of military use and military advantage before an object may be attacked, one must add the obligation to respect the *principle of proportionality*.[16] The importance of this principle when we are concerned with 'dual use objects', which are those objects that are able to serve civilian as well as military purposes, can be easily appreciated. Strictly speaking, almost all objects can be for dual purposes. However, some categories of objects are more important in this context as they are more likely to have dual uses. Thus, for example, a bridge or a railway line can transport civilians and civilian goods, but can also transport military personnel or arms. Depending upon their concrete use, they are civilian or military objectives. If the object is used for military purposes, it becomes a military objective and may be attacked if there is a military advantage to be gained by attacking it: we have seen that this advantage must be definite and must be judged on a case-by-case basis, dependant upon the concrete circumstances. If we assume that there is a concrete military advantage to be gained by targeting such a facility, the attacker must still consider proportionality. Is the military advantage important enough to outweigh the possible incidental civilian losses that may occur during the attack on that object? Are the means of the attack chosen appropriate, with a view to avoiding, or at least minimising, incidental civilian casualties or damage? In situations where the assessment of proportionality is complex and it is open to debate whether or not the attack is proportionate, the interests of the civilian population should be given a high priority. It should be kept in mind that IHL requires that a belligerent takes constant care to spare the civilian population, civilians and civilian objects. We will discuss an example in due course.

12. Finally, the *principle of precaution* should be stated. This important principle imposes several obligations on belligerents, such as: (1) the decisions as to targeting should be taken at command level by experienced officers; (2) the attack must be carefully planned and various factors affecting its impact on the civilian population taken into account; for example the risk of civilian casualties may be different according to the day or the time the that attack takes place or according to the type of weapons used and so on; (3) an attack must be stopped or suspended while in progress if it appears that the incidental damage to the civilian population or to civilian objects is significantly higher than expected; (4) advance warning of the attack must be given, to the extent that this is feasible; and (5) if there is a choice between several military objectives in order to obtain a similar military advantage,

---

[16] Additional Protocol I Art 51(5)(b).

the objective which may be expected to cause the least danger to civilian lives and to civilian objects should be attacked.[17]

Article 57 of Additional Protocol I is of crucial importance in defining the scope of the principle of precaution:

Precautions in attack

1. In the conduct of military operations, constant care shall be taken to spare the civilian population, civilians and civilian objects.

2. With respect to attacks, the following precautions shall be taken:

(a) those who plan or decide upon an attack shall:

   (i)   do everything feasible to verify that the objectives to be attacked are neither civilians nor civilian objects and are not subject to special protection but are military objectives within the meaning of paragraph 2 of Article 52 and that it is not prohibited by the provisions of this Protocol to attack them;
   (ii) take all feasible precautions in the choice of means and methods of attack with a view to avoiding, and in any event to minimizing, incidental loss or civilian life, injury to civilians and damage to civilian objects;
   (iii) refrain from deciding to launch any attack which may be expected to cause incidental loss of civilian life, injury to civilians, damage to civilian objects, or a combination thereof, which would be excessive in relation to the concrete and direct military advantage anticipated;

(b) an attack shall be cancelled or suspended if it becomes apparent that the objective is not a military one or is subject to special protection or that the attack may be expected to cause incidental loss of civilian life, injury to civilians, damage to civilian objects, or a combination thereof, which would be excessive in relation to the concrete and direct military advantage anticipated;

(c) effective advance warning shall be given of attacks which may affect the civilian population, unless circumstances do not permit.

3. When a choice is possible between several military objectives for obtaining a similar military advantage, the objective to be selected shall be that the attack on which may be expected to cause the least danger to civilian lives and to civilian objects.

4. In the conduct of military operations at sea or in the air, each Party to the conflict shall, in conformity with its rights and duties under the rules of international law applicable in armed conflict, take all reasonable precautions to avoid losses of civilian lives and damage to civilian objects.

5. No provision of this article may be construed as authorizing any attacks against the civilian population, civilians or civilian objects.

13. At this juncture a short case study may be useful in order to illustrate the practical application of the principles that have been set out in abstract above. For this example we will use the attack by US air forces on the broadcasting building housing RTS (Radio-Television of Serbia) situated in Belgrade, which was launched during the armed conflict between NATO and Serbia in 1999.[18] The

---

[17] See also: ch 23 para 1(b) below

[18] For an account of this attack, see Final Report to the Prosecutor by the Committee Established to Review the NATO Bombing Campaign Against the Federal Republic of Yugoslavia (2000) 39 ILM 1279 paras [71]–[79].

attack was launched in the early hours, at approximately 02.20, and resulted in 16 civilian deaths and approximately 20 civilian wounded. First, we must ask ourselves if a broadcasting station can be a military objective. The answer is affirmative to the extent that this station, in the particular circumstances, effectively served a military purpose. A television or radio station is typically a dual-use object. The United States claimed that RTS, in effect, served, alongside its civilian broadcasting role, to transmit military messages. If this was true, the object was a military objective. One may also recall that Article 8 of the Hague Convention on the Protection of Cultural Property in the Event of Armed Conflict expressly classifies broadcasting stations as objects liable to attack as military objectives.[19] Now we have determined that RTS represents a military objective, we must examine the next two questions: first, does the attack offer a definite military advantage, in the circumstances? Secondly, is the attack proportionate when taking into account the probable civilian casualties? It appears doubtful that the destruction of RTS offered a concrete military advantage. First, there existed tens of other broadcasting stations in Belgrade. It has not been shown that the neutralisation of the RTS building in particular could effectively stop or hamper transmission of military messages. If this was the case, the destruction of the RTS building seemed militarily useless. Secondly, the attack on the building was unlikely to cause any great disruption to broadcasting. In actuality, it took roughly three hours for the Serb technicians to repair the damage and for RTS to resume broadcasting. The military advantage gained by interrupting broadcasting, and therefore the transmission of military messages, for a few hours, if we assume that there was such interruption, which for the reasons mentioned above is implausible, seems too slight when compared to the number of civilian casualties. The death of 16 civilians, and the injury of roughly 20 more, in return for approximately three hours of interruption to broadcasting does not appear to be proportionate. Conversely, if RTS was attacked not in order to interrupt military messages, but rather in order to symbolically hit a conspicuous means of broadcasting propaganda and thus to deal a blow to the morale of the Serb population, there is no direct contribution to military purposes emanating from the RTS building and further there is no direct military advantage to be gained from the destruction of the station. The destruction of the morale of the population cannot be made a military objective: otherwise, civilians could be attacked directly, in order to break their morale. Moreover, the fact that civilians take part in the dissemination of propaganda does not turn them into a part of the military branch. Thus, one cannot say that they are serving military purposes. Otherwise, all civilians who contribute to some extent to the war effort, for example by producing food which is fed to the army, would be seen as military objectives. If we view RTS as a legitimate military objective, CNN and the BBC would have been liable to be attacked if Yugoslavia had had the power to do so. It is highly unlikely that the Western powers would have accepted this as an exercise of legitimate belligerent targeting. Thus, because of the fundamental equality of the belligerents in the LOAC, the same must be true for the RTS building. The above

---

[19] Convention for the Protection of Cultural Property in the Event of Armed Conflict (adopted 14 May 1954, entered into force 7 August 1956) 249 UNTS 240 Art 8.

analysis of the available information indicates that the RTS building was not liable to attack as a military objective under the LOAC. A key lesson that should be taken from this example is that the answer to the question of whether something is a military objective depends on a careful examination of the available information.

In order to illustrate the importance of a careful consideration of contextual factors and the relative nature of the judgement of whether a particular object is a military objective, we will now introduce some variations into our example. First, assume that the attack is conducted after a warning, which allows the building to be evacuated. In this case, we can assume that there would be no civilian casualties, either dead or injured, but some damage would be caused to the building. Let us also assume that the reason for targeting the building was to interrupt the transmission of military messages. In this example, the calculation underlying the proportionality test is altered. If it is to be expected that the station will be repaired within three hours, it would still appear that the concrete military advantage gained by the attack is minimal. However, if it may be expected that the repair will take more time, a concrete military advantage may exist. This will be the case, for example, if certain messages can be transmitted only from that building and not from others because of its more modern installations. Let us introduce a second variation. Assume that a military operation is about to be launched by US/NATO forces somewhere in Yugoslavia and that a warning could only be transmitted to the Serb forces from the RTS building. In such a case, interruption of broadcasting for three hours, and indeed even for less, could offer a decisive military advantage which would allow the effective and successful execution of that particular military operation. In this case, the 16 dead and 20 wounded are not necessarily excessive: one must weigh them up carefully against the magnitude of the concrete military advantage expected from the successful execution of the operation. One can easily see that if the operation is expected to be decisive or to lead to an important breakthrough in the armed conflict, the proportionality principle would be respected even though 36 civilian casualties, including 16 dead, resulted from the attack. One could introduce further variations, each of which would affect the calculation to be made when determining whether the targeting was legitimate. The point of these examples is to show that full consideration of the specific context is necessary in order to understand whether a particular object falls within the concept of 'military objective'.

THE PROHIBITION PLACED ON INDISCRIMINATE ATTACKS

14. It is logical that a law that wishes to uphold the principle of distinction between civilians and civilian objects on the one hand and military objectives on the other must proscribe attacks that hit one or the other indiscriminately. However, as we shall see, this prohibition is not absolute. It must be assessed in the particular context. Some attacks which result in so-called collateral damage to civilians are not unlawful. The prohibition is set out in Article 51(4) of Additional Protocol I in the following terms:

Indiscriminate attacks are prohibited. Indiscriminate attacks are:

(a) those which are not directed at a specific military objective;
(b) those which employ a method or means of combat which cannot be directed at a specific military objective; or
(c) those which employ a method or means of combat the effects of which cannot be limited as required by this Protocol;

and consequently, in each such case, are of a nature to strike military objectives and civilians or civilian objects without distinction.

Thus, for example, it is prohibited to use weapons that cannot be specifically targeted at military objectives because their action is inherently indiscriminate. This applies, in particular, to biological and bacteriological weapons.[20] Moreover, if an attack uses a weapon that could be used in a way that distinguishes between civilians and combatants, it is prohibited to use that weapon in a way that is indiscriminate, for example to have recourse to area bombing instead of directing the bombs to specific objectives.

15. Additional Protocol I specifies two ways in which an attack can be indiscriminate. These are set out in Article 51(5):

Among others, the following types of attacks are to be considered as indiscriminate:

(a) an attack by bombardment by any methods or means which treats as a single military objective a number of clearly separated and distinct military objectives located in a city, town, village or other area containing a similar concentration of civilians or civilian objects;

and

(b) an attack which may be expected to cause incidental loss of civilian life, injury to civilians, damage to civilian objects, or a combination thereof, which would be excessive in relation to the concrete and direct military advantage anticipated.

Article 51(5)(a) concerns situations where several military objectives are scattered within an area in which they are surrounded and separated by civilian objects. In such a case, a belligerent must not treat the whole area as a single military objective; rather, the separate military objectives must be targeted individually. Hence, area bombing is prohibited.

Article 51(5)(b) concerns more complex situations. In these cases a military objective is targeted, but the attack on the objective is likely to cause some collateral losses, either to civilians themselves or to civilian objects. In such a case, the two predominant principles are proportionality and precaution.[21] The difficulty in calculating whether a particular attack will be proportionate is explained by the fact that expected civilian losses cannot normally be foreseen with any precision. There is a military objective that can be targeted, the destruction of which offers a definite military advantage; there is a certain risk for civilians, but that risk is difficult to calculate; the balancing exercise between these two remains hypothetical until the attack is carried out. If everything works out ideally, no civilian losses may result;

---

[20] See also: *Nuclear Weapons*, n 5, para [92].
[21] Additional Protocol I Art 57.

alternatively, if things do not go as anticipated, for example, by chance on the day of the attack a school class is passing close to the attacked facility, there may be a dramatic amount of civilian casualties, which could not have been foreseen. Of course, a belligerent cannot be expected to foresee the unforeseeable. However, he or she is required by the LOAC to engage in careful and diligent preparations for the attack, utilising all of the information that is in his or her possession, and hence, if reasonably possible, to become aware of the fact that school classes pass near that military objective every Wednesday and Thursday and, for this reason, this particular military objective should not be attacked on these days; or that fewer civilian casualties would result if the facility was attacked at night, if such an attack is militarily feasible. Moreover, a belligerent is expected to engage in a detailed bona fide balancing act between the military advantage that will accrue from the attack on the military objective and the expected civilian losses. If the civilian losses appear to be disproportionate to the military advantage to be gained from the attack, the attack must not go ahead. It should be clear that such complex and detailed assessments can only be performed by military commanders. It is on this level that targeting decisions should be taken.

16. One may further ask to what extent a belligerent that possesses precision munitions, which if used will limit the number of collateral civilian losses, is bound to use such arms either exclusively or in preference to any non-precision weapons in their arsenal. The LOAC has not yet developed to the point where it assesses the legality each attack according to the technical capabilities of the weapons available to the belligerent. There is always a danger when exceptions are introduced into the principle of equality of belligerents. However, a belligerent which possesses precision weapons should carefully consider the possibility of using such weapons in all situations where collateral damages can be expected, even if such weapons are more costly. To be sure, under the law as it stands today there is no legal obligation to use such arms. However, there would appear to be at least moral grounds for careful consideration of the matter. Thus, if laser-guided bombs, or munitions guided in some other way, had been used in Iraq in 1991, many thousands of civilian casualties could probably have been avoided.

Comprehension check:

a) What is the definition of 'military objective'? How must one assess whether a certain entity is a military objective?

b) Consider the following situation. An aircraft receives a mission to bomb and destroy a bridge carrying a railway. The reason is that the bridge serves to transport troops and ammunitions by train. However, the bridge also serves for the passage of civilian trains. The pilot proceeds on his mission and targets the bridge. By accident a train is just coming out of the tunnel which precedes the bridge. The pilot had not established whether a train was in the tunnel. Thus, during his attack, he hits the train, which happens to be a civilian object and carrying civilians. Seeing that he did not destroy the bridge on the first bombing run, he returns on the spot and bombs that bridge for a second time. Because of the smoke caused by the first bombing run, the pilot accidentally hits the train for a second time. There are between 10 and 30 civilian casualties. How should we evaluate these events from the point of view of the LOAC?

c)   In case of doubt as to the character of a facility, is it presumed that the facility is civilian or that it is a military objective?

d)   Are there peacetime obligations for states with respect to the protection of civilians against adverse targeting?

e)   What are the arguments against the use of atomic bombs from the point of view of the rules on targeting?

Answers:

a)   'Military objective' is defined in Article 52(2) of Additional Protocol I: military objectives are limited to those objects which by their nature, location, purpose or use make an effective contribution to military action and whose total or partial destruction, capture or neutralisation, in the circumstances ruling at the time, offers a definite military advantage. The test is thus based on two essential and cumulative elements, that: (i) an object or person makes a effective and direct contribution to military action; and (ii) its attack offers, in the concrete circumstances, a direct and distinct military advantage. The test is thus concrete and contextual. There are no military objectives per se from the point of view of targeting. An attack is possible only if both of the mentioned criteria are met. The military contribution and the advantage have to be direct. Indirect or hypothetical contributions and advantages cannot be taken into consideration when assessing the legality of an attack on a particular object, since this would put too heavy a strain on the principle of distinction.

b)   This case reveals a violation of the principle of precaution as enshrined in Article 57 of Additional Protocol I. First of all, the pilot should have, to the extent feasible, ascertained whether a train was passing through the tunnel. If the air control was precarious, that verification could have been difficult. However, with the complete air superiority of his side, and also with good weather and visibility, confirming that a train was in the tunnel should not have been difficult. Hence, such confirmation was required. Further, there is a violation of Article 57(2)(b) which requires that an attack be suspended or cancelled if it becomes apparent that it causes incidental loss to civilian life, injury to civilians, damage to civilian objects or a combination thereof, which would be excessive in relation to the concrete and direct military advantage anticipated. This clearly seems to be the case here.

c)   The rule is that a facility, which normally serves civilian purposes, such as a school, an administrative building, or a factory, will be presumed not to serve military purposes (Article 52(3)). The presumption is thus in favour of the civilian character of objects, but only for objects that normally serve civilian purposes. Obviously, this is the case regarding the majority of objects. The presumption is founded on the idea that this is the only way that the principle of distinction can be sufficiently upheld. Otherwise, a 'shoot first, ask questions later' logic would result; this would entail heavy civilian suffering and a de facto reduction in the extent of the immunity granted of civilians.

d)   Yes, see Article 58 of Additional Protocol I, which provides:

> The Parties to the conflict shall, to the maximum extent feasible: (a) without prejudice to Article 49 of the Fourth Convention, endeavour to remove the civilian population, individual civilians and civilian objects under their control from the vicinity of military objectives; (b) avoid locating military objectives within or near densely populated areas; (c) take the other necessary precautions to protect the civilian population, individual civilians and civilian objects under their control against the dangers resulting from military operations.

Note that (b) is especially relevant during peacetime.

e)   The main argument against the atomic bomb under the rules on targeting is that it has indiscriminate effects, which are rendered unlawful by Article 51(4) of Additional Protocol I. These weapons are indiscriminate because their effect cannot be limited to military objectives alone. Thus, according to Articles 51(4)(b) and 51(4)(c), indiscriminate attacks are:

> (b) those which employ a method or means of combat which cannot be directed at a specific military objective; or (c) those which employ a method or means of combat the effects of which cannot be limited as required by this Protocol.

This means, in other words, that nuclear weapons do not respect the principle of distinction and they are therefore, considering the rules on targeting, contrary to a fundamental principle of the LOAC. In reality, one knows that nuclear weapons have received special treatment because of their pivotal role in the policy of nuclear deterrence. However, that their use would, in most cases, violate the LOAC cannot be disputed.

18

OTHER OBJECTIVES SPECIFICALLY PROTECTED AGAINST ATTACK

Learning objectives: To understand which objectives, other than civilians and civilian objects, which were addressed in the last chapter, enjoy a specific immunity from attack under the LOAC.

1. Other than the targeting rules that deal with civilians, addressed in the last chapter, there are certain localities or installations which enjoy immunity from attack, at least under certain conditions. The following are the most important:

a) *Undefended, or open, towns or non-defended localities.* This is a category which has traditionally received protection within the LOAC. By a unilateral proclamation of one belligerent, which has to be acknowledged by the adverse party, a certain locality, which is generally a town, can be declared 'undefended'. All combatant personnel will be evacuated from that locality and all mobile military material will be removed. Fixed military buildings or installations will not serve any hostile purpose. In exchange for this 'neutralisation', the adverse belligerent accepts an obligation to spare the undefended area from attack. With the withdrawal of the military power of the belligerent the locality is open for belligerent occupation by the enemy without resistance. This is the reason why such localities were also called, in the past, 'open towns'. Moreover, the belligerents may enter into agreements that render further non-defended localities immune from attack, even if the conditions that provided for in the LOAC for the recognition of a locality as 'undefended' are not fulfilled. If the conditions for the recognition of undefended status are fulfilled, a party may declare a location undefended and the other party must accept this course; however, if the conditions are not fulfilled, the parties may still, by special agreement, agree to spare further areas from combat by declaring them 'undefended'. The negotiations that precede the completion of such an agreement may conveniently be conducted through the good offices of the ICRC. The evident aim of declaring a locality undefended is to spare the civilian population from the suffering and damage that is unavoidable if the place was subject to a military assault. The relevant provisions in this area of the law are found in the

Hague Regulations and in Additional Protocol I.[1] Article 59 of Additional Protocol I, which is quite detailed, reads as follows:

Non-defended localities

1. It is prohibited for the Parties to the conflict to attack, by any means whatsoever, non-defended localities.

2. The appropriate authorities of a Party to the conflict may declare as a non-defended locality any inhabited place near or in a zone where armed forces are in contact which is open for occupation by an adverse Party. Such a locality shall fulfil the following conditions:

(a) all combatants, as well as mobile weapons and mobile military equipment must have been evacuated;

(b) no hostile use shall be made of fixed military installations or establishments;

(c) no acts of hostility shall be committed by the authorities or by the population; and

(d) no activities in support of military operations shall be undertaken.

3. The presence, in this locality, of persons specially protected under the Conventions and this Protocol, and of police forces retained for the sole purpose of maintaining law and order, is not contrary to the conditions laid down in paragraph 2.

4. The declaration made under paragraph 2 shall be addressed to the adverse Party and shall define and describe, as precisely as possible, the limits of the non-defended locality. The Party to the conflict to which the declaration is addressed shall acknowledge its receipt and shall treat the locality as a non-defended locality unless the conditions laid down in paragraph 2 are not in fact fulfilled, in which event it shall immediately so inform the Party making the declaration. Even if the conditions laid down in paragraph 2 are not fulfilled, the locality shall continue to enjoy the protection provided by the other provisions of this Protocol and the other rules of international law applicable in armed conflict.

5. The Parties to the conflict may agree on the establishment of non-defended localities even if such localities do not fulfil the conditions laid down in paragraph 2. The agreement should define and describe, as precisely as possible, the limits of the non-defended locality; if necessary, it may lay down the methods of supervision.

6. The Party which is in control of a locality governed by such an agreement shall mark it, so far as possible, by such signs as may be agreed upon with the other Party, which shall be displayed where they are clearly visible, especially on its perimeter and limits and on highways.

7. A locality loses its status as a non-defended locality when its ceases to fulfil the conditions laid down in paragraph 2 or in the agreement referred to in

[1] Regulations concerning the Laws and Customs of War on Land annexed to Hague Convention IV (adopted 18 October 1907, entered into force 26 January 1910) (1907) 205 CTS 227 (Hague Regulations) Art 25, Protocol. Additional to the Geneva Conventions of 12 August 1949, and relating to the Protection of Victims of International Armed Conflicts (adopted 8 June 1977, entered into force 7 December 1978) 1125 UNTS 3 (Additional Protocol 1) Art 59.

paragraph 5. In such an eventuality, the locality shall continue to enjoy the protection provided by the other provisions of this Protocol and the other rules of international law applicable in armed conflict.

b) *Hospital and safety zones, demilitarised zones.* It may be useful, either in advance, or once the fighting has produced many civilian victims, who are displaced by, and in flight from, the armed clashes, to organise some safe haven areas where displaced persons can be grouped together, cared for and protected from attack. Ideally, such zones are created by agreements that are put in place during peacetime. In most cases, however, this ideal situation does not reflect reality, and these zones are created by way of special agreements made under the pressures and constraints of war. These areas are known as 'safety zones' or 'demilitarised zones'. Such areas were first created in Madrid in 1936 during the Spanish Civil War, then in Shanghai in 1937 during the Japanese bombardment, and again in Jerusalem in 1948. This practice was codified by Article 23 of Geneva Convention I and Article 14 of Geneva Convention IV.[2] Contrary to the rather restrictive wording of these provisions, practice has shown that persons who, in a strict sense, do not fulfil the conditions for admission to these zones, for example men able to bear arms, are often admitted to them, provided that they need help and that they abstain from any act of hostility. Clearly, arms cannot be carried into such areas. Article 23 of Geneva Convention I reads as follows:

> Art. 23. In time of peace, the High Contracting Parties and, after the outbreak of hostilities, the Parties thereto, may establish in their own territory and, if the need arises, in occupied areas, hospital zones and localities so organized as to protect the wounded and sick from the effects of war, as well as the personnel entrusted with the organization and administration of these zones and localities and with the care of the persons therein assembled.

> Upon the outbreak and during the course of hostilities, the Parties concerned may conclude agreements on mutual recognition of the hospital zones and localities they have created. They may for this purpose implement the provisions of the Draft Agreement annexed to the present Convention, with such amendments as they may consider necessary.

> The Protecting Powers and the International Committee of the Red Cross are invited to lend their good offices in order to facilitate the institution and recognition of these hospital zones and localities.

c) *Neutralised zones.* During armed conflicts there is often an immediate need to create some zones near to the frontline where fleeing civilians, wounded combatants or other persons who find themselves in need of help and shelter may find refuge. By ad hoc agreement between the belligerents, specific areas may be immunised from attack in order to receive these persons and provide them with assistance and help. In practice, the difference between such zones

---

[2] Geneva Convention I for the Amelioration of the Condition of the Wounded and Sick in Armed Forces in the Field (adopted 12 August 1949, entered into force 21 October 1950) 75 UNTS 31 (Geneva Convention I) Art 23; Geneva Convention IV Relative to the Protection of Civilian Persons in Time of War (adopted 12 August 1949, entered into force 21 October 1950) 75 UNTS 287 (Geneva Convention IV) Art 14.

and the 'safety or hospital zones' previously discussed has never been clearly worked out. In principle, neutralised zones are more temporary, smaller, nearer the front and based more on urgent ad hoc agreements than 'hospital and safety zones'. In practice, many of these neutralised areas have been created. Normally, the process of creating such zones involves the ICRC serving as intermediary and as organising agency. Neutralised zones have been created in this manner in, for example, Dacca in 1971, Nicosia in 1974, Phnom Penh in 1975, Managua in 1979, N'Djamena in 1980 and Tripoli in Lebanon in 1983. These zones have been created in IACs as well as in NIACs. Article 15 of Geneva Convention IV was the first conventional provision to allow for the creation of such zones,[3] and Article 60 of Protocol I codifies the matter again.[4] These provisions read as follows:

Geneva Convention IV, Article 15.

Any Party to the conflict may, either direct or through a neutral State or some humanitarian organization, propose to the adverse Party to establish, in the regions where fighting is taking place, neutralized zones intended to shelter from the effects of war the following persons, without distinction:

(a) wounded and sick combatants or non-combatants;
(b) civilian persons who take no part in hostilities, and who, while they reside in the zones, perform no work of a military character.

When the Parties concerned have agreed upon the geographical position, administration, food supply and supervision of the proposed neutralized zone, a written agreement shall be concluded and signed by the representatives of the Parties to the conflict. The agreement shall fix the beginning and the duration of the neutralization of the zone.

Additional Protocol I, Article 60. Demilitarized zones

1. It is prohibited for the Parties to the conflict to extend their military operations to zones on which they have conferred by agreement the status of demilitarized zone, if such extension is contrary to the terms of this agreement.

2. The agreement shall be an express agreement, may be concluded verbally or in writing, either directly or through a Protecting Power or any impartial humanitarian organization, and may consist of reciprocal and concordant declarations. The agreement may be concluded in peacetime, as well as after the outbreak of hostilities, and should define and describe, as precisely as possible, the limits of the demilitarized zone and, if necessary, lay down the methods of supervision.

3. The subject of such an agreement shall normally be any zone which fulfils the following conditions:

(a) all combatants, as well as mobile weapons and mobile military equipment, must have been evacuated;

---

[3] Geneva Convention IV Art 15.
[4] Additional Protocol I Art 60.

(b) no hostile use shall be made of fixed military installations or establishments;

(c) no acts of hostility shall be committed by the authorities or by the population; and

(d) any activity linked to the military effort must have ceased.

The Parties to the conflict shall agree upon the interpretation to be given to the condition laid down in subparagraph (d) and upon persons to be admitted to the demilitarized zone other than those mentioned in paragraph 4.

4. The presence, in this zone, of persons specially protected under the Conventions and this Protocol, and of police forces retained for the sole purpose of maintaining law and order, is not contrary to the conditions laid down in paragraph 3.

5. The Party which is in control of such a zone shall mark it, so far as possible, by such signs as may be agreed upon with the other Party, which shall be displayed where they are clearly visible, especially on its perimeter and limits and on highways.

6. If the fighting draws near to a demilitarized zone, and if the Parties to the conflict have so agreed, none of them may use the zone for purposes related to the conduct of military operations or unilaterally revoke its status.

7. If one of the Parties to the conflict commits a material breach of the provisions of paragraphs 3 or 6, the other Party shall be released from its obligations under the agreement conferring upon the zone the status of demilitarized zone. In such an eventuality, the zone loses its status but shall continue to enjoy the protection provided by the other provisions of this Protocol and the other rules of international law applicable in armed conflict.

d) *Cultural property.* The LOAC protects against attack of moveable or immovable property of great importance to the cultural heritage of every people, such as important pieces of architecture, art or history, whether these are religious or secular, as well as the buildings in which such property is located.[5] Thus, not only are the Coliseum in Rome and the Pyramids in Egypt protected objects, but so is the library of the *Stiftskirche* in St Gall. Special protection is granted to refuges intended to shelter moveable cultural property in the event of armed conflict, provided that they are situated at an adequate distance from any large industrial centre or from any important military objective.[6] It is left to the State Parties to the Cultural Property Convention to decide which objects situated on their territory shall be considered cultural property. In order to facilitate the protection of these cultural items, lists are prepared and the locations of the objects are marked on maps. Moreover, the objects may be provided, in case of armed conflict, with a distinctive emblem so as to facilitate their recognition.[7] The immunity

---

[5] Convention for the Protection of Cultural Property in the Event of Armed Conflict (adopted 14 May 1954, entered into force 7 August 1956) 249 UNTS 240 (Cultural Property Convention) Art 1. Customary International Law also protects cultural property: *Central Front—Eritrea's Claims 2, 4, 6, 7, 8 & 22 (Eritrea v Ethiopia)* Eritrea-Ethiopia Claims Commission (28 April 2004) at <http://www.pca-cpa.org/upload/files/Eritrea%20Central%20Front%20award.pdf> accessed 15 May 2008 para [113].

[6] *Ibid*, Art 8.

[7] *Ibid*, Art 6.

granted to cultural property is, however, not absolute. A protected object may be attacked if there is an 'imperative military necessity',[8] or if the protected object is used for military ends.[9] Article 53 of Additional Protocol I repeats, in a more concise form, the principle of protection. It does not contain any wording that permits derogation from the protection, but it reserves the Hague Convention of 1954, which does so. Therefore, one may assume that the exceptions stipulated in 1954 continue to be applicable, even in cases where the parties to a conflict are parties to Additional Protocol I.[10] Finally, the Second Protocol to the Hague Convention attempts a more precise definition of the exception of military necessity; provides for a new regime of enhanced protection; reinforces individual criminal responsibility for violations; and extends application to NIAC.[11]

The most important new feature contained in Protocol II is the tighter definition of military necessity. In Article 6 of the Protocol, it is stated that:

> [A] waiver [of protection] pursuant to Article 4(2) of the [Cultural Property] Convention may only be invoked to direct an act of hostility against cultural property when and for long as:
>
> (i) that cultural property has, by its function, been made into a military objective; and
> (ii) there is no feasible alternative to obtain a similar military advantage to that offered by directing an act of hostility against that objective.[12]
>
> Moreover, the decision to invoke imperative military necessity shall only be taken by an officer commanding a force the equivalent of a battalion in size or larger, or a force smaller in size where circumstances do not permit otherwise.[13] Furthermore, a new regime of enhanced protection for cultural heritage objects of the greatest importance for humanity is provided for by the Protocol,[14] where the exceptions of immunity are even more narrowly defined.[15]

e) *Protection of objects indispensable for the survival of the civilian population.* It would be pointless to protect the civilian population from attack if the life of civilians could be jeopardised indirectly by cutting them off from indispensable means of survival, such as foodstuffs or water. For this reason, the LOAC prohibits starvation as a means of warfare.[16] Moreover, it prohibits attacks which will result in a civilian population being cut off from the necessities for survival.[17] It has been confirmed that this provision

---

[8] *Ibid*, Art 4(2).

[9] *Ibid*, Art 11.

[10] For further discussion of the relationship between the Cultural Property Convention and Additional Protocol I, see *Prosecutor v Strugar* (Trial Judgment) IT-01-42-T (31 January 2005) paras [298]–[312].

[11] Second Protocol to the Hague Convention of 1954 for the Protection of Cultural Property in the Event of Armed Conflict (adopted 26 March 1999, entered into force 9 March 2004) (1999) 38 ILM 769 (Second Cultural Property Protocol).

[12] *Ibid*, Art 6(1).

[13] *Ibid*, Art 6(3).

[14] *Ibid*, Arts 10*ff*.

[15] *Ibid*, Art 13.

[16] Additional Protocol I Art 54(1).

[17] *Ibid*, Art 54(2).

has the status of customary law.[18] Article 54 of Additional Protocol I reads as follows:

Protection of objects indispensable to the survival of the civilian population

1. Starvation of civilians as a method of warfare is prohibited.

2. It is prohibited to attack, destroy, remove or render useless objects indispensable to the survival of the civilian population, such as food-stuffs, agricultural areas for the production of food-stuffs, crops, livestock, drinking water installations and supplies and irrigation works, for the specific purpose of denying them for their sustenance value to the civilian population or to the adverse Party, whatever the motive, whether in order to starve out civilians, to cause them to move away, or for any other motive.

3. The prohibitions in paragraph 2 shall not apply to such of the objects covered by it as are used by an adverse Party:

(a) as sustenance solely for the members of its armed forces; or
(b) if not as sustenance, then in direct support of military action, provided, however, that in no event shall actions against these objects be taken which may be expected to leave the civilian population with such inadequate food or water as to cause its starvation or force its movement.

4. These objects shall not be made the object of reprisals.

5. In recognition of the vital requirements of any Party to the conflict in the defense of its national territory against invasion, derogation from the prohibitions contained in paragraph 2 may be made by a Party to the conflict within such territory under its own control where required by imperative military necessity.

f) *Protection of the natural environment*. The modern LOAC tries to protect the natural environment from the worst effects of particular means of warfare. The defoliant chemical agents used by the United States during the Vietnam War are an important example of means of warfare being turned against the environment, and it was this occurrence that brought the potential problem to light. The level of protection afforded to the environment, however, remains minimal and its precise extent controversial. When considering sources that deal with this problem, one must consider the Convention on the Prohibition of Military or Other Hostile Uses of Environmental Modification Techniques,[19] and Article 55 of Additional Protocol I.[20] This latter Article reads as follows:

---

[18] *Western Front, Aerial Bombardment and Related Claims—Eritrea's Claims 1, 3, 5, 9–13, 14, 21, 25 & 26 (Ethiopia v Eritrea)* Eritrea-Ethiopia Claims Commission (19 December 2005) at <http://www.pca-cpa.org/upload/files/FINAL%20ER%20FRONT%20CLAIMS.pdf> accessed 15 May 2008 paras [104]–[105].

[19] Convention on the Prohibition of Military or any Other Hostile use of Environmental Modification Techniques (adopted 10 December 1976, entered into force 5 October 1978) 1108 UNTS 151.

[20] See also: Additional Protocol I Art 35(3). For the customary position, see J-M Henckaerts and L Doswald-Beck (eds), *Customary International Humanitarian Law Volume 1: Rules* (Cambridge, CUP, 2005) ('*ICRC Customary Study*') Rules 43–45.

Art 55. Protection of the natural environment

1. Care shall be taken in warfare to protect the natural environment against widespread, long-term and severe damage. This protection includes a prohibition of the use of methods or means of warfare which are intended or may be expected to cause such damage to the natural environment and thereby to prejudice the health or survival of the population.

2. Attacks against the natural environment by way of reprisals are prohibited.

This text makes clear that only the infliction of 'widespread, long-term and severe damage' to the environment is prohibited. The criteria are cumulative, and require that the damage must be widespread, long-term and severe. The effects on the environment must last for months or years in order to be termed 'long-term'. They must be severe, which requires that they endanger the health or the survival of the civilian population. Furthermore, the damage must be geographically extensive and not merely confined to a localised area. The protection afforded to the environment is thus insufficient as the law stands. Only most severe measures will be contrary to Article 55. The use of *Agent Orange* by the United States in Vietnam would have been an example for a violation of the quoted provisions, and also the setting aflame of over 700 oil wells by Iraqi armed forces during the Gulf War in 1991, a practice that was condemned by the UN Security Council in its Resolution 687 of 1991.[21] Conversely, the use of armour-piercing weaponry containing uranium cannot be classified in this category with any certainty.[22] The possible deleterious effects of these weapons are still controversial. As far as the environment is concerned, the effects would not necessarily fit the strict criteria of Article 55.

g) *Protection of works and installations containing dangerous forces.* Some installations, such as nuclear plants or dykes, can set free devastating forces if they are made the object of attack. For this reason the LOAC grants them immunity from attack.[23] This immunity is regulated by the rather detailed Article 56 of Additional Protocol I in the following terms:

Art 56. Protection of works and installations containing dangerous forces

1. Works or installations containing dangerous forces, namely dams, dykes and nuclear electrical generating stations, shall not be made the object of attack, even where these objects are military objectives, if such attack may cause the release of dangerous forces and consequent severe losses among the civilian population. Other military objectives located at or in the vicinity of these works or installations shall not be made the object of attack if such attack may cause the release of dangerous forces from the works or installations and consequent severe losses among the civilian population.

2. The special protection against attack provided by paragraph 1 shall cease:

---

[21] UN Doc S/RES/687.

[22] Final Report to the Prosecutor by the Committee Established to Review the NATO Bombing Campaign Against the Federal Republic of Yugoslavia (2000) 39 ILM 1279 para [26].

[23] On the customary status of this immunity, see *ICRC Customary Study*, n 20, Rule 42.

(a) for a dam or a dyke only if it is used for other than its normal function and in regular, significant and direct support of military operations and if such attack is the only feasible way to terminate such support;

(b) for a nuclear electrical generating station only if it provides electric power in regular, significant and direct support of military operations and if such attack is the only feasible way to terminate such support;

(c) for other military objectives located at or in the vicinity of these works or installations only if they are used in regular, significant and direct support of military operations and if such attack is the only feasible way to terminate such support.

3. In all cases, the civilian population and individual civilians shall remain entitled to all the protection accorded them by international law, including the protection of the precautionary measures provided for in Article 57. If the protection Ceases and any of the works, installations or military objectives mentioned in paragraph 1 is attacked, all practical precautions shall be taken to avoid the release of the dangerous forces.

4. It is prohibited to make any of the works, installations or military objectives mentioned in paragraph 1 the object of reprisals.

5. The Parties to the conflict shall endeavour to avoid locating any military objectives in the vicinity of the works or installations mentioned in paragraph 1. Nevertheless, installations erected for the sole purpose of defending the protected works or installations from attack are permissible and shall not themselves be made the object of attack, provided that they are not used in hostilities except for defensive actions necessary to respond to attacks against the protected works or installations and that their armament is limited to weapons capable only of repelling hostile action against the protected works or installations.

6. The High Contracting Parties and the Parties to the conflict are urged to conclude further agreements among themselves to provide additional protection for objects containing dangerous forces.

7. In order to facilitate the identification of the objects protected by this article, the Parties to the conflict may mark them with a special sign consisting of a group of three bright orange circles placed on the same axis, as specified in Article 16 of Annex I to this Protocol [Article 17 of Amended Annex]. The absence of such marking in no way relieves any Party to the conflict of its obligations under this Article.

This provision lists some dangerous installations, but its list is not exhaustive. Further installations containing dangerous forces could be added, such as chemical plants. The use of the word 'namely' to introduce the list tends to show that this list is not exhaustive and that other installations may be protected under Article 56. Moreover, one will notice that immunity from attack is not absolute. First, an exception is implicitly made for attacks on such objects, to the extent that they are military objectives, if these attacks cannot, and do not, cause the release of the dangerous force. The United States argued that this implicit exception applied when they attacked some Iraqi nuclear installations during the Gulf War in 1991. Secondly, an attack is allowed if such an installation significantly and directly supports military operations, and if the attack is the only way to terminate such support. However, in the planning and execution of an attack allowed by this exception all the precautionary principles provided for in Article 57 of Additional Protocol I and the principle of proportionality set out in Article 51(5)(b) of Additional Protocol I are applicable and must be taken into account. Taking these into account, it would hardly ever seem proportionate to attack a nuclear installation, thereby unleashing radiation such as that released at Chernobyl, in order to stop some support that the attacked plant may give to a military operation. Further details as to the practical application of this protection can be gathered from an attentive reading of the text of Article 56.

Comprehension check:

a) What are the main localities or installations protected against attack?
b) How do these special immunities from attack relate to the general rule of immunity of civilian objectives?
c) Are attacks against such immunised localities and installations possible in the form of reprisals?
d) Are attacks against such immunised localities and installations possible in case of urgent military necessities?
e) Do these immunities apply also to NIAC?

Answers:

a) The main protected localities and installation are: (1) civilian persons and objects, according to the general rule set out in Additional Protocol I[24]; (2) non-defended localities[25]; (3) hospital and security zones[26]; (4) neutralised zones[27]; (5) cultural property[28]; (6) objects indispensable to the survival of the civilian population[29]; (7) the natural environment[30]; and (8) works and installations containing dangerous forces.[31]
b) These rules do not derogate from the general rule on protection of civilian objects, but add some specific protections to the general rule. These special rules thus do not detract from the general protection: a locality or installation cannot be attacked if it does not serve military purposes, and is therefore not a military objective. What, then, is the proper role of the special rules? First, to particularly stress some protections in particular contexts where they are especially important. Secondly, to tighten the conditions under which such localities and installations can be attacked even if they incidentally or directly

---

[24] Additional Protocol I Art 48.
[25] *Ibid*, Art 59.
[26] Geneva Convention I Art 23; Geneva Convention IV Art 14; and Additional Protocol I Art 60.
[27] Geneva Convention IV Art 15; and Additional Protocol I Art 60.
[28] Cultural Property Convention n 5; Second Cultural Property Protocol n 11; and Additional Protocol I Art 53.
[29] Additional Protocol I Art 54.
[30] *Ibid*, Art 55.
[31] *Ibid*, Art 56.

serve military purposes, taking account, for example, of the dangerous forces they contain.[32]

c) Reprisals against such localities and installations are in many, but not in all, cases ruled out by the applicable conventional norms. Hence, no reprisals are allowed in the context of cultural property,[33] of objects indispensable to the survival of the civilian population,[34] of the natural environment[35] or of works and installations containing dangerous forces.[36] In the other cases, the general rules against reprisals against protected persons have to be applied.[37]

d) In the modern LOAC, the plea of military necessity in order to derogate from a rule of the law is admissible only if that rule allows derogation in cases of military necessity. If the rule is silent on this point, any derogation on the basis of military necessity is prohibited. This point has been settled since the post World War II trials of Axis war criminals.[38] One has thus to look at the specific rules to discover if allowance is made for military necessity. As we have seen, in the context of cultural property, the 1954 Cultural Property Convention makes such allowance, and even the more recent Second Additional Protocol to that convention maintains a certain sphere in which this plea can operate. The same is true for Article 54(5) of Protocol I with respect to the objects indispensable to the survival of the civilian population. Conversely, Geneva Convention IV does not allow attacks against protected persons, including safety or neutralised zones, in cases of military necessity.[39] Likewise, Article 55 of Additional Protocol I contains no military necessity derogation clause with respect to the natural environment.

e) Yes: first, by way of customary LOAC, which extends these prohibitions to both types of conflict[40]; secondly, by conventional law, since Additional Protocol II of 1977 reproduces the most important provisions of Protocol I in these areas, albeit in a shorter form.[41] However, there are some gaps: thus, there is no norm corresponding to Article 55 of Additional Protocol I in Additional Protocol II; and therefore the natural environment

---

[32] See, eg: Additional Protocol I Art 56.

[33] Additional Protocol I Art 53(c).

[34] *Ibid*, Art 54(4).

[35] *Ibid*, Art 55(2).

[36] *Ibid*, Art 56(4).

[37] *Prosecutor v Kupreskic* (Trial Judgment) IT-95-16-T (14 January 2000) paras [521]–[536] and ch 22 below.

[38] *United States v Krupp* (1948) 15 AD 622, 628.

[39] Geneva Convention IV Art 27.

[40] See, eg: *ICRC Customary Study*, n 20, Rules 35–40 and 42–43, and *Prosecutor v Tadic* (Decision on the Defence Motion for Interlocutory Appeal on Jurisdiction) IT-49-1-AR72 (2 October 1995) paras [96]–[127], in particular para [97], which states: 'Why protect civilians from ... the wanton destruction of *hospitals, churches, museums* ... when two sovereign States are engaged in war, and yet refrain from enacting the same bans or providing the same protection when armed violence has erupted "only" within the territory of a sovereign State' (author's emphasis) and para [127], which refers to cultural property.

[41] Protocol Additional to the Geneva Conventions of 12 August 1949, and relating to the Protection of Victims of Non-International Armed Conflicts (adopted 8 June 1977, entered into force 7 December 1978) 1125 UNTS 609 Arts 13*ff*.

is not specifically protected by Additional Protocol II. In such cases one must refer to customary international law, which has in the meantime produced equivalent prohibitions to those contained in the law applicable to IAC. Thus, today, in this area, the law of NIAC is aligned with the law that governs IAC.

19

PROHIBITED WEAPONS

Learning objectives: To understand the principles and rules that govern the acceptability or unacceptability of the use of weapons.

1. Some weapons cause 'superfluous' injury, 'unnecessary' suffering or 'excessive' damage when compared with their military utility. Thus, certain conventional weapons, as well as weapons of mass destruction, are prohibited by the LOAC. Unlike the protections examined above,[1] their use is not only prohibited if directed against civilians, but generally in warfare. The soldiers of the adverse belligerent are also protected from unnecessary suffering. The LOAC makes clear that the licence to kill an enemy in combat under certain conditions is not a licence to kill with whatever means and with whatever cruelty.[2]

2. The rules of the LOAC that regulate weapons are multi-layered. At the most general level, there are general principles and rules which apply to all weapons and govern the acceptability or unacceptability of their use. More specifically, a series of detailed conventions explicitly prohibit particular weapons or classes of weapons. Finally, Article 36 of Additional Protocol I places some constraints on the development of new weapons. This article requires the state parties to determine, when engaged in the study or development of any new weapon, means or method of warfare, whether the employment of the weapon, means or method would, in some or all circumstances, be prohibited by the Protocol or by any other rule of international law. This makes clear that the rules of the LOAC are applicable to new weapons. It cannot be argued that a new weapon is not covered by IHL because it did not exist at the time the rules were framed, and thus could not be envisaged, at that time, by the drafters of the rules. Let us first examine the general principles restraining the use of weapons.

3. The LOAC applies some general rules or principles to all weapons and to all means and methods of warfare. These rules furnish general criteria which must be considered by the parties to a conflict in order to decide whether or not a particular weapon or means of warfare is allowed. The three main principles are that: (1) weapons and means which would render the death of adverse personnel inevitable

---

[1] For example in ch 17.

[2] Protocol Additional to the Geneva Conventions of 12 August 1949, and relating to the Protection of Victims of International Armed Conflicts (adopted 8 June 1977, entered into force 7 December 1978) 1125 UNTS 3 (Additional Protocol 1) Art 35 states, 'the right of the Parties to the conflict to choose methods and means of warfare is not unlimited'.

are prohibited[3]; (2) weapons and means which would uselessly aggravate the sufferings of adverse personnel are prohibited[4]; and (3) weapons and means which have indiscriminate effects, hitting military and civilian objectives alike, are prohibited.[5] These principles, which permeate the modern law of warfare, originate in the 1868 St Petersburg Declaration.[6] In the preamble to this old but seminal text, the theoretical underpinnings of these principles may be found:

> Considering ... That the only legitimate object which States should endeavor to accomplish during war is to weaken the military forces of the enemy; That for this purpose it is sufficient to disable the greatest possible number of men; That this object would be exceeded by the employment of arms which uselessly aggravate the sufferings of disabled men, or render their death inevitable; That the employment of such arms would, therefore, be contrary to the laws of humanity.

The philosophy that motivates the general principles is very aptly stated in this passage. The aim of war is to overpower the enemy and to submit him or her to one's own will. In order to achieve this, it is sufficient to break his or her resistance, which can be equally well accomplished by disabling enemy combatants—thus preventing these persons from continuing the fight—rather than by killing them. Whilst militarily both measures are equivalent; from a humanitarian perspective they are not. Therefore, the principle of necessity suggests that a belligerent must limit him- or herself, to the maximum extent possible, to the milder measure (disabling) rather than the more severe one (killing).[7] If it is possible to disable the opposing belligerent's troops in the prevailing circumstances, killing is unnecessary as it will not add anything to the achievement of the war aim, namely the overpowering of the enemy. The same is true for weapons that cause 'unnecessary suffering'. It is forbidden to use a weapon that causes painful or incurable wounds when the desired result of placing opposing troops *hors de combat* (by inflicting disabling injuries or even killing those troops) can be obtained by weapons which do not cause such suffering. This principle is now stated in Article 35(1) of Additional Protocol I, which states:

> It is prohibited to employ weapons, projectiles and material and methods of warfare of a nature to cause superfluous injury or unnecessary suffering.

Conversely, the principle which forbids indiscriminate weapons flows from the general principle of distinction between military and civilian objectives.[8] Now we have examined the theoretical underpinnings of the principles, we should explore these principles somewhat more in detail.

a) *Weapons and means rendering the death inevitable.* This prohibition on weapons causing certain death flows from the modern conception that the aim of war is to cause the minimum rather than the maximum evil in relation to

---

[3] St Petersburg Declaration Renouncing the Use, in Time of War, of Explosive Projectiles Under 400 Grammes Weight (signed 11 December 1868, entered into force 11 December 1868) (1868–69) 138 CTS 297 Preamble, para 4.

[4] *Ibid*; *Legality of the Threat or Use of Nuclear Weapons (Advisory Opinion)* [1996] ICJ Rep 226 (*Nuclear Weapons*) para [78].

[5] Additional Protocol 1 Art 51(4); *Nuclear Weapons, ibid*, para [78].

[6] St Petersburg Declaration.

[7] See generally: ch 7 above.

[8] Additional Protocol 1 Arts 48–56; *Nuclear Weapons*, n 4, para [78].

the goal of overpowering the enemy. Hence, a weapon or means that inevitably results in the death of an adversary must be prohibited. This is so because this death goes beyond what is necessary to achieve the legitimate goal of the war. Consequently, this prohibition could also be grounded in the 'principle of necessity', used as a limitation of measures allowed in warfare. Obviously, any weapon that is used in the intended way may, and in many cases inevitably will, result in casualties. Such a proper use of a weapon, thus causing casualties, is not prohibited. The point is rather to prohibit those weapons leaving no chance of survival to all the persons who find themselves within a certain perimeter of the place of impact. Examples of such weapons are 'depression bombs', which create a vacuum and lead to asphyxia, and 'fuel-air explosives', which, with a given perimeter, create shockwaves akin to those created by an atomic bomb.

b) *Weapons causing unnecessary suffering.* This rule is now stated in both Additional Protocol I[9] and in the Certain Conventional Weapons Convention,[10] which recalls that this prohibition flows from a 'principle of international law'. This prohibition is clearly part of customary international law and the International Court of Justice (ICJ) in the *Nuclear Weapons* advisory opinion expressed as follows:

> [I]t is prohibited to cause unnecessary suffering to combatants: it is accordingly prohibited to use weapons causing them such harm or uselessly aggravating their suffering. In application of that second principle, States do not have unlimited freedom of choice of means in the weapons they use. [...] In conformity with the aforementioned principles, humanitarian law, at a very early stage, prohibited certain types of weapons either because of their indiscriminate effect on combatants and civilians or because of the unnecessary suffering caused to combatants, that is to say, a harm greater than that unavoidable to achieve legitimate military objectives.[11]

Under the LOAC it is forbidden to increase the suffering of the adverse combatants by the use of weapons that cause suffering greater than necessary when placing enemy troops *hors de combat*. It is thus not prohibited to cause suffering, but only to cause 'unnecessary' suffering. Suffering is unnecessary when, in the circumstances, another practicable militarily means, causing less suffering to the adverse combatants, could have been used to place the adversary *hors de combat*. An example concerning the use of projectiles which flatten or fragment themselves when entering the human body may be given. Such projectiles cause severe suffering. Projectiles which flatten cause severe wounds by destroying significantly bigger parts of the body and organs with which they impact than projectiles that do not flatten; projectiles fragmenting cause incurable wounds because, almost inevitably, the fragments cannot be extracted and thus perpetually impair the proper functioning of the parts of the body affected. Such projectiles are unnecessary when considered from the

---

[9] Art 35(2).

[10] UN Convention on Prohibitions or Restrictions on the Use of Certain Conventional Weapons which may be deemed to be Excessively Injurious or to Have Indiscriminate Effects (adopted 10 October 1980, entered into force 2 December 1983) 1342 UNTS 137 (CCW Convention) Preamble, para 3.

[11] *Nuclear Weapons*, n 4, para [78]

point of view of the war aim: an ordinary projectile would have been equally efficient in placing the adverse combatant *hors de combat*; but it would not have caused such grave wounds. Hence, the excess in suffering beyond that which would be caused by an ordinary projectile can be called 'unnecessary'. Other examples of weapons causing unnecessary suffering are lances or spears with a barbed head; serrated-edged bayonets; poisoned weapons; projectiles smeared with substances that inflame wounds; projectiles filled with broken glass; and blinding laser weapons.[12] Moreover, one should interpret the principle of humanity to prohibit the infliction of cruel sufferings by the use of arms which notoriously cause such sufferings—whatever the military advantage gained.[13] This advantage can only be slight; whereas the sufferings to the individual adverse belligerent are grave and often permanent.

c) *Weapons and methods having indiscriminate effects.* This rule flows from the principle of distinction between military and civilian objectives.[14] The general rule is now contained in Article 48 of Additional Protocol 1:

> In order to ensure respect for and protection of the civilian population and civilian objects, the Parties to the conflict shall at all times distinguish between the civilian population and combatants and between civilian objects and military objectives and accordingly shall direct their operations only against military objectives.

Thus, indiscriminate attacks, which strike military as well as civilian objectives, are prohibited.[15] An attack can be indiscriminate in two basic ways. These are described in Article 51(4) of Additional Protocol I:

> Indiscriminate attacks are prohibited. Indiscriminate attacks are:
>
> (a) those which are not directed at a specific military objective;
> (b) those which employ a method or means of combat which cannot be directed at a specific military objective; or
> (c) those which employ a method or means of combat the effects of which cannot be limited as required by this Protocol;
>
> and consequently, in each such case, are of a nature to strike military objectives and civilians or civilian objects without distinction.

Letter (a) refers to attacks with weapons which could be directed at a military objective, but which are not so used in the concrete circumstances: they are not, in a specific case, directed at a specific military objective. An example of such a weapon would be the classical air bomb. It can be used in a way that allows it to be targeted at a military objective alone; but it can also be used indiscriminately in so-called area bombing. These weapons are not prohibited on account of their nature; instead particular military operations

---

[12] See further examples cited in J-M Henckaerts and L Doswald-Beck (eds), *Customary International Humanitarian Law Volume 1: Rules* (Cambridge, CUP, 2005) ('*ICRC Customary Study*'),Commentary to Rule 70.

[13] See generally: ch 7 above.

[14] Ch 7 above; *Nuclear Weapons*, n 4, para [78].

[15] This prohibition is clearly customary, *Western Front, Aerial Bombardment and Related Claims—Eritrea's Claims 1, 3, 5, 9–13, 14, 21, 25 & 26 (Ethiopia v Eritrea)* Eritrea-Ethiopia Claims Commission (19 December 2005) at <http://www.pca-cpa.org/upload/files/FINAL%20ER%20FRONT%20CLAIMS.pdf> para [95].

using the weapons are prohibited when the weapons are employed in such a way that they cause indiscriminate damage. Letter (b) is concerned with attacks that employ a weapon or a method or means of combat which by their very nature cannot be directed at a specific military objective, such as unguided missiles which are fired at enemy territory (for example the famous V2 rockets used at the end of World War II). The point is here that where a certain weapon cannot, inherently, be used in a way that complies with the principle of distinction, it is prohibited. Paragraph (c) is a general clause reinforcing the content of letter (b). Hence, a bacteriological weapon would be prohibited because it is inherently indiscriminate under both letters (b) and (c).

4. The LOAC has not limited itself to statements of general principles when determining the lawfulness of particular weapons or means of warfare. It has also specifically prohibited certain weapons and means in a series of single issue treaties and more comprehensive arms conventions. The choice of subjects of these specific prohibitions is based on the general principles: a weapon is specifically prohibited precisely because it causes excessive suffering, leaves no chance of survival or has indiscriminate effects. For reasons of space all of the existing specific prohibitions cannot be discussed here. A list of the most important prohibited arms must suffice:

a) expanding bullets[16];
b) explosive bullets[17];
c) poisoned weapons[18];
d) biological and bacteriological weapons[19];
e) chemical weapons[20];
f) weapons injuring by non-detectable fragments[21];
g) booby-traps[22];

---

[16] *ICRC Customary Study* Rule 77.
[17] *ICRC Customary Study* Rule 78.
[18] *ICRC Customary Study* Rule 72 and Regulations concerning the Laws and Customs of War on Land annexed to Hague Convention IV (adopted 18 October 1907, entered into force 26 January 1910) (1907) 205 CTS 227 Art 23(a).
[19] *ICRC Customary Study* Rule 73. See also Geneva Protocol for the Prohibition of the Use in War of Asphyxiating, Poisonous or Other Gases, and of Bacteriological Methods of Warfare (signed 17 June 1925, entered into force 8 February 1928) 94 LNTS 65 ('Geneva Gas Protocol'); and Convention on the Prohibition of Development, Production and Stockpiling of Bacteriological (Biological) and Toxin Weapons and on Their Destruction (adopted 16 December 1971, entered into force 26 March 1975) 1015 UNTS 164.
[20] *ICRC Customary Study* Rules 74–76. See also Geneva Gas Protocol and Convention on the Prohibition of the Development, Production, Stockpiling and Use of Chemical Weapons and on Their Destruction (adopted 3 September 1992, entered into force 29 April 1997) 1974 UNTS 45.
[21] *ICRC Customary Study* Rule 79. See also Protocol I to the UN Convention on Prohibitions or Restrictions on the Use of Certain Conventional Weapons which may be deemed to be Excessively Injurious or to Have Indiscriminate Effects concerning Non-Detectable Fragments (adopted 10 October 1980, entered into force 2 December 1983) 1342 UNTS 137.
[22] *ICRC Customary Study* Rule 80. See also Protocol II to the UN Convention on Prohibitions or Restrictions on the Use of Certain Conventional Weapons which may be deemed to be Excessively Injurious or to Have Indiscriminate Effects concerning Prohibitions or Restrictions concerning the Use of Mines, Booby-traps and Other Devices (adopted 10 October 1980, entered into force 2 December 1983) 1342 UNTS 137 (CCW Protocol II); and Amended Protocol to the UN Convention on Prohibitions or

h) landmines, under certain conditions[23];
i) incendiary weapons, under certain conditions, especially when used indiscriminately[24]; and
j) blinding laser weapons.[25]

5. The nuclear weapon has a special status in international law. The question of whether nuclear weapons may be lawfully used in certain circumstances has remained very controversial. If the question is analysed on the basis of the foundational legal principles of the *jus in bello*, the use of nuclear weapons must be regarded as contrary to the fundamental norms that underlie the LOAC. Not only does the use of a nuclear weapon render the death of many persons inevitable; not only does it cause horrific suffering for those dying and for those remaining alive, and even for unborn members of future generations; it first of all indiscriminately targets military and civilian objectives and is thus contrary to the fundamental principle of distinction. However, because of the long-established political doctrine of nuclear deterrence, also known as mutual assured destruction, or MAD, which requires a credible threat of use of nuclear weapons as a means of ensuring that no other states will use their stockpiles of nuclear weapons, the nuclear states have always resisted to any attempt to outlaw such weapons directly. During the negotiations surrounding the drafting of the Additional Protocols, the states which possessed nuclear weapons insisted that the rules being set out Protocols, in particular Articles 48–58 of Additional Protocol I, could not be used to imply the illegality of nuclear weapons. The question of the legality of nuclear weapons was simply bracketed out of the deliberations, as a precondition to the participation of the nuclear powers. Thus, the position regarding nuclear weapons is somewhat unsatisfactory. Their use seems in most, if not in all, cases to be clearly contrary to many rules of international law, in particular the foundational principles of the LOAC, and still more particularly the principle of distinction. However, there is a political penumbra covering the matter, since the nuclear states, especially the Western nuclear states, have not agreed to completely rule out, at the very least, a first strike use of nuclear weapons.

Therefore, when the ICJ was asked to consider the question of whether 'the threat or use of nuclear weapons [is] in any circumstance permitted under

---

Restrictions on the Use of Certain Conventional Weapons which may be deemed to be Excessively Injurious or to Have Indiscriminate Effects concerning the Use of Mines, Booby Traps and Other Devices (adopted 3 May 1996, 3 December 1998) (1996) 35 ILM 1206 (Amended CCW Protocol II).

[23] *ICRC Customary Study* Rules 81–83, CCW Protocol II, *ibid*, Amended CCW Protocol II, *ibid*, and Convention on the Prohibition of the Use, Stockpiling, Production and Transfer of Anti-Personnel Mines and on their Destruction (adopted 18 September 1997, entered into force 1 March 1999) 2056 UNTS 211. On the customary status of these prohibitions: *Western Front, Aerial Bombardment and Related Claims*, n 15, para [15].

[24] *ICRC Customary Study* Rules 84–85. See also Protocol III to the UN Convention on Prohibitions or Restrictions on the Use of Certain Conventional Weapons which may be deemed to be Excessively Injurious or to Have Indiscriminate Effects concerning Prohibitions or Restrictions on the Use of Incendiary Weapons (adopted 10 October 1980, entered into force 2 December 1983) 1342 UNTS 137.

[25] *ICRC Customary Study* Rule 86. See also Protocol IV to the UN Convention on Prohibitions or Restrictions on the Use of Certain Conventional Weapons which may be deemed to be Excessively Injurious or to Have Indiscriminate Effects concerning Blinding Laser Weapons (adopted 13 December 1995, entered into force 30 July 1998) (1996) 35 ILM 1218.

international law',[26] the answer that the court gave could be only ambiguous. The court analysed the question in its *Nuclear Weapons* Advisory Opinion.[27] In the operative part of the decision, the court expressed as follows:

> A threat or use of nuclear weapons should [...] be compatible with the requirements of the international law applicable in armed conflict, particularly those of the principles and rules of international humanitarian law [...]. It follows from the above-mentioned requirements that the threat or use of nuclear weapons would generally be contrary to the rules of international law applicable in armed conflict, and in particular the principles and rules of humanitarian law; However, in view of the current state of international law, and of the elements of fact at its disposal, the Court cannot conclude definitively whether the threat or use of nuclear weapons would be lawful or unlawful in an extreme circumstance of self-defence, in which the very survival of the State would be at stake.[28]

In simple terms, this means that the use of nuclear weapons is normally illegal, because of its incompatibility with the principles of the *jus in bello*, but that in extreme circumstances where the state survival is at stake, the illegality under international law is not conclusively established because of the policy of nuclear deterrence.

The best solution would be for the Western nuclear states to commit themselves to never using nuclear weapons as a first strike, as Russia and China did in the mid-1990s. This would be perfectly compatible with a true policy of 'deterrence'. It would unambiguously spell out the idea that a nuclear strike is only permissible when made in response to a nuclear attack. If such a declaration were made, it would be possible to rule out the use of such weapons in all cases, with only one exception. This exception would not be the vague 'survival of the state' exception postulated by the ICJ. Instead the exception would be clear-cut, only allowing nuclear weapons to be used as reprisals for a nuclear attack. It must be stressed once more that this is a proposal for the development of the law: it does not reflect the actual legal position.

Comprehension check:

a) Under what conditions will a weapon, ammunition or a means of warfare be prohibited by the LOAC?
b) Why is it prohibited to hide explosives in everyday objects, such as toys ('booby-traps')?
c) Is the use of nuclear weapons prohibited?
d) Is it possible to use a prohibited weapon or means by way of reprisals? (This question is not answered in the present chapter; if necessary, please refer to the chapter on belligerent reprisals.[29])

---

[26] UNGA Res 49/75K (15 December 1994) Un Doc/A/Res/49/75K.
[27] *Nuclear Weapons*, n 4, paras [23]*ff.*
[28] *Ibid*, para [105] (D) and (E).
[29] Ch 22 below.

Answers:

a) Weapons or means of warfare are prohibited because they either: (1) leave no chance of survival and thus have excessive effects; (2) cause grave and unnecessary suffering, not conducive to any real military advantage because a lesser means would have achieved the result of placing the adversary *hors de combat*; or (3) have indiscriminate effects, ie hit military and civilian objects without distinguishing between them. These rules are the foundations of all the concrete prohibitions.

b) The rules on this point are to be found in Article 6 of Protocol II of the Conventional Weapons Convention. The main reason for this prohibition is that such hidden arms cause injuries mainly to civilians, and are thus indiscriminate.

c) As a rule, the use of nuclear weapons is prohibited, because such weapons are unable to be used in a manner that discriminates between civilian and military objectives. According to the ICJ, the principal judicial organ of the United Nations and of the international community, there are, however, extreme cases where it cannot be said with certainty that the use of a nuclear weapon is prohibited in international law. In particular, it is not possible to say that the use of a nuclear weapon would be prohibited in an extreme circumstance of self-defence, where the very survival of the state is at stake.

d) Reprisals that target protected persons, either those that are *hors de combat* or civilian, have been ruled out by the Geneva Conventions and the Additional Protocols.[30] Against combatants, reprisals have not been ruled out. However, such reprisals are subjected to stringent conditions. These conditions are mainly the following: (1) the purpose of the reprisals may only be to secure future law-compliance, not to punish for a violation of the law; (2) reprisals must be a measure of last resort; (3) reprisals must be proportionate to the wrong suffered; (4) the decision to take reprisals must be made at the highest level of government; and (5) reprisals must cease as soon as the adversary complies with the law.[31]

[30] Geneva Convention I for the Amelioration of the Condition of the Wounded and Sick in Armed Forces in the Field (adopted 12 August 1949, entered into force 21 October 1950) 75 UNTS 31 Art 46; Geneva Convention II for the Amelioration of the Condition of Wounded, Sick and Shipwrecked Members of Armed Forces at Sea (adopted 12 August 1949, entered into force 21 October 1950) 75 UNTS 85 Art 47; Geneva Convention III relative to the Treatment of Prisoners of War (adopted 12 August 1949, entered into force 21 October 1950) 75 UNTS 135 Art 13(3); and Geneva Convention IV Relative to the Protection of Civilian Persons in Time of War (adopted 12 August 1949, entered into force 21 October 1950) 75 UNTS 287 Art 33(3) with respect to protected persons hors de combat and Additional Protocol I Arts 51(6), 51(1) 53(c), 54(4), 55(2) and 56(4) for reprisals against the civilian population.

[31] *ICRC Customary Study* Rule 145.

20

PERFIDY AND RUSES

Learning objectives: To discuss one particular prohibited means of warfare.

1. Since time immemorial, it has been part of military art to induce the adversary to fall into traps and/or to make errors in order to obtain a military advantage. However, some acts aimed at deceiving an adversary are prohibited because they constitute a breach of faith. Such prohibited acts of deceit are called 'perfidy'. The definition of perfidy and its prohibition are spelled out in clear terms in Article 37 of Additional Protocol I of 1977.[1] This provision reflects customary international law and extends, today, to NIAC.[2] Article 37 states as follows:

Art 37. Prohibition of Perfidy

1. It is prohibited to kill, injure or capture an adversary by resort to perfidy. Acts inviting the confidence of an adversary to lead him to believe that he is entitled to, or is obliged to accord, protection under the rules of international law applicable in armed conflict, with intent to betray that confidence, shall constitute perfidy. The following acts are examples of perfidy:

(a) the feigning of an intent to negotiate under a flag of truce or of a surrender;
(b) the feigning of an incapacitation by wounds or sickness;
(c) the feigning of civilian, non-combatant status; and
(d) the feigning of protected status by the use of signs, emblems or uniforms of the United Nations or of neutral or other States not Parties to the conflict.

2. Study of this provision allows us to appreciate the primary motivation that underlies the prohibition of perfidy. The point is that one party gains a specific military advantage by taking advantage of the good faith of an adverse party to the conflict by a mistaken belief of that latter party as to the existence of a situation giving rise to protection under the LOAC. One party takes advantage of the duty of the adverse party to respect the laws of warfare and uses this in order to gain a specific military advantage. Thus, in an attempt to gain a military advantage, a belligerent's combatants may make the adverse party believe that it is obliged to

---

[1] Protocol Additional to the Geneva Conventions of 12 August 1949, and relating to the Protection of Victims of International Armed Conflicts (adopted 8 June 1977, entered into force 7 December 1978) 1125 UNTS 3 (Additional Protocol 1).

[2] J-M Henckaerts and L Doswald-Beck (eds), *Customary International Humanitarian Law Volume 1: Rules* (Cambridge, CUP, 2005) (hereinafter *ICRC Customary Study*) Rule 65 and *Prosecutor v Tadic* (Decision on the Defence Motion for Interlocutory Appeal on Jurisdiction) IT-49-1-AR72 (2 October 1995) para [125]. See also Rome Statute of the International Criminal Court (adopted 17 July 1998, entered into force 1 July 2002) 2187 UNTS 90 Art 8(2)(e)(ix).

grant a protection under the LOAC. For example, surrender may be simulated by hoisting a white flag. In reality, the operation has the objective of bringing the troops of the adversary out of their positions. When they approach the entrenchment of those having hoisted the white flag, in order to take as prisoners the persons purportedly surrendering, find themselves under fire. Thus, the combatants feigning surrender gain an opportunity to attack under best conditions. They profit from the rule that surrender entitles them to prisoner of war status, and that they may not be attacked in such a situation (unless they commit hostile acts).[3]

3. Three elements are constitutive of perfidy:

 a) an act of deception as to the applicability of a protection under the LOAC;
 b) with the aim of gaining a military advantage; and
 c) when the military advantage consists in killing, injuring or capturing an adversary.

All three elements must cumulatively be present in order for the belligerent to commit an act of perfidy. Thus, for example, a soldier who feigns sickness because he or she no longer wishes to fight does not thereby commit an act of perfidy. He or she does not use his or her deception in this situation in order to gain an advantage relative to an adverse belligerent, but only, for example, to be captured and brought off the battlefield. This soldier assuredly feigns sickness. However, he or she does not do so in order to obtain a military advantage; he or she does so only in order to save his or her life. However, even a soldier who feigns sickness in order to be transported in to the camp of the enemy and to perform acts of espionage there is not committing an act of perfidy. He or she feigns a protected status and does so in order to gain, for his or her party, a military advantage. However, the modern definition of perfidy restricts the military advantages to killing, injuring or capturing adverse forces. This is not the case here. The advantage sought is purely strategic. The fact that this strategic advantage can lead, in due course, to death, injury or capture of adverse forces is immaterial. All military advantages indirectly serve that purpose. If interpreted so broadly, the phrase 'killing, injuring or capturing' contained in Article 37 of the Protocol would be deprived of all meaning.

Perfidy is prohibited in order that belligerents adhere to the provisions of the LOAC. If it were not, all of the protections of the LOAC would become inapplicable. If any belligerent has reason to fear that at any moment there may be a misuse of these protections, he or she would no longer be ready to grant them. Thus, the whole effort undertaken by the LOAC to humanise warfare to the maximum extent possible would become nugatory.

4. Several examples of perfidious acts are mentioned in Article 37 of Additional Protocol I: (1) feigning of surrender or intent to negotiate, with the aim of breaching the confidence inspired in the adverse party and using such breach to kill, injure or capture an adversary; (2) feigning of incapacitation or wounds with the same aim; (3) feigning of non-combatant status with the same aim; (4) misuse of

---

[3] Geneva Convention III relative to the Treatment of Prisoners of War (adopted 12 August 1949, entered into force 21 October 1950) 75 UNTS 135 (Geneva Convention III) Art 13.

protected emblems, signs or uniforms with the same aim. This list is not exhaustive; other situations exist.

Articles 38 and 39 of the Protocol prohibit certain acts akin to perfidy:

Art 38. Recognized emblems

1. It is prohibited to make improper use of the distinctive emblem of the red cross, red crescent or red lion and sun or of other emblems, signs or signals provided for by the Conventions or by this Protocol. It is also prohibited to misuse deliberately in an armed conflict other internationally recognized protective emblems, signs or signals, including the flag of truce, and the protective emblem of cultural property.

2. It is prohibited to make use of the distinctive emblem of the United Nations, except as authorized by that Organization.

Art 39. Emblems of nationality

1. It is prohibited to make use in an armed conflict of the flags or military emblems, insignia or uniforms of neutral or other States not Parties to the conflict.

2. It is prohibited to make use of the flags or military emblems, insignia or uniforms of adverse Parties while engaging in attacks or in order to shield, favour, protect or impede military operations.

3. Nothing in this Article or in Article 37, paragraph 1 (d), shall affect the existing generally recognized rules of international law applicable to espionage or to the use of flags in the conduct of armed conflict at sea.

As can be seen, these particular prohibitions are cast in more absolute terms. These provisions reflect customary international law.[4] For example, the use of emblems of neutral states is prohibited generally, at all time and in all situations, not only when it is used with the intent to gain the specific military advantage required in Article 37.

5. For the sake of completeness, it must be added that the prohibition of perfidy has ancient roots. Apart from longstanding prohibition found in customary international law,[5] the prohibition of perfidy can also be found in Articles 23(b) and (f) of the Hague Regulations.[6] Article 23(b) is the general provision. It reads: '[It is forbidden:] To kill or wound treacherously individuals belonging to the hostile nation or army'.

Article 23(f) forbids in specific terms:

To make improper use of a flag of truce, of the national flag or the military insignia and uniform of the enemy, as well as distinctive badges of the Geneva Convention [of 1864].

The misuse of the emblem of the Red Cross is also specifically prohibited in Geneva Conventions I and II.[7]

---

[4] *ICRC Customary Study* Rules 58–63.

[5] *ICRC Customary Study* Rule 65.

[6] Regulations concerning the Laws and Customs of War on Land annexed to Hague Convention IV (adopted 18 October 1907, entered into force 26 January 1910) (1907) 205 CTS 227 Art 23.

[7] Geneva Convention I for the Amelioration of the Condition of the Wounded and Sick in Armed Forces in the Field (adopted 12 August 1949, entered into force 21 October 1950) 75 UNTS 31 Art 54; and Geneva Convention II for the Amelioration of the Condition of Wounded, Sick and Shipwrecked

6. Whilst perfidy is prohibited, ruses of war are not.[8] The kernel of a ruse of war consists in deceiving the adversary on a point of fact—for example, on the strength or the direction of an armed column—in order to gain a military advantage. The essential point that differentiates a ruse from perfidy is that there is here no deceit about the applicability of a protection under the LOAC. The deceit takes places on a point of fact (on the military operations) and not on a point of law (the protections under the LOAC). There are many famous historical examples of such war ruses. One of them is the Trojan Horse.

The ICRC, in its commentary to the Additional Protocols, gave examples of such permitted 'stratagems', as they are also called, which will not amount to perfidy:

> [S]etting up surprise attacks, ambushes, retreats, simulated operations on land, in the air or at sea; simulating quiet and inactivity; camouflaging troops, weapons, depots or firing positions in the natural or artificial environment; taking advantage of the night or favourable weather conditions (fog, etc.); constructing installations that will not be used; putting up dummy aerodromes or placing in position dummy canon and dummy armoured vehicles, and laying dummy mines; use of small units to simulate large forces and equipping them with a strong avant-garde or numerous advances bases; transmitting misleading messages by radio or in the press; knowingly permitting the enemy to intercept false documents, plans of operations, dispatches or news items which actually bear no relation to reality; using the enemy wavelengths, passwords and wireless codes to transmit false instructions; pretending to communicate with reinforcements which do not exist; organizing simulated parachute drops and supply operations; moving land marks and route markers or altering road signs; removing the signs indicating rank, unit, nationality or special function from uniforms; giving members of one military unit the signs from other units to make the enemy believe that it is faced with a more important force; using signals for the sole purpose of deceiving the adversary; resorting to psychological warfare methods by inciting the enemy soldiers to rebel, to mutiny or desert, possibly taking weapons and transportation.[9]

Comprehension check:

a) What is the essential difference between war ruses and perfidy?
b) If a bomb is hidden within a foodstuff, is that perfidy?
c) Is it perfidy to hoist the true flag of nationality of the attacker at the last moment before the attack, while before that moment the flag of the adversary was used in order to secure a better approach?
d) Is it perfidy to use the Red Cross Flag in order to engage in espionage?

Answers:

a) The essential difference is that in case of war ruses, the deceit of the adversary does not relate to a protection of the LOAC, but only to a fact; whereas in the

---

Members of Armed Forces at Sea (adopted 12 August 1949, entered into force 21 October 1950) 75 UNTS 85 Art 45.

[8] *ICRC Customary Study* Rule 57.
[9] ICRC, *Commentary on the Additional Protocols of 8 June 1977 to the Geneva Conventions of 12 August 1949* (ICRC, Geneva 1987) 443–4.

case of perfidy, the deception holds out that the belligerent is entitled to protection under the LOAC. That is the reason why perfidy is prohibited and war ruses are not. If perfidious acts were permitted, the whole of the LOAC would become inoperative. Acts of perfidy constitute war crimes.[10]

b)   There are no rules of protection under the LOAC as to where bombs may or may not be put: thus, no deceit can take place on a protection of the LOAC and the act is not perfidious. However, the act is still contrary to the LOAC, because the method of putting bombs in such daily-use objects infringes the principles of prohibition of indiscriminate attacks. That is why Protocol II of the Certain Conventional Weapons Convention, in its Article 6, explicitly prohibits such 'booby-traps'.[11]

c)   No situation of Article 39(2) is at stake here. Moreover, there is no general protection of the flag of the enemy under the LOAC. Thus the act is not prohibited.

d)   This act is not perfidy in the sense of Article 37 of Protocol I of 1977, since the aim of the use is not to 'kill, injure, or capture an adversary'. However, the act is prohibited under Article 38(1) of Protocol I, which reflects customary international law.[12]

---

[10] Additional Protocol 1 Art 85(3)(f) and *Tadic*, n 2.

[11] Protocol II to the UN Convention on Prohibitions or Restrictions on the Use of Certain Conventional Weapons which may be deemed to be Excessively Injurious or to Have Indiscriminate Effects concerning Prohibitions or Restrictions on the Use of Mines, Booby-traps and Other Devices (adopted 10 October 1980, entered into force 2 December 1983) 1342 UNTS 137 Art 6.

[12] *ICRC Customary Study*, n 2, Rule 59 and *Re Hagendorf* (1948) 13 War Crimes Reports 146.

SOME OTHER PROHIBITED MEANS AND METHODS OF WARFARE

Learning objectives: To discuss prohibited means and methods of warfare in general.

1. Means of warfare are essentially weapons or physical devices used in combat.[1] Methods of warfare are tactical or strategic devices designed to weaken the adversary. In other words, the means of warfare are material objects used by one belligerent to damage another, whereas the methods are those non-physical techniques used by the belligerents to gain a military advantage.[2] The limitations or prohibitions placed on the resort to specific means or methods of warfare contained in the LOAC derive from three basic premises[3]:

a) the choice of the means and methods of warfare is not unlimited[4];
b) the use of means and methods of a nature to cause unnecessary suffering or superfluous injury are forbidden[5];
c) the only legitimate object of war is to overpower or to weaken the military forces of the enemy in order that the enemy may be subjected to the will of the victor, not to destroy and kill as many members of the opposing military forces as possible.[6]

2. From these general principles flow a series of detailed rules as to the prohibited means and methods of warfare. In the case of prohibited weapons we have already seen this process in action.[7] However, the LOAC does not list in detail which methods are allowed. It begins from the assumption that the parties are allowed to use all methods of warfare that are not prohibited. In this sense, one may say that

---

[1] Prohibited weapons were discussed above, ch 19.
[2] Perfidy and ruses, discussed in ch 20 above are examples of methods of warfare.
[3] For more detailed discussion of these principles, see ch 19 above.
[4] Regulations concerning the Laws and Customs of War on Land annexed to Hague Convention IV (adopted 18 October 1907, entered into force 26 January 1910) (1907) 205 CTS 227 (Hague Regulations) Art 22; and Protocol Additional to the Geneva Conventions of 12 August 1949, and relating to the Protection of Victims of International Armed Conflicts (adopted 8 June 1977, entered into force 7 December 1978) 1125 UNTS 3 (Additional Protocol 1) Art 35(1).
[5] Hague Regulations Art 23(e) and Additional Protocol 1 Art 35(2).
[6] St Petersburg Declaration Renouncing the Use, in Time of War, of Explosive Projectiles Under 400 Grammes Weight (signed 11 December 1868, entered into force 11 December 1868) (1868–69) 138 CTS 297 Preamble.
[7] Ch 19 above.

all acts that are not prohibited are allowed.[8] However, keen attention is necessary on this point. The fact that a means or method of warfare is not *specifically* prohibited by a concrete provision of the LOAC, such as a treaty specifically banning that method, does not mean that this means or method is lawful. It has first to be asked if that means or method is compatible with the general principles of the LOAC, for example the principle of distinction (prohibition of indiscriminate attacks),[9] and with the principle of humanity as enshrined in the rule prohibiting 'unnecessary suffering'[10] or in the Martens clause.[11] Only if the means and methods at stake do not infringe either a specific prohibition or these general principles can it be said that the LOAC does not prohibit them and that they are, therefore, lawful.

3. A partial list of prohibited means and methods of warfare can be found in Article 8 of the Rome Statute.[12] Article 8 bears the title 'war crimes'. Violation of substantive rules of the LOAC are termed 'war crimes' in international criminal law. Thus, the list contained in Article 8 provides a good indication of the customary law prohibiting means and methods, but due to the Rome negotiating process it is incomplete.[13] Only by the application of the tests discussed above can it be determined whether a further particular means or method is lawful. It is worth quoting the Article at length and subjecting it to a through reading.[14] Reproduced below is Article 8(2), which governs crimes in international armed conflict:

Article 8, War Crimes

(2)(b) Other serious violations of the laws and customs applicable in international armed conflict, within the established framework of international law, namely, any of the following acts:

(i)   Intentionally directing attacks against the civilian population as such or against individual civilians not taking direct part in hostilities;
(ii)   Intentionally directing attacks against civilian objects, that is, objects which are not military objectives;
(iii)   Intentionally directing attacks against personnel, installations, material, units or vehicles involved in a humanitarian assistance or peacekeeping mission in accordance with the Charter of the United Nations, as long as they are entitled to the protection given to civilians or civilian objects under the international law of armed conflict;

---

[8] See generally: *The Case of the SS Lotus* (*Turkey v France*) PCIJ Rep Series A No 10, 19.

[9] Additional Protocol 1 Art 51(4).

[10] Additional Protocol 1 Art 35(2).

[11] Convention (IV) respecting the Laws and Customs of War on Land (adopted 18 October 1907, entered into force 26 January 1910) (1907) 205 CTS 227 Preamble and ch 9 above.

[12] Rome Statute of the International Criminal Court (adopted 17 July 1998, entered into force 1 July 2002) 2187 UNTS 90 Art 8.

[13] For example, slavery and forced labour are not listed as war crimes in Art 8, despite being recognised as such in the jurisprudence of the International Criminal Tribunal for Yugoslavia, *Prosecutor v Kronjelac* (Trial Judgment) IT-97-25-T (15 March 2003) paras [350]–[360] and *Prosecutor v Naletelic and Martinovic* (Trial Judgment) IT-98-34-T (31 March 2003) paras [250]–[261]. Further, the use of chemical weapons is not listed as a war crime despite clearly being prohibited at customary law, *Prosecutor v Tadic* (Decision on the Defence Motion for Interlocutory Appeal on Jurisdiction) IT-49-1-AR72 (2 October 1995) paras [120]–[124].

[14] For more detailed information on the crimes contained in Art 8, see K Dörmann, *Elements of War Crimes under the Rome Statute of the International Criminal Court* (Cambridge, CUP, 2003).

(iv)   Intentionally launching an attack in the knowledge that such attack will cause incidental loss of life or injury to civilians or damage to civilian objects or widespread, long-term and severe damage to the natural environment which would be clearly excessive in relation to the concrete and direct overall military advantage anticipated;

(v)   Attacking or bombarding, by whatever means, towns, villages, dwellings or buildings which are undefended and which are not military objectives;

(vi)   Killing or wounding a combatant who, having laid down his arms or having no longer means of defence, has surrendered at discretion;

(vii)   Making improper use of a flag of truce, of the flag or of the military insignia and uniform of the enemy or of the United Nations, as well as of the distinctive emblems of the Geneva Conventions, resulting in death or serious personal injury;

(viii)   The transfer, directly or indirectly, by the Occupying Power of parts of its own civilian population into the territory it occupies, or the deportation or transfer of all or parts of the population of the occupied territory within or outside this territory;

(ix)   Intentionally directing attacks against buildings dedicated to religion, education, art, science or charitable purposes, historic monuments, hospitals and places where the sick and wounded are collected, provided they are not military objectives;

(x)   Subjecting persons who are in the power of an adverse party to physical mutilation or to medical or scientific experiments of any kind which are neither justified by the medical, dental or hospital treatment of the person concerned nor carried out in his or her interest, and which cause death to or seriously endanger the health of such person or persons;

(xi)   Killing or wounding treacherously individuals belonging to the hostile nation or army;

(xii)   Declaring that no quarter will be given;

(xiii)   Destroying or seizing the enemy's property unless such destruction or seizure be imperatively demanded by the necessities of war;

(xiv)   Declaring abolished, suspended or inadmissible in a court of law the rights and actions of the nationals of the hostile party;

(xv)   Compelling the nationals of the hostile party to take part in the operations of war directed against their own country, even if they were in the belligerent's service before the commencement of the war;

(xvi)   Pillaging a town or place, even when taken by assault;

(xvii)   Employing poison or poisoned weapons;

(xviii) Employing asphyxiating, poisonous or other gases, and all analogous liquids, materials or devices;

(xix)   Employing bullets which expand or flatten easily in the human body, such as bullets with a hard envelope which does not entirely cover the core or is pierced with incisions;

(xx)   Employing weapons, projectiles and material and methods of warfare which are of a nature to cause superfluous injury or unnecessary suffering or which are inherently indiscriminate in violation of the international law of armed conflict, provided that such weapons, projectiles and material and methods of warfare are the subject of a comprehensive prohibition and are included in an annex to this Statute, by an amendment in accordance with the relevant provisions set forth in articles 121 and 123;

(xxi)   Committing outrages upon personal dignity, in particular humiliating and degrading treatment;

(xxii)   Committing rape, sexual slavery, enforced prostitution, forced pregnancy, as defined in article 7, paragraph 2 (f), enforced sterilization, or any other form of sexual violence also constituting a grave breach of the Geneva Conventions;

(xxiii) Utilizing the presence of a civilian or other protected person to render certain points, areas or military forces immune from military operations;

(xxiv) Intentionally directing attacks against buildings, material, medical units and transport, and personnel using the distinctive emblems of the Geneva Conventions in conformity with international law;

(xxv) Intentionally using starvation of civilians as a method of warfare by depriving them of objects indispensable to their survival, including wilfully impeding relief supplies as provided for under the Geneva Conventions;

(xxvi) Conscripting or enlisting children under the age of fifteen years into the national armed forces or using them to participate actively in hostilities.

4. For NIAC, the list of prohibited means and methods given in Article 8(2)(e) is somewhat shorter.[15] It should be noted that this list fails to include as war crimes many of the means and methods which give rise to criminal liability when used in international armed conflicts.[16] This must not be taken to mean that these means and methods are allowed in NAIC, as the general principles underlying the prohibition of these means and methods in international armed conflict continue to apply.[17] Article 8(2)(e) is reproduced below:

e) Other serious violations of the laws and customs applicable in armed conflicts not of an international character, within the established framework of international law, namely, any of the following acts:

(i)   Intentionally directing attacks against the civilian population as such or against individual civilians not taking direct part in hostilities;

(ii)   Intentionally directing attacks against buildings, material, medical units and transport, and personnel using the distinctive emblems of the Geneva Conventions in conformity with international law;

(iii)   Intentionally directing attacks against personnel, installations, material, units or vehicles involved in a humanitarian assistance or peacekeeping mission in accordance with the Charter of the United Nations, as long as they are entitled to the protection given to civilians or civilian objects under the international law of armed conflict;

(iv)   Intentionally directing attacks against buildings dedicated to religion, education, art, science or charitable purposes, historic monuments, hospitals and places where the sick and wounded are collected, provided they are not military objectives;

(v)   Pillaging a town or place, even when taken by assault;

(vi)   Committing rape, sexual slavery, enforced prostitution, forced pregnancy, as defined in article 7, paragraph 2 (f), enforced sterilization, and any other form of sexual violence also constituting a serious violation of article 3 common to the four Geneva Conventions;

(vii)   Conscripting or enlisting children under the age of fifteen years into armed forces or groups or using them to participate actively in hostilities;

(viii) Ordering the displacement of the civilian population for reasons related to the conflict, unless the security of the civilians involved or imperative military reasons so demand;

(ix)   Killing or wounding treacherously a combatant adversary;

---

[15] Rome Statute Art 8(2)(e). See also *Tadic,* n 13, paras [96]–[127] for discussion of those means and methods that are prohibited in non-international armed conflicts.

[16] Rome Statute Art 8(2)(b)(xvii)–(xx) above has no counterparts in Art 8(2)(e).

[17] *Tadic,* n 13, para [119].

(x)   Declaring that no quarter will be given;

(xi)   Subjecting persons who are in the power of another party to the conflict to physical mutilation or to medical or scientific experiments of any kind which are neither justified by the medical, dental or hospital treatment of the person concerned nor carried out in his or her interest, and which cause death to or seriously endanger the health of such person or persons;

(xii)   Destroying or seizing the property of an adversary unless such destruction or seizure be imperatively demanded by the necessities of the conflict.

5. For reasons of space, it is impossible to comment in detail on each of these prohibited means and methods. However, three of them are worthy of short comment.

a) *The refusal of quarter is prohibited.* This rule is first found in The Hague Regulations[18] and is restated in Additional Protocol 1. Article 40 of Additional Protocol 1 reads as follows:

> It is prohibited to order that there shall be no survivors, to threaten an adversary therewith or to conduct hostilities on this basis.

The idea underpinning this provision is that surrendering enemy soldiers must be spared and taken as prisoners of war.[19] They may not be assaulted or killed. Moreover, it is prohibited to announce that 'no prisoners will be taken' in order to provoke the flight of the adverse army. Giving such an order, putting in danger adverse soldiers and/or lowering the law-abidingness of the commander's own forces is a war crime.[20]

b) *The forced conscription of nationals of the adverse party* to make them fight against their country is forbidden. This method was first proscribed in the Hague Regulations[21] and later restated in the Geneva Conventions.[22]

c) *Children under the age of 15 shall not be conscripted* in order to serve actively in hostilities or in the army.[23]

Comprehension check:

a) What are the main reasons for prohibiting certain means and methods of warfare?

b) Give some examples of prohibited means and methods of warfare.

---

[18] Regulations concerning the Laws and Customs of War on Land annexed to Hague Convention IV (adopted 18 October 1907, entered into force 26 January 1910) (1907) 205 CTS 227 Art 32(d).

[19] Geneva Convention III relative to the Treatment of Prisoners of War (adopted 12 August 1949, entered into force 21 October 1950) 75 UNTS 135(Geneva Convention III) Art 12.

[20] Rome Statute Arts 8(2)(b)(xii) and 8(2)(e)(x).

[21] Hague Regulations Art 23(h).

[22] Geneva Convention III Art 130 and Geneva Convention IV Relative to the Protection of Civilian Persons in Time of War (adopted 12 August 1949, entered into force 21 October 1950) 75 UNTS 287 Art 147.

[23] Additional Protocol 1 Art 77(2), concerning international armed conflicts, or Protocol Additional to the Geneva Conventions of 12 August 1949, and relating to the Protection of Victims of Non-International Armed Conflicts (adopted 8 June 1977, entered into force 7 December 1978) 1125 UNTS 609 Art 4(3)(c) for non-international armed conflicts; and see also *Prosecutor v Norman* (Decision on Preliminary Motion Based on Lack of Jurisdiction (Child Recruitment)) SCSL-04-14-AR72(E)-131 (31 May 2004); *Prosecutor v Brima, Kamara and Kanu* (Trial Judgment) SCSL-04-16-T (20 June 2007) para [728]; and *Prosecutor v Fofana and Kondewa* (Trial Judgment) SCSL-04-14-T (2 August 2007) para [197].

c)   Is it lawful to announce that 'no prisoners shall be taken'?

Answers:

a)   The main reason for limiting the means and methods of warfare is to avoid 'total war', ie to put some limitation on the barbarity of the war and to assure a minimum of humanity in warfare. More specific reasons to prohibit certain methods and means of warfare are to avoid unnecessary suffering (from the point of view of what is necessary to achieve the war aim) and to proscribe indiscriminate attacks that hit civilians as well as military objectives.

b)   Examples of prohibited means and methods can be found in the list of war crimes contained in Article 8 of the ICC Statute. You may mention a combination of them, for example, perfidy, refusal of quarter, poisoned or biological weapons, etc.

c)   No. This is what is called 'refusal of quarter', which is a war crime.[24]

---

[24] Additional Protocol 1 Art 40, and Rome Statute Arts 8(2)(b)(xii) and 8(2)(e)(x).

22

BELLIGERENT REPRISALS

Learning objectives: To explore the difficult question of the extent to which a belligerent may commit a violation of the LOAC in response to a previous violation of the LOAC committed by an adverse belligerent, in order to induce the adverse belligerent to comply with the violated norm of the LOAC.

1. The extent to which belligerent reprisals are allowed under the LOAC is a highly controversial question. A belligerent reprisal is, roughly, a violation of the LOAC committed in response to a violation of the LOAC by the other party, in order to induce that other party to comply with the law. Western states have traditionally resorted to belligerent reprisals as a means to enforce compliance with the LOAC, for example in World War II, when reprisals were used as a justification for the bombardment the Germany cities.

Western states continue to defend the legality of reprisals, albeit under strict conditions.[1] The main argument for the continuing legality of reprisals is that due to the weaknesses of enforcement mechanisms of the LOAC,[2] belligerent reprisals are the most efficient, and often the only, means available to induce compliance with the LOAC by the adversary, or at least prevent being placed at a military disadvantage with respect to an adverse belligerent who egregiously violates the law. In contrast to the attitude taken by the Western states, the so-called third world states, or 'Group of 77,' have always claimed that belligerent reprisals should be regarded as illegal in most cases. Their main argument is that reprisals are primitive means of assuring compliance. Such means are, according to their views, inherently barbarian, because they injure the innocent in order to indirectly influence the behaviour of the guilty. They inevitably lead to uncontrolled violence, provoke 'counter-reprisals' and result in the escalation of violence.

2. The law bears the stamp of this controversy. It is to some extent torn between the two poles of attempting to abolish reprisals on the one hand and giving them some minimum role on the other, on account of a realistic assessment of military necessities. As a general proposition, it can be said that during the past century, the categories of persons and objects that may be made subject to reprisals has been constantly reduced. Reprisal action against certain persons and objects is now prohibited by the LOAC. Further, state practice shows that reprisals have hardly

---

[1] UK Ministry of Defence, *The Manual of the Law of Armed Conflict* (Oxford, OUP, 2004) (hereinafter *UK Manual*) paras [16.16]–[16.19.2].

[2] See generally: ch 35 below.

been resorted to as a means of law enforcement in the last two decades. The last war where reprisals were invoked significantly was the Iran-Iraq War, which took place between 1981 and 1988. However, the idea of reprisal was also prominent during the Israel/Lebanon war in 2006. Overall, this trend tends to show that reprisals are now seen as a very ambiguous and problematic means of law enforcement, the use of which should be avoided as much as possible. The impact and success of reprisal as a means of enforcement is more than uncertain, whereas the danger that resort to reprisal will provoke a grave escalation of violence is almost certain. On this basis it is understandable that reprisals should be avoided as much as possible.

3. The LOAC does not prohibit belligerent reprisals generally, but contains a series of special prohibitions. These prohibitions are today so broad that the space left in which states can resort to reprisals is narrow indeed. Thus, belligerent reprisals are prohibited against the following persons and objects:

   a) the wounded, sick or shipwrecked combatants, and all other persons covered by Geneva Conventions I and II[3];
   b) prisoners of war under Geneva Convention III[4];
   c) civilians which find themselves in the hands of a party to the conflict of which they are not nationals, ie protected civilians outside of warfare situations, for example in internment or occupied territory[5];
   d) the wounded, sick or shipwrecked military persons or civilians covered by Part II of Additional Protocol I[6];
   e) civilians during hostilities, particularly in the context of targeting[7]—this is a most important limitation—it means that all the limitations placed on targeting due to the principle of distinction must be obeyed at all times and can no longer be ignored in the context of reprisals;
   f) civilian objects during hostilities, particularly in the context of targeting[8];
   g) historic monuments, works of art or places of worship which constitute the cultural or spiritual heritage of peoples[9];
   h) objects indispensable to the survival of the civilian population[10];
   i) the natural environment[11]; and
   j) works and installations containing dangerous forces.[12]

---

[3] Geneva Convention I for the Amelioration of the Condition of the Wounded and Sick in Armed Forces in the Field (adopted 12 August 1949, entered into force 21 October 1950) 75 UNTS 31 Art 46; Geneva Convention II for the Amelioration of the Condition of Wounded, Sick and Shipwrecked Members of Armed Forces at Sea (adopted 12 August 1949, entered into force 21 October 1950) 75 UNTS 85 Art 47.
[4] Geneva Convention III relative to the Treatment of Prisoners of War (adopted 12 August 1949, entered into force 21 October 1950) 75 UNTS 135 Art 13(3).
[5] Geneva Convention IV Relative to the Protection of Civilian Persons in Time of War (adopted 12 August 1949, entered into force 21 October 1950) 75 UNTS 287 Art 33(3).
[6] Protocol Additional to the Geneva Conventions of 12 August 1949, and relating to the Protection of Victims of International Armed Conflicts (adopted 8 June 1977, entered into force 7 December 1978) 1125 UNTS 3 (Additional Protocol 1) Art 20.
[7] Additional Protocol I Art 51(6).
[8] Additional Protocol I Art 52(1).
[9] Additional Protocol I Art 53(c).
[10] Additional Protocol I Art 54(4).
[11] Additional Protocol I Art 55(2).
[12] Additional Protocol I Art 56(4).

The prohibition of reprisals against protected persons, namely persons *hors de combat* or non-combatants in the hands of the adverse party, under the four Geneva Conventions and the prohibition of reprisals against civilian persons and objects under Additional Protocol I, in the context of attack and targeting, have reduced the scope of admissible reprisals to a dramatic extent. Which belligerent reprisals thus remain allowed?

4. Reprisals against military and combatant personnel during warfare remain admissible under the law as it stands today. In particular, reprisals against military objectives remain possible. It could be argued that such objectives may be attacked anyway, and that the permissibility of reprisals does not allow the attacking belligerent to do anything that it could not do otherwise. However, this is not certain. Thus, a military objective could perhaps be targeted by way of reprisals if the attack on the target does not present a concrete military advantage, which would not be the case if the attack was not a reprisal.[13] Furthermore, attacks against combatants using prohibited means of warfare, such as chemical agents, may be undertaken as reprisals. Finally, reprisals are still probably admissible in the law of maritime and air warfare when we are concerned with attacks from an aircraft to another aircraft; or from a ship to a ship; or from a ship to an aircraft; or conversely from an aircraft to a ship. Additional Protocol I is only concerned with land warfare, including attacks from ships or aircraft against land objectives, but does not directly concern attacks that are limited to the air or to the sea. However, it appears that customary international law prohibits attacks on civilian aircraft or civilian ships even by way of reprisals.

Recent jurisprudence clearly points in the direction of a general prohibition of reprisals against civilian persons. Thus, the International Criminal Tribunal for the former Yugoslavia (ICTY), in the *Kupreskic* case, considered that under customary international law all civilians are protected against belligerent reprisals in all circumstances.[14] The ICTY trial chamber relied on a series of arguments to conclude that such a general prohibition exists. The chamber invoked the fundamental principle of humanity; the absence of a need for reciprocity in the fundamental protections of IHL, which must be respected in all circumstances independently from the respect given to the LOAC norms by other party, asking the question of why further innocent civilians should die because the other party has violated the rule of protection in a specific case?; and the moderns tendencies of state practice, including the negative reaction of the UN General Assembly to cases of reprisals. Thus, the rule against reprisals in the context of civilian persons must, today, probably be considered to be applicable in all circumstance.[15] It is moreover hardly possible to find any civilians who are not protected either by Article 33(3) of Geneva Convention IV or by Article 51(6) of Additional Protocol I, as either protected persons in the hands of the enemy or civilians who must not be targeted. It is inevitable that a belligerent reprisal that is aimed at civilians will hit civilians either as protected persons or through combat means: to stage reprisals against

---

[13] See generally: ch 17 above.

[14] *Prosecutor v Kupreskic* (Trial Judgment) IT-95-16-T (14 January 2000) paras [527]*ff*.

[15] Against: *UK Manual*, n 1, para [16.19.2] and fn 62, which explicitly rejects the conclusion of the trial chamber in *Kupreskic*.

civilians in either of these ways is prohibited. There remains only the small area of civilians at sea and in the air. It would be wholly against the trend of increasing protection for there to be a loophole into the law in this particular context.

5. To the extent that belligerent reprisals are still admissible under the LOAC, five strict conditions apply to their use[16]:

a) the purpose of the reprisals may only be to secure future law-compliance, not, for example, to punish for a violation of the law;

b) reprisals must be a measure of last resort (*ultima ratio*); no other, less intrusive, means for securing law-compliance must be available;

c) reprisals must be proportionate to the wrong suffered;

d) the decision to take reprisals must be made at the highest level of government; and

e) reprisals must cease as soon as the adversary complies with the law.

These strict criteria limiting the scope of admissible reprisals make it even more difficult to conceive that reprisals against a civilian population or civilian persons are still admissible.

It is sometimes contended that at least as far as civilian objects, as opposed to civilian persons, are concerned, the law is, and should be, less strict. This may be true to some extent. However, even in this context, it is hard to envision many situations in which, due to the preceding strict criteria, an intentional attack on civilian objects could be rendered lawful because it was carried out as a belligerent reprisal.

6. The question of whether reprisals are lawful in NIAC is highly controversial. To support the position that reprisals are unlawful in the LOAC the argument is made that Common Article 3 to the Geneva Conventions and Article 4(2) of Additional Protocol II[17] oblige states not to attack persons *hors de combat* or non-combatants 'at any time and in any place whatsoever'. It is inferred from this wording that belligerent reprisals, at least against non-combatant personnel, are prohibited. This argument was used by the ICTY in the *Martic* case.[18] It has also been suggested that belligerent reprisals have, as a concept, never extended to the law of NIAC as a device of law enforcement. Rather, in the law of NIAC the protection of civilians has always been given high priority.[19] On the other hand, several states claim to have a sovereign power to adopt measures of reprisal within their territory, as there is no prohibition in the LOAC against such measures in the context of NIAC.

It cannot be said that the point is as yet clearly settled in the law. It remains controversial. In any case, the restrictive criteria for the admissibility of reprisals developed in the context of IAC must also apply to reprisals in NIAC, since they are bound up with the very concept of reprisals in the modern law of armed

---

[16] *UK Manual, ibid*, para [16.17] and *Prosecutor v Martic* (Trial Judgment) IT-95-11-T (12 June 2007) paras [465]–[467].

[17] Protocol Additional to the Geneva Conventions of 12 August 1949, and relating to the Protection of Victims of Non-International Armed Conflicts (adopted 8 June 1977, entered into force 7 December 1978) 1125 UNTS 609.

[18] *Prosecutor v Martic* (Rule 61 Decision) IT-95-11-R61 (8 March 1996) para [1264].

[19] J-M Henckaerts and L Doswald-Beck (eds), *Customary International Humanitarian Law Volume 1: Rules* (Cambridge, CUP, 2005) ('*ICRC Customary Law Study*') 527–529.

conflicts. Hence, there are some stringent limitations placed on the exercise of reprisals in NIAC, if one admits them at all.

Comprehension check:

a) What are reprisals and what are belligerent reprisals?
b) Would the bombing of cities like Coventry, London, Dresden, Leipzig and Hiroshima be lawful today if undertaken as a reprisal?
c) Where essentially do belligerent reprisals remain lawful today?

Answers:

a) Reprisals (or counter-measures) are measures which would normally be contrary to the international obligations of an injured state vis-a-vis a state responsible for a violation of the law, if they were not taken by the former in response to an internationally wrongful act by the latter in order to procure cessation and reparation.[20] The term 'belligerent reprisal' refers to such measures when they are taken during an armed conflict and involve the use of military force. Obviously, during a time of armed conflict, peaceful counter-measures, reprisals, can be adopted by one state against another. However, such measures do not interest us here, as they are not covered by the LOAC. The same is true for 'retorsion', which is an unfriendly act that is not inconsistent with any international obligation of the state engaging in it even though it may be a response to an internationally wrongful act. An example is the withdrawal of an embassy.
b) No, such bombings would no longer be permissible under Article 51(6) of Additional Protocol I. This provision reflects customary international law.[21]
c) Belligerent reprisals remain admissible, in particular, against military objectives. The doctrine of reprisals may mean that a belligerent does not have to show that a specific military advantage would be gained from attacking a military object, to the extent that he or she relies on reprisals. Conversely, reprisals against civilian persons, and to a large extent, civilian objects, should be regarded as in principle ruled out by the modern law of armed conflicts.

---

[20] See generally ILC Articles on Responsibility of States for Internationally Wrongful Acts UNGA Res 56/83 (12 December 2001) UN Doc A/RES/56/83 available at <http://untreaty.un.org/ilc/texts/instruments/english/draft%20articles/9_6_2001.pdf > (last accessed 24th May 2008) Arts 22 and 49–54.
[21] *ICRC Customary Law Study* Rule 146.

23

COMMAND RESPONSIBILITY

Learning objectives: To learn about the responsibilities, duties and liabilities of commanders of belligerent armed forces.

1. The doctrine of command responsibility strictly relates to military law and international criminal law more than it does to the LOAC. It is, primarily, a doctrine devoted to the apportionment of criminal liability for breaches of the LOAC norms, and only as a corollary to this are international duties imposed upon commanders. Therefore, only some provisions of the LOAC and international criminal law consider the duties that are placed on commanders, whereas the rules and regulations applicable to a responsible commander as a matter of internal law may impose duties that are far more extensive. Of course, the responsibilities exist for many more reasons than merely avoiding criminal liability, and are, in part, imposed due to the honour of the position of command.

We must first examine the general responsibilities of commanders, before moving on to consider the responsibility of commanders for the actions of those under their command. Members of the armed forces who have powers of command, at any level, but particularly those with a higher level of command, are under a duty to do the following:

a) *Exercise operational command*, to turn a mission given to them by higher command into reality by making a battle plan. To that end, a commander must assess all of the factors relevant at the time of the mission that may influence how the mission is carried out, such as: the strength, structure and location of enemy forces; the strength, structure and location of the commander's own forces; logistical considerations; the availability of reinforcements; the terrain; alternative courses of action, and so on. To appropriately assess all of the relevant data, the commander will need ample intelligence information. Such information is important to enable a commander to live up to the duty to take precautions.[1] This information must be up to date. The strength and efficacy of intelligence services is an essential element in military success, as well as an important influence on the ability to fulfil the duties imposed by the LOAC. Of course, such intelligence information cannot be obtained from adverse prisoners of war or civilians through torture or physical coercion. In particular, prisoners of war are only obliged to

---

[1] See (b) below.

give their: name and surname; regimental, personal or serial number; rank; and date of birth.[2] Further, any battle plan that is devised by a commander must take into account the necessities of IHL, such as the evacuation of wounded combatants, from both the commander's own forces and the adverse forces,[3] and the treatment of any captured prisoners of war and their transfer to a camp located at some distance from the front and marked, if possible, with the letters 'PW' or 'PG'.[4]

b) During the early phase of planning an attack, a high-level commander has an obligation to ensure that the operation complies with the duty to take *precautions in attack*, which is laid down by Article 57 of Additional Protocol I.[5] This important provision contains several relevant facets.

   i) First, everything feasible must be done to verify that the objectives to be attacked are neither civilian nor enjoy special protection, such as that accorded to cultural property or installations containing dangerous forces. 'Feasible' in this context means that everything practically and reasonably possible shall be done.[6] The question may be particularly relevant when 'dual-use' objects, which may serve either civilian or military purposes, are attacked.

   ii) Secondly, if there is the potential that civilians will suffer incidentally from an attack against a military objective, the commander must assess the ways in which the attack may be planned to take all feasible precautions with regard to the choice of means and methods of attack with a view to avoiding, and in any event to minimising, these incidental losses. This may mean that precision weaponry should be used instead of cheaper but more imprecise weaponry, if the use of such weaponry will reduce the risk of the attack striking a group of civilians. The necessity to take precautions may also mean that an attack should be made at a certain time of the day, at a time when, under normal circumstances, the concentration of civilians around the object is lowest. Or conversely, it can suggest avoiding certain days, when the concentration of civilians is normally highest. In order to make these assessments, information or intelligence is required.

   iii) Thirdly, the commander should refrain from deciding to launch any attack which may be expected, according to the information held, to cause incidental loss of civilian life, injury to civilians or damage to

---

  [2] Geneva Convention III relative to the Treatment of Prisoners of War (adopted 12 August 1949, entered into force 21 October 1950) 75 UNTS 135 (Geneva Convention III) Art 17(1).

  [3] Geneva Convention I for the Amelioration of the Condition of the Wounded and Sick in Armed Forces in the Field (adopted 12 August 1949, entered into force 21 October 1950) 75 UNTS 31 and ch 24 below.

  [4] Geneva Convention III and ch 26 below.

  [5] Protocol Additional to the Geneva Conventions of 12 August 1949, and relating to the Protection of Victims of International Armed Conflicts (adopted 8 June 1977, entered into force 7 December 1978) 1125 UNTS 3 (Additional Protocol 1) Art 57.

  [6] *Prosecutor v Galic* (Trial Judgment) IT-98-29-T (5 December 2003) para [58] and fn 105; and *Western and Eastern Fronts—Ethiopia's Claims 1 & 3 (Ethiopia v Eritrea)* Eritrea-Ethiopia Claims Commission (19 December 2005) at <http://www.pca-cpa.org/upload/files/FINAL%20ET%20FRONT%20CLAIMS(1).pdf> accessed 15 May 2008 para [33].

civilian objects which would be excessive in relation to the concrete and direct military advantage anticipated.[7] In simpler words, if it appears that the civilian losses are excessive with respect to the advantage to be gained by the attack, the commander should refrain from ordering such an attack. This duty supposes a good faith effort to put into balance the military and civilians interests and to refrain from systematically over-emphasising military benefit over the life and physical integrity of adverse civilians.

iv) Fourthly, a commander should immediately cancel or suspend an attack if it becomes apparent that the objective is not a military objective or is entitled to specific protection, or that the attack may be expected to cause excessive collateral losses to civilians.[8] Hence, even once the attack has started, the commander must take a continuing interest in the course of events. He or she has to react to the situations as they evolve, and in particular immediately suspend an attack if the assumptions upon which the attack was based turn out to be wrong or imprecise, or if excessive damage is otherwise caused to protected persons and/or objects.

v) Fifthly, the commander must contemplate the possibility of giving effective advance warning when an attack may affect the civilian population.[9] This duty is a relative one. It does not exist if the circumstances do not permit the giving of such warning. In some cases, if advance warning is given, the efficacy and safety of the operation may be put at grave jeopardy. In this situation, advance warning will not be reasonably feasible. However, if the efficacy of the operation is not put at risk, for example, because the attacker has complete air superiority and it is impossible for the enemy to organise anti-aircraft defences in the warned area within the time between the warning and the attack, there will be an obligation to give an advance warning when it allows the civilian population to be spared from death and injury through evacuation.

vi) Sixthly, Article 57(6) of Additional Protocol I states that:

> When a choice is possible between several military objectives for obtaining a similar military advantage, the objective to be selected shall be that the attack on which may be expected to cause the least danger to civilian lives and to civilian objects.

If more than one objective can be attacked in order to secure the same military advantage, the object of the attack must be the objective which is likely to cause the fewest civilian losses. Take a simple example. A commander is given a mission which has the objective of cutting off a route which is being used to supply arms and ammunitions to the adverse army. In order to achieve this objective, the commander could order the destruction of either one of two bridges which carry the route over large rivers. One of these bridges is situated within a small town, whereas the

---

[7] Additional Protocol I Art 51(5)(b).
[8] Additional Protocol I Art 57(2)(b).
[9] Additional Protocol I Art 57(2)(c).

other is situated in a non-populated region. If the commander knows that if he or she orders a strike on the bridge passing through the small town, the attack is likely to cause between 10 and 50 civilian casualties; if he or she orders a strike on the bridge in the non-populated region, no collateral civilian damage will result. In this case, if the military advantage gained by the two attacks is the same, the commander must order the attack to be made on the bridge in the non-populated area.

c) The next duty of the commander is to *issue orders*, which pass the battle plan on to the subordinates who are to carry out the plan. Such orders must be clear and precise. They shall not be open to misinterpretations. The orders must not contain wording that is not meant, for example, they should not contain jokes or phrasing that only serves to demonstrate bravado. The orders will lay down clear parameters for conducting the operation and will often contain rules of engagement. The orders issued must clearly indicate all localities and objects to be spared from attack. They shall also contain a statement setting out the duties of the subordinates under the LOAC and the way in which these duties can be complied with, if necessary, such as details regarding the evacuation of the wounded and as to the treatment of captured prisoners of war. Orders may also be addressed to the civilian population by, for example, giving civilians an order to evacuate certain areas. An order that is given must not be contrary to the LOAC. If orders are given that are contrary to the LOAC, not only will the commander face international criminal responsibility, but the subordinates are required, in grave cases, to refuse to obey orders, or face international criminal responsibility themselves.[10]

d) The next duty of the commander relates to *control of the execution of the orders* and the overall implementation of the battle plan. The main purpose of requiring control by the commander is to ensure that orders are carried out according to the plan. Commanders remain responsible throughout the conduct of the operation. As we have seen, they must, according to the circumstances, give the order to immediately suspend an operation when it turns out that an objective attacked is not, in reality, a military objective, or that unexpected and excessive collateral damage to civilians is being caused by the operation. Thus, the commander may have to directly communicate with his or her subordinates, for example by means of radio, to correct a course of action that is not in accordance with the plan, or with the LOAC. That means that a commander has to remain in constant contact with those who carry out his or her orders. For example, if a commander has ordered his or her subordinates to gain control of a building in order to use it for defensive fire in support of the artillery, but as the troops tasked with this mission approach the building it becomes clear that it is a hospital marked by the Red Cross,[11] the commander must immediately order the troops not to attack the objective and cancel the mission to capture the building. The

---

[10] Rome Statute of the International Criminal Court (adopted 17 July 1998, entered into force 1 July 2002) 2187 UNTS 3 Art 33.

[11] And is therefore immune from attack, Geneva Convention I Art 19.

commander has a general responsibility to ensure that the personnel under his or her command are not violating the LOAC.[12]

e) Lastly, it may be recalled that the commander has a duty to maintain firm, but fair, *discipline* among his or her subordinates.

2. As has already been said, a commander has a general responsibility to ensure that the personnel under his or her command are not violating the LOAC. Therefore, a commander must be sure that his or her personnel are trained in the LOAC and order them to always respect these rules. Moreover, a commander has to control the adherence of subordinates to the rules. The principle is that every member of the armed forces, whatever his or her rank, has a personal responsibility to comply with the LOAC. However, commanders have an additional duty to control their subordinates and ensure that they comply with the rules of the LOAC, and to take action when violations are encountered. Thus, a commander must make full use of the machinery available to him or her to investigate and suppress violations of the LOAC.[13] He or she cannot just say, 'I did not know'. This may require the commander to punish subordinates who have breached the LOAC or may entail a duty to report any violations committed by subordinates, or even, in some cases, by the enemy, to a higher authority competent to take action against those who have committed the LOAC violations.[14] Article 87 of Additional Protocol I clearly spells out these duties:

Art 87. Duty of commanders

1. The High Contracting Parties and the Parties to the conflict shall require military commanders, with respect to members of the armed forces under their command and other persons under their control, to prevent and, where necessary, to suppress and to report to competent authorities breaches of the Conventions and of this Protocol.

2. In order to prevent and suppress breaches, High Contracting Parties and Parties to the conflict shall require that, commensurate with their level of responsibility, commanders ensure that members of the armed forces under their command are aware of their obligations under the Conventions and this Protocol.

3. The High Contracting Parties and Parties to the conflict shall require any commander who is aware that subordinates or other persons under his control are going to commit or have committed a breach of the Conventions or of this Protocol, to initiate such steps as are necessary to prevent such violations of the Conventions or this Protocol, and, where appropriate, to initiate disciplinary or penal action against violators thereof.

If the commander fails to live up to these duties, he or she will be liable, before either national or international tribunals, for the war crimes committed by personnel under his or her command.[15]

---

[12] See further para 2 below.

[13] See, eg: *Prosecutor v Halilovic* (Trial Judgment) IT-01-48-T (16 November 2005) paras [97]–[100] and in particular para [98].

[14] See, eg: *Prosecutor v Oric* (Trial Judgment) IT-03-68-T (30 June 2006) para [336].

[15] See also: *Prosecutor v Hadzihasanovic* (Decision on Interlocutory Appeal Challenging Jurisdiction in Relation to Command Responsibility) IT-01-47-AR72 (16 July 2003) including Partially Dissenting Opinion of Judge Shahabuddeen and Separate and Partially Dissenting Opinion of Judge Hunt, in particular Judge Shahabuddeen at para [33]; and *Oric*, *ibid*, para [294] for a discussion of the nature of such responsibility.

3. A commander is personally responsible under the law if he or she 'knew, or should have known' that subordinates were planning to violate the LOAC at some point in the future or had actually violated the LOAC at some time in the past, but did nothing to prevent or to suppress such action. There are thus two aspects to command responsibility: actual knowledge and constructive knowledge. Actual knowledge does not pose any problems for the law: if it was reported to the commander that breaches of the law were taking place, then it is clear that he or she knew about them. A more difficult question arises when it is asked whether a commander 'should have known' about violations of the LOAC committed by those under his or her command. Article 86(2) of Additional Protocol I attempts to answer this question. This provision provides that a commander 'should have known' about violations committed by his subordinates when he or she was 'put on notice' regarding the breaches in one way or another. A commander will be put on notice when information regarding the conduct of the subordinates is in his or her possession. Thus, according to the Protocol, he or she is not placed under a duty to search for information regarding the conduct of subordinates him- or herself. It is necessary that, for example, a subordinate, another commander, public opinion or newspaper articles put him or her on notice. Article 86(2) reads as follows:

> The fact that a breach of the Conventions or of this Protocol was committed by a subordinate does not absolve his superiors from penal or disciplinary responsibility, as the case may be, if they knew, or had information which should have enabled them to conclude in the circumstances at the time, that he was committing or was going to commit such a breach and if they did not take all feasible measures within their power to prevent or repress the breach.

The International Criminal Tribunal for the former Yugoslavia (ICTY), after some hesitation,[16] has interpreted the requirement that the commander must be 'put on notice' literally. It decided that the commander must actually 'be put on notice by some form of information'. In the *Galic* case, for example, it was decided that for a commander to be held responsible for the acts of his or her subordinates it must be shown that a superior had some general information in his or her possession which would put him or her on notice of possible unlawful acts by his or her subordinates.[17] However, in another case, it was made clear that knowledge may be presumed if the commander had the means of obtaining the relevant information, but deliberately refrained from doing so, so-called wilful blindness.[18] The measures that a commander can take in order to obtain information are obviously limited by the circumstance in which the commander finds him- or herself at time when he or she acted or omitted to act. The standard thus remains quite exacting for a duty-bound commander. The only thing which the law, as expounded by the ICTY, does not require, is that the commander him- or herself engages in investigations to establish whether there has been any violation of the law. In the earlier jurisprudence, after World War II, if a commander was negligent as to the means taken to inform

---

[16] *Prosecutor v Blaskic* (Trial Judgment) IT-95-14-T (3 March 2000) para [332], overturned on appeal, *Prosecutor v Blaskic* (Appeal Judgment) IT-95-14-A (29 July 2004) paras [58]–[64].

[17] *Prosecutor v Galic* (Trial Judgment) IT-98-29-A (5 December 2003) para [175], following *Prosecutor v Delalic et al* (Appeal Judgment) IT-96-21-A (20 February 2001) para [238].

[18] *Prosecutor v Brdjanin* (Trial Judgment) IT-99-36-T (1 September 2004) para [278].

him- or herself about the conduct of subordinates, this could be sufficient to fix that commander with a breach of his or her duty of responsible command and therefore render the commander liable for the acts of his or her subordinates before national or international tribunals.[19] Such an approach has now been explicitly rejected.[20]

4. In any event, a good commander should always remain informed and control the execution of orders by his or her subordinates. Hence, it is best practice for a commander to, at least, after any operation check that the LOAC, and his or her orders, have been scrupulously been complied with in sample cases. Such actions become even more important when it is appreciated that Article 28 of the Rome Statute could be interpreted as a return to the imposition of a more exacting standard of care on commanders. Negligence by a commander in obtaining information regarding the actions of subordinates may be seen as sufficient to trigger his or her criminal responsibility. This provision reads as follows, with the passage that is most relevant to the commander's possible duty to obtain information about the actions of his subordinates italicised:

Responsibility of commanders and other superiors

In addition to other grounds of criminal responsibility under this Statute for crimes within the jurisdiction of the Court:

(a) A military commander or person effectively acting as a military commander shall be criminally responsible for crimes within the jurisdiction of the Court committed by forces under his or her effective command and control, or effective authority and control as the case may be, as a result of his or her failure to exercise control properly over such forces, where:

(i)   *That military commander or person either knew or, owing to the circumstances at the time, should have known that the forces were committing or about to commit such crimes*; and

(ii) That military commander or person failed to take all necessary and reasonable measures within his or her power to prevent or repress their commission or to submit the matter to the competent authorities for investigation and prosecution.

(b) With respect to superior and subordinate relationships not described in paragraph (a), a superior shall be criminally responsible for crimes within the jurisdiction of the Court committed by subordinates under his or her effective authority and control, as a result of his or her failure to exercise control properly over such subordinates, where:

(i)   The superior either knew, or consciously disregarded information which clearly indicated, that the subordinates were committing or about to commit such crimes;

(ii) The crimes concerned activities that were within the effective responsibility and control of the superior; and

(iii) The superior failed to take all necessary and reasonable measures within his or her power to prevent or repress their commission or to submit the matter to the competent authorities for investigation and prosecution.

---

[19] *Prosecutor v Yamashita* (1946) 13 AD 269.
[20] *Prosecutor v Bagilishema* (Appeal Judgment) ICTR-95-IA-A (Appeal Judgement) paras [34]–[35]; and *Halilovic*, n 13, para [71].

5. Finally, the question of the effect of *superior orders* on liability for breaches of the LOAC must be discussed. The rule is simple enough in principle: it is no defence in a prosecution for a war crime that the act was committed in compliance with a superior order.[21] A soldier who carries out an order, which is illegal under the LOAC, is guilty of a war crime, provided that the act was of some gravity and that he or she was aware of the circumstances which made that order unlawful, or at least should have been aware of these circumstances. The principle is recalled in simple terms in Article 7(4) of the Statute of the ICTY[22]:

> The fact that an accused person acted pursuant to an order of a Government or of a superior shall not relieve him of criminal responsibility, but may be considered in mitigation of punishment.

Obedience to superior order may mitigate the sentence, but it does not provide a complete defence to a criminal prosecution.[23] Thus, if an order is plainly unlawful, a soldier has a duty not to carry it out. Conversely, the commander who gives an order breaching the LOAC cannot require his subordinate to carry it out. In professional, well-trained armed forces, such situations should not occur, although we know that, in the real world, they do. To summarise, it can be said that a solider owes a loyalty to the law that is of a higher order than the loyalty the solider owes to a commander.

Comprehension check:

a)   What are the main duties of a commander?

b)   What are the duties of a commander with respect to the LOAC?

c)   A troop that is progressing according to the orders given reaches a building that is marked as protected cultural property under Article 53 of Additional Protocol I, when it suddenly comes under fire from that building, which kills 10 members of the troop. What should or could the commander do?

Answers:

a)   The commander has five main duties: (1) to exercise operational command and prepare military operations by organising and assessing all relevant information; (2) to weigh up all possible precautions in attack as required by Article 57 of Additional Protocol I; (3) to issue orders that clearly spell out the mission and the standards of behaviour expected of subordinates, such as the requirement to comply with duties under the LOAC; (4) to control the application of his or her orders and to react to changed circumstances by adapting, suspending or cancelling some orders; and (5) to maintain discipline.

b)   The main duties with respect to the LOAC are: (1) to ensure that the subordinates know the relevant rules of the LOAC; (2) to give orders which conform with the LOAC; (3) to always specify to subordinates that during the military

---

[21] See, eg: *The Llandovery Castle* (1922) 16 *American Journal of International Law* 708; and *Judgment of the Nuremburg International Military Tribunal 1946* (1947) 41 *American Journal of International Law* 172, 221.

[22] Statute of the International Criminal Tribunal for the Former Yugoslavia (adopted 25 May 1993) 32 ILM 1192. See also Rome Statute Art 33.

[23] See generally: *Prosecutor v Erdemovic* (Appeal Judgment) IT-96-22-A (7 October 1997).

operations they must respect the rules of the LOAC; (4) to react to new infor-mation by cancelling an attack or suspending it once it has started if the LOAC so requires, for example if it turns out that the attack on a military objective will cause excessive collateral damages to civilians with respect to the military advantage to be gained; and (5) to investigate and suppress violations of the LOAC by his or her subordinates. To this end, the commander has to organise channels of information to keep him or her up to date with the actions of his or her subordinates.

c) The commander must first be aware that the building is under special protection as cultural property. However, in our case that building is used militarily, in breach of the duties under the LOAC. When a piece of cultural property is used in this manner it becomes liable to proportionate and necessary counter-attack.[24] In order to decide whether to stage such a counter-attack, the commander would have to weigh up several considerations: the magnitude of the military advantage gained by neutralising the enemy fire from this particular property on the one hand, for example, must the fire from this building be neutralised because it controls the only route which the troop can take to reach the place where the main operation is to be performed, and that main operation is of a high priority; or, can the building be left aside and skirted around, as it is clearly a secondary place of skirmish?; and the extent of the probable damage that would be inflicted by an attack in relation to the importance of the cultural property that would be attacked, for example, the degree of damage expected with respect to the arms that could be used to stop the fire and the precise location of the enemy forces in the building, and so on. In any case, the commander has a duty to try to use the minimum force and cause the minimum damage possible to the building if he or she chooses to engage in an operation designed to neutralise his or her opponents. As is so often the case, the essential role of the commander in this situation is to carefully balance the different factors.

---

[24] Convention for the Protection of Cultural Property in the Event of Armed Conflict (adopted 14 May 1954, entered into force 7 August 1956) 249 UNTS 240 Art 4(2); and Second Protocol to the Hague Convention of 1954 for the Protection of Cultural Property in the Event of Armed Conflict (adopted 26 March 1999, entered into force 9 March 2004) (1999) 38 ILM 769 Art 6.

24

ASSISTANCE, RESPECT AND PROTECTION OF WOUNDED AND SICK MILITARY PERSONS

Learning objectives: To learn about the duties that belligerents owe to wounded, sick and shipwrecked combatants.

1. The modern LOAC, since its birth on the field at Solferino, has been preoccupied by the fate of wounded, sick and shipwrecked combatants or other military personnel. The LOAC, in particular Geneva Conventions I and II, contains a series of norms protecting these personnel and requiring belligerents to grant them assistance. The paramount duty with respect to the wounded, sick and shipwrecked is not to target injured personnel or engage in hostile action directed towards them: as soon as they are *hors de combat*, such persons may no longer be made the object of any attack or assault whatsoever.[1] Further important duties require adverse belligerents to: (i) respect, (ii) protect and (iii) care for *hors de combat* wounded and/or sick and/or shipwrecked military personnel once they are under the control of that belligerent.[2]

The requirement to 'respect' the *hors de combat* military personnel connotes the idea of abstention. Belligerents must not engage in hostile acts against such persons, which includes a requirement to abstain from threats, intimidation and harassment directed against those placed *hors de combat*. If the concept underlying the duty of respect could be summed up in one word, it is that wounded, sick and shipwrecked persons should be spared.

The duty of 'protection' connotes an active preservation of the *hors de combat* personnel from evils and dangers. The requirement extends to dangers that are a result of the armed conflict and those that are the result of other external causes, such as illness or the elements. The wounded, sick and shipwrecked personnel should be sheltered and treated humanely.

Finally, the obligation to 'care' for the *hors de combat* personnel requires each belligerent to search for and collect the wounded and sick without discrimination

---

[1] Geneva Convention I for the Amelioration of the Condition of the Wounded and Sick in Armed Forces in the Field (adopted 12 August 1949, entered into force 21 October 1950) 75 UNTS 31 (Geneva Convention I) Art 12; and Geneva Convention II for the Amelioration of the Condition of Wounded, Sick and Shipwrecked Members of Armed Forces at Sea (adopted 12 August 1949, entered into force 21 October 1950) 75 UNTS 85 (Geneva Convention II) Art 12.

[2] Geneva Convention I Art 12; and Geneva Convention II Art 12.

based on nationality or on other irrelevant criteria, such as sex, religion or political opinions.[3] Moreover, it requires the wounded and sick to be cared for medically, according to the practical possibilities and the material available.[4]

These fundamental duties are spelled out in Geneva Conventions I and II, the first of which applies to land warfare and the second of which relates to warfare at sea and thus includes provisions concerning the protection of the shipwrecked military personnel. These conventions do not cover injured and sick civilians, where Geneva Convention IV applies.[5]

The most relevant provisions in Geneva Convention I are Articles 12 and 15, which are extracted below:

Art. 12. Members of the armed forces and other persons mentioned in the following Article, who are wounded or sick, shall be respected and protected in all circumstances.

They shall be treated humanely and cared for by the Party to the conflict in whose power they may be, without any adverse distinction founded on sex, race, nationality, religion, political opinions, or any other similar criteria. Any attempts upon their lives, or violence to their persons, shall be strictly prohibited; in particular, they shall not be murdered or exterminated, subjected to torture or to biological experiments; they shall not wilfully be left without medical assistance and care, nor shall conditions exposing them to contagion or infection be created.

Only urgent medical reasons will authorize priority in the order of treatment to be administered.

Women shall be treated with all consideration due to their sex. The Party to the conflict which is compelled to abandon wounded or sick to the enemy shall, as far as military considerations permit, leave with them a part of its medical personnel and material to assist in their care.

Art. 15. At all times, and particularly after an engagement, Parties to the conflict shall, without delay, take all possible measures to search for and collect the wounded and sick, to protect them against pillage and ill-treatment, to ensure their adequate care, and to search for the dead and prevent their being despoiled.

Whenever circumstances permit, an armistice or a suspension of fire shall be arranged, or local arrangements made, to permit the removal, exchange and transport of the wounded left on the battlefield.

Likewise, local arrangements may be concluded between Parties to the conflict for the removal or exchange of wounded and sick from a besieged or encircled area, and for the passage of medical and religious personnel and equipment on their way to that area.

The position is recapitulated in Article 10 of Additional Protocol I, which is reproduced below:

---

[3] Geneva Convention I Art 15; and Geneva Convention II Art 15.

[4] *Prisoners of War—Eritrea's Claim 17* (*Eritrea v Ethiopia*) Eritrea-Ethiopia Claims Commission (1 July 2003) at <http://www.pca-cpa.org/upload/files/ER17.pdf> accessed 15 May 2008 paras [64]–[65]; *Prisoners of War—Ethiopia's Claim 4* (*Ethiopia v Eritrea*) Eritrea-Ethiopia Claims Commission (1 July 2003) at <http://www.pca-cpa.org/upload/files/ET04.pdf> paras [69]–[70].

[5] Geneva Convention IV Relative to the Protection of Civilian Persons in Time of War (adopted 12 August 1949, entered into force 21 October 1950) 75 UNTS 287 Arts 16*ff.*

Protection and care

1. All the wounded, sick and shipwrecked, to whichever Party they belong, shall be respected and protected.

2. In all circumstances they shall be treated humanely and shall receive, to the fullest extent practicable and with the least possible delay, the medical care and attention required by their condition. There shall be no distinction among them founded on any grounds other than medical ones.[6]

Similar obligations apply to the parties in non-international armed conflict. These duties are set out, in a much more succinct and less detailed fashion, in Article 3 common to the Geneva Conventions and in Article 7 of Additional Protocol II.[7] These provisions reduce the obligations contained in Geneva Conventions I and II to their minimum common core.

2. The duties of respect, protection and care primarily place obligations on the parties to the conflict. Every state must organise, either within its army, or complementary to its army, a medical service with the role of caring for wounded and sick combatants in case of armed conflict. This duty is not dependent on the existence of an armed conflict and is imposed on states in times of peace in order to ensure that there is no period of time during an armed conflict where such a service does not exist. The civilian population of a state has no direct duty of protection and care for enemy combatants. However, the civilian population has a duty to respect the wounded, sick and shipwrecked, and this must be translated by the states into their municipal law, requiring that there shall be no attacks on the wounded or sick enemy combatants.[8] Civilians who spontaneously care for wounded and sick enemy combatants shall not be liable to criminal prosecution for these acts.[9] For example, such civilians shall not be prosecuted for treason. Of course, the authorities of the state, and in particular also the military authorities, can call upon the civilian population to collect and care for adverse combatants, appealing thus to their charity.[10] However, they are under no LOAC obligation to respond, but if they do they will be granted the necessary protection and facilities.[11]

3. Once the wounded and sick are collected by the competent medical services of a belligerent, information concerning the combatant must be gathered as soon as possible.[12] Collected data should, if possible, include: designation of the state of origin of the combatant; army, regimental, personal or serial number; surname; first name or names; date of birth; any other particulars shown on his or her identity card or disc; date and place of capture and/or death; particulars concerning wounds

---

[6] Protocol Additional to the Geneva Conventions of 12 August 1949, and relating to the Protection of Victims of International Armed Conflicts (adopted 8 June 1977, entered into force 7 December 1978) 1125 UNTS 3 (Additional Protocol I) Art 10.

[7] Protocol Additional to the Geneva Conventions of 12 August 1949, and relating to the Protection of Victims of Non-International Armed Conflicts (adopted 8 June 1977, entered into force 7 December 1978) 1125 UNTS 609 Art 7.

[8] Geneva Convention I Art 18.

[9] *Ibid.*

[10] *Ibid.*

[11] *Ibid.*

[12] Geneva Convention I Art 16; and Geneva Convention II Art 19.

or illness, or cause of death.[13] Then, as soon as possible, the belligerent is obliged to forward this information to the Information Bureau for Prisoners of War, described in Geneva Convention III and operated by the International Committee of the Red Cross (ICRC).[14] The Information Bureau will transmit these particulars to the power of origin of the wounded or sick combatant, and in particular to his or her family.

4. During situations of armed conflict, it happens very often that the number of victims by far exceeds the amount that the ordinarily equipped medical service of the army can handle. For this reason, the LOAC provides a four-tier system in order to guarantee that adequate care can be given to the wounded and sick. First, as has been examined above, the primary duty to care for the wounded and sick, of whatever nationality, is placed upon the medical services of the army. Secondly, the National Red Cross Society of the belligerent, the medical service of which is overburdened, will be able to offer invaluable services in assistance of that medical service through its medical personnel, material and expertise. Thirdly, if the needs of the wounded and sick exceed the capacities of both the medical service of the belligerent and the National Red Cross Society of the belligerent, the ICRC will request that National Red Cross Societies of neutral states render assistance to their under-resourced sister society within the territory stricken by the war. Hence, a series of Red Cross Societies will send medical personnel and material to the war zone. Thereby, they will increase considerably numbers of personnel and equipment able to assist the wounded and sick. This practice began during the Franco-Prussian War of 1870, and has been a feature of subsequent armed conflicts. Finally, the ICRC itself may organise some help, for example by sending medical material or qualified personnel to locations where there is a shortage. In the past, during the Yom Kippur War in 1973 and during the Indo-Pakistani War of 1971, the ICRC has hired aircraft in order to transport material to places where it is desperately needed. To summarise, the four tiers of aid for the wounded and sick are thus:

a) the medical services of the army of the belligerent and any civilian medical services controlled by the belligerent;
b) the medical services of the National Red Cross Society of the territory of the belligerent;
c) the medical services of National Red Cross Societies from neutral states that offer their assistance, often at the request of the ICRC; and
d) the medical services of the ICRC.

5. The cardinal rule that governs the provision of care to the wounded, sick and shipwrecked is that of *non-discrimination*. When deciding which wounded or sick combatant should be treated first, only medical factors, particularly the urgency of the need for treatment, may be taken into account.[15] Thus, a heavily injured person should be treated in priority to a person with lesser injuries; a combatant who is at risk of death due to his or her injuries must receive priority over those with wounds

---

[13] Geneva Convention I Art 16.

[14] Geneva Convention I Art 16(2); and Geneva Convention III relative to the Treatment of Prisoners of War (adopted 12 August 1949, entered into force 21 October 1950) 75 UNTS 135 Art 122.

[15] Geneva Convention I Art 12.

that are not life-threatening; and so on. Conversely, it is accepted that adverse distinction on the basis of nationality, sex, race, religion, political opinion or similar criteria is prohibited.[16] The cardinal rule remains that assistance and care must be provided equally, with distinction between the wounded and sick made only on the basis of urgency and need. It is clear that the duty of non-discrimination requires that the soldiers owing allegiance to the power of origin of the treating medical service or to the 'enemy' power the must be treated equally. It may not always be easy to live up to this duty in practice, since it may mean that adverse soldiers have to be treated in priority to soldiers from the country of the treating medical personnel. However, the duty is taken exceptionally seriously by members of a medical service, and may be seen as a reflection of the requirements imposed on them by medical ethics.

Moreover, the requirement to make decisions on the basis of clinical need makes clear that material assistance given by, for example, the ICRC need not be distributed in arithmetically equal parts to all participants in the conflict. Whilst the quality of medical supplies supplied should be the same, it would be absurd to provide the same quantity of material to both a party with a well-equipped medical service who is not in need of supplies and to a party whose medical service is badly equipped, with an urgent requirement for more provisions. However, it may be politically difficult to persuade the parties to the conflict to accept such 'distinctive' treatment. Thus, during the Spanish Civil War, medical and humanitarian aid was distributed on the basis of strict equality, even if the needs were unequal.

6. Medical personnel have to operate in and be, along with their material, trans-ported to, positions near to the front line of an armed conflict, possibly even inside the combat zone, as many of the wounded and sick suffer injuries that would not withstand transport to a place of greater safety. In order to protect these medical personnel and their material they are granted immunity from attack, with the belligerents placed under an affirmative duty not to make 'fixed establishments and mobile medical units' the object of attack.[17] In order to ensure that the personnel and material entitled to protection from attack can be distinguished by the adverse belligerent, they must be visibly marked as a medical unit. To this effect, and in order to ensure uniformity amongst the medical services of state parties, a particular protective emblem was specified in Geneva Conventions I and II.[18] It is the heraldic emblem of the red cross on white ground, or the red crescent on white ground.[19] A new protective emblem was added to those which may be worn by medical services by Additional Protocol III to the Geneva Conventions. It is composed of a red frame in the shape of a square on edge on a white ground. [20]

7. In armed conflicts at sea, covered by Geneva Convention II, special protection is granted to *hospital ships*.[21] These ships are devoted to the collection and provision

---

[16] *Ibid.*

[17] Geneva Convention I Arts 19 and 24*ff*.

[18] See generally: ch 26 below.

[19] Geneva Convention I Art 38; and Geneva Convention II Art 41.

[20] Protocol additional to the Geneva Conventions of 12 August 1949, and relating to the Adoption of an Additional Distinctive Emblem (adopted 8 December 2005, entered into force 14 January 2007) Art 2(2).

[21] Geneva Convention II Arts 22*ff*.

of care to wounded, sick and shipwrecked military personnel. The key provision with respect to these ships is Article 22 of Geneva Convention II, which reads as follows:

> Military hospital ships, that is to say, ships built or equipped by the Powers specially and solely with a view to assisting the wounded, sick and shipwrecked, to treating them and to transporting them, may in no circumstances be attacked or captured, but shall at all times be respected and protected, on condition that their names and descriptions have been notified to the Parties to the conflict ten days before those ships are employed.[22]

The notification that is required by this article before protection is granted to hospital ships may be effected either by direct contact between the belligerent parties or through the channels of the protecting power or the ICRC. In order that the belligerents can satisfy themselves that the privileged status granted to hospital ships is not being abused, the warships of a belligerent can search adverse hospital ships and may exercise a control over matters such as the course taken by the hospital ship or its ability to communicate with other ships.[23] If the privileged status of the hospital ship is abused for the purposes of hostile action, the ship may be captured as a prize, once an order to stop the hostile action has been given and a reasonable time for compliance has lapsed.[24] The best method of guaranteeing proper use of such ships is to place a neutral observer aboard the hospital ship.[25] Such an observer may be sourced through the protecting power or may even be sent by the ICRC. Neutral states may offer hospital ships to the belligerents. In such cases, the hospital ship must be put under the command of a belligerent and be notified to opposing belligerents to benefit from protection under Geneva Convention II.[26] Such ships will then fly the flags of both their state of origin and the belligerent with whom they are affiliated. By requiring that a ship be placed under the control of a belligerent, these provisions aim to ensure that neutrally flagged hospital ships will not hamper in any way military operations at sea, and thus put themselves in danger. The drafters of Geneva Convention II felt that only the 'incorporation' of neutrally flagged hospital ships within the forces of a belligerent was sufficient to guarantee the avoidance of such a danger. Whilst other entities may also charter ships to undertake philanthropic missions, devoted to the provision of care and help to the wounded, sick and shipwrecked of the armed conflict, unless the provisions of Article 25 of Geneva Convention II are complied with such ships will not be hospital ships able to avail themselves of the protection granted to such ships under Geneva Convention II. However, this does not mean that such ships are without protection. As civilian objects these ships are not liable to attack or seizure. This point is emphasised in Hague Convention XI, which codifies certain customary law restrictions on the right of capture in navel warfare,

---

[22] Geneva Convention II Art 22.
[23] Geneva Convention II Art 31.
[24] Geneva Convention II Art 34; and L Doswald-Beck (ed), *San Remo Manual on International Law Applicable to Armed Conflicts at Sea* (Cambridge, CUP, 1995) available at <http://www.icrc.org/ihl> accessed 15 May 2008 paras [49]–[50].
[25] Geneva Convention II Art 31(4).
[26] Geneva Convention II Art 25.

and states in Article 4 that, '[v]essels charged with religious, scientific, or philan-thropic missions are … exempt from capture'.[27]

Comprehension check:

a)   Who must care for the wounded and sick combatants?
b)   If there is lack of medical personnel and material, who can provide useful help?
c)   How does one guarantee that medical units, personnel or material are not attacked?
d)   What happens if a medical unit or establishment is abused for military (hostile) purposes?
e)   Does a medical unit lose its protection under Geneva Convention I if the medical personnel are armed?

Answers:

a)   First, the medical services of the army (or, more generally, of the belligerent); secondly, the Red Cross (or Red Crescent) Society of the belligerent, in cooperation with the armed services of that belligerent; thirdly, the Red Cross (or Red Crescent) Societies of neutral states, called upon by the ICRC; and lastly, the ICRC itself. Obviously, all of these sources of assistance may intervene and provide care for the wounded and sick at the same time. There is no strict hierarchy which governs the timing of assistance; however, the first entity to act will normally be the national medical service (which you will recall must exist!).
b)   Foreign Red Cross or Red Crescent Societies and the ICRC. In such cases the ICRC should be contacted immediately.
c)   Through the use of protective emblems, the red cross on white ground, the red crescent on white ground or the red frame in the shape of a square on edge on a white ground.
d)   If the protection granted to a medical unit or establishment is abused and it takes part in hostile action, it loses its immunity from attack and seizure. Geneva Convention I requires, even in such cases, that a due warning be given, naming, in appropriate cases, a reasonable time limit and allowing measures to be taken against the medical unit only after such warning has remained unheeded.[28] Moreover, only proportionate measures should be taken, taking into account the possible impact of an attack on the persons cared for by the medical unit or in the medical establishment. What is proportionate depends on the circumstances.[29]
e)   This case is explicitly regulated in Geneva Convention I, Article 22 of which reads:

---

[27] Hague Convention XI Relative to Certain Restrictions with regard to the Exercise of the Right of Capture in Naval Warfare (adopted 18 October 1907, entered into force 26 January 1910) (1907) 205 CTS 367 Art 4. See also San Remo Manual para [47(f)].
[28] Geneva Convention I Art 21(1).
[29] Additional Protocol I Art 51(5)(b).

The following circumstances shall not be considered as depriving a medical unit or establishment of the protection ... (1) That the personnel of the unit or establishment are armed, and that they use the arms in their own defence, or in that of the wounded and sick in their charge.[30]

---

[30] Geneva Convention I Art 22(1).

25

THE DEFINITION OF COMBATANTS

Learning objectives: To learn who is entitled to combatant status, and therefore entitled to prisoner of war status, and who is not entitled to such a status, remaining what is sometimes called an 'irregular combatant'.

1. The right to take part in armed conflict is not unlimited. The LOAC places limits on the classes of people who are entitled to take part in hostilities. Some people are clearly entitled to take part, such as members of the regular armed forces of belligerent parties. Others may only participate if they fulfil certain stringent conditions. If these other persons participate in the hostilities without satisfying these conditions, they may be prosecuted for having taken part in the conflict. Therefore, it is important for us to examine the categories of person that are recognised by International Humanitarian Law ('IHL') as possessing the status of 'regular combatant' and therefore having the right to take part in hostilities. There are essentially three categories of regular combatants:

a) *Regular members of the armed forces.* Regular members of the armed forces are all the persons incorporated into the army of a state. If they are engaged in a mission that sees them actively take part in hostilities, they are 'combatants'.[1] The requirement of active participation in hostilities does not necessitate that the member of the armed force be involved in the actual fighting. Commanders, including members of the general staff of an army who play the role of shaping strategy for the armed conflict are also combatants, even if they never leave their office and do not take part in the actual fighting. The same is true, for example, for the commander of a prisoner of war (POW) camp, even if they never take part in actual fighting. As a member of the regular armed forces of a state, such a commander possesses combatant status. Certain members of the armed forces do not have a combat mission and are therefore not considered to be 'combatants'. This special regime applies eg to medical personnel and chaplains. They are covered by Article 33 of Geneva Convention III.[2] If captured, they must be granted a regime at

---

[1] Note, however, that members of the regular armed forces may lose their regular combatant status if they fail to fulfil the conditions that are normally required of irregular forces (see below) whilst on a mission: *Mohamed Ali v Public Prosecutor* [1969] AC 430 (PC), 449–54.

[2] Geneva Convention III relative to the Treatment of Prisoners of War (adopted 12 August 1949, entered into force 21 October 1950) 75 UNTS 135 (Geneva Convention III).

least as favourable as that granted to POWs.[3] Moreover, militias or volunteer corps may be incorporated into the regular army of a belligerent state through the municipal law of that state. Such militias and volunteer corps then become a part of the army and therefore regular combatants. This may also be the case for police forces. Such forces are not normally entitled to regular combatant status under the LOAC. However, they can, in case of armed conflict, be wholly or partially incorporated into the armed forces of a belligerent state by a decision taken under municipal law. If this is done by a state, and notified to the other party, these police forces will become regular combatants. Article 4(A)(1) of Geneva Convention III defines this overall category of regular combatants as follows:

> Members of the armed forces of a Party to the conflict as well as members of militias or volunteer corps forming part of such armed forces.

Police forces are not part of the armed forces, unless so notified to the adverse party.

The non-recognition of one belligerent by another has no effect on combatant status. Thus, if state A, as a matter of politics, does not recognise state B and both states become involved in an armed conflict on opposing sides, the non-recognition has no influence on the combatant status of the soldiers of either party, and hence it has no influence on the duty to grant POW status to the combatants of the other party who are captured. Article 4(A)(3) of Geneva Convention III thus includes within the category of regular combatants:

> Members of regular armed forces who profess allegiance to a government or an authority not recognized by the Detaining Power.

This may also be true for a government in exile, if it commands the allegiance of troops who participate in the fighting.

b) *Civilians participating in a 'levée en masse'.* This is a traditional category, which came to prominence due to the experiences of the 1789 French Revolution. Today, it is no longer of any great practical importance. This category affords combatant status to all civilians who spontaneously take up arms to defend their national soil against invaders during the short period of time that a foreign army is advancing onto the territory of their state. However, mindful of the fact that these persons engaged in combat are in reality civilians, the LOAC requires them to distinguish themselves from non-combatant civilians in order that the principle of distinction between military and civilian objectives can operate effectively. Thus, Article 4(A)(6) of Geneva Convention III grants regular combatant status to:

> Inhabitants of a non-occupied territory, who on the approach of the enemy spontaneously take up arms to resist the invading forces, without having had time to form themselves into regular armed units, provided they carry arms openly and respect the laws and customs of war.

---

[3] On the regime applicable to POWs, see generally ch 26 below.

As can be seen, the *levée en masse* concerns actions in a very short and transient phase of hostilities. It cannot be used to give combatant status to those who are engage in resistance within an occupied territory. The relevant provision of Geneva Convention III, quoted above, clearly speaks of acts of hostility in 'non-occupied territory'. Thus combatant status for civilians during a *levée en masse* only applies during a spontaneous fight against an invader, when that invader is still involved in actions intended to take possession of the territory. In other words, *levée en masse* does not apply once the invader is in effective control of the territory. Moreover, the civilians involved in the *levée en masse* must have had no time to either organise themselves into a regular army corps or to have constituted a militia. If these conditions are met, any civilian who openly takes up arms, thereby visibly identifying him- or herself as a combatant, and respects the rules of the LOAC, is entitled to take part in hostilities as a regular combatant, and hence to POW status if captured.

c) *Resistance movements and militias not incorporated into the regular army of a belligerent.* We have already seen that a militia can be incorporated into the regular army. The status of its members as regular combatants is then placed beyond doubt. However, cases may also arise where militias or resistance movements are formed spontaneously, especially in occupied territories. In these cases it will not be possible to attach such movements to the regular army in the manner contemplated above, as the regular army has been removed from the occupied territory by the enemy forces. However, the modern LOAC recognises that, under some quite strict conditions, civilians who take up the arms as part of resistance forces may qualify as regular combatants. Thus, Article 4(A)(2) of Geneva Convention III reads:

> Members of other militias and members of other volunteer corps, including those of organized resistance movements, belonging to a Party to the conflict and operating in or outside their own territory, even if this territory is occupied, provided that such militias or volunteer corps, including such organized resistance movements, fulfil the following conditions: (a) that of being commanded by a person responsible for his subordinates; (b) that of having a fixed distinctive sign recognizable at a distance; (c) that of carrying arms openly; (d) that of conducting their operations in accordance with the laws and customs of war.

If looked at closely, this provision requires persons to fulfil five criteria before they can be granted regular combatant status.[4] The first is that a militia is linked to a party to the conflict. In the words of the above provision it is required that the militia is one, 'belonging to a Party to the conflict'. The idea is that only militias fighting for the cause of a belligerent, for example with the aim of ensuring the liberation of national territory, should be entitled to regular combatant status. Groups fighting for private ends, and in some cases for criminal ends, should not come within the reach of the

---

[4] It has been suggested that a sixth criterion exists; that, in order to be a regular combatant, the member of the militia must not owe allegiance to the state against whom he takes up arms: *Public Prosecutor v Koi* [1968] 1 All ER 419 (PC), 425.

LOAC.[5] The link with a state can be secured by formal recognition, for example a connection with a government in exile, or simply through effective support afforded to the group by the state. The other four conditions are listed in letters (a) to (d) of the above provision. It should be noted that the criteria are quite strict. The members of the militia or resistance movement must be militarily organised, and in particular must have a fixed distinctive sign recognisable at distance. Furthermore, they must carry their arms openly. That limits such movements to situations where they actually control parts of national territory, such as during World War II, when irregular movements controlled parts of the mountain regions in occupied Yugoslavia and Greece. In other cases it is impracticable to carry arms openly and to have fixed signs visible at a distance. In situations where the occupier has effective control it is likely that they would simply arrest the people wearing fixed distinctive signs and carrying arms openly and put them to death.

2. With regard to the classification as combatants of the last mentioned class of persons, those involved in resistance movements, an evolutionary step in the law was secured by Additional Protocol I.[6] Many so-called 'third world states', which, in no small measure, had gained their independence thanks to guerrilla warfare, wanted to see those engaged in this type of resistance recognised as 'regular combatants' and not branded as criminals or terrorists. Once they became independent states, they pushed forcefully to change the LOAC in that direction. Of course, when combatants are engaged in guerrilla warfare it seems impracticable to require a fixed distinctive sign visible at distance and the continuous open display of arms. Moreover, the fifth condition required by Geneva Convention III, namely that a member of a militia must comply with the rules of the LOAC in order to be entitled to claim POW status, was attacked as discriminatory. In effect, it was argued that members of the regular army do not have to comply with these rules to be able to claim POW status.[7] Why should a resistance fighter be placed in a worse position? This new international environment explains the reforms in the qualifications for combatant status that were instituted mainly through Article 44 of Additional Protocol I.

a) First, *respect for the rules of the LOAC is no longer a condition precedent to regular combatant status* and hence for the right to POW status. Under Additional Protocol I this applies to all combatants, whether they are regular soldiers or members of a militia not incorporated into the armed forces of a belligerent state. If rules of the LOAC are not respected, persons expose themselves to criminal prosecution for war crimes. If convicted, they will serve their sentence and all privileges they enjoy as regular combatants, and therefore POWs, may be limited to the extent necessary in order for the punishment to be carried out. However, such crimes do not provide a reason to deprive the

---

[5] See, eg: *Military Prosecutor v Kassam* (1968) 42 ILR 470, 476–8.
[6] Protocol Additional to the Geneva Conventions of 12 August 1949, and relating to the Protection of Victims of International Armed Conflicts (adopted 8 June 1977, entered into force 7 December 1978) 1125 UNTS 3 (Additional Protocol 1).
[7] But see *Mohamed Ali*, n 1.

war criminal of POW status. Hence, Article 44(2) of Additional Protocol I reads:

> While all combatants are obliged to comply with the rules of international law applicable in armed conflict, violations of these rules shall not deprive a combatant of his right to be a combatant or, if he falls into the power of an adverse Party, of his right to be a prisoner of war.

b) Secondly, *the requirement that a combatant wear a fixed distinctive sign visible at distance* is abolished, while the condition of *openly carrying arms* is limited to the period that the combatant is involved in an active engagement. Article 44(3) of Additional Protocol I thus reads:

> In order to promote the protection of the civilian population from the effects of hostilities, combatants are obliged to distinguish themselves from the civilian population while they are engaged in an attack or in a military operation preparatory to an attack. Recognizing, however, that there are situations in armed conflicts where, owing to the nature of the hostilities an armed combatant cannot so distinguish himself, he shall retain his status as a combatant, provided that, in such situations, he carries his arms openly: (a) during each military engagement, and (b) during such time as he is visible to the adversary while he is engaged in a military deployment preceding the launching of an attack in which he is to participate.

Letter (b), in particular, has given rise to much discussion, because it may be interpreted in either a strict or extended manner. In any event, this provision considerably enlarges the scope of regular combatancy. Finally, it should be noted that if a combatant fails to accord to the conditions set out in Additional Protocol I, that combatant is not entitled to POW status if captured. However, in this case, Article 44(4) of Additional Protocol I requires the detaining power to grant combatants who have forfeited their right to POW status protections equivalent to those accorded to prisoners of war. Taken together, the reforms embodied in Additional Protocol I represent a considerable improvement in the protection of those involved in guerrilla warfare, and may represent a legitimisation of these tactics.

3. The reforms embodied in Additional Protocol I have been criticised by some states as a terrorist's charter. Such a fierce indictment of Additional Protocol I seems, however, somewhat excessive. It is true that guerrilla warfare implies surprise attacks: the combatants 'hit and run', dissolving themselves quickly in the mass of civilians, which can be seen as antithetical to the principle of distinction. However, the alternative of completely ruling out the possibility of lawful guerrilla warfare is not very attractive. Each state, or armed group representing a state, fights with the arms that it has. Modern day armed conflicts are increasingly marked by asymmetry in strength between the belligerents; it is inevitable that, in these cases, the weaker party will resort to guerrilla tactics. These are the only means that such groups can use. Denying guerrilla combatants the right to lawfully take part in hostilities, without any attempt to regulate, and possibly restrict, the use of such tactics would not be realistic. It would simply mean that much of the fighting in modern armed conflicts remained unaddressed by the LOAC.

Moreover, one must be aware of the fact that all guerrilla warfare cannot simply be labelled as terrorism. This is too simple an equation. First, the guerrilla groups, members of which are recognised as lawful combatants, must be groups fighting for the cause of a state party and recognised, either formally or informally, by that state. The requirement that the combatant has a link to a state, which is set out in the chapeau to Article 4 of Geneva Convention III, remains valid under Additional Protocol I. A private group of persons, asserting that they fight in furtherance of some self-proclaimed cause, could not come within the reach of the Protocol.[8] Secondly, Additional Protocol I applies only to international armed conflict (IAC). Thus, in reality Article 44 is applicable only in occupied territories. Conversely, the lawfulness of guerrilla warfare in non-international armed conflict (NIAC) or in situations of internal tensions and disturbances is not addressed by Article 44. Thirdly, guerrilla warfare cannot necessarily be equated with terrorism if the participants only target military objectives, which will usually be the forces belonging to the occupying power. It is clear that placing a bomb in the market place of a city, thereby targeting civilians, is not an act that may be lawfully performed during armed conflict. If such an act is committed by a lawful combatant, who is thus entitled to POW status, he or she shall be tried and sentenced for that act. However, if the acts of guerrilla warfare only strike against military installations or forces of the occupant, it is not obvious that this can be called terrorist action within the framework of IHL. The designation of the act as 'lawful' or 'terrorist' is obviously in the eye of the beholder: occupants will find that such actions are characteristically 'terrorist', as the Germans did in the occupied territories during World War II. However, the essential criterion should be that if the acts conform to the principle of distinction between military and civilian objectives, attacking only the former and sparing the latter, in accordance with the rules set out in Articles 48*ff* of Additional Protocol I, these attacks should be seen as lawful under the LOAC, and therefore not labelled 'terrorist'. Fourthly, it is difficult to maintain that Additional Protocol I, by way of Article 44(3), sustains terrorism if one takes into account that the very same protocol prohibits terrorist acts. Thus, Article 51(2) of Additional Protocol I reads, '[a]cts or threats of violence the primary purpose of which is to spread terror among the civilian population are prohibited'.[9]

It may be said, at least in Western eyes, that Article 44 of Additional Protocol I opens the floodgates to means of warfare which are felt to be problematic since they are based on guerrilla warfare tactics. The reason for this hostility to guerrilla warfare is that the Western Powers have often found themselves as 'occupiers' of territories, be it in the colonial context, in Palestine or elsewhere. In these contexts the Western Powers felt the effects, and also the strength, of the guerrilla methods that were used against them. Hence, these powers were not very sympathetic to reforms that appeared to legitimise this type of warfare. However, it suffices to recall the situation during World War II to see how transitory such perspectives and interests are. During World War II, the Western Powers considered that the

---

[8] For example, the groups in *United States of America v Buck and Shakur* (1988) 690 F Supp 1291 and *Public Prosecutor v Folkerts* (1977) 74 ILR 695 would not benefit from the right of lawful combatancy afforded by Additional Protocol I.

[9] This prohibition is customary: *Prosecutor v Galic* (Judgement) IT-98-29-A (30 November 2006) paras [79]–[90].

resistance movements in the territories occupied by Germany were 'freedom fighters' entitled to POW protection if captured, whereas Germany considered them to be 'terrorists'. Overall, the balance struck by Additional Protocol I does not seem excessive.

During the so-called 'war against terrorism' following 11 September, the LOAC does not, in large part, apply. The greater part of the military action that has been taken against terrorism since 2001 has not taken place in the context of an IAC. Thus Geneva Convention III and Additional Protocol I are not applicable. Arresting supposed terrorists, extraditing them and even abducting them falls under the law of peace and not under the LOAC. Therefore, these 'terrorists' are not entitled to POW status. The only exceptions are the militias who fought on the battlefield in Afghanistan on the side of the Taliban Government, some of whom were apparently members of al-Qaeda. If such persons were captured on the battlefield while they were taking part in fighting as regular combatants, POW status had to be granted to them. They could not be prosecuted for having fought against US forces in Afghanistan. However, if individual persons could be charged with crimes committed during the armed conflict in Afghanistan or terrorist acts committed before the war in Afghanistan, such persons could be prosecuted under criminal law by the detaining power.[10] During the war on terror, it is thus only this small class of persons captured in Afghanistan who are entitled to POW status; and even this status does not preclude criminal prosecution for prior terrorist acts or war crimes.

4. The main *effect of the grant of the status of regular combatant* is twofold.[11] First, such persons enjoy combatant immunity: they cannot be prosecuted under criminal law simply for having taken part in the hostilities. They may be prosecuted for war crimes or common crimes that they have committed. However, they cannot be punished for having taken part in the hostilities. Secondly, when captured, these persons have a right to POW status. This status gives them a series of rights and duties, which are spelled out in the substantive provisions of Geneva Convention III.[12]

5. If the *status of a person is uncertain*; if it is not clear whether or not he or she fulfils the conditions of a combatant, he or she shall be provisionally granted POW status unless, and until, a competent court of the detaining power has decided whether he or she is entitled to such a status.[13] Thus, Article 5(2) of Geneva Convention III reads:

> Should any doubt arise as to whether persons, having committed a belligerent act and having fallen into the hands of the enemy, belong to any of the categories enumerated in Article 4, such persons shall enjoy the protection of the present Convention until such time as their status has been determined by a competent tribunal.

---

[10] *US v Noriega* (1997) 99 ILR 143, 167–171, which makes clear that POW status does not bar prosecution by the detaining power for ordinary crimes committed prior to capture.

[11] *US v Khadr* (Opinion of the Court and Action on Appeal by the United States Filed Pursuant to 10 USC § 950d) (24 September 2007) United States Court of Military Commission Review, available at <http://www.defenselink.mil/news/Sep2007/KHADR%20Decision%20(24%20Sep%2007)(25%20pages).pdf> accessed 15 May 2008 5.

[12] Arts 12–125 and see generally ch 26 below.

[13] *Koi*, n 4.

Additional Protocol I reinforces that presumption in favour of POW status in Article 45(1):

> A person who takes part in hostilities and falls into the power of an adverse Party shall be presumed to be a prisoner of war, and therefore shall be protected by the Third Convention, if he claims the status of prisoner of war, or if he appears to be entitled to such status, or if the Party on which he depends claims such status on his behalf by notification to the detaining Power or to the Protecting Power. Should any doubt arise as to whether any such person is entitled to the status of prisoner of war, he shall continue to have such status and, therefore, to be protected by the Third Convention and this Protocol until such time as his status has been determined by a competent tribunal.

The presumption of regular combatant status in case of doubt is sensible. If belligerents were entitled to avoid the protection given to those afforded such a status when cases of doubt arose, the intentions of the Convention could be frustrated. A number of captives who are, in reality, entitled to POW status could be deprived of the protections under the Convention, leaving room for manipulation. For example, if POW status could be denied pending a decision by a competent court, some regular combatants would not benefit from the guarantees found in the Convention, thus opening a gap in protection and providing an incentive for belligerents to slow down judicial proceedings. Some states tend to argue that in a particular case there is no true 'doubt' and thus deprive a captive of POW status. If such an argument was used liberally, the presumption of Article 5(2) would be rendered otiose. That is why Additional Protocol I attempts to link the presumption to the claim of the captured person or the claim of his or her power of origin. If a person avers that he or she is a regular combatant, POW status should be provisionally granted to him or her, unless and until a competent court, in accordance with due process of law, has decided that he or she is not entitled to such a status. The practice of the United States with regard to persons captured in Afghanistan was problematic in this respect. It tried to deny POW status on the basis of the simplistic argument that these were cases that did not give rise to any 'doubts' regarding the true status of the captured combatants.

6. If a person who takes part in armed conflict does not fulfil the conditions for being a 'regular combatant', what is his or her status under the LOAC? Such persons are sometimes called 'irregular' or 'unlawful' combatants. We must, however, note that the LOAC Conventions do not explicitly make reference to such a status. According to the practice of the International Criminal Tribunal for the Former Yugoslavia (ICTY), such persons are not entitled to the benefit of the protections accorded by Geneva Convention III because they are not regular combatants. However, given that Geneva Conventions I–III and Geneva Convention IV were drafted to ensure that there were no gaps in the protections afforded, a person who does not fall within Geneva Conventions I–III thus automatically falls within Geneva Convention IV. Therefore, the tribunal held that irregular combatants were 'civilians' under Geneva Convention IV.[14] As such they are entitled to protection if they fulfil the conditions of Article 4 of Geneva

---

[14] *Prosecutor v Brdjanin* (Trial Judgment) IT-99-36-T (1 September 2004) para [125].

Convention IV. This is the solution that is favoured by the ICRC; it is the better solution.

However, some states have claimed that persons taking part in the fight could not be regarded as 'civilians' under Geneva Convention IV. In making this argument they placed reliance on the exception found in Article 5(1) of Geneva Convention IV, which reads:

> Where in the territory of a Party to the conflict, the latter is satisfied that an individual protected person is definitely suspected of or engaged in activities hostile to the security of the State, such individual person shall not be entitled to claim such rights and privileges under the present Convention as would, if exercised in the favour of such individual person, be prejudicial to the security of such State.

These states, including the United States, claim that 'irregular combatants' fall neither within the reach of Geneva Convention III nor within the reach of Geneva Convention IV. Only minimum guarantees apply to them. This means that it is necessary to explore the minimum standards for treatment of irregulars. First of all, human rights law guarantees apply. Secondly, some minimum guarantees under the LOAC—especially the minimum humane treatment and fair trial rights enshrined in Common Article 3 to the four Geneva Conventions and Article 75 of Protocol I—apply.[15] Article 5(3) of Geneva Convention IV restates these minimum rights:

> In each case, such persons shall nevertheless be treated with humanity and, in case of trial, shall not be deprived of the rights of fair and regular trial prescribed by the present Convention. They shall also be granted the full rights and privileges of a protected person under the present Convention at the earliest date consistent with the security of the State or Occupying Power, as the case may be.

This provision shows that any limitations placed on the protections given to captured combatants should be as temporary as possible and should never fall below the humanitarian minimum.

7. Finally, it must be stressed that these rules were developed for IAC and not for NIAC. Within NIAC, there is no clear definition of 'combatant'.[16] There is no regular combatant status, the possession of which gives rise to combatant immunity and the secondary status of POW. In NIAC governmental forces confront rebel armed groups. If captured, rebels may be treated as criminals; conversely, if rebels capture members of the armed forces, there are no rules of the LOAC that apply to their treatment. Thus, this is a matter which often gives rise to the conclusion of ad hoc special agreements, which attempt to give some legal status, often on the basis of reciprocity, to the respective captives.[17] The ICRC has often interceded between the parties to assist in the negotiation and conclusion of such agreements. It is clear, however, that wounded and sick 'combatants' on either side must be spared and cared for, within the limits of what is possible in the particular situation.[18]

---

[15] *Hamdan v Rumsfeld* (2006) 126 S Ct 2749.

[16] Additional Protocol II (1977), Art 13(3), uses the concept of 'direct participatin in hostilities' in the context of the principle of distinction between civilian and military objectives.

[17] See generally: ch 15 above.

[18] Geneva Conventions I–IV common Art 3 and Protocol Additional to the Geneva Conventions of 12 August 1949, and relating to the Protection of Victims of Non-International Armed Conflicts (adopted 8 June 1977, entered into force 7 December 1978) 1125 UNTS 609 Arts 7–12.

Comprehension check:

a) Who is considered to be a regular combatant under the LOAC?
b) What are the essential rights and privileges of the regular combatant?
c) What is the legal position of the so-called 'irregular combatant'; a person taking part in hostilities who would not be entitled to do so under the LOAC?
d) Are terrorists 'regular combatants'?

Answers:

a) Three categories of persons are considered to be regular combatants under the law of IAC: (1) ordinary members of the armed forces as well as militias incorporated into the armed forces, with the exception of chaplains and medical personnel; (2) Civilians taking part in a *levee en masse*; and (3) militias or resistance movements not formally incorporated into the armed forces of a belligerent, under certain conditions. The conditions of Article 4 of Geneva Convention III have been somewhat softened by Article 44 of Additional Protocol I, in order to take account of the spread of guerrilla warfare as a war tactic. Article 4 of Geneva Convention III requires a link to a party to the conflict, responsible command assuring military discipline, a fixed and distinctive sign visible at distance, the open carrying of arms and the conduct of the military operations in accordance with the LOAC. Protocol I maintains unaltered only the first two criteria. The necessity for a fixed sign disappears. Arms must be carried openly only during military engagement and deployment. The respect for the LOAC is no longer a condition for combatant status. It has always been a controversial question whether this new rule has hardened into customary international law. Taking into account recent states practice and *opinio juris*, this seems to be the case, even if some important states still dissent, in particular the United States.

b) There are two essential rights and privileges: (1) combatant immunity—the prohibition on the prosecution of the regular combatant for having taken up the arms and having participated in the conflict; and (2) POW status if captured by adverse armed forces. POW status assures the combatant of a series of rights and duties under Geneva Convention III.

c) These persons are to be considered as civilians despite having being irregular combatants. The consequence of this is that they can be prosecuted for having taken part in hostilities and they are not entitled to POW status. It is controversial whether irregular combatants are entitled to the protection of the whole of Geneva Convention IV, as civilians, or only to the humanitarian minimum as codified in Common Article 3 to Geneva Conventions I–IV and Article 75 of Additional Protocol I. The ICTY and the ICRC, as well as significant proportion of academic literature, is in favour of the first option. However, some states, for example the United States, and some authors suggest that only the minimum guarantees must be given. In any case, acts of torture, unfair trial, or other human rights violations would remain prohibited.

d) This question cannot be answered in the abstract, particularly as it is not clear if a person accused of being a 'terrorist' is really one or not. In almost all cases, 'terrorists' are not regular combatants. They do not take part in an IAC and they are unable to trigger such a conflict by their deeds. Hence, they remain ordinary criminals liable to criminal prosecution. The only exception is to be found in cases where persons accused of terrorism participate in an IAC, as was the case in Afghanistan in 2002, and are caught in that context while respecting the conditions required to obtain regular combatant status. In this case, they must be granted POW status. However, they can be prosecuted for 'terrorist' acts. There is thus no immunity for the POW with regard to crimes he may have committed. Even if convicted for a crime, such persons would retain their POW status. However, the privileges flowing from that status can be curtailed during the period of their sentence.

26

PROTECTION OF PRISONERS OF WAR

Learning objectives: To understand the essential protections that must be granted to prisoners of war.

1. Once members of the armed forces of belligerents, other lawful combatants and persons entitled by analogy to a prisoner of war status (religious and medical personnel) have been captured, [1] they enjoy a series of rights and are bound by a series of duties with respect to the belligerent power that detains them. These rights and duties are spelled out in detail in Geneva Convention III, much of which has obtained customary status.[2] The combination of the customary and conventional law provides 'an extremely detailed and comprehensive code for the treatment of POWs'.[3] It is impossible to go into full detail regarding the legal regime, but the main elements will be presented.

The general rules that concern the protection of detainees are to be found in Articles 12 to 16 of Geneva Convention III under the title 'General Protection of Prisoners of War'. They are motivated by the all pervading general principle of humanity and of humane treatment.[4] They cover what the Eritrea-Ethiopia Claims Commission has called the 'core' of the Geneva Convention III regime, 'the legal obligations to keep POWs alive and in good health'.[5] Articles 13 to 16 contain the most important general rules. Article 13 concerns the 'absolutely fundamental' duty of humane treatment[6]; Article 14 covers respect for the integrity of the person and their honour; Article 15 deals with the duty to maintain and provide medical care to the prisoners free of charge; and Article 16 concerns the duty to treat detainees equally, excepting well-founded distinctions such as rank, sex or professional qualifications. These articles are set out in full below, and repay full reading:

---

[1] Geneva Convention III relative to the Treatment of Prisoners of War (adopted 12 August 1949, entered into force 21 October 1950) 75 UNTS 135 (Geneva Convention III) Arts 4 and 33, see generally ch 25 above.

[2] *Prisoners of War—Eritrea's Claim 17* (*Eritrea v Ethiopia*) Eritrea-Ethiopia Claims Commission (1 July 2003), available at <http://www.pca-cpa.org/upload/files/ER17.pdf> accessed 15 May 2008 paras [39]–[41]; and see also *Prisoners of War—Ethiopia's Claim 4* (*Ethiopia v Eritrea*) Eritrea-Ethiopia Claims Commission (1 July 2003) at <http://www.pca-cpa.org/upload/files/ET04.pdf> accessed 15 May 2008 paras [30]–[32].

[3] *Eritrea's Claim 17, ibid*, para [54].

[4] See generally: ch 7 above.

[5] *Eritrea's Claim 17* para [55].

[6] *Ibid*, para [54].

Art 13. Prisoners of war must at all times be humanely treated. Any unlawful act or omission by the Detaining Power causing death or seriously endangering the health of a prisoner of war in its custody is prohibited, and will be regarded as a serious breach of the present Convention. In particular, no prisoner of war may be subjected to physical mutilation or to medical or scientific experiments of any kind which are not justified by the medical, dental or hospital treatment of the prisoner concerned and carried out in his interest.

Likewise, prisoners of war must at all times be protected, particularly against acts of violence or intimidation and against insults and public curiosity.

Measures of reprisal against prisoners of war are prohibited.

Art 14. Prisoners of war are entitled in all circumstances to respect for their persons and their honour.

Women shall be treated with all the regard due to their sex and shall in all cases benefit by treatment as favourable as that granted to men.

Prisoners of war shall retain the full civil capacity which they enjoyed at the time of their capture. The Detaining Power may not restrict the exercise, either within or without its own territory, of the rights such capacity confers except in so far as the captivity requires.

Art 15. The Power detaining prisoners of war shall be bound to provide free of charge for their maintenance and for the medical attention required by their state of health.

Art 16. Taking into consideration the provisions of the present Convention relating to rank and sex, and subject to any privileged treatment which may be accorded to them by reason of their state of health, age or professional qualifications, all prisoners of war shall be treated alike by the Detaining Power, without any adverse distinction based on race, nationality, religious belief or political opinions, or any other distinction founded on similar criteria.

These provisions, which illustrate the prime concerns of the Geneva Convention scheme, constitute a sort of mini-code for the protection of prisoners of war.

2. However, the Convention contains a series of more detailed provisions covering the following activities or situations:

a) *Rules as to the beginning of captivity.* These deal with matters such as the legitimate extent of questioning and interrogation of prisoners of war and their evacuation from the zone of combat. Article 17 is the most important provision. It stipulates that the military authorities of the detaining power can question the prisoner, but that he or she is only obliged to respond to certain points.[7] Further questions may obviously be asked, but the prisoner is free to refuse to answer. However, the detaining power is prohibited from using force or threats of force to make a detainee respond to any questions, whether or not the detainee is obliged to answer. If the prisoner refuses to answer those questions to which he or she is in principle required to respond,[8] no sanctions

---

[7] *Ibid*, para [70].
[8] Surname, first names, rank, date of birth and serial number, Geneva Convention III Art 17.

can be enforced against him or her. However, he or she may then suffer from a restriction of privileges accorded to his or her rank and status, because they will remain unknown as he or she has failed to answer questions regarding these. It must be stressed that a prisoner of war suspected to have committed either a war crime or a common crime for which he or she does not possess combatant immunity can be subjected to criminal prosecution.[9] Article 17 is not applicable to such criminal proceedings. However, if a prisoner persistently refuses to cooperate in the criminal proceedings, he or she cannot be forced to change his or her stance since torture and physical pressure, or threat of such, are prohibited. The prohibition of torture is not only applicable to prisoners of war, but also exists under general human rights law.[10] Article 17 is reproduced below:

> Art 17. Every prisoner of war, when questioned on the subject, is bound to give only his surname, first names and rank, date of birth, and army, regimental, personal or serial number, or failing this, equivalent information.
>
> If he wilfully infringes this rule, he may render himself liable to a restriction of the privileges accorded to his rank or status.
>
> Each Party to a conflict is required to furnish the persons under its jurisdiction who are liable to become prisoners of war, with an identity card showing the owner's surname, first names, rank, army, regimental, personal or serial number or equivalent information, and date of birth. The identity card may, furthermore, bear the signature or the fingerprints, or both, of the owner, and may bear, as well, any other information the Party to the conflict may wish to add concerning persons belonging to its armed forces. As far as possible the card shall measure 6.5 x 10 cm. and shall be issued in duplicate. The identity card shall be shown by the prisoner of war upon demand, but may in no case be taken away from him.
>
> No physical or mental torture, nor any other form of coercion, may be inflicted on prisoners of war to secure from them information of any kind whatever. Prisoners of war who refuse to answer may not be threatened, insulted, or exposed to unpleasant or disadvantageous treatment of any kind.
>
> Prisoners of war who, owing to their physical or mental condition, are unable to state their identity, shall be handed over to the medical service. The identity of such prisoners shall be established by all possible means, subject to the provisions of the preceding paragraph.
>
> The questioning of prisoners of war shall be carried out in a language which they understand.

The rules as to evacuation of prisoners of war from the combat area are in Articles 19 and 20 of Geneva Convention III.[11] The material parts of these articles read as follows:

---

[9] *US v Noriega* (1997) 99 ILR 143, 167–171.

[10] See, eg: Convention against Torture and Other Cruel, Inhuman or Degrading Treatment or Punishment (adopted 10 December 1984, entered into force 26 June 1987) 1465 UNTS 85.

[11] See generally *Eritrea's Claim 17* paras [66]–[69] and *Ethiopia's Claim 4* paras [71]–[74].

Art 19. Prisoners of war shall be evacuated, as soon as possible after their capture, to camps situated in an area far enough from the combat zone for them to be out of danger.

Only those prisoners of war who, owing to wounds or sickness, would run greater risks by being evacuated than by remaining where they are, may be temporarily kept back in a danger zone.

Prisoners of war shall not be unnecessarily exposed to danger while awaiting evacuation from a fighting zone.

Art 20. The evacuation of prisoners of war shall always be effected humanely and in conditions similar to those for the forces of the Detaining Power in their changes of station.

b) *Rules as to the internment of prisoners of war.* The rules concerning the conditions of detention of prisoners of war are to be found in Articles 21–48 of Geneva Convention III. These rules are, in the main, also rules of customary international law.[12] They touch upon such questions as: security; quarters; food and clothing;[13] hygiene and medical attention;[14] religious, intellectual and physical activities; discipline; respect due to the rank of prisoners of war; and transfer of prisoners of war after their arrival in camp.[15] By way of example, Article 29 of Geneva Convention III, which contains obligations relating to hygiene in prisoner of war camps, is set out below:

Art 29. The Detaining Power shall be bound to take all sanitary measures necessary to ensure the cleanliness and healthfulness of camps and to prevent epidemics.

Prisoners of war shall have for their use, day and night, conveniences which conform to the rules of hygiene and are maintained in a constant state of cleanliness. In any camps in which women prisoners of war are accommodated, separate conveniences shall be provided for them.

Also, apart from the baths and showers with which the camps shall be furnished prisoners of war shall be provided with sufficient water and soap for their personal toilet and for washing their personal laundry; the necessary installations, facilities and time shall be granted them for that purpose.

Article 30 deals with medical attention and provides as follows:

Art 30. Every camp shall have an adequate infirmary where prisoners of war may have the attention they require, as well as appropriate diet. Isolation wards shall, if necessary, be set aside for cases of contagious or mental disease.

Prisoners of war suffering from serious disease, or whose condition necessitates special treatment, a surgical operation or hospital care, must be admitted to any military or civilian medical unit where such treatment can be given, even if their repatriation is contemplated in the near future. Special facilities

---

[12] *Eritrea's Claim 17*, n 2, para [87].
[13] On food: *Eritrea's Claim 17*, n 2, paras [106]–[114].
[14] On the standard of medical care required in camps: *Eritrea's Claim 17*, n 2, paras [115]–[138].
[15] See generally *Ethiopia's Claim 4*, n 2, paras [135]–[138].

shall be afforded for the care to be given to the disabled, in particular to the blind, and for their. rehabilitation, pending repatriation.

Prisoners of war shall have the attention, preferably, of medical personnel of the Power on which they depend and, if possible, of their nationality.

Prisoners of war may not be prevented from presenting themselves to the medical authorities for examination. The detaining authorities shall, upon request, issue to every prisoner who has undergone treatment, an official certificate indicating the nature of his illness or injury, and the duration and kind of treatment received. A duplicate of this certificate shall be forwarded to the Central Prisoners of War Agency.

The costs of treatment, including those of any apparatus necessary for the maintenance of prisoners of war in good health, particularly dentures and other artificial appliances, and spectacles, shall be borne by the Detaining Power.

c) *Rules on labour of prisoners of war.* In Articles 49–57, the Convention seeks to prohibit certain forms of labour, in particular work that is either dangerous or humiliating. It also attempts to secure proper working conditions, such as maximum duration of working hours per day, minimum rates of payment for work undertaken, response to occupational incidents and allocation to labour detachments.[16] The general rule is set out in Article 49:

The Detaining Power may utilize the labour of prisoners of war who are physically fit, taking into account their age, sex, rank and physical aptitude, and with a view particularly to maintaining them in a good state of physical and mental health.

Non-commissioned officers who are prisoners of war shall only be required to do supervisory work. Those not so required may ask for other suitable work which shall, so far as possible, be found for them.

If officers or persons of equivalent status ask for suitable work, it shall be found for them, so far as possible, but they may in no circumstances be compelled to work.

Types of work explicitly authorised can be found in Article 50(1):

Besides work connected with camp administration, installation or maintenance, prisoners of war may be compelled to do only such work as is included in the following classes:

(a) agriculture;
(b) industries connected with the production or the extraction of raw materials, and manufacturing industries, with the exception of metallurgical, machinery and chemical industries; public works and building operations which have no military character or purpose;
(c) transport and handling of stores which are not military in character or purpose;

---

[16] See generally *Ethiopia's Claim 4*, n 2, paras [126]–[134]. Labour undertaken in breach of these conditions will be unlawful, even if it is of a type that is explicitly authorised in Art 50(1): *Prosecutor v Naletelic and Martinovic* (Trial Judgment) IT-98-34-T (31 March 2003) para [323].

    (d) commercial business, and arts and crafts;

    (e) domestic service;

    (f) public utility services having no military character or purpose.[17]

Article 52 concerns prohibited labour:

> Unless he be a volunteer, no prisoner of war may be employed on labour which is of an unhealthy or dangerous nature.

> No prisoner of war shall be assigned to labour which would be looked upon as humiliating for a member of the Detaining Power's own forces.

> The removal of mines or similar devices shall be considered as dangerous labour.

d) *Rules on financial resources of prisoners of war.* Articles 58–68 of Geneva Convention III deal with the financial resources of detained prisoners of war. The norms contained in these articles concern the income of prisoners and how they possess monetary resources. The objective is to allow prisoners to purchase the services or commodities they need whilst in detention. Apart from some restrictions aiming at avoidance of excessive inequalities among prisoners, which, of course, have the potential to lead to frictions, the detaining power must accept payment of sums of money to the prisoners, even if the payment emanates from an opposing belligerent power. These payments are in addition to the sums that the detaining power is required to provide to the prisoners under the conventions. Article 61 thus reads:

> The Detaining Power shall accept for distribution as supplementary pay to prisoners of war sums which the Power on which the prisoners depend may forward to them, on condition that the sums to be paid shall be the same for each prisoner of the same category, shall be payable to all prisoners of that category depending on that Power, and shall be placed in their separate accounts, at the earliest opportunity, in accordance with the provisions of Article 64. Such supplementary pay shall not relieve the Detaining Power of any obligation under this Convention.[18]

e) *Rules on the relations of the prisoners of war with the exterior.* Articles 69–77 of the Convention cover various aspects of the relations of POWs with the world outside the camp. They touch upon questions such as the sending of a capture card to the family of the prisoner,[19] correspondence[20] and exemptions from postal charges.[21] Perhaps the most important set of provisions relates to the relief shipments, which played a vital role during World War II. Article 72 thus reads as follows:

> Prisoners of war shall be allowed to receive by post or by any other means individual parcels or collective shipments containing, in particular, foodstuffs, clothing, medical supplies and articles of a religious, educational or

---

[17] The building of roads is presumed to fall within this category unless a military purpose can be shown, *Ethiopia's Claim 4*, n 2, para [133].

[18] Geneva Convention III Art 61.

[19] *Ibid*, Art 70.

[20] *Ibid*, Art 71.

[21] *Ibid*, Art 74.

recreational character which may meet their needs, including books, devotional articles, scientific equipment, examination papers, musical instruments, sports outfits and materials allowing prisoners of war to pursue their studies or their cultural activities.

Such shipments shall in no way free the Detaining Power from the obligations imposed upon it by virtue of the present Convention.

The only limits which may be placed on these shipments shall be those proposed by the Protecting Power in the interest of the prisoners themselves, or by the International Committee of the Red Cross or any other organization giving assistance to the prisoners, in respect of their own shipments only, on account of exceptional strain on transport or communications.

The conditions for the sending of individual parcels and collective relief shall, if necessary, be the subject of special agreements between the Powers concerned, which may in no case delay the receipt by the prisoners of relief supplies. Books may not be included in parcels of clothing and foodstuffs. Medical supplies shall, as a rule, be sent in collective parcels.

f) *Rules on relations between prisoners of war and the authorities.* Articles 78–108 concern the treatment of complaints and requests by prisoners of war[22]; the representation of prisoners in their dealings with the detaining power; and the penal and disciplinary sanctions that may be imposed on prisoners. Article 79(1) deals with the representatives of the prisoners of war. It reads as follows:

> In all places where there are prisoners of war, except in those where there are officers, the prisoners shall freely elect by secret ballot, every six months, and also in case of vacancies, prisoners' representatives entrusted with representing them before the military authorities, the Protecting Powers, the International Committee of the Red Cross and any other organization which may assist them. These prisoners' representatives shall be eligible for re-election.

An important part of the Convention is devoted to the penal and disciplinary sanctions. Prisoners of war may be prosecuted for war crimes or other common crimes under the legislation of the detaining power[23]; however, such trials must follow due process of law and must conform to the fair trial guarantees found in the Convention.[24] Even if convicted, the prisoner of war retains the status and rights granted to him or her by Geneva Convention III.[25] Special restrictions are put upon the death penalty.[26] One must distinguish those sanctions imposed for breaches of the disciplinary regulations applicable to the camp or for attempts to escape from criminal sanctions for conduct in breach of either international law or the criminal law applicable to the armed forces of the detaining power. This section of the Convention is too detailed to be quoted in detail here. It should be read in full. However, it is worthwhile setting out one of the provisions of paramount importance,

---

[22] *Ethiopia's Claim 4*, n 2, paras [147]–[150].
[23] Geneva Convention III Art 82.
[24] Geneva Convention III Arts 86 and 99*ff*.
[25] Geneva Convention III Art 85 and *US v Noriega*, n 9.
[26] Geneva Convention III Arts 100–101.

Article 105, which spells out the guarantees of fair trial in the context of a proper criminal defence:

> The prisoner of war shall be entitled to assistance by one of his prisoner comrades, to defence by a qualified advocate or counsel of his own choice, to the calling of witnesses and, if he deems necessary, to the services of a competent interpreter. He shall be advised of these rights by the Detaining Power in due time before the trial.
>
> Failing a choice by the prisoner of war, the Protecting Power shall find him an advocate or counsel, and shall have at least one week at its disposal for the purpose. The Detaining Power shall deliver to the said Power, on request, a list of persons qualified to present the defence. Failing a choice of an advocate or counsel by the prisoner of war or the Protecting Power, the Detaining Power shall appoint a competent advocate or counsel to conduct the defence.
>
> The advocate or counsel conducting the defence on behalf of the prisoner of war shall have at his disposal a period of two weeks at least before the opening of the trial, as well as the necessary facilities to prepare the defence of the accused. He may, in particular, freely visit the accused and interview him in private. He may also confer with any witnesses for the defence, including prisoners of war. He shall have the benefit of these facilities until the term of appeal or petition has expired.
>
> Particulars of the charge or charges on which the prisoner of war is to be arraigned, as well as the documents which are generally communicated to the accused by virtue of the laws in force in the armed forces of the Detaining Power, shall be communicated to the accused prisoner of war in a language which he understands, and in good time before the opening of the trial. The same communication in the same circumstances shall be made to the advocate or counsel conducting the defence on behalf of the prisoner of war.
>
> The representatives of the Protecting Power shall be entitled to attend the trial of the case, unless, exceptionally, this is held in camera in the interest of State security. In such a case the Detaining Power shall advise the Protecting Power accordingly.

g) *Rules as to the termination of captivity.* Articles 109–121 contain norms that govern the end of the relationship between the detaining power and the detainee. These rules cover the possibility of internment of prisoners in a neutral country, if an agreement can be reached between the detaining power and a neutral country[27]; the repatriation of seriously wounded or sick prisoners during the continuing hostilities, it being understood that such prisoners will no longer be able to participate in the armed conflict[28]; the repatriation of prisoners at the general close of hostilities[29]; and the end of captivity by the death of a prisoner of war.[30] The question of repatriation after the general close of hostilities has often given rise to problems. First, it has often happened that prisoners have not been released for some time after

---

[27] *Ibid*, Art 111.
[28] *Ibid*, Arts 109*ff*.
[29] Geneva Convention III Arts 118–119 and see generally *Eritrea's Claim 17*, n 2, paras [143]–[163].
[30] Geneva Convention III Arts 120–121 and see generally *Ethiopia's Claim 4*, n 2, paras [139]–[141].

the end of the conflict, on the basis of a number of different, and often overlapping, arguments such as the pretext of continuation of 'working contracts'; non-termination of the armed conflict by or against a co-belligerent; or the absence of a formalised peace treaty. Article 118 was drafted in mandatory terms to prevent such procrastination and to require immediate release of the prisoners at the end of active hostilities. The objective in 1949 of the drafters of Geneva Convention III was to avoid all of those dilatory pretexts for delaying the liberation of the prisoners at the end of the hostilities. The objective of the prompt release of prisoners in all cases has not been achieved in practice. An important question arises as to the temporal situation of the 'general close of hostilities'. It would seem, taking a literal approach, that the cessation of fighting brought about by a general armistice is enough to trigger the application of Article 118.[31] However, in this case some marginal fighting may still occur. Further, the Eritrea-Ethiopia Claims Commission has commented that:

> [A]s a practical matter, and as indicated by state practice, any state that has not been totally defeated is unlikely to release all the POWs it holds without assurance that its own personnel held by its enemy will also be released, and it is unreasonable to expect otherwise.[32]

Secondly, there is the potential for a situation to arise where certain prisoners do not want to be sent back to their home state. This situation especially arose during the Korean War. In such cases, detainees professed fear of persecution by the regime in power in the state for which they fight. Since this point, international practice has modified the application of Article 118: it is no longer an imperative duty, owed to the adverse belligerent, to send the prisoner back to his or her home state. The primacy of this principle has been displaced by the controlling norm that a prisoner shall not be sent back to his or her home state (or to any other state) contrary to his or her will. The ICRC will individually interview the detainees prior to their return and try to find out their non-coerced will. The modified norm thus provides that the POWs will be repatriated 'without delay after the cessation of active hostilities', provided that they do not express a freely held wish to remain in the territory of the detaining power or to be sent to the territory of a third state. Thus, a series of Iraqi prisoners were not sent back to Iraq after the Gulf War (1991), because they feared persecution by Saddam Hussein's regime.

The key provision governing end-of-hostilities repatriation is to be found in Article 118, which is set out below, modified by practice to the extent previously explained:

> Prisoners of war shall be released and repatriated without delay after the cessation of active hostilities.

> In the absence of stipulations to the above effect in any agreement concluded between the Parties to the conflict with a view to the cessation of hostilities, or failing any such agreement, each of the Detaining Powers shall itself establish

---

[31] See generally: ch 14 above.
[32] *Eritrea's Claim 17*, n 2, para [148] (footnote omitted).

and execute without delay a plan of repatriation in conformity with the principle laid down in the foregoing paragraph.

In either case, the measures adopted shall be brought to the knowledge of the prisoners of war.

The costs of repatriation of prisoners of war shall in all cases be equitably apportioned between the Detaining Power and the Power on which the prisoners depend. This apportionment shall be carried out on the following basis:

(a) If the two Powers are contiguous, the Power on which the prisoners of war depend shall bear the costs of repatriation from the frontiers of the Detaining Power.
(b) If the two Powers are not contiguous, the Detaining Power shall bear the costs of transport of prisoners of war over its own territory as far as its frontier or its port of embarkation nearest to the territory of the Power on which the prisoners of war depend. The Parties concerned shall agree between themselves as to the equitable apportionment of the remaining costs of the repatriation. The conclusion of this agreement shall in no circumstances justify any delay in the repatriation of the prisoners of war.

The relevant provision setting out the procedure in case of death of a prisoner of war is spelled out in Articles 120 and 121[33]:

Art 120. Wills of prisoners of war shall be drawn up so as to satisfy the conditions of validity required by the legislation of their country of origin, which will take steps to inform the Detaining Power of its requirements in this respect. At the request of the prisoner of war and, in all cases, after death, the will shall be transmitted without delay to the Protecting Power; a certified copy shall be sent to the Central Agency.

Death certificates, in the form annexed to the present Convention, or lists certified by a responsible officer, of all persons who die as prisoners of war shall be forwarded as rapidly as possible to the Prisoner of War Information Bureau established in accordance with Article 122. The death certificates or certified lists shall show particulars of identity as set out in the third paragraph of Article 17, and also the date and place of death, the cause of death, the date and place of burial and all particulars necessary to identify the graves.

The burial or cremation of a prisoner of war shall be preceded by a medical examination of the body with a view to confirming death and enabling a report to be made and, where necessary, establishing identity.

The detaining authorities shall ensure that prisoners of war who have died in captivity are honourably buried, if possible according to the rites of the religion to which they belonged, and that their graves are respected, suitably maintained and marked so as to be found at any time. Wherever possible, deceased prisoners of war who depended on the same Power shall be interred in the same place.

Deceased prisoners of war shall be buried in individual graves unless unavoidable circumstances require the use of collective graves. Bodies may be cremated only for imperative reasons of hygiene, on account of the religion of the

---

[33] See generally: *Ethiopia's Claim 4*, n 2, paras [139]–[141]. These norms are customary.

deceased or in accordance with his express wish to this effect. In case of cremation, the fact shall be stated and the reasons given in the death certificate of the deceased.

In order that graves may always be found, all particulars of burials and graves shall be recorded with a Graves Registration Service established by the Detaining Power. Lists of graves and particulars of the prisoners of war interred in cemeteries and elsewhere shall be transmitted to the Power on which such prisoners of war depended. Responsibility for the care of these graves and for records of any subsequent moves of the bodies shall rest on the Power controlling the territory, if a Party to the present Convention. These provisions shall also apply to the ashes, which shall be kept by the Graves Registration Service until proper disposal thereof in accordance with the wishes of the home country.

Art 121. Every death or serious injury of a prisoner of war caused or suspected to have been caused by a sentry, another prisoner of war, or any other person, as well as any death the cause of which is unknown, shall be immediately followed by an official enquiry by the Detaining Power.

A communication on this subject shall be sent immediately to the Protecting Power. Statements shall be taken from witnesses, especially from those who are prisoners of war, and a report including such statements shall be forwarded to the Protecting Power.

If the enquiry indicates the guilt of one or more persons, the Detaining Power shall take all measures for the prosecution of the person or persons responsible.

Comprehension check:

a) What are the main protections afforded to a prisoner of war?
b) If a prisoner of war dies, what is the procedure to be followed?
c) If a prisoner of war is handed over to a third state (eg a neutral state), does he or she keep his or her status as prisoner of war or does he or she lose it? (The answer to this question does not figure in the text of this chapter, but may be discovered from a reading of Geneva Convention III.)

Answers:

a) The main guarantees provided to POWs are presented in Articles 12–16 of Geneva Convention III and relate to the basic requirements of humane treatment. Other specific guarantees relate to food, clothing, medical supplies, intellectual and physical activities, treatment equivalent to the rank, labour conditions, disposal of financial resources, relations with the exterior, including with the power of origin or the family of the POW, election of representatives, fair trial rights and rights with respect to repatriation or end of captivity by other means. Geneva Convention III therefore represents a code of rights and duties for the POW.
b) The procedure to be followed in the case of the death of a POW whilst in captivity is spelled out in Articles 120–121 of Geneva Convention III, which are quoted above. As can be seen, the Convention attempts to secure that no

suspect deaths occur. First, it requires the completion of a detailed death certificate, which is set out in the annex of the Convention. This certificate contains many details as to the cause of death, personal effects, caring personnel having had direct contact with the prisoner during the last stage of their life, place of burial, etc. Secondly, it mandates an official inquiry in cases of 'suspect' death.

c) This aspect of the protection afforded to POWs has not been discussed in the text above, but an answer is still possible. It must, of course, be sought in Geneva Convention III. The provision dealing with this aspect is situated in the area of the Convention that deals with the general protections afforded to POWs under the marginal title 'Responsibility for the treatment of prisoners'. Article 12(2) provides that:

> Prisoners of war may only be transferred by the Detaining Power to a Power which is a party to the Convention and after the Detaining Power has satisfied itself of the willingness and ability of such transferee Power to apply the Convention. When prisoners of war are transferred under such circumstances, responsibility for the application of the Convention rests on the Power accepting them while they are in its custody.

The rule is thus: once prisoner of war, always prisoner of war, until the final repatriation or death.[34] This rule is motivated by a desire to prevent evasion or circumvention of the protections contained in Geneva Convention III. The guarantees contained in the Convention would be of little value if they could be rendered naught by the mere act of transferring the prisoners from the detaining power to another power.

---

[34] See also: *US v Noriega* (Order Dismissing Defendant's 'Petition for Writ of Habeas Corpus Pursuant to 28 USC § 2241' and Order Lifting Stay of Extradition) (7 September 2007) US District Court, Southern District of Florida, available at <http://www.flsd.uscourts.gov/viewer/viewer.asp?file=/cases/pressDocs/188cr00079_1720.pdf> accessed 15 May 2008.

27

GENERAL PROTECTION OF CIVILIANS

Learning objectives: To discover how the rights of civilian non-combatants are protected in the modern LOAC.

1. Prior to the drafting of Geneva Convention IV in 1949,[1] civilians were subject to only very limited protection under the LOAC. They were the object of a general immunity from attack[2] and possessed certain rights in the context of belligerent occupation of territory.[3] However, if further protection from the exigencies of armed conflict was extended to civilians, it was due to humanitarian initiatives on the part of the International Committee of the Red Cross (ICRC). As an example, one may refer to the enormous relief operations conducted by the ICRC, in cooperation with the Swedish Red Cross, in 1942 and 1943, designed to relieve the suffering of the starving civilian population in occupied Greece. Following the adoption of Geneva Convention IV regarding the protection of the civilian population in times of war, the level of protection afforded to civilians greatly increased.

2. Civilians need protection in wartime in two different situations:

   a) *Civilians as protected persons.* Civilians caught up in armed conflict need protection if they fall into the hands of 'enemy forces'. These enemy armed forces could, for example, arrest them, ill-treat them, harass them, confiscate their property or not provide them with food or medical supplies. These situations exist not when the civilian is exposed to active armed conflict, but when armed forces come into contact with civilians who owe allegiance to the 'enemy' outside the context of ongoing hostilities. This usually happens outside active 'war zones'. The aim of the law in these cases is to protect civilians from arbitrary acts by the opposing forces under whose control they find themselves. This control may flow mainly from the presence of a civilian on the territory of an adverse belligerent or within territory occupied by an

---

[1] Geneva Convention IV Relative to the Protection of Civilian Persons in Time of War (adopted 12 August 1949, entered into force 21 October 1950) 75 UNTS 287 (Geneva Convention IV).

[2] Regulations concerning the Laws and Customs of War on Land annexed to Hague Convention (IV) respecting the Laws and Customs of War on Land (adopted 18 October 1907, entered into force 26 January 1910) (1907) 205 CTS 227 (Hague Regulations) Art 25.

[3] Hague Regulations Arts 47*ff*. See generally: ch 28 below.

adverse belligerent. Geneva Convention IV aims to provide protection for civilians in these situations.[4]

b) *Civilians as targets during warfare.* Civilians also need protection during the active phase of warfare. Whilst they are not directly in the hands or under the control of the enemy, they may face bomb attacks on their towns or have excessive damage inflicted upon them by attacks that fail to have sufficient regard to the collateral damage caused to civilians by such attacks. The rules that attempt to protect civilians against the effect of active hostilities are mainly contained in the Hague Regulations[5] and in Additional Protocol I.[6]

3. The scope of applicability of Geneva Convention IV is defined in Article 4. This important provision reads as follows:

> Persons protected by the Convention are those who, at a given moment and in any manner whatsoever, find themselves, in case of a conflict or occupation, in the hands of a Party to the conflict or Occupying Power of which they are not nationals.

> Nationals of a State which is not bound by the Convention are not protected by it. Nationals of a neutral State who find themselves in the territory of a belligerent State, and nationals of a co-belligerent State, shall not be regarded as protected persons while the State of which they are nationals has normal diplomatic representation in the State in whose hands they are.[7]

It is useful to explore the personal applicability of the protections granted to civilians by the convention. Who do they usually protect? Geneva Convention IV ordinarily applies to 'enemy civilians' because they are thought to be in need of protection on account of their adverse allegiance, and due to the fact that they cannot be protected by the normal mechanism of diplomatic representation as these ties are severed on account of the situation of armed conflict between the belligerents. Enemy civilians, considered from the standpoint of a particular belligerent, are those having the nationality of, or owing allegiance to, an adverse belligerent. Geneva Convention IV governs the relations of such enemy civilians with the belligerent opposed to the state to which they owe allegiance, in cases where that opposed belligerent exercises control over them.

Whilst such civilians were contemplated to be the beneficiaries of protection under Geneva Convention IV when it was drafted, state practice has extended the protections to 'stateless persons'. These people do not have the benefit of diplomatic protection from any state. They will have the benefit of the protections granted by Geneva Convention IV if they were established, or living permanently, in the territory of a belligerent that is opposed to the belligerent whose control they are subject to. That belligerent state in whose power they find themselves may then consider such persons hostile, despite them not owing nationality-allegiance to any state, and they therefore require protection against any arbitrary actions that may be taken against them.

---

[4] For civilians in territory subject to belligerent occupation, see also ch 28 below.

[5] See, eg: Hague Regulations Art 25.

[6] Protocol Additional to the Geneva Conventions of 12 August 1949, and relating to the Protection of Victims of International Armed Conflicts (adopted 8 June 1977, entered into force 7 December 1978) 1125 UNTS 3 Arts 48*ff*. These rules are discussed in more detail in ch 17 concerning targeting above.

[7] Geneva Convention IV Art 4.

Finally, Geneva Convention IV covers civilians of third states if they no longer enjoy the diplomatic protection of their home state and thus find themselves in need of a guarantee against arbitrary acts by a state that has them in its power.

Generally, Geneva Convention IV does not protect civilians of one belligerent, in relations to the actions of that same belligerent. It grants no protection against the acts of a civilian's own national state. However, Part II of Geneva Convention IV[8] is an exception to this general rule. This part applies to all civilians on the territories of the belligerents[9] and deals with general protection of civilians against certain consequences of war, through mechanisms such as the establishment of safety and hospital zones for refuge,[10] the establishment and protected status of civilian hospitals[11] and the protection of vehicles and aircraft carrying the wounded and sick.[12]

4. Article 4 of Geneva Convention IV contains, either explicitly or implicitly, three further important elements that delineate its scope of application.

a)   *Civilian*: the term 'civilian' has been given a wide and generous definition in practice. This aims to increase to the maximum extent the breadth of humanitarian protection granted by the LOAC in this area. The term 'civilian' covers all non-combatant persons, roughly speaking all those who are not members of the armed forces. In circumstances where civilians take part in armed conflict as irregulars, who illegally take up arms, they should be considered as civilians during the time that they do not actively participate in the armed conflict as 'irregular combatants'.[13] In any event, in cases where there is doubt as to the civilian or non-civilian status of a person, the person should be presumed to be a civilian.

b)   *'In the hands of'*: the International Criminal Tribunal for the former Yugoslavia (ICTY) has interpreted this notion very widely. All persons in an area controlled by the adverse belligerent are said to be in the hands of that adverse belligerent. Therefore, the rights and duties set out in Geneva Convention IV cover not only persons under arrest, but also all of the persons finding themselves in an occupied territory.[14]

c)   *'Of which they are not nationals'*: The requirement that civilians have a separate nationality from the state into whose hands they fall has been loosely interpreted. It covers not only 'enemy civilians' in the strict sense, but also: stateless persons; persons from neutral states without diplomatic protection; and those persons whose effective allegiance, if not nationality, lies with the adverse belligerent and who find themselves in the hands of the opposed belligerent, even if there is no difference of nationality between the civilian and the belligerent who has them in its power. The ICTY has made

---

[8] Geneva Convention IV Arts 13–26.

[9] Geneva Convention IV Art 13.

[10] Geneva Convention IV Arts 14–15.

[11] Geneva Convention IV Articles 18-20.

[12] Geneva Convention IV Arts 21–22.

[13] *Prosecutor v Brdjanin* (Trial Judgment) IT-99-36-T (1 September 2004) para [125]. See generally: ch 25 above.

[14] *Prosecutor v Tadic* (Trial Judgment) IT-49-1-T (7 May 1997) para [579]; and *Prosecutor v Delalic* (Trial Judgment) IT-96-21-T (16 November 1998) para [246].

clear that this is the case in decisions concerning the protection of civilians during the Yugoslav Wars of dissolution, and particularly the conflict in Bosnia. There, persons found themselves detainees in camps set up and run by the adverse forces, either Bosno-Serb or Bosno-Croat-Muslim, despite their nationality being formally the same as those detaining them (Bosnian). As the armed conflict was considered to be an international armed conflict, the ICTY applied Geneva Convention IV by utilising the criterion of 'allegiance' to an adverse party to the conflict, or non-allegiance to the detaining party, as the qualifying condition for the application of the protections contained in Geneva Convention IV instead of the clearly inapplicable 'nationality'. The protection of Geneva Convention IV was thereby extended to captives on the opposite side of the conflict in Bosnia to the forces by whom they were held, despite the fact that their nationality did not differ from that of the detaining forces.[15]

5. The substantive rules governing the protection of civilians under Geneva Convention IV are tripartite.

   a) First, Geneva Convention IV contains some *general rules* that either apply generally to all protected persons, without distinction of nationality,[16] or in particular to the protected persons as defined by Article 4, being enemy civilians; stateless persons; persons from neutral states without diplomatic protection; and those persons whose effective allegiance, if not nationality, lies with the adverse belligerent.[17] The rules applying to all civilians concern essentially refuge zones, evacuations and medical care.[18] The rules applying in particular to those protected persons defined in Article 4 essentially concern guarantees of humane treatment, for example, freedom from harassment, torture and arbitrary measures.[19]

   b) Secondly, the Convention contains rules applying to enemy *civilians (and other protected aliens) who find themselves in the territory of a party to the conflict*.[20] Two questions are important in this context: the right of such persons to leave the hostile territory;[21] and the question of their internment.[22]

   c) Thirdly, the Geneva Convention includes rules that govern the situation of *civilians finding themselves in occupied territory*.[23] These rules will be discussed in a separate chapter.[24]

Geneva Convention IV thus aims to provide a complete code protecting civilians in their direct relations with enemy forces during armed conflict. In order to prevent the

---

[15] *Prosecutor v Tadic* (Appeal Judgment) IT-49-1-A (15 July 1999) paras [163]–[171]; and *Delalic*, n 14, paras [247]–[266].

[16] Geneva Convention IV Arts 13–26.

[17] Geneva Convention IV Arts 27–34.

[18] Geneva Convention IV Arts 13–26 and text to n 8 above.

[19] See, eg: Geneva Convention IV Art 27.

[20] Geneva Convention IV Arts 35–46.

[21] Geneva Convention IV Arts 35–6.

[22] See especially: Geneva Convention IV Arts 41–3 and 79–135.

[23] Geneva Convention IV Arts 47–78.

[24] See generally: ch 28 below.

loopholes it provides, as already pointed out: (1) some general rules providing protection to all; (2) rules that deal with the situation of those who are on the territory of an adverse belligerent; and (3) rules that regulate the condition of those who are in territory that at the beginning of armed conflict belongs to the state to whom they owe allegiance, but during the struggle is occupied by an adverse belligerent.

6. The general rules contained in Part III, Section I of Geneva Convention IV apply to all those who are protected persons within Article 4, whether they are in the territory of an adverse belligerent or in occupied territory. These fundamental common rules add flesh to the general duty to comply with the principle of humanity during contact with civilians. To illustrate, we may quote Articles 27, 33 and 34:

> **Art. 27**. Protected persons are entitled, in all circumstances, to respect for their persons, their honour, their family rights, their religious convictions and practices, and their manners and customs. They shall at all times be humanely treated, and shall be protected especially against all acts of violence or threats thereof and against insults and public curiosity.
>
> Women shall be especially protected against any attack on their honour, in particular against rape, enforced prostitution, or any form of indecent assault.
>
> Without prejudice to the provisions relating to their state of health, age and sex, all protected persons shall be treated with the same consideration by the Party to the conflict in whose power they are, without any adverse distinction based, in particular, on race, religion or political opinion.
>
> **Art. 33**. No protected person may be punished for an offence he or she has not personally committed. Collective penalties and likewise all measures of intimidation or of terrorism are prohibited.
>
> Pillage is prohibited.
>
> Reprisals against protected persons and their property are prohibited.
>
> **Art. 34**. The taking of hostages is prohibited.

7. The next section of Geneva Convention IV is devoted to *alien civilians on the territory of a belligerent*.[25] At the beginning of the hostilities, some civilians living abroad will become 'enemy civilians' with respect of the state on whose territory they find themselves. Geneva Convention IV attempts to give them protection, particularly in two important areas.

First, Article 35 stipulates that all protected persons who desire to leave the territory at the outset of, or during, the conflict are entitled to do so, unless their departure is contrary to the national interest of the state on whose territory they find themselves.[26] Departure may be contrary to the national interest of the state on whose territory the protected person is situated if the person desiring repatriation is a man of such an age that he would be able to take part in military action during

---

[25] Geneva Convention IV Arts 35–46.
[26] Geneva Convention IV Art 35(1).

the armed conflict. In any case, the refusal to grant leave to depart the state must be subject to regular procedures and to periodic judicial review.[27]

Secondly, Articles 41 and 42 are concerned with internment. This is the most severe measure of restriction of freedom that may be imposed on adverse civilians. Protected persons may only be made subject to internment on the basis of compelling security considerations.[28] Possession of 'enemy' nationality or simple suspicion that the protected person may be acting against the territorial state is not enough. In order to be justified, internment must be absolutely necessary in order to satisfy compelling security requirements and no milder measure must be available that would achieve the same security aim.[29] All cases must be considered individually and collective measures are not allowed. Moreover, the internment must be conducted with procedural fairness, with the opportunity for review by a court or administrative board exercising judicial powers.[30] Whilst the internment lasts, a periodical review of the continued necessity for detention must take place at least twice a year.[31] If a protected person is interned, the conditions of their internment are regulated in detail by Articles 79 to 135 of Geneva Convention IV. This regime is similar to that concerning prisoners of war,[32] with some relaxation on account of the civilian character of the persons.

8. Whilst similarly concerned with the protection of civilians, the next section of the Geneva Convention IV concerns the protection of civilians in *occupied territories*.[33] On account of the importance of this question, it is appropriate to devote a separate chapter to it.[34]

Comprehension check:

a) What is the general system of protection of Geneva Convention IV?
b) Does Geneva Convention IV protect civilians who are caught in fighting between opposing armies?
c) If a specific rule cannot be found in the part of Geneva Convention IV that deals with occupied territories, for example the rule prohibiting pillage, can it then be said that this rule does not apply to occupied territories?

Answers:

a) The system of protection of Geneva Convention IV is divided into four parts. First, there are some general rules for all civilians, regardless of nationality, on the territories of the belligerent parties. These rules concern general protection of the civilians, such as hospital zones and the evacuation of wounded and sick civilians. Secondly, there are some general rules that apply to protected

---

[27] Geneva Convention IV Art 35(2).
[28] Geneva Convention IV Art 42(1).
[29] This requirement has been very strictly interpreted, *Prosecutor v Kordic and Cerkez* (Trial Judgment) IT-95-14/2-T (26 February 2001) paras [273]–[285], in particular para [284].
[30] Geneva Convention IV Art 43.
[31] *Ibid.*
[32] See generally: ch 26 above.
[33] Geneva Convention IV Arts 47*ff.*
[34] See generally: ch 28 below.

persons in the narrower sense, as defined in Article 4 of Geneva Convention IV, which apply wherever these persons find themselves. Thirdly, there are special rules that apply to 'enemy' civilians, and some other protected civilians, who find themselves on the territory of an opposed belligerent. These rules principally aim to regulate the right to leave the enemy territory and the exercise by the belligerents of the power to intern 'enemy' civilians situated on their territory. Fourthly, there are rules that govern the relationship between 'enemy' civilians, and some other protected civilians, and the armed forces of adverse belligerents in occupied territories.

b)   The Geneva Convention does not purport to cover such situations, which it leaves to be regulated by the 'Hague Law'. Rules on the protection of civilians during hostilities, which essentially forbid the deliberate targeting of civilians and regulate collateral damage that may be caused to civilians during attacks on legitimate military targets, may thus be found in the Hague Regulations[35] and Additional Protocol I.[36] Geneva Convention IV applies to the phase outside active hostilities, essentially when enemy civilians come into contact with the opposing belligerent.

c)   No. First, there are some general rules contained in Geneva Convention IV that apply in situations of belligerent occupation.[37] Further, the rules contained in the Hague Regulations continue to apply.[38] Moreover, customary international law and, potentially, human rights law will apply to the situation in occupied territory. The rule on pillage, in particular, can be found within the general rules on protected persons.[39] These rules apply both on the territory of the belligerents and in occupied territory.

---

[35] See especially: Hague Regulations Art 25.
[36] Additional Protocol I Arts 48*ff*.
[37] Geneva Convention IV Arts 13*ff* and 27*ff*.
[38] Hague Regulations Art 47.
[39] Geneva Convention IV Art 33(2).

28

OCCUPIED TERRITORIES (BELLIGERENT OCCUPATION)

Learning objectives: To learn about both the definition of belligerent occupation and the law applicable in territory that is occupied by an adverse belligerent.

1. During armed conflict, one belligerent may advance whilst the other may retreat. This has the potential to create a situation where the armed forces of a belligerent come to exercise control over territories not belonging to that belligerent, either due to the exercise of force in the armed conflict or because the opposed party offers no resistance.[1] In both cases, there is a hostile occupation of territory by the army of another state. This situation is known as 'belligerent occupation'. Belligerent occupation must be distinguished from peaceful occupation. If the occupation is the result of an agreement that is freely entered into between the territorial state where an armed force is deployed and the state that deploys the armed force, this is not a situation of belligerent occupation, but only a situation of peaceful occupation. The LOAC does not apply in these cases. Furthermore, the extent to which UN forces, or UN-mandated forces, for example under a mandate of civil administration, can be considered as occupants is doubtful. Thus, when Kosovo was placed under the administration of the United Nations Interim Administration Mission in Kosovo (UNMIK), it was not considered to be belligerently occupied and therefore the duties that exist under the LOAC did not apply.

2. The main sources of the law that governs belligerent occupation are: (1) the Hague Regulations on Land Warfare[2]; and (2) Geneva Convention IV.[3] The Hague Regulations are primarily, but not exclusively, concerned with the administrative rights and duties of the occupying power, whereas the Geneva Convention has greatest concern for the rights granted for the protection of the civilian population. Moreover, the Hague Regulations are composed of relatively few short articles, which means that they fail to provide a comprehensive elucidation of the norms applying to occupied territories, whereas the Geneva Convention attempts to create a complete and detailed code setting out the rights and duties applicable in

---

[1] Geneva Convention IV Relative to the Protection of Civilian Persons in Time of War (adopted 12 August 1949, entered into force 21 October 1950) 75 UNTS 287 (Geneva Convention IV) Art 2(2).

[2] Regulations concerning the Laws and Customs of War on Land annexed to Hague Convention (IV) respecting the Laws and Customs of War on Land (adopted 18 October 1907, entered into force 26 January 1910) (1907) 205 CTS 227 Arts 42*ff*.

[3] Geneva Convention IV Arts 47*ff*.

occupied territory, thus completing the work begun in the Hague Regulations. When the Hague Regulations were drafted in 1907, they were based on the conduct of wars in the nineteenth century. It was considered that occupation was to be a short transitory phase, where the contacts between the foreign army and the local civilians would be sporadic and minimal, and that war would tend to spare the civilian population because this population did not participate in any way in the war and was consequently not considered hostile. Therefore, only minimal regulation was necessary. The experience of World War II with the tremendous abuses committed by German and Japanese occupying forces in the territories they controlled showed the international community engaged in drafting the Geneva Conventions that the law governing conduct in occupied territories instituted in 1907 was inadequate and some fresh regulation, imposing tighter controls on occupiers, was needed.

3. A *belligerent occupation starts* when a hostile army penetrates into territory under the sovereignty of another state, or at least not under the sovereignty of its own state, and begins to exercise effective and exclusive control over it. This test is set out in Article 42 of the Hague Regulations thus, '[t]erritory is considered occupied when it is actually placed under the authority of the hostile army'.[4] Control by a foreign army can occur in different ways. First, the most normal occurrence is that during warfare one army retreats while the other advances onto foreign soil. The occupation is here the result of hostilities. The occupation formally begins when the resistance of the adverse army is broken and the active phase of hostilities is terminated. Secondly, the control may be the consequence of invasion of a foreign state without any resistance on the part of its armed forces. In such cases, the occupation is not the result of an 'armed conflict'. However, it is belligerent occupation.[5] Thirdly, it is possible that a peaceful occupation turns into a belligerent occupation. If the armed forces of a foreign state are invited by the territorial state to display some control over parts of its territory and if these foreign armed forces effectively do so, but at a certain moment the territorial sovereign asks them to leave but the foreign armed forces remain, the territorial state no longer consents to their presence. Thus, a peaceful occupation turns into a belligerent occupation.

4. Similarly, a *belligerent occupation ends* when the hostile armed forces cease to control the occupied territory. This can occur either because they retreat after an armistice or peace treaty, or because the warfare resumes in the occupied territory in such a manner that the foreign army no longer exercises effective control over it.

A third way in which the belligerent occupation can come to an end is that it is turned into a peaceful occupation. The occupying troops can be requested to remain on the foreign soil by way of an agreement with the territorial state. This happened in the years following World War II with the Allied troops being requested to remain in Japan and Germany in 1952 and 1955 respectively. This

---

[4] The test has customary status, *Legal Consequences of the Construction of a Wall in the Occupied Palestinian Territory (Advisory Opinion)* [2004] ICJ Rep 136 para [78].
[5] Geneva Convention IV Art 2(2).

means of ending an occupation can obviously be problematic. The agreement must be entered into freely by an autonomous local government.[6] The question of autonomy of the government may be very difficult to decide, since the occupying army in fact controls the territory and may be able to force self-serving agreements on a local government only apparently independent from it. Thus, for example, was the elected Iraqi Government sufficiently independent from the US command to be able to freely 'invite' the US troops to stay in the country as they did in 2004? Doubts may be entertained.[7]

Finally, Article 6(3) of Geneva Convention IV stipulates that some provisions of the Convention will cease to apply one year after the general close of military operations. This provision was based on particular situations that existed in the immediate post-World War II era (Germany, Japan) that provided the backdrop to the negotiations of the conventions. This provision has now been rendered obsolete by developments in customary international law. At customary international law, the applicability of which is clearly reflected in Article 3(b) of Additional Protocol I, the occupation ends with loss of effective control or with transformation of a belligerent occupation into a peaceful occupation, discussed above. The one-year limit at least no longer restricts the applicability of the norms of Geneva Convention IV, which have been transformed into norms of customary law.

5. There are two main features of the law of belligerent occupation that characterise the regime of rights and duties that arises from the Hague Regulations and Geneva Convention IV.

a) *Maintenance, as far as possible, of the status quo in the occupied territory.* Occupation law is based upon the general idea that the occupying army should modify the status of the territory as sparingly as possible and change as few of the local laws and institutions as practicable.[8] The reason is simply that the territory does not belong to it. It is to be hoped that the belligerent occupation will be transient and short. Moreover, it is for the local people and their representatives, in exercise of the right of self-determination, to decide on questions of the status of territory, not the occupying army. It is therefore understandable that the occupying power can be described as having an obligation to permit life to continue as normally as possible in the occupied territories. This obligation to maintain the status quo with respect to the laws and institutions is spelled out in Article 43 of the Hague Regulations on Land Warfare of 1907:

> The authority of the legitimate power having in fact passed into the hands of the occupant, the latter shall take all the measures in his power to restore, and ensure, as far as possible, public order and safety, while respecting, unless absolutely prevented, the laws in force in the country.

---

[6] Coercion is a ground that vitiates an agreement at customary international law: Vienna Convention on the Law of Treaties (adopted 23 May 1969, entered into force 27 January 1980) 1155 UNTS 331 Arts 51–2.

[7] See R Kolb, 'Occupation in Iraq since 2003 and the Pwers of the UN Security Council' (2008) 90 *International Review of the Red Cross* 29.

[8] Hague Regulations Art 43. There are exceptions; see, eg *Christian Society for the Holy Places v Minster of Defence* (1972) 52 ILR 512.

Practically, this means that with an exception for the protection of the occupying power's security, local laws remain in force[9] and local courts remain competent.[10] Except when rendered absolutely necessary by military operations, private property may not be destroyed.[11] It may only be confiscated under local legislation that existed prior to the occupation.[12] Public property, other than that of the municipalities, which is considered to be private property,[13] can no longer be administrated by the ordinary sovereign and will therefore be administrated by the occupying power, but only under the rules of usufruct, which means, in general, that the substance of the property must not be depleted as a function of the method by which it is used. It is clear, at least, that the occupier may not exploit previously unexploited resources that belong to the state whose territory is occupied.

However, the occupying power may have the authority, and in some cases the duty, to take some positive action to alter the complexion of the local law. First, it may abrogate oppressive laws which are contrary to international human rights standards and/or to the rights that are guaranteed to the population of the occupied territory by Geneva Convention IV.[14] Thus, the Allied Forces were perfectly within their rights, and were possibly subject to a duty, as occupiers, to abrogate the Nuremberg Laws of 1933, which institutionalised racial discrimination against the Jewish population of Germany. Secondly, the occupying power must take necessary measures to protect law and order in the occupied territory, as well as for ensuring public hygiene and health, food and medical supplies.[15] This power to ensure public order and safety has been used in a wide range of circumstances, including changes to legislation aimed at ensuring continuance of the economic, social and commercial life of the occupied community.[16] Thirdly, the occupying power is entitled to adopt rules to ensure the security of its armed forces.[17] In this context, it may establish tribunals responsible for punishing violations of the newly established security regulations.[18] These tribunals may even be given jurisdiction to punish violations of security regulations that amount to war crimes.

The maintenance of the status quo has one further aspect: The status of the occupied territory may not be altered, for example by annexation to the occupant. This rule has a double foundation. First, under *jus ad bellum*, a territory may no longer be annexed. Since the entry into force of Article 2(4) of the UN Charter,[19] prohibiting the use of force, the ban placed upon

---

[9] Hague Regulations Art 43 and Geneva Convention IV Art 64.
[10] Geneva Convention IV Art 64.
[11] Geneva Convention IV Art 53.
[12] Hague Regulations Art 46.
[13] Hague Regulations Art 56.
[14] See, eg *Christian Society for the Holy Places*, n 7.
[15] Hague Regulations Art 43 and Geneva Convention IV Arts 55–6.
[16] *Grahame v Director of Prosecutions (British Military Courts in Germany)* (1947) 14 AD 228, 232. See also: *US v List (The Hostages Case)* (1948) 15 AD 632.
[17] Geneva Convention IV Art 64(2), and see also *Christian Society for the Holy Places*, n 7.
[18] Geneva Convention IV Art 66.
[19] Charter of the United Nations (adopted 26 June 1945, entered into force 24 October 1945) 892 UNTS 119.

obtaining territory by conquest is absolute. Even if the use of force is legal, such as in a proper exercise of self-defence under Article 51, annexation remains unlawful. Thus, when Israel purported to annex a part of the Golan Heights, the UN Security Council considered that annexation void.[20] The same is true for the annexation of Kuwait by Iraq in 1990, which the UN Security Council declared of 'no legal validity' and 'null and void'.[21] Under *jus in bello*, an annexation cannot deprive the civilian population in the occupied territory of its protections under IHL.[22] Under both branches of the law, annexation is therefore made of no effect, once as such, under the *jus ad bellum*, and in the *jus in bello* with respect to any legal effects on the civilian population.

b) *Respect for individual rights of the civilian population.* Geneva Convention IV contains a series of provisions granting the civilian population rights as against the occupier. The aim is to prevent abuse of the civilian population by the occupying power. In this area we can see the overlap between the LOAC and international human rights law, which both apply in occupied territory. Thus, the International Court of Justice applied both the LOAC and human rights law to the situation in the Israeli occupied territories.[23]

Some particular obligations that are imposed on the occupying power and rights that are granted to the civilian population are listed below. However, Geneva Convention IV repays close reading to discover all the rights granted to the population.

i) prohibition of deportation or individual or collective forced transfers[24];
ii) prohibition of 'colonisation' of occupied territory—'[t]he Occupying Power shall not deport or transfer parts of its own civilian population into the territory it occupies'[25];
iii) prohibition of compulsory service in the occupying armed forces or their auxiliaries[26];
iv) prohibition of destruction of private property, except when rendered absolutely necessary by military operations[27];
v) prohibition of collective penalties, pillage and reprisals[28];
vi) prohibition of hostage taking[29];
vii) right to due process in judicial proceedings[30];
viii) duty of the occupying power to ensure food and medical supplies to the fullest extent, given the means available[31];

---

[20] UNSC Res 497 (17 December 1981) UN Doc/S/Res/497 para [1].
[21] UNSC Res 662 (9 August 1990) UN Doc/S/Res/662 para [1].
[22] Geneva Convention IV Art 47.
[23] *Wall Opinion*, n 4, paras [89]–[113]. See also: *Armed Activities on the Territory of the Congo (Democratic Republic of Congo v Uganda)* [2006] ICJ Rep 6, paras [181]*ff*, particularly paras [216]–[221].
[24] Geneva Convention IV Art 49(1).
[25] Geneva Convention IV Art 49(6).
[26] Geneva Convention IV Art 51(1).
[27] Geneva Convention IV Art 53.
[28] Geneva Convention IV Art 33.
[29] Geneva Convention IV Art 34.
[30] Geneva Convention IV Arts 64*ff*.
[31] Geneva Convention IV Art 55.

ix)   duty of the occupying power to maintain hygiene and public health, for example through hospital establishments, to the fullest extent, given the means available[32];

x)   duty of the occupying power to allow relief operations by other states or humanitarian organisms, such as the ICRC, if the civilian population of the occupied territory is inadequately supplied.[33]

Comprehension check:

a)   Which are the essential principles for deciding if and when a territory is under belligerent occupation?

b)   Which legal sources apply to occupied territories and how are they related?

c)   Which are the essential substantive obligations imposed on the occupier under the law of belligerent occupation?

d)   Was it lawful, under the law of occupation, to establish in Germany a series of criminal tribunals in order to judge Axis war criminals?

e)   Is the law of belligerent occupation well adapted to situations of prolonged occupation, lasting, say, 40 years?

Answers:

a)   The essential principles are those of 'effectiveness' and of 'consent'. First, effectiveness: if a territory is in fact under the control of a hostile army, it is occupied in the sense of belligerent occupation—whether or not there is a state of war or armed conflict existing between the occupied power and the occupier.[34] Secondly, consent: if the occupying force is on the foreign territory at the invitation, or with the consent of the local sovereign, and the consent has been freely given, this is peaceful and not belligerent occupation. In this case, the Hague Regulations and Geneva Convention do not apply.

b)   The four main sources are the following: (1) The Hague Regulations on Land Warfare, Articles 42*ff*; (2) Geneva Convention IV, Articles 47*ff*; (3) customary international humanitarian law; and (4) human rights law. Customary law is for the most part aligned with the conventional law. Human Rights Law applies in parallel to the LOAC without contradicting it on any point. As far as the relationship between the Hague Regulations and Geneva Convention IV are concerned, Geneva Convention IV expressly mentions the Hague Regulations, which it makes clear that it supplements, but from which it does not purport to derogate. Article 154 of Geneva Convention IV reads:

> In the relations between the Powers who are bound by the Hague Conventions respecting the Laws and Customs of War on Land [...] and who are parties to the present Convention, this last Convention shall be supplementary to Sections II and III of the Regulations annexed to the above-mentioned Conventions of The Hague.

---

[32] Geneva Convention IV Art 56.
[33] Geneva Convention IV Art 59.
[34] Hague Regulations Art 42 and Geneva Convention IV Art 2(2).

c) Roughly speaking these are twofold: (1) maintenance of the status quo in the territory with respect to the laws, institutions, etc; (2) respect and protection of rights of the civilian population, which implies abstention from certain actions on the one hand and a positive obligation to act in certain cases on the other. For example, whereas collective punishments are prohibited, occupying powers have an obligation to provide food and medical material.

d) Under customary international law, the occupant may establish tribunals in the occupation zones to try offences against the security regulations it creates. These tribunals may also be given the competence, under international law, to try war crimes and other international crimes such as genocide and crimes against humanity.[35]

e) The case of prolonged occupation places the principle of maintenance of the status quo in the occupied territory under a great deal of strain. If the occupation is short, a moratorium on local reforms is justified in order to let the local sovereign, returning in due course to the territory, make any necessary decisions. If the occupation lasts for long a time, the proper administration of the territory requires, for example, economic and social reform so that the territory keeps pace with inevitable changes and evolutions in society. IHL is therefore well equipped to protect the status quo of occupied territories, but is weak in responding to new needs of the population of the occupied territories as time passes. The longer the occupation lasts, the more shortcomings may appear in the status quo. However, if the occupier was given the right to undertake structural reforms in the occupied territory subject to prolonged occupation, the door may be opened to potential abuses and the fundamental principle of self-determination of peoples would be curtailed.

---

[35] Geneva Convention IV Arts 66 and 146–7.

29

THE 'INTANGIBLE' NATURE OF THE LOAC RIGHTS

Learning objectives: To obtain an appreciation that rights granted to protected persons by Geneva Conventions I–IV cannot be waived, derogated from or otherwise diminished. These rights are due in all circumstances.

1. There is always a risk that a belligerent may conclude some agreement with another belligerent to diminish the rights of protected persons. Alternatively, there is a risk that a belligerent may put pressure on a protected person, such as a prisoner of war, to renounce his or her conventional protections. Historic precedent exists for such agreements. During World War II, agreements were concluded between Germany and the puppet government of Vichy France allowing the deportation of civilians from France to Germany. If this were to happen today, should the civilians lose their rights under, amongst others, Article 49 of Geneva Convention IV because 'their' government decided to collaborate and make an agreement with an opposing belligerent? Furthermore, during World War II, in Germany many prisoners of war were pressured into renouncing their conventional protections under the 1929 Geneva Convention by exchanging their status as prisoners of war for status as a 'civilian workers' under contract. These persons were then exploited under inhumane conditions in German industries, and lost all protection that they possessed as a result of their POW status, in particular the protection afforded to them as a result of supervision by the ICRC. If this were to happen today, should the POW lose their protection under Geneva Convention III because, under duress, they made an agreement with their detaining power?

A desire to avoid repetition of such incidents led the states to insert into the Geneva Conventions some provisions aiming at entrenching the conventional rights and obligations as the minimum baseline of protection to be given protected persons. Therefore, the rights of protected persons are rendered 'untouchable' by the Geneva Conventions. However, this word does not precisely capture the nature of the entrenchment of the rights given to protected persons by the Geneva Conventions. It is accepted that the rights of the protected persons may be increased: thus, a prisoner of war may be given more pay for his or her work than the minimum set down in the Convention; or, he or she may receive more hours of rest or a greater facility to correspond with the external world. Such improvements of the status of protected persons are obviously not prohibited, since such prohibition would be contrary to the humanitarian and protective aim of the

Conventions. In that sense, the rights are not untouchable. They can be augmented; but they cannot be diminished.[1]

2. There are two Common Articles in the four Geneva Conventions dealing with this aspect: Common Article 6/6/6/7[2] and Common Article 7/7/7/8.[3]

    a) Common Article 6/6/6/7 deals with *special agreements*.[4] The belligerents may conclude such agreements in order to regulate more in detail the implementation of an obligation or obligations imposed by one (or more) of the Conventions or to provide for the implementation of such obligations in a specific context. They may also conclude such agreements to provide additional rights to the protected persons either supplementary to the rights granted to the protected persons by the Conventions or in relation to matters not covered by conventional regulations. However, such special agreements may only execute the Geneva Conventions or improve the situation of the protected persons. They must not diminish the rights granted by the Conventions. In Geneva Convention III, the Common Article reads as follows:

> In addition to the agreements expressly provided for in Articles 10, 23, 28, 33, 60, 65, 66, 67, 72, 73, 75, 109, 110, 118, 119, 122 and 132, the High Contracting Parties may conclude other special agreements for all matters concerning which they may deem it suitable to make separate provision. No special agreement shall adversely affect the situation of prisoners of war, as defined by the present Convention, nor restrict the rights which it confers upon them.[5]

    b) Common Article 7/7/7/8 deals with the *renunciation of rights* by the protected persons. It stipulates that such renunciation is invalid in all circumstances, unless specifically allowed by the Conventions. In Geneva Convention III, this Article reads as follows:

> Prisoners of war may in no circumstances renounce in part or in entirety the rights secured to them by the present Convention, and by the special agreements referred to in the foregoing Article, if such there be.[6]

3. The potential for rights given to protected persons by the Conventions to be taken away by subterfuge has always been greatest in occupied territories. The

---

[1] Sometimes, it may be possible to depart from the letter of a provision if that serves, in a specific context, to enhance the protection of the persons concerned. The agreement of the ICRC can be a potent indication of appropriateness of such action. For an example, see R Kolb, 'Jus cogens, intangibilité, intransgressibilité, dérogation "positive" et "négative"' (2005) 109 *RGDIP* 311.

[2] Geneva Convention I for the Amelioration of the Condition of the Wounded and Sick in Armed Forces in the Field (adopted 12 August 1949, entered into force 21 October 1950) 75 UNTS 31 (Geneva Convention I) Art 6; Geneva Convention II for the Amelioration of the Condition of Wounded, Sick and Shipwrecked Members of Armed Forces at Sea (adopted 12 August 1949, entered into force 21 October 1950) 75 UNTS 85 (Geneva Convention II) Art 6; Geneva Convention III relative to the Treatment of Prisoners of War (adopted 12 August 1949, entered into force 21 October 1950) 75 UNTS 135 (Geneva Convention III) Art 6; Geneva Convention IV Relative to the Protection of Civilian Persons in Time of War (adopted 12 August 1949, entered into force 21 October 1950) 75 UNTS 287 (Geneva Convention IV) Art 7.

[3] Geneva Convention I Art 7; Geneva Convention II Art 7; Geneva Convention III Art 7; Geneva Convention IV Art 8.

[4] See generally: ch 15 above.

[5] Geneva Convention III Art 6(1).

[6] Geneva Convention III Article 7.

occupying power may profit from a government that engages in collaboration, or install a puppet government, and then adopt repressive measures by presenting them as measures 'autonomously' decided by the local government (which in fact it controls). Furthermore, the occupying power could attempt to subvert the protection of the LOAC by proclaiming the territory annexed and arguing that once the formerly occupied territory became its own national territory, occupation law would cease to apply to it and the civilian residents, who had previously been protected persons, cease to enjoy the protections of Geneva Convention IV. World War II provides many examples of such subterfuges; in Croatia, in occupied France and Norway; in Czechoslovakia. This is why the states negotiating Geneva Convention IV ensured that Article 47 forcefully restated the inability of such inventive mechanisms, whatever they may be, to diminish the rights of the protected persons. This important provision reads as follows:

> Protected persons who are in occupied territory shall not be deprived, in any case or in any manner whatsoever, of the benefits of the present Convention by any change introduced, as the result of the occupation of a territory, into the institutions or government of the said territory, nor by any agreement concluded between the authorities of the occupied territories and the Occupying Power, nor by any annexation by the latter of the whole or part of the occupied territory.[7]

It should be noted that this provision, in addition to the situations explicitly mentioned, states that the protections cannot be diminished, 'in any case or in any manner whatsoever'. The guarantees given to civilians in the event of belligerent occupation should therefore be sacrosanct. However, the question arises whether the UN Security Council could, by virtue of its powers under Chapter VII and Article 103 of the UN Charter,[8] dispense from the application of some of the rules of occupation law; or qualify a situation as not being an occupation, if the effect of such a determination would be that civilians lose protections they would otherwise be entitled to under Convention IV. This is a difficult question—which the occupation of Iraq in 2003 has rendered more acute—and one to which no clear answer has been given up until now.

Comprehension check:

a) In 1949, why did it appear necessary to guarantee the protections of the Conventions against diminishment by special agreement between the belligerents and against renunciation by the protected persons themselves?
b) In what area of the LOAC are the protected person's rights under particular danger of being shrunk or done away with completely?

Answers:

a) The Geneva Conventions 1949 aim to guarantee certain rights given to persons in danger of suffering from arbitrary or adverse acts by an opposing belligerent. These are the protected persons, ie wounded, sick or shipwrecked

---

[7] Geneva Convention IV Art 47.
[8] Charter of the United Nations (adopted 26 June 1945, entered into force 24 October 1945) 892 UNTS 119 Arts 39–51 and 103.

military persons, prisoners of war and protected civilians. Certain minimum rights should be secured in all circumstances, so as to ensure a minimum baseline of humanity. Therefore, the Geneva Conventions attempt to close down all of the loopholes that could be used to jeopardise this minimum protection or render it illusory. One way in which the minimum conventional guarantees could be flouted is through the use of special agreements derogating from them, or by ad hoc renunciations, made by the protected persons themselves, usually under duress. World War II gave ample illustration and showed that those fears are well founded. Hence, the Geneva Conventions close the potential loophole by declaring that such acts (agreements, renunciations, changes of government, annexations, etc) shall in any case not have the effect of diminishing or annulling those rights of the protected persons guaranteed by the Conventions.

b)   The rights guaranteed by the Conventions are particularly in danger in occupied territories, because there the civilian population is particularly prone to be seen by the occupant as a hostile unit, responsible for resistance against them. That is why Article 47 of Geneva Convention IV contains a specific provision concerning the 'untouchable' nature of rights in the context of occupied territories.

PROTECTIVE EMBLEMS

Learning objectives: To understand the form and function of protective emblems today.

1. Persons and objects entitled to special protection against attack must be visibly identifiable to the adverse belligerent in order to avoid being targeted. The adverse belligerents signal that particular objects are entitled to special protection through the use of identification signs or symbols, called 'emblems'. During armed conflict, the emblem serves a protective function. It enables the combatants to identify certain persons and objects protected by the Conventions and the Additional Protocols, such as medical personnel, medical units, medical means of transport, relief convoys, civil defence units, cultural property, installations containing dangerous forces, etc. In order to be effective, an emblem must be both commonly accepted and, moreover, it must be large and visible. The proliferation of emblems jeopardises protection. The interest of the International Committee of the Red Cross (ICRC) is thus to keep the main distinctive signs as reduced in number as possible. Finally, in order to avoid undermining the protection offered by the emblem, its misuse must be suppressed. In some cases, misuse of an emblem will constitute a war crime.[1] Moreover, the emblem may neither be imitated nor used for private or commercial purposes.[2] States parties to the Geneva Conventions have a duty to implement legislation regulating the appropriate use of the emblem and suppressing any improper use during in peacetime.[3]

2. There are today three main emblems that may be used to protect those engaged in medical and caring action during warfare. Furthermore, there are a series of special emblems protecting particular objects, such as cultural property under the Hague Convention on Cultural Property[4] and Additional Protocol I,[5] or installations containing dangerous forces.[6]

---

[1] Protocol Additional to the Geneva Conventions of 12 August 1949, and relating to the Protection of Victims of International Armed Conflicts (adopted 8 June 1977, entered into force 7 December 1978) 1125 UNTS 3 (Additional Protocol I) Arts 37(1) and 85(3)(f) and *Re Hagendorf* (1948) 13 WCR 146.

[2] Geneva Convention I for the Amelioration of the Condition of the Wounded and Sick in Armed Forces in the Field (adopted 12 August 1949, entered into force 21 October 1950) 75 UNTS 31 (Geneva Convention I) Arts 53 and 54.

[3] Geneva Convention I Art 54.

[4] Hague Convention for the Protection of Cultural Property in the Event of Armed Conflict (adopted 14 May 1954, entered into force 7 August 1956) 249 UNTS 240 (Hague Cultural Property Convention).

[5] Additional Protocol 1 Art 53.

[6] Additional Protocol 1 Art 56.

a) The main emblems are those of the *Red Cross and Red Crescent Movement*, which are inserted into the Conventions. These emblems have a general protective use. They serve mainly to distinguish medical and religious personnel, whether serving with the army or acting as members of a humanitarian organisation affiliated with the Red Cross and Crescent Movement, such as the ICRC[7]; to distinguish medical units and establishments[8]; to distinguish the medical units belonging to neutral countries lending their services to a belligerent[9]; to distinguish hospital ships[10]; to distinguish civilian hospitals and their staff[11]; to distinguish convoys of vehicles, trains or aircraft employed for the removal of wounded and sick civilians[12]; and, although not specifically mandated by the Conventions, these emblems have been used to mark convoys of foodstuffs for the benefit of the civilian population, even during non-international armed conflict (NIAC), eg during in the Spanish Civil War (1936–39).

In the Convention system, there are currently four equivalent emblems authorised to fulfil the general protective purpose; but only three are effectively used:

i)   the red cross on white background;
ii) the red crescent on white background;
iii) the red lion and sun on a white background (Persia); the Red Lion is no longer in use;
iv) the red frame in the shape of a square on edge on a white ground (which was introduced at insistence of Israel through the Third Additional Protocol to the Geneva Conventions of 1949, adopted in 2005[13]).

The emblems look as follows:

Red cross:

Red crescent:

---

[7] Geneva Convention I Art 40
[8] Geneva Convention I Art 42.
[9] Geneva Convention I Art 43.
[10] Geneva Convention II for the Amelioration of the Condition of Wounded, Sick and Shipwrecked Members of Armed Forces at Sea (adopted 12 August 1949, entered into force 21 October 1950) 75 UNTS 85 (Geneva Convention II) Art 43.
[11] Geneva Convention IV Relative to the Protection of Civilian Persons in Time of War (adopted 12 August 1949, entered into force 21 October 1950) 75 UNTS 287 (Geneva Convention IV) Arts 18 and 20.
[12] Geneva Convention IV Arts 21 and 22.
[13] Protocol additional to the Geneva Conventions of 12 August 1949, and relating to the Adoption of an Additional Distinctive Emblem (adopted 8 December 2005, entered into force 14 January 2007).

Red frame:

Red lion and sun:

b) Besides these general protective emblems, there are a series of emblems signalling *particular protected objects*. Some 'emblems' may consist of just letters. Thus, to the maximum extent feasible, and where military considerations permit, the large visible letters 'PW' or 'PG', ie 'prisoners of war' or 'prisonniers de guerre', must mark a prisoner of war camp.[14] However, there are also a series of pictorial, or 'heraldic', emblems. The most important are the following:

i) *Hospital zones under Geneva Convention IV*, ie civilian hospital zones, may be marked either by the red cross/crescent, or by means of oblique red bands on a white ground[15]:

ii) *Protected cultural property*[16]: The emblem is described in Hague Cultural Property Convention as follows:

> [A] shield, pointed below, per saltire blue and white (a shield consisting of a royal blue square, one of the angles of which forms the point of the shield, and of a royal-blue triangle above the square, the space on either side being taken up by a white triangle).[17]

iii) *Works and installations containing dangerous forces*[18]: objects containing dangerous forces are, for example, dams, dykes or nuclear power stations. The protective emblem is a group of three bright orange circles of equal

---

[14] Geneva Convention III relative to the Treatment of Prisoners of War (adopted 12 August 1949, entered into force 21 October 1950) 75 UNTS 135 (Geneva Convention III) Art 23.

[15] Geneva Convention IV Annex I Art 6(1).

[16] Hague Cultural Property Convention Art 16 and Additional Protocol 1 Art 53.

[17] Hague Cultural Property Convention Art 16.

[18] Additional Protocol 1 Art 56 and Annex 1 Art 17.

size, placed on the same axis, the distance between each circle being one radius:

iv) *Civil defence*: civil defence units of the army have non-combatant tasks such as: warning; evacuation; rescue and management of shelters for the civilian population; first aid; detection, marking and decontamination of danger areas; emergency repair of indispensable facilities and emergency disposal of the dead; etc.[19] These forces are granted immunity from attack.[20] The specific protective emblem allocated to forces performing a civil defence role enhances their protection. It consists of an equilateral blue triangle on an orange background[21]:

Comprehension check:

a) What is the function of the protective emblems? In other words, to what ends are they used?
b) What is the protective emblem that is used to identify cultural property?
c) What is the protective emblem that is used to identify installations containing dangerous forces?
d) Can a belligerent choose to mark whatever he or she wishes with a red cross because he or she thinks that this object should not be attacked?

Answers:

a) During wartime, the function of the emblems is protective. It means that the objects marked are properly used for certain tasks protected by the Conventions (such as medical establishments) or are installations entitled to special protection (such as cultural property or works containing dangerous forces). Thus, the main function of the emblem is to give information to assist belligerent forces to respect the duty not to attack protected objects by signalling that an object is protected. The objects signalled by the emblem should not be attacked. Exceptions exist only when the emblem is misused, ie when the object in effect serves military purposes.
b) It is a shield consisting of a royal-blue square, one of the angles of which forms the point of the shield, and of a royal-blue triangle above the square, the space on either side being taken up by a white triangle.

---

[19] Additional Protocol 1 Arts 61*ff*.
[20] Additional Protocol 1 Art 62.
[21] Additional Protocol 1 Annex 1 Art 16.

c)   It is a group of three bright orange circles or equal size, placed on the same axis, the distance between each circle being one radius.

d)   No. The use of the emblem is strictly regulated by the Conventions. Any use not covered by the Conventions is a misuse which has to be suppressed by national legislation.[22] Some forms of misuse, performed in order to gain military advantages, constitute a war crime.[23] However, if there is agreement among the parties and the ICRC, the red cross/crescent emblem may be used for some caring purposes going beyond that foreseen by the Conventions. The condition is that such uses are in keeping with the spirit of the sign. Thus, protective emblems can be used in a NIAC by analogy, or they can be used for convoys of foodstuffs organised by the ICRC or a national Red Cross Society.

---

[22] Geneva Convention I Art 54.
[23] Additional Protocol 1 Arts 37(1) and 85(3)(f).

31

SEA WARFARE

Learning objectives: To learn the essentials of the law applicable to naval warfare.

1. The part of the LOAC that regulates sea, or naval, warfare can be split into two parts. First, there is that part that regulates the means and methods of combat between ships (ship/ship) and, since the advent of aircraft, also between aircraft and ships (air/ship; ship/air). This part of naval LOAC also regulates the behaviour of belligerents with regard to foreign, both belligerent and neutral, commercial vessels and deals with the treatment of those vessels responsible for carrying contraband. Thus, the entirety of the law of prize, which concerns the arrest of ships carrying contraband, must be considered under this head. Secondly, naval LOAC also concerns itself with the treatment of protected persons, namely wounded, sick and shipwrecked military personnel.[1] Thus we return again to the classical partition between 'Hague' and 'Geneva' Law, this time on the sea. The norms governing treatment of the wounded, sick and shipwrecked has been alluded to previously.[2] However, given its importance, let us quickly repeat that lesson.

2. *Geneva Law*. In armed conflicts at sea, governed by Geneva Convention II, hospital ships receive special protection.[3] These ships are devoted to the collection, assistance, and transportation of and provision of care to wounded, sick and shipwrecked military personnel.[4] The first paragraph of Article 22 of Geneva Convention II reads as follows:

> Military hospital ships, that is to say, ships built or equipped by the Powers specially and solely with a view to assisting the wounded, sick and shipwrecked, to treating them and to transporting them, may in no circumstances be attacked or captured, but shall at all times be respected and protected, on condition that their names and descriptions have been notified to the Parties to the conflict ten days before those ships are employed.

The notification that is required by this Article before protection is granted to hospital ships may be effected either by direct contact between the belligerent parties, or through the channels of the protecting power or the International Committee of

---

[1] Geneva Convention II for the Amelioration of the Condition of Wounded, Sick and Shipwrecked Members of Armed Forces at Sea (adopted 12 August 1949, entered into force 21 October 1950) 75 UNTS 85 (Geneva Convention II).

[2] Ch 24 para 7.

[3] Geneva Convention II Art 22.

[4] *Ibid*, Arts 22*ff*.

the Red Cross (ICRC). In order that the belligerents can satisfy themselves that the privileged status granted to hospital ships is not being abused, the warships of a belligerent can search adverse hospital ships and may exercise a control over matters such as the course taken by the hospital ship or its ability to communicate with other ships.[5] If the privileged status of the hospital ship is abused for the purposes of hostile action, the ship may be captured as a prize, once an order to stop the hostile action has been given and a reasonable time for compliance has lapsed.[6] The best method of guaranteeing proper use of such ships is to place a neutral observer aboard the hospital ship.[7] Such an observer may be sourced through the protecting power or may even be sent by the ICRC. Neutral states may offer hospital ships to the belligerents. In such cases, the hospital ship must be put under the command of a belligerent and be notified to opposing belligerents to benefit from protection under Geneva Convention II.[8] Such ships will then fly the flags of both their state of origin and the belligerent with whom they are affiliated. By requiring that a ship be placed under the control of a belligerent these provisions aim to ensure that neutrally flagged hospital ships will not hamper in any way military operations at sea, and thus put themselves in danger. The drafters of Geneva Convention II felt that only the 'incorporation' of neutrally flagged hospital ships within the forces of a belligerent was sufficient to guarantee the avoidance of such a danger. Whilst other entities may also charter ships to undertake philanthropic missions, devoted to the provision of care and help to the wounded, sick and shipwrecked of the armed conflict, unless the provisions of Article 25 of Geneva Convention II are complied with, such ships will not be hospital ships able to avail themselves of the protection granted to such ships under Geneva Convention II. However, this does not mean that such ships are without protection. As civilian objects these ships are not liable to attack or seizure. This point is emphasised in Hague Convention XI, which codifies certain customary law restrictions on the right of capture in navel warfare, and states in Article 4 that, '[v]essels charged with religious, scientific, or philanthropic missions are ... exempt from capture'.[9]

3. *Hague Law.* The laws governing naval warfare, and certain connected questions, were partially codified in a series of Conventions negotiated at the 1907 Hague Peace Conference. These Conventions are now largely outdated, although some of their provisions have attained customary law status.[10] They tackle the following activities:

---

[5] Geneva Convention II Art 31.

[6] Geneva Convention II Art 34 and L Doswald-Beck (ed), *San Remo Manual on International Law Applicable to Armed Conflicts at Sea* (Cambridge, Cambridge University Press, 1995) available at <http://www.icrc.org/ihl> accessed 20 May 2008 (hereinafter, San Remo Manual) paras [49]–[50].

[7] Geneva Convention II Art 31(4).

[8] Geneva Convention II Art 25.

[9] Hague Convention XI Relative to Certain Restrictions with regard to the Exercise of the Right of Capture in Naval Warfare (adopted 18 October 1907, entered into force 26 January 1910) (1907) 205 CTS 367 (Hague Convention XI) Art 4. See also San Remo Manual para [47(f)].

[10] See, eg: *Corfu Channel Case (UK v Albania)* (Merits) [1949] ICJ Rep 4, 22; and *Military and Paramilitary Activities in and against Nicaragua (Nicaragua v United States of America)* (Merits) [1986] ICJ Rep 14, para [215], discussing submarine contact mines in times of peace.

a) the status of enemy merchant ships at the outbreak of hostilities[11];

b) the conversion of merchant ships into war-ships[12];

c) the laying of automatic submarine contact mines[13];

d) the bombardment by naval forces in time of war[14];

e) the restrictions with regard to the exercise of the right of capture in naval war[15];

f) the creation of an international prize court[16]; and

g) the rights and duties of neutral powers in naval war.[17]

Conventions VI and XII never came into force. The other Conventions are today largely obsolete; they are geared towards the conditions of naval warfare of the nineteenth century, before the advent of aircraft, submarine warfare and substantial advances in weapons technology, innovations which fundamentally changed the nature of naval warfare. The most important modern text relating to armed conflicts at sea is the San Remo Manual on International Law Applicable to Armed Conflict at Sea.[18] Whilst this manual is not a convention, but a private work of codification prepared by international lawyers and naval experts, brought together under the auspices of the Institute of Humanitarian Law, based in San Remo, the text largely reflects customary international law and can thus be consulted in order to identify the rules applicable to armed conflicts at sea. A further advantage of this text, apart from the advantage of being up to date, is that in contrast to the Hague Conventions, the San Remo Manual is intended to present a complete codification of naval LOAC. It touches upon all of the questions relevant in the conduct of sea warfare. In addition to these advantages, and similarly to Additional Protocol I relating to land warfare, this text merges into unity the 'Hague Law' aspects of the law of naval warfare concerning the means and methods to be adopted and humanitarian 'Geneva Law' aspects of the law governing war at sea, previously contained in Geneva Convention II[19] and Additional Protocol I.[20]

With regard to content, the primary importance of the San Remo Manual is that it clarifies that the essential rules of the law of armed conflicts on land are also applicable to warfare taking place at sea. Thus, for example, the principle of distinction between civilian and military objectives, the definition of military

---

[11] Hague Convention VI Relating to the Status of Enemy Merchant Ships at the Outbreak of Hostilities (adopted 18 October 1907, not yet in force) (1907) 205 CTS 305.

[12] Hague Convention VII Relating to the Conversion of Merchant Ships into Warships (adopted 18 October 1907, entered into force 26 January 1910) (1907) 205 CTS 319.

[13] Hague Convention VIII Relative to the Laying of Automatic Submarine Contact Mines (adopted 18 October 1907, entered into force 26 January 1910) (1907) 205 CTS 331.

[14] Hague Convention IX Concerning Bombardment by Naval Forces in Time of War (adopted 18 October 1907, entered into force 26 January 1910) (1907) 205 CTS 345.

[15] Hague Convention XI Relative to Certain Restrictions with Regard to the Exercise of the Right of Capture in Naval War (adopted 18 October 1907, entered into force 26 January 1910) (1907) 205 CTS 367.

[16] Hague Convention XII Relative to the Creation of an International Prize Court (adopted 18 October 1907, not yet in force) (1907) 205 CTS 381.

[17] Hague Convention XIII Concerning the Rights and Duties of Neutral Powers in Naval War (adopted 18 October 1907, entered into force 26 January 1910) (1907) 205 CTS 395.

[18] See n 6.

[19] See n 1.

[20] Protocol Additional to the Geneva Conventions of 12 August 1949, and relating to the Protection of Victims of International Armed Conflicts (adopted 8 June 1977, entered into force 7 December 1978) 1125 UNTS 3.

objective and the duty to take precautionary measures when attacking are all applicable to naval warfare. Moreover, the San Remo Manual addresses some issues specifically relating to maritime warfare, such as the use of sea mines and torpedoes,[21] the hostilities between ships and aircraft[22] and the existence of maritime war zones.[23] Some of these key issues will now be considered.

4. *War zones.* Hostile actions by belligerent forces are forbidden in the territorial waters, meaning internal waters and territorial sea,[24] of neutral states. Elsewhere, the parties to the conflict are free to engage in acts of war.[25] The belligerent may undertake hostilities within the exclusive economic zone of neutral states that have proclaimed such a zone, extending up to 200 nautical miles from the coast.[26] However, belligerent states must have due regard for the economic activities of the coastal state.[27] Where the rule of immunity of neutral waters is violated, the neutral state is under an obligation to intervene in order to terminate the encroachment into its waters.[28] First, it must order the belligerent ships to leave its waters immediately. If that request is not honoured, it must take action in order to force the belligerent vessels out of its territorial waters or to intern the ships that violated its neutrality. The neutral state must not give refuge to warships of a belligerent, although this rule is subject to exceptions, for example, in some cases where the life of the crew is in danger because of the unseaworthiness of the ship or bad weather.[29] The permissible conduct of warships in neutral waters is regulated exhaustively in the San Remo Manual.[30]

A belligerent may establish a special war zone, for example an 'exclusion zone' reserved for the conduct of hostilities where commercial ships, even those that fly the flag of a neutral state, should either not enter, or enter at their own risk. Such zones were proclaimed during both the Falklands War and the Iran-Iraq War. Even in this situation the ordinary LOAC applies. Hence, a belligerent cannot proclaim that he or she will automatically and indiscriminately attack any vessel entering that zone and, for example, civilian ships remain protected.[31]

5. *Military objectives.* The general principle of distinction between civilian and military persons and objectives applies to sea warfare.[32] The San Remo Manual provides a list of vessels immune from attack.[33] These are as follows:

    a) hospital ships[34];

---

[21] Regarding Sea Mines, San Remo Manual paras [80]–[92] and for Torpedoes, San Remo Manual para [79].

[22] See, eg: San Remo Manual paras [62]–[64].

[23] San Remo Manual paras [105]–[108].

[24] See generally: United Nations Convention on the Law of the Sea (adopted 10 December 1982, entered into force 16 November 1994) 1833 UNTS 3 Pt II for definitions.

[25] San Remo Manual para [14].

[26] San Remo Manual para [10].

[27] San Remo Manual para [34].

[28] San Remo Manual para [22].

[29] San Remo Manual para [20].

[30] San Remo Manual paras [19]*ff.*

[31] San Remo Manual paras [105]–[108].

[32] San Remo Manual para [39].

[33] San Remo Manual para [47].

[34] Geneva Convention II Arts 22*ff.*

b) small craft used for coastal rescue operations and medical transport;

c) vessels granted safe conduct by agreement between the belligerent parties, such as cartel vessels engaged in the transport of prisoners of war, or vessels engaged in humanitarian missions;

d) vessels engaged in transporting cultural property under special protection;

e) passenger vessels when engaged only in carrying civilian passengers;

f) vessels charged with religious, non-military scientific or philanthropic missions[35];

g) small coastal fishing vessels and small boats engaged in local coastal trade, subject to the regulations of a belligerent naval commander;

h) vessels designated or adapted exclusively for responding to pollution incidents;

i) vessels which have surrendered; and

j) life rafts and life boats.[36]

However, the San Remo Manual provides that such vessels may lose their immunity if[37]:

a) they are not employed in their original role, but are used for military purposes, always subject to the principle of necessity and proportionality; or

b) they refuse to submit to identification and inspection when required, subject to the rules of necessity and proportionality; or

c) they intentionally hamper the movement of combatants and do not obey orders to stop or move out of the way when required.

The conditions that must be fulfilled before a hospital ship loses the benefit of immunity from attack are considerably more stringent, since a higher degree of necessity and proportionality is required before putting at risk the lives of the wounded and sick.[38]

Whilst the above discussion has focused on those seagoing craft that may not be the object of an attack, except in the absence of special circumstances, it is necessary to consider which ships may be subjected to violence. Clearly, in most cases, the warships of an opposed belligerent will fall within the definition of a military objective and therefore may be attacked.[39] Any attacks must comply with the basic rules that govern all hostile actions at sea.[40] The warships of a neutral state, however, may not be attacked, unless they are performing a service which breaches their duty of neutrality. Other ships flying the belligerent flag and engaging in some military service, such as acting as fleet auxiliaries, may be attacked if they conform to the definition of 'military objectives',[41] a concept that was discussed during the consideration of targeting in the law of land warfare.

---

[35] See generally: *The Paklat* (1915) 1 British and Colonial Prize Cases 515.

[36] See further: *The Llandovery Castle* (1922) 16 AJIL 704; and *Re Eck (The Peleus)* (1946) 13 AD 248.

[37] San Remo Manual para [48].

[38] San Remo Manual para [49].

[39] San Remo Manual para [65].

[40] San Remo Manual para [66].

[41] San Remo Manual paras [40] and [65].

6. *Means and methods of warfare.* The restrictions that are imposed on means and methods of warfare during armed conflicts on land[42] also apply to warfare conducted at sea.[43] Thus, for example, the use of indiscriminate means of warfare is forbidden[44]; there is a requirement that precautions must be taken when planning and engaging in attacks[45]; refusal of quarter and perfidy are prohibited.[46]

The proclamation of a maritime blockade is a method of warfare unique to the naval situation.[47] The object of such a blockade is to ensure that all maritime shipping that has the aim of docking in an enemy state is interrupted, subject to the duty to allow passage of certain humanitarian convoys.[48] In order for a blockade to be properly utilised as a method of warfare, it must satisfy certain criteria:

a) A blockade must be declared and notified to all belligerents and neutral states.[49]

b) The blockade must be effective, which means that the naval forces, including aircraft, of the belligerent power which declares that the blockade is in existence must be able to enforce that blockade.[50] The question of effectiveness is one of fact. A paper blockade, which is unable to be enforced by the naval forces of the power that declares its existence, is illegal.

c) The blockade must be enforced at a distance near to the coast. Long-distance blockades, whereby a vessel may be arrested wherever it is met on the sea provided there is a suspicion that it could be bound to the blockaded coast, are illegal.

d) The blockade must be applied impartially to all vessels of all states.[51]

7. *Visit and search; capture of vessels.* There may be a belief that a vessel which flies a neutral flag is, in reality, an enemy vessel, or at least carries goods for the benefit of the opposed belligerent. Similarly, a vessel with a supposed commercial or philanthropic purpose may, in actuality, perform military services for the benefit of the enemy. In cases of suspicion, only a visit on board the ship can dispel the doubts.[52] In accordance with our discussion of the areas in which warfare may be conducted, above, the warships of a belligerent can visit and search a ship on the high seas or in the exclusive economic zone of a state, but not in the territorial sea or internal waters of a neutral state.[53] The right of visit and search does not extend to neutral warships. Moreover, a merchant vessel is exempt from the duty to submit to visit and search if it navigates under the convoy of a neutral warship, is bound for a neutral port, and certifies that it does not transport contraband by providing the information that could be obtained by visit and search.[54] If a visit and search of

---

[42] Additional Protocol I Art 35.
[43] San Remo Manual paras [38]*ff* and see generally ch 19 above.
[44] San Remo Manual para [42(b)].
[45] San Remo Manual para [46].
[46] San Remo Manual para [111].
[47] See generally: San Remo Manual paras [93]–[104].
[48] San Remo Manual [104].
[49] San Remo Manual [93]–[94].
[50] San Remo Manual [95].
[51] San Remo Manual para [100].
[52] San Remo Manual Section II.
[53] San Remo Manual para [118].
[54] San Remo Manual para [120].

a commercial vessel at the point of interception cannot be performed for reasons of danger, the commercial vessel may be diverted to a more safe location where the visit and search may be performed.[55] If a ship subject to visit and search is found either to have been engaged in the transport of contraband, which are goods that are ultimately destined for territory under control of the enemy and which are susceptible to use in the armed conflict, and which moreover are found on a prohibited contraband list published by the belligerent; presents false identification documents; violates a blockade; or is being used for military purposes, then that ship may be captured as a prize.[56] In extreme cases, a captured vessel may be destroyed, but only under the strictest conditions.[57]

The law relating to these questions is fraught with complications. In order to highlight the difficulties, one example to note is the practice of camouflaging contraband carried aboard a neutral ship, thereby decreasing the chance that it will be seized. This practice consists of interposing a series of neutral ports between the port of origin of the goods and their port of final destination. The aim of this ruse is to disguise the ultimate destination, an enemy port, from adverse warships for as long as possible. In order to ensure that the rules of naval LOAC cannot be evaded, the doctrine of 'continuous voyage' has developed.[58] The voyage is considered to be 'continuous' up until the port of final destination, and not fragmented by the route taken including neutral intercalated ports. If goods are bound for an enemy port, they may be seized. Although the doctrine addresses the issue, a problem of evidence remains: is it certain that the goods are effectively destined for an enemy port?

Let us return to more simple rules. The most important of them is that whenever a ship or goods are captured and made a prize, such capture must be upheld by a judgment of a special national prize court in the belligerent state.[59] Each prize taken must be adjudicated. Such prize courts, albeit being national tribunals of a belligerent, adjudicate the capture according to rules of international law and often show a great deal of procedural and substantive fairness to the foreign commercial actor involved.[60] They closely scrutinise the justification advanced for the taking of the prize.

A prize may be liberated by a warship of an opposed belligerent, especially by a warship of its state of affiliation. This is known as 'recapture', or 'rescousse' in French.

8. *Sea warfare in NIAC.* There is a great deal of uncertainty as to the content of the rules applicable to non-international armed conflict (NIAC) sea warfare. Whilst such non-international sea warfare is a rare occurrence in situations where there has not been an express or implied recognition of belligerency, an example can be found in the civil war in Sri Lanka. Whilst it is clear that the parties involved in such sea warfare are bound to respect the 'common core of humanity' that is applicable to

---

[55] San Remo Manual para [121].
[56] San Remo Manual para [146].
[57] San Remo Manual para [151].
[58] See especially: *The Kim* [1915] P 215, 272–275.
[59] San Remo Manual para [116].
[60] See, eg: *The Zamora (No 1)* [1916] 2 AC 77 (PC).

both international and non-international sea warfare,[61] it is submitted that the best solution to the question of applicability is to make this matter the subject of special agreements between the parties,[62] which would ideally provide that the parties to the conflict recognise the applicability of all or part of the rules applicable to sea warfare under international armed conflict.

Comprehension check:

a) What are the basic principles when comparing the law of sea warfare to the law of land warfare? Which of these principles are common to both areas and which differ?
b) Which vessels may not be attacked?
c) If contraband is seized and a vessel is captured, may the belligerent capturing those goods and vessels dispose of them as he or she wishes?
d) Under what conditions is it lawful to proclaim a maritime blockade?

Answers:

a) The basic principle is that the main rules of land warfare apply also to sea warfare by analogy. For example, this is true as to the rules that govern prohibited weapons or other means and methods of warfare; as to the principle of distinction between military and civilian objectives; as to the rule on precautions in attack; as to the rules on perfidy and refusal of quarter; and as to the rules on protection of the wounded and sick or shipwrecked. There are obviously also some specialised rules which arise due to a proper appreciation of the difference in nature between the sea and the land. Thus, the rules relating to visit and search, capture and prize adjudication and the doctrine of continuous voyage, are special laws framed for seagoing vessels. Analogous rules cannot be found in land warfare.

b) There are many such vessels. You may just mention some of them[63]:
    i)   hospital ships[64];
    ii)   small craft used for coastal rescue operations and medical transport;
    iii) vessels granted safe conduct by agreement between the belligerent parties, such as cartel vessels, engaged in the transport of prisoners of war, or vessels engaged in humanitarian missions;
    iv)   vessels engaged in transporting cultural property under special protection;
    v)   passenger vessels when engaged only in carrying civilian passengers;
    vi)   vessels charged with religious, non-military scientific or philanthropic missions;
    vii) small coastal fishing vessels and small boats engaged in local coastal trade, subject to the regulations of a belligerent naval commander;

---

[61] See especially: *Corfu Channel*, n 10, 22; *Nicaragua*, n 10, para [218]; and *Prosecutor v Tadic* (Decision on the Defence Motion for Interlocutory Appeal on Jurisdiction) IT-49-1-AR72 (2 October 1995) para [98].

[62] See generally: ch 15 above.

[63] San Remo Manual para [47].

[64] Geneva Convention II Arts 22*ff*.

viii) vessels designated or adapted exclusively for responding to pollution incidents;

ix) vessels which have surrendered; and

x) life rafts and life boats.

Remember that under some conditions, even such vessels may be attacked, for example if they engage in military activities.[65]

c) No. The principle rule in this context is that a special court of municipal law, called a prize court, must always adjudicate the lawfulness of the seizure. Hence, the goods and vessel seized may not be disposed of before such adjudication takes place. Destruction of the vessel or its goods is possible under extreme circumstances, but only when some extremely strict conditions have been complied with.[66] Even in such a case, an adjudication of the lawfulness of the destruction must take place before a prize court.

d) The maritime blockade is an act of war. Hence, it can be used within an armed conflict. Conversely, a proclamation of a blockade outside such a conflict (and without the authorisation of the Security Council of the United Nations) is an act of aggression. Apart from this last aspect relating to *jus ad bellum*, the principle rule is that the warships of the power which declares the blockade must be able to effectively enforce the blockade (no paper blockade). Furthermore, the blockade may not extend too far into the sea (no long-distance blockade). These restrictions aim to create a balance and avoid excessively infringing the commercial interests of the neutral powers by allowing arbitrary and fictitious blockades to be proclaimed too easily, or by allowing visit and search to take place everywhere on the high seas at the discretion of commanders of warships.

---

[65] San Remo Manual para [48].
[66] San Remo Manual para [151].

32

NON-INTERNATIONAL ARMED CONFLICTS IN PARTICULAR

Learning objectives: To discover the rules applicable during non-international armed conflicts.

1. Non-international armed conflicts (NIAC) are, roughly speaking, civil wars. In the period prior to the 1990s, the law of NIAC was poorly developed. Whilst the law of international armed conflicts (IAC) contained detailed conventional rules that governed almost all questions relating to protection and means and methods of warfare, the law concerning NIAC contained only a few rudimentary rules, such as Article 3 common to the Geneva Conventions,[1] and many gaps. Indeed, in the years before the negotiation of the Geneva Conventions in 1949, the matter was wholly unregulated. It was left to the government caught in the civil war and to third states to grant some form of recognition of belligerency to the rebels if they wanted to apply rules of the LOAC to them. Hence, third states sometimes granted recognition to the rebels in order to be entitled to apply rules of neutrality to both belligerents. In this period, when a civil war was the cause of unnecessary suffering to the civilian population, the responsibility for relief initiatives often rested with the humanitarian initiative of the International Committee of the Red Cross (ICRC). These initiatives sometimes gave rise to ad hoc agreements between the warring parties, providing for some protection for particular groups of persons. The ICRC initiatives had no conventional basis. They were undertaken by virtue of the ICRC's general customary right to propose humanitarian solutions in cases of crises.[2]

The reason why the law of NIAC has been neglected and under-regulated for so long is the sensitivity of states to third-party interference in questions related to their internal security and sovereignty. In the pre-1949 period, many states preferred to remain completely free to treat rebellion and sedition as a crime under domestic law rather than to give international law rights and duties to the rebels under the LOAC. Developing the law of NIAC was perceived as upgrading the moral, legal and political position of the rebels. It was moreover considered that such a development would grant an unwelcome right of intervention to foreign entities such as a 'protecting powers', third states, the ICRC or even the 'international community' in general.

---

[1] Geneva Conventions I–IV Art 3.
[2] See generally: ch 16 above.

2. In the 1990s, under the impulsion of the growing amount of human rights law and the practice of international organs such as the Security Council and the International Criminal Tribunal for the former Yugoslavia (ICTY),[3] the law of NIAC quickly developed, on a case-by-case basis. It now tends to largely merge into the law of IAC. The main reason for this evolution is that, in current circumstances, most conflicts are inextricably mixed. Modern conflicts have the characteristics of IAC with respect to certain types of hostilities in certain places and at the same time retain the complexion of a NIAC with respect to other war, or warlike, actions. The armed conflict following the dissolution of Yugoslavia is a case in point. The conflict was either international or non-international depending on: the particular stage of the conflict being considered; the actors involved; and the specific area where the fighting was taking place. The international and non-international aspects of the armed conflict were so intertwined that it was difficult to separate them. Moreover, the international community was attempting to ensure maximum protection for those affected by the war, and therefore a separation would have been unwelcome. Separating areas and actions according to the type of conflict, international or non-international, would have meant discriminating in the protection given to those who were in desperate need of such protection. Here, in one particular valley, the conflict at the relevant time happened to be international because of the involvement of a foreign state. In that valley, the persons to be protected enjoyed the coverage of the much more precise and generous law of IAC. Then, in a nearby valley, the conflict at the relevant time remained non-international, since there was no foreign involvement. Thus, the persons who required the protection of the LOAC would lose most of the protective guarantees, since the law of NIAC is replete with low standards and gaps. This discrimination was considered to be deeply unsatisfactory. From the humanitarian point of view, the same rules should protect victims of IAC and of NIAC.[4] Similar problems arise and the victims need similar protection. This argument appears with even more strength in the case of a mixed armed conflict, where any attempt at separation of the various aspects and phases of a conflict must appear to be deeply arbitrary.

Following the outbreak of the armed conflict in the former Yugoslavia, there has been a steady push in the direction of a merger of both branches of the law, NIAC and IAC. We are in this context confronted with a paradigm shift. What was considered to be normal in the past under the aegis of state sovereignty is now considered to be inadmissible from the perspective of human rights. According to the ICTY and to a series of authors, there has been a revolution; we have moved from a LOAC based on state sovereignty towards a LOAC based on the protection of the human person.[5]

A further advantage of the merged approach is that it avoids the complication of deciding whether a particular armed conflict has an international or

---

[3] See, eg: *Prosecutor v Tadic* (Decision on the Defence Motion for Interlocutory Appeal on Jurisdiction) IT-94-1-AR72 (2 October 1995) paras [96]–[127]; *Prosecutor v Galic* (Judgment) IT-98-29-A (30 November 2006) paras [79]–[90]; *Prosecutor v Furundzija* (Trial Judgment) IT-95-17/1-T (10 December 1998); and *Prosecutor v Krstic* (Trial Judgment) IT-98-33-T (2 August 2001).

[4] *Tadic*, n 3, para [97].

[5] *Ibid*, para [97], which states, '[g]radually the maxim of Roman law *hominum causa omne jus constitutum est* (all law is created for the benefit of human beings) has gained a firm foothold in the [LOAC]'.

non-international character. This exercise may be quite exacting, as the chapter devoted to the distinction between IAC and NIAC has shown.[6] Moreover, the qualification of a conflict as either international or non-international is often politically delicate. Take the example of secession. If it is decided that the law of NIAC applies in such a case, this implies that the secession has not yet achieved its aims and that the seceding entity is still legally and factually attached to the central state. This will be unacceptable for the secessionist authorities. Conversely, applying the law of IAC will imply that the secession has succeeded and that the secessionist entity has been legally and factually severed from the central state. This will be intolerable for the central authorities. Therefore, when making the decision one has the potential to end up in a quagmire.

3. Where do we stand today? In the last two decades the law applying to NIAC has moved progressively closer to the law applying to IAC. A neat and clear distinction between the law applicable to the two types of conflict exists today only in two areas: (1) the status of combatants and prisoners of war; and (2) occupied territories. Both of the mentioned concepts do not apply automatically in cases of NIAC. First, there is no prisoner of war status under NIAC. The state where the non-international armed conflict takes place can treat the rebels as simple criminals and try them for having taken up the arms against the government, contrary to the criminal law of that state. Obviously, the state can accept an obligation to treat all or some of them as having a status equivalent to prisoners of war. However, this concession rests on a special grant by the state or on a special agreement between the parties to the conflict. This happened in Spain during the civil war between 1936 and 1939. Secondly, there are obviously no occupied territories in NIAC. The government does not occupy a territory if it retakes it from rebel control, nor do the rebels occupy the governmental territory over which they exercise power. Only foreign territory can be occupied. Further, there is one other area where some doubts remain as to the unity of the law applicable in IAC and NIAC: the prohibition of certain weapons. States for a long time resisted extending prohibitions on particular weapons to NIAC. Only recently have states become willing to narrow the gaps between the two types of conflict in this area.

For all the other rules of the LOAC, there is now at least a presumption that they apply to NIAC as well as to IAC. This is true, for example, for the norms concerning means and methods of warfare, for the principle of distinction between civilian and military objectives and for those rules that govern the provision of relief assistance.[7] This progressive 'merger' of NIAC and IAC has been consolidated by several factors:

a) the jurisprudence of the ICTY and the International Criminal Tribunal for Rwanda (ICTR), which has contributed to the development of customary international law applicable in non-international armed conflicts[8];

[6] See generally: ch 10 above. For an example of a decision on the character of a conflict, see, eg: *Prosecutor v Tadic* (Appeal Judgment) IT-94-1-A (15 July 1999) paras [88]–[162].

[7] See generally: J-M Henckaerts and L Doswald-Beck (eds), *Customary International Humanitarian Law Volume 1: Rules* (Cambridge, CUP, 2005) (*ICRC Customary Study*).

[8] See especially: *Tadic*, n 3, paras [96]–[127].

b) the definition of war crimes in the Rome Statute of the International Criminal Court[9];

c) states having accepted that recent treaties on prohibition of certain weapons[10] and on the protection of cultural objects[11] apply during both categories of conflicts; and

d) the growing influence of human rights law.[12]

The evolutionary merger is reflected in the ICRC customary law study.[13]

4. The overall result of this recent evolution is that conventional law explicitly applicable to NIAC lags behind the customary international law that is applicable in situations of NIAC. Thus, in order to facilitate and simplify the application of the LOAC in situations of NIAC, a new convention should be adopted that codifies and develops the law applicable in NIAC. Such a convention should compile all of the rules applicable in NIAC by analogy to the law of IAC. Practically speaking, except for the law that applies to prisoners of war and during belligerent occupation, one should today always refer to the rules of IAC in conjunction with the sources that specifically apply to NIAC. Where the text of conventions applicable to NIAC does not contain sufficient details to allow the rights and duties of belligerent parties in NIAC to be ascertained in detail, reference must be made by analogy to the law of IAC. Thus, for example, the principle of distinction applies during NIAC. However, the conventional norms that apply this principle to NIAC do not define military objectives or civilian status.[14] These definitions must be construed by way of analogy to the law of IAC.

5. The main conventional sources that apply to non-international armed conflicts in particular are the following:

a) *Human rights law*, especially those core rules that are applicable in times of emergency. There are some rules of human rights law that cannot be derogated from even in time of emergencies.[15] These are called 'non-derogable human rights', and include the right to life and the right to freedom from torture. A non-international armed conflict is an emergency that allows human rights that are derogable to be suspended. If a government involved in a NIAC does not proclaim the suspension of certain rights because of an

---

[9] Rome Statute of the International Criminal Court (adopted 17 July 1998, entered into force 1 July 2002) 2187 UNTS 3 Art 8, and in particular Art 8(2)(e).

[10] Amended Art 1 to The Convention on Prohibitions or Restrictions on the Use of Certain Conventional Weapons Which May be Deemed to be Excessively Injurious or to Have Indiscriminate Effects adopted at Geneva on the 10 October 1980 (adopted 21 December 2001, entered into force 18 May 2004) UN Doc CCW/CONF.II/2.

[11] Second Protocol to the Hague Convention of 1954 for the Protection of Cultural Property in the Event of Armed Conflict (adopted 26 March 1999, entered into force 9 March 2004) (1999) 38 ILM 769 Arts 3(1) and 22(1).

[12] See generally: ch 33 below.

[13] *ICRC Customary Study*, n 7.

[14] Protocol Additional to the Geneva Conventions of 12 August 1949, and relating to the Protection of Victims of Non-International Armed Conflicts (adopted 8 June 1977, entered into force 7 December 1978) 1125 UNTS 609 (Additional Protocol II) Arts 13–14.

[15] See, eg: International Covenant on Civil and Political Rights (adopted 16 December 1966, entered into force 23 March 1976) 999 UNTS 171 (ICCPR) Art 4(2).

emergency situation, then all of the human rights ordinarily applicable to its territory in time of peace will remain in force.

b) *Common Article 3 of Geneva Conventions I–IV.* This Article is known as a 'common article' because it has the same text in all four Geneva Conventions. This provision has been, and still is, of huge importance. It applies not only to NIAC, but also in all situations where there are gaps in the protection granted by the LOAC. It forms a minimum standard beneath which no belligerent should ever fall, no matter what the circumstances.[16] Common Article 3 thus presents a 'minimum humanitarian standard', a universal rule setting out the minimum requirements of humanity applicable in all situations and in all circumstances.[17] Common Article 3 reads as follows:

> In the case of armed conflict not of an international character occurring in the territory of one of the High Contracting Parties, each Party to the conflict shall be bound to apply, as a minimum, the following provisions:
>
> (1) Persons taking no active part in the hostilities, including members of armed forces who have laid down their arms and those placed hors de combat by sickness, wounds, detention, or any other cause, shall in all circumstances be treated humanely, without any adverse distinction founded on race, colour, religion or faith, sex, birth or wealth, or any other similar criteria. To this end, the following acts are and shall remain prohibited at any time and in any place whatsoever with respect to the above-mentioned persons:
>
> (a) violence to life and person, in particular murder of all kinds, mutilation, cruel treatment and torture;
> (b) taking of hostages;
> (c) outrages upon personal dignity, in particular humiliating and degrading treatment;
> (d) the passing of sentences and the carrying out of executions without previous judgement pronounced by a regularly constituted court, affording all the judicial guarantees which are recognized as indispensable by civilized peoples.
>
> (2) The wounded and sick shall be collected and cared for.
>
> An impartial humanitarian body, such as the International Committee of the Red Cross, may offer its services to the Parties to the conflict.
>
> The Parties to the conflict should further endeavour to bring into force, by means of special agreements, all or part of the other provisions of the present Convention.
>
> The application of the preceding provisions shall not affect the legal status of the Parties to the conflict.

Common Article 3 thus contains four essential normative injunctions.

---

[16] *Military and Paramilitary Activities in and against Nicaragua (Nicaragua v United States of America)* (Merits) [1986] ICJ Rep 14 para [218].

[17] Rules applicable in IAC may be used to interpret the guarantees given in Common Article 3, *Hamdan v Rumsfeld* (2006) 126 S Ct 2749, where Common Article 3 was interpreted by reference to Protocol Additional to the Geneva Conventions of 12 August 1949, and relating to the Protection of Victims of International Armed Conflicts (adopted 8 June 1977, entered into force 7 December 1978) 1125 UNTS 3 (Additional Protocol 1) Art 75.

i)   First, the *principle of humanity without adverse distinction*. All persons *hors de combat* have to be humanely treated without discrimination on the basis of race, colour, religion, faith, sex, birth, wealth or any similar criteria. Nationality is not mentioned as a ground of equality because the applicable conflict is considered to be a NIAC, where all fighters have the same nationality. The principle of humanity set out in Common Article 3 gives rise to the most fundamental duties which must be obeyed by all parties to the NIAC at all times.

ii) Secondly, *a series of precise prohibitions* flow from the general principle of humanity. These are mentioned in letters (a) to (d) of Common Article 3(1). These specific prohibitions make clear that violence to life and limb, outrages to personal dignity, taking of hostages and unfair trial shall always be prohibited in NIACs.

iii) Thirdly, the *wounded and sick shall be collected and cared for*. This provision does not specify the manner in which this duty must be carried out. It miniaturises to the maximum extent possible the contents of Geneva Conventions I and II.

iv) Fourthly, the customary *right of humanitarian initiative* possessed by impartial humanitarian bodies, namely the ICRC, is recognised. This provision codifies an important customary principle, which has in the past been integral to the humanitarian protection of civilians in non-international armed conflicts.

c) *Additional Protocol II*. This convention, which was originally drafted as a comprehensive code of the LOAC applicable in NIAC, was reduced to a mere skeleton during the diplomatic conference that led to the adoption of Additional Protocol II in 1977 by a series of states, in particular the so-called 'third world states', which wished to jealously guard their unimpaired sovereignty. However, despite its much reduced form, Additional Protocol II develops the protections contained in Common Article 3 to the Geneva Conventions. Its contents are twofold: first, it adds more detail to the minimum provisions set out in Common Article 3; secondly, it introduces 'Hague Law' provisions, regulating the means and methods of warfare, into the conventional law applicable to NIAC. Summing up, Additional Protocol II contains three main normative injunctions:

i)   The *principle of humane treatment* is again mentioned. However, the list of specifically prohibited acts is considerably extended.[18] Moreover, special protection is granted to persons deprived of their liberty and obligations relating to fair trial are set out.[19] Article 4, which is of great importance, is set out below:

Fundamental guarantees

1. All persons who do not take a direct part or who have ceased to take part in hostilities, whether or not their liberty has been restricted, are enti-

---

[18] Additional Protocol II Art 4.
[19] Additional Protocol II Arts 5–6.

tled to respect for their person, honour and convictions and religious practices. They shall in all circumstances be treated humanely, without any adverse distinction. It is prohibited to order that there shall be no survivors.

2. Without prejudice to the generality of the foregoing, the following acts against the persons referred to in paragraph I are and shall remain prohibited at any time and in any place whatsoever:

(a) violence to the life, health and physical or mental well-being of persons, in particular murder as well as cruel treatment such as torture, mutilation or any form of corporal punishment;
(b) collective punishments;
(c) taking of hostages;
(d) acts of terrorism;
(e) outrages upon personal dignity, in particular humiliating and degrading treatment, rape, enforced prostitution and any form or indecent assault;
(f) slavery and the slave trade in all their forms;
(g) pillage;
(h) threats to commit any or the foregoing acts.

3. Children shall be provided with the care and aid they require, and in particular:

(a) they shall receive an education, including religious and moral education, in keeping with the wishes of their parents, or in the absence of parents, of those responsible for their care;
(b) all appropriate steps shall be taken to facilitate the reunion of families temporarily separated;
(c) children who have not attained the age of fifteen years shall neither be recruited in the armed forces or groups nor allowed to take part in hostilities;
(d) the special protection provided by this Article to children who have not attained the age of fifteen years shall remain applicable to them if they take a direct part in hostilities despite the provisions of subparagraph (c) and are captured;
(e) measures shall be taken, if necessary, and whenever possible with the consent of their parents or persons who by law or custom are primarily responsible for their care, to remove children temporarily from the area in which hostilities are taking place to a safer area within the country and ensure that they are accompanied by persons responsible for their safety and well-being.

ii) The provision in Common Article 3 as to the *treatment and care of the wounded, sick and shipwrecked* is considerably developed, by analogy to the rules of IAC. This is the object of Articles 7–12 of Additional Protocol II. These provisions read as follows:

Art 7. Protection and care

1. All the wounded, sick and shipwrecked, whether or not they have taken part in the armed conflict, shall be respected and protected.

2. In all circumstances they shall be treated humanely and shall receive to the fullest extent practicable and with the least possible delay, the medical care and attention required by their condition. There shall be no distinction among them founded on any grounds other than medical ones.

Art 8. Search

Whenever circumstances permit and particularly after an engagement, all possible measures shall be taken, without delay, to search for and collect the wounded, sick and shipwrecked, to protect them against pillage and ill-treatment, to ensure their adequate care, and to search for the dead, prevent their being despoiled, and decently dispose of them.

Art 9. Protection of medical and religious personnel

1. Medical and religious personnel shall be respected and protected and shall be granted all available help for the performance of their duties. They shall not be compelled to carry out tasks which are not compatible with their humanitarian mission.

2. In the performance of their duties medical personnel may not be required to give priority to any person except on medical grounds.

Art 10. General protection of medical duties

1. Under no circumstances shall any person be punished for having carried out medical activities compatible with medical ethics, regardless of the person benefiting therefrom.

2. Persons engaged in medical activities shall neither be compelled to perform acts or to carry out work contrary to, nor be compelled to refrain from acts required by, the rules of medical ethics or other rules designed for the benefit of the wounded and sick, or this Protocol.

3. The professional obligations of persons engaged in medical activities regarding information which they may acquire concerning the wounded and sick under their care shall, subject to national law, be respected.

4. Subject to national law, no person engaged in medical activities may be penalized in any way for refusing or failing to give information concerning the wounded and sick who are, or who have been, under his care.

Art 11. Protection of medical units and transports

1. Medical units and transports shall be respected and protected at all times and shall not be the object of attack.

2. The protection to which medical units and transports are entitled shall not cease unless they are used to commit hostile acts, outside their humanitarian function. Protection may, however, cease only after a warning has been given, setting, whenever appropriate, a reasonable time-limit, and after such warning has remained unheeded.

Art 12. The distinctive emblem

Under the direction of the competent authority concerned, the distinctive emblem of the red cross, red crescent or red lion and sun on a white ground shall be displayed by medical and religious personnel and medical units, and on medical transports. It shall be respected in all circumstances. It shall not be used improperly.

iii) Finally, Additional Protocol II contains provisions concerning the *protection of the civilian population and special objects from attack*. These norms are set out in Articles 13–18. These provisions reproduce, in a shortened form, the corresponding provisions contained in Additional Protocol I.[20] One should not hesitate, in interpreting the rules contained in Additional Protocol II, to compare by analogy the text of the Additional Protocol I provisions. The Protocol II provisions read as follows:

Art 13. Protection of the civilian population

1. The civilian population and individual civilians shall enjoy general protection against the dangers arising from military operations. To give effect to this protection, the following rules shall be observed in all circumstances.

2. The civilian population as such, as well as individual civilians, shall not be the object of attack. Acts or threats of violence the primary purpose of which is to spread terror among the civilian population are prohibited.

3. Civilians shall enjoy the protection afforded by this part, unless and for such time as they take a direct part in hostilities.

Art 14. Protection of objects indispensable to the survival of the civilian population

Starvation of civilians as a method of combat is prohibited. It is therefore prohibited to attack, destroy, remove or render useless for that purpose, objects indispensable to the survival of the civilian population such as food-stuffs, agricultural areas for the production of food-stuffs, crops, livestock, drinking water installations and supplies and irrigation works.

Art 15. Protection of works and installations containing dangerous forces

Works or installations containing dangerous forces, namely dams, dykes and nuclear electrical generating stations, shall not be made the object of attack, even where these objects are military objectives, if such attack may cause the release of dangerous forces and consequent severe losses among the civilian population.

Art 16. Protection of cultural objects and of places of worship

Without prejudice to the provisions of the Hague Convention for the Protection of Cultural Property in the Event of Armed Conflict of 14 May 1954, it is prohibited to commit any acts of hostility directed against historic monuments, works of art or places of worship which constitute the cultural or spiritual heritage of peoples, and to use them in support of the military effort.

Art 17. Prohibition of forced movement of civilians

---

[20] Additional Protocol 1 Arts 48–60.

1. The displacement of the civilian population shall not be ordered for reasons related to the conflict unless the security of the civilians involved or imperative military reasons so demand. Should such displacements have to be carried out, all possible measures shall be taken in order that the civilian population may be received under satisfactory conditions of shelter, hygiene, health, safety and nutrition.

2. Civilians shall not be compelled to leave their own territory for reasons connected with the conflict.

Art 18. Relief societies and relief actions

1. Relief societies located in the territory of the High Contracting Party, such as Red Cross (Red Crescent, Red Lion and Sun) organizations may offer their services for the performance of their traditional functions in relation to the victims of the armed conflict. The civilian population may, even on its own initiative, offer to collect and care for the wounded, sick and shipwrecked.

2. If the civilian population is suffering undue hardship owing to a lack of the supplies essential for its survival, such as food-stuffs and medical supplies, relief actions for the civilian population which are of an exclusively humanitarian and impartial nature and which are conducted without any adverse distinction shall be undertaken subject to the consent of the High Contracting Party concerned.

Comprehension check:

a) Why was the law of NIAC traditionally less developed than the law of IAC? Where do we stand today if we compare the content of the two branches of the law, NIAC and IAC?

b) Is it reasonable to bring the two branches of the law, IAC and NIAC, ever closer?

c) In what main areas do there remain clear differences between the law of NIAC and the law of IAC?

d) Which are the main sources applicable to NIAC?

e) If a gap in the law applicable to a NIAC appears, where would you look to find the rule that applies in a particular situation?

Answers:

a) The difference in development was due to the fact that an IAC, typically a war between states, has always been an intrinsically international phenomenon requiring some international law regulation of the relationship between the belligerents. Conversely, NIAC was seen as a purely internal matter for the state confronted with a rebellion. It was felt that no international rules should intervene in such internal affairs and no third states or international institutions should have any say. Today, the two branches of the law have merged considerably, mainly under the impulsion of customary international law, as applied by the ICTY and ICTR. The reason for this evolution is that the distinction between law applicable in IAC and law applicable in NIAC is felt to be impracticable or excessively complicated in many situations, particularly mixed conflicts; to sometimes be politically delicate; and to be arbitrary in the sense that the protection of a person largely depends on the qualification of the conflict, which is largely a technical accident. This discrimination in protection on the basis of a technicality is felt to be outdated and is no longer easily accepted.

b) This is a question for discussion, and different answers can be given to it. On the one hand, for those arguing from the standpoint of state freedom of action and of the protection of internal affairs, the merger approach may be unwelcome. It lessens the autonomy of the government on the question of how to treat rebels and how to conduct the warfare against them. Moreover, it politically and morally upgrades the rebels, possibly giving even some incentive for them to undertake their rebellious action. On the other hand, those arguing from the viewpoint of humanitarian protection, and possibly also those who desire simplicity in the law, will find the development welcome, since it enhances protection and regulates warfare for the benefit of the potential or actual war victims.

c) There are two main areas where the difference is clearly maintained and is likely to be maintained. (1) Combatant status and prisoner of war status. There are no recognised combatants in NIAC; all rebels can be criminally prosecuted for having taken up the arms; they do not enjoy prisoner of war status. (2) Belligerent occupation. There are no occupied territories if the armed conflict takes place within the borders of a single state.

d) Apart from customary international law and human rights law, two main conventional sources must be mentioned: (1) Common Article 3 to the Geneva Conventions; (2) Additional Protocol II. It is possible to briefly describe the contents of these two conventional sources.

e) If there is no conventional provision dealing with the law that applies to a particular situation during NIAC, it is necessary to examine customary law, as presented by the *ICRC Customary Study* and contained in military manuals and writings on the LOAC.[21] According to the type of question asked, applicable human rights law may also provide an answer. In any case, you should compare the rule applying to the situation which is found in the law of IAC and ask yourself if it is suitable for NIAC. It may be possible to apply the IAC rule by analogy.

---

[21] *ICRC Customary Study*, n 7.

33

THE RELATIONSHIP BETWEEN THE LOAC AND HUMAN RIGHTS LAW

Learning objectives: To learn about the relationship between the LOAC and international human rights law.

1. International Human Rights Law (IHRL), despite its prominence in contemporary discourse, is still a young branch of public international law (PIL). Created after World War II, in response to the egregious atrocities of the Axis Powers, it has enriched the body of international law. IHRL grants a series of individual, or collective, fundamental rights aimed at providing a certain level of protection to every individual who finds him- or herself on the territory, or otherwise in the control, of a state. The individual is protected from arbitrary or excessive interference by the state with the rights granted; and he or she is granted certain rights of positive action by the state, to their benefit. Two categories of fundamental rights and freedoms may be discussed. First, we can examine the so-called 'civil and political' rights.[1] Within this category, the 'civil' rights are particularly important in the context of armed conflict. These include the right to life; the right to physical integrity; the right to freedom from arbitrary arrest and detention, roughly equivalent to the right to *habeas corpus*; and the right to a fair trial or due process of law. Secondly, one may consider the 'economic, social and cultural' rights.[2] These are more vaguely formulated and constitute, for the most part, general criteria for the shaping of a proper policy.

2. For a long time these two branches of public international law, the LOAC and IHRL, remained separated. However, due to an increase in the number of non-international armed conflicts and the rise of situations of prolonged belligerent occupation, these branches of public international law have been progressively brought together. During non-international armed conflicts, the war affects the civilian population to a huge extent. Thus, it is understandable that in these situations IHRL was seen as a particularly apt vehicle for enhancing the protection given to civilians. This tendency was particularly marked in NIAC because the LOAC

---

[1] See, eg: International Covenant on Civil and Political Rights (adopted 16 December 1966, entered into force 23 March 1976) 999 UNTS 171.

[2] See, eg: International Covenant on Economic, Social and Cultural Rights (adopted 16 December 1966, entered into force 3 January 1976) 993 UNTS 3.

applicable in this area has traditionally displayed many gaps. The same is true for occupied territories. It is not an accident that, in the part dealing with belligerent occupation, Geneva Convention IV contains many provisions that appear to mirror a human rights approach.[3] Thus, for example, Article 49 sets out that deportation is prohibited; this rule could also be formulated as a fundamental right not to be displaced. This simple shift in expression shows the closeness of the formulation of a norm of the LOAC to the formulation of a norm of IHRL.

3. Today, the LOAC and IHRL intersect in many important ways. One may mention three of them in particular. The first is coordination by way of subsidiary application. The second is coordination by way of '*renvoi*' or reference from one branch of PIL to the other. The third is a sort of merger by which new law, permeated by both branches, is shaped. These three different approaches illustrate three facets of interaction between these two branches of PIL. Some short examples may be given for each approach.

THE 'SUBSIDIARY APPLICATION' APPROACH

4. Whilst the LOAC is only applicable during situations of armed conflict, IHRL is applicable in all situations, whether peace or war. Thus, international humanitarian law (IHL) does not apply, for example, during situations of internal disturbances and tensions, such as riots, isolated and sporadic acts of violence, or terrorist attacks. However, IHRL will apply to such situations. In these circumstances, IHRL formulates a subsidiary rule, which fills the 'gap' in protection left open by the inapplicability of the LOAC. Thus, one may say that IHRL borders on all parts of the LOAC and assures a humanitarian standard in all cases where IHL does not apply. Once the boundaries that govern the applicability of IHL are crossed, one ends up in the province of IHRL, which assures the subsidiary application of certain humanitarian standards.

That is not to say that IHRL applies only when IHL does not apply. We will see that both may apply contemporaneously. However, a distinctive function of IHRL is to remain the sole body of applicable international law rules that cover questions of humanity when IHL is no longer applicable. The famous Martens clause can today be read as providing the basis for such a function of human rights law.[4] This clause recalls that:

> [I]n cases not covered by the law in force, the human person remains under the protection of the principles of humanity and the dictates of public conscience.[5]

However, it has to be borne in mind that IHL may also apply by way of special agreements, even where legally it would not automatically apply. The parties can agree to apply some rules of IHL to situations beyond their formal scope of

---

[3] Geneva Convention IV Relative to the Protection of Civilian Persons in Time of War (adopted 12 August 1949, entered into force 21 October 1950) 75 UNTS 287 (Geneva Convention IV) Arts 47*ff*.

[4] See generally: ch 9 above.

[5] Protocol Additional to the Geneva Conventions of 12 August 1949, and relating to the Protection of Victims of Non-International Armed Conflicts (adopted 8 June 1977, entered into force 7 December 1978) 1125 UNTS 609, Preamble.

application.[6] Thus, the protections due to prisoners of war may be extended to the benefit of some captives in a non-international armed conflict, as was done during the Spanish Civil War. In these situations the scope of application of IHL is extended, although the effect of the extension is limited to a single case. In these cases the rules of IHL and IHRL again apply contemporaneously, through the choice of the concerned party.

5. Examples of the subsidiary application of IHRL when IHL does not apply can be found in all cases of 'public emergency' not amounting to an armed conflict, such as in Greece between 1967 and 1969 after the *coup d'état* by a military junta, or in the numerous Latin American situations of emergency, such as that in Uruguay in the 1970s.

THE RENVOI APPROACH

6. The technique of 'renvoi', or reference, is used mostly by the LOAC to make indirect reference, often as a guide to interpretation, to IHRL.[7] Thus, when IHL guarantees a 'fair trial' or otherwise sets out norms governing legal proceedings,[8] IHRL norms and jurisprudence may be invaluable in order to define more precisely the requirements of such a 'fair trial'. When IHL provides for detention of persons,[9] IHRL may help to concretise the rights and duties involved by offering its own rich experience. Sometimes the implicit reference may be bolder. In the case of occupation, the fundamental guarantees afforded to the civilians are a mix of IHL and IHRL. Practice with respect to Israeli occupied territories illustrates this point very clearly.[10]

7. Obviously, the *renvoi* can be reversed, with the LOAC used to interpret IHRL norms. Thus, according to the International Court of Justice, the non-derogable 'right to life' enshrined in Article 6 of the International Covenant on Civil and Political Rights (ICCPR) continues to apply in times of armed conflict.[11] However, its precise content is influenced by the armed conflict situation. According to the court, IHL constitutes in this situation a *lex specialis* which must be taken into account in order to be able to determine what constitutes an 'arbitrary deprivation of life' in this context.[12] This is so because killing is not generally prohibited in time of war: some deprivation of life is inherent in the nature of armed conflict. In this

---

[6] Geneva Conventions I–IV, Common Art 6/6/6/7 and ch 15 above.

[7] See, eg: *Prosecutor v Kunarac* (Trial Judgment) IT-96-23-T (2 February 2001) paras [465]–[497]; and *Prosecutor v Kronjelac* (Trial Judgment) IT-97-25-T (15 March 2002) paras [181]–[188], which use the case law of the European Court of Human Rights to define 'torture' in a LOAC context.

[8] See, eg: Geneva Conventions I–IV, Common Article 3; Geneva Convention III relative to the Treatment of Prisoners of War (adopted 12 August 1949, entered into force 21 October 1950) 75 UNTS 135 Arts 5(2) and 99*ff*; Geneva Convention IV Art 43.

[9] See, eg: Geneva Convention III Arts 21*ff*; Geneva Convention IV Arts 76, 78 and 79*ff*.

[10] See, eg: *Beit Sourik Village Council v The Government of Israel* HCJ/2056/04 (30 June 2004), Supreme Court of Israel, sitting as the High Court of Justice, available at <http://elyon1.court.gov.il/files_eng/04/560/020/A28/04020560.a28.pdf> accessed 20 May 2008 para [35], which states, referring to the law of belligerent occupation, that, '[t]hese provisions create a single tapestry of norms that recognizes both human rights and the needs of the local population as well recognizing security needs from the perspective of the military commander'.

[11] International Covenant on Civil and Political Rights Art 6.

case, both branches of the law and their norms are simply coordinated as a matter of interpretation. It is not so much a matter of allowing one, more specialised, source to override the other, which is the traditional meaning of the *lex specialis* rule, but rather using both sources of law in a complementary manner in order to obtain a proper interpretation. This approach is more properly described as one of *renvoi* rather than one of *lex specialis*.

8. References from one branch of PIL to the other take place when questions arise concerning those rights that are protected by both sources. Rights that benefit from such double protection include the right to life, as against arbitrary deprival; the prohibition against inhumane and degrading treatment and the prohibition of assaults on physical and mental integrity; the right to be free from arbitrary arrest and detention; rights related to judicial guarantees; rights related to the use of firearms by enforcement officials; and rights related to medical assistance and ethics.

THE 'MERGER' APPROACH

9. A movement that called for the respect of 'human rights in times of armed conflict' started in 1968 within the UN, at the Tehran Conference on Human Rights.[13] The general idea was to extend IHRL to situations of armed conflict in order to improve the protection of the civilian population and the detained persons. This new movement produced various texts at the international level, including a great series of relevant resolutions.[14] Thus, a peculiar branch of IHRL was developed, namely an IHRL that applied in situations of emergency and armed conflict. The various IHRL bodies soon had to consider applications that concerned alleged human rights violations first in the context of civil war, and later of international armed conflict. This has been the case for the UN Treaty bodies, in particular the Committee under the Covenant on Civil and Political Rights, the Inter-American Commission and Court of Human Rights,[15] the African Commission on Human Rights,[16] and even the European Court of Human Rights.[17] For fear that they will engage in too bold an action in a branch of law, the LOAC, on which they lack subject-matter jurisdiction and expertise, regional human rights bodies have generally showed studied restraint in their use of IHL,

---

[12] *Legality of the Threat or Use of Nuclear Weapons (Advisory Opinion)* [1996] ICJ Rep 226 para [25]; and *Legal Consequences of the Construction of a Wall in the Occupied Palestinian Territory (Advisory Opinion)* [2004] ICJ Rep 136 para [106].

[13] Human Rights in Armed Conflicts, Resolution XXIII adopted by the International Conference on Human Rights, Teheran (12 May 1968), available at <http://www.icrc.org/ihl.nsf/FULL/430?Open Document> accessed 20 May 2008.

[14] See, eg: Respect for Human Rights in Armed Conflict UNGA Res 2444 (XXIII) (19 December 1968); Basic Principles for the Protection of Civilian Populations in Armed Conflicts UNGA Res 2675 (XXV) (9 December 1970); and Declaration on the Protection of Women and Children in Emergency and Armed Conflict UNGA Res 3318 (XXIX) (14 December 1974).

[15] See, eg: *Coard v US* Case 10.951, Report No 109/99 (29 September 1999) available at <http://www1.umn.edu/humanrts/cases/us109-99.html> accessed 20 May 2008.

[16] *Commission Internationale des Droits de l'homme et des Libertés v Chad*, African Commission on Human and Peoples' Rights, Comm. No. 74/92 (1995) available at (1997) 18 *Human Rights Law Journal* 34.

and have generally refused to directly apply IHL. They have normally held that their jurisdiction is limited to the rights enshrined in the human rights treaty over whose application they have to control, and their ability to scrutinise states does not extend to questions of breach of the LOAC. A converse example is the *La Tablada* case decided by the Inter-American Commission of Human Rights.[18] In this case IHL, namely Article 3 common to the Geneva Conventions, was directly applied.[19] To a large extent the body of law dealing with 'human rights in armed conflicts' has simply taken the place of IHL in non-international armed conflicts. There is here only a partial merger of the two branches of PIL in these cases. However, the degree of merger could be reinforced by future evolution.

A more pronounced merger has taken place through the medium of UN reports, whether those concerning extra-judicial executions or those focused on specific armed conflicts, such as Iraq or Sudan. Unlike human rights bodies, UN organs are not constrained as to the material scope of their jurisdiction by treaty restrictions. These reports take into account both branches of the law by substantively combining the rights at stake.

10. Norms from the sphere of human rights law have been applied in many cases arising out of armed conflict. The precise conditions for the applicability of IHRL and its scope have been progressively spelled out. To gain a flavour of these cases one may quote, as for the European Court of Human Rights, the Cyprus cases,[20] the Turkish cases and nowadays the Chechnya cases[21]; for cases within the inter-American system, one may quote *La Tablada*,[22] *Las Palmeras*[23] or *Coard*[24]; and for the African Commission on Human Rights we can examine *Commission internationale des droits de l'homme et des libertés v Chad*.[25]

11. In the last few years, human rights bodies have found themselves concerned with cases arising from international armed conflicts, rather than merely being concerned with cases arising in NIAC. For example, the *Bankovic* case before the European Court of Human Rights arose from the NATO bombing of Serbia in 1999.[26] We may also consider the various human rights actions that concern the detention centre at Guantanamo Bay.[27] One may also think of cases that have considered the human rights implications of the acts of the occupying forces in Iraq.[28]

---

[17] See, eg: *Isayeva v Russia* (App no 57947-49/00) (2005) 41 EHRR 39; and *Bankovic v Belgium* (App no 52207/99) ECHR 12 December 2001 (2007) 44 EHRR SE5.

[18] *Abella v Argentina* Case 11.137, Report No 55/97 (18 November 1997) OEA/Ser.L/V/II.95 available at <http://www.cidh.org/annualrep/97eng/argentina11137.htm> accessed 20 May 2008.

[19] *Ibid*, paras [146]–[189], but see *Bámaca-Velásquez v Guatemala* (Merits) Inter-American Court of Human Rights Series C No 70 (25 November 2000) para [208], which states that the Inter-American Commission and court do not have 'competence to declare that a State is internationally responsible for the violation of international treaties that do not grant [them] such competence'.

[20] *Cyprus v Turkey* (2002) 35 EHRR 30.

[21] See, eg: *Isayeva*, n 17.

[22] Above, n 18.

[23] *Las Palmeras v Colombia* (Preliminary Objections) Inter-American Court of Human Rights Series C No 67 (4 February 2000).

[24] Above, n 15.

[25] Above, n 16.

[26] Above, n 17.

12. Finally, one must take notice of the emergence of 'minimum humanitarian standards' based on a complex mix of IHL and IHRL. The desire for such minimum standards came about because the interaction of IHRL and the LOAC gave rise to a paradox. In cases of national emergency which do not amount to an armed conflict, by remaining merely at the level of internal disturbances and tensions, states are allowed to suspend the application of some parts of IHRL. When these allowed suspensions of human rights operate in peacetime, this may bring about standards of protection which are lower than those which would exist if a fully fledged armed conflict had arisen. In other words, non-derogable human rights applicable in all cases of emergency proved in some cases weaker than the norms of IHL that applied in non-international armed conflicts. This is paradoxical because the law is more protective in an armed conflict situation where it seems that, on account of the gravity of the circumstances, states should be afforded more freedom to act.

In order to resolve this paradox, there has been an attempt to create minimum rules applicable to any situation within the continuum: rules that are applicable whether it is peacetime, an emergency, or an armed conflict. These proposed 'minimum rules' consist of a complex merger of IHRL and IHL. The heyday of this effort was reached in 1990 with the *Turku Declaration*, which was adopted by an expert meeting in Finland and proposed as a model to be taken into consideration by the UN and other international organisations.[29] This declaration is concerned with: issues of fair trial; limitations on means and methods of combat; prohibition of displacement and deportation; and guarantees of humane treatment. It has not yet achieved the success that its drafters had hoped it would have. However, efforts aimed at the creation of such minimum standards, based on a merger approach, are likely to be fuelled by recent events that have revealed the uncertainties concerning intermediate situations between peace and war: the situations in Afghanistan and Iraq spring to mind.

13. Recent practice thus reveals a rich array of relationships between IHL and IHRL. These relationships are designed to reinforce the separate branches of the law by combined action with the other branch. The evolution since 1945 has thus been one from mutual suspicion and disinterest to one of mutual cooperation and progressive inter-penetration of IHL and IHRL.

Comprehension check:

a) Why did IHRL and IHL converge in the modern world?
b) What functions does IHRL fulfil in the context of situations of armed conflict?
c) What is the most ordinary interaction of IHL and IHRL?

---

[27] *Decision on Request for Precautionary Measures (Detainees at Guantanamo Bay, Cuba)* [2002] 14 ILM 553, Inter-American Commission on Human Rights; and *Response of the United States to Request for Precautionary Measures (Detainees in Guantanamo Bay, Cuba)* [2002] 14 ILM 1015.

[28] See especially: *Al-Skeini v Secretary of State for Defence* [2007] UKHL 26, [2007] 3 WLR 33.

[29] (1991) 232 *International Review of the Red Cross* 330; UN Doc E/CN.4/Sub.2/1991/55.

Answers:

a) With the drafting of the Geneva Conventions in 1949, the 'protected person' and his or her rights against the enemy belligerent became an important new focus in the LOAC. Thus, some convergence with the emergent human rights movement became inevitable. The evolutions in international society in the post-World War II period did the rest. In particular, there has been a tremendous rise in numbers of NIAC and the occurrence of some difficult and prolonged occupation situations, such as that of the Palestinian occupied territories. These situations brought about great sufferings for the civilian populations. It was thus inevitable that IHRL would step in, alongside IHL, in order to strengthen the protection afforded to those persons. Finally, IHRL has developed tremendously over the last 30 years, so that a linkage with IHL was again unavoidable. As the LOAC and IHRL both protect the human person, either generally or in a particular context, the progressively stronger interaction of these two branches of PIL comes as no surprise.

b) IHRL has three distinctive functions. *First*, it assures some subsidiary rules are applicable in situations where IHL does not apply. This is the case, for example, when strife has not risen to the level of an armed conflict or an armed conflict no longer exists, but a state is racked by disturbances and tensions; or if an armed force is no longer a belligerent occupant but remains on a foreign territory on invitation of the local government. *Secondly*, it allows a proper application of some concepts within the LOAC, which can only be properly construed when the IHRL experience is examined. One may think of the notion of 'fair trial', but also of the rules on 'detention'. *Thirdly*, IHRL and IHL may partially merge together to produce a single set of rules applicable in armed conflict, or even in all situations of conflict as a sort of minimum standard. In any case, if there is not a specifically applicable rule of IHL, it is possible that IHRL may still provide some useful guidance.

c) The most ordinary interaction between the LOAC and IHRL is the parallel application of both strands of PIL to the same set of facts, each judging these facts through its own requirements. This is how the International Court of Justice approached the question in the *Israeli Wall* opinion,[30] and in the *Armed Activities* case.[31] It stands to reason that such a parallel application may imply that certain notions from one branch of the law will be taken into account in order to apply notions found in the other: for example the 'right to life' found in IHRL is influenced by the situation of warfare and is interpreted according to IHL considerations.

---

[30] See n 12, paras [89]*ff* and [102]*ff*.

[31] *Armed Activities on the Territory of the Congo (Democratic Republic of the Congo v Uganda)* [2006] ICJ Rep 6 paras [181]*ff*, particularly [216].

34

NEUTRALITY

Learning objectives: To learn about the law regulating the relationship between belligerent states and those third states that do not participate in the conflict.

1. When an armed conflict is fought, or war is declared, between two or more belligerent states, third states must make a political decision to either participate in the conflict or to remain aloof. If a third state decides to participate, they will become belligerents on the side of one or more other states, and become subject to the rights and duties of a party to the armed conflict; if they decide to remain aloof, they may obtain the status of neutrals if they comply with the duties that accompany this status, which are discussed in this chapter. The term neutrality originates from the Latin term '*ne-uter*', which means 'neither with the one nor with the other'.

2. This chapter is concerned with the rights and duties of neutral states in relation to belligerent states. However, two further questions arise that will not be discussed substantively:

a) First, the question of whether a state may remain neutral or not is a question that arises in the realm of the *jus ad bellum*, which is now governed by the Charter of the United Nations.[1] This difficult and controversial question is not part of the *jus in bello*, the law relating to the conduct of armed conflicts, and therefore we need not devote detailed consideration to it. However, briefly, it may be said that ordinary neutrality is ruled out by the Charter if the United Nations undertakes enforcement action against a state under Chapter VII of the Charter in the context of a threat to the peace, a breach of the peace or an act of aggression.[2] However, until the point that United Nations decides to take such action, neutrality remains possible. This means that a Member State of the United Nations can choose not to intervene in a conflict. A case in point is the Iraq War of 2003. The United Nations did not authorise that action under Chapter VII of the Charter. Thus, it is generally acknowledged that the action was undertaken outside the Charter, and, possibly, even in breach of it. However, as the United Nations did not determine the action to be a threat to the peace, breach of the peace or act of aggression, each state could decide if it wanted to participate in the conflict,

---

[1] Charter of the United Nations (adopted 26 June 1945, entered into force 24 October 1945) 892 UNTS 119 Arts 2(4) and 51.

[2] *Ibid*, Arts 2(5) and 39.

thus potentially participating in the violation of international law, or if it wanted to remain neutral.

b) Secondly, the question of neutrality under the LOAC arises for states each time an armed conflict begins. In fact, the question arises only when there is an armed conflict. At the moment that the conflict begins, all third states have to decide whether they want to participate in the conflict as belligerents or whether they prefer to claim the status of neutrality. However, there is the particular situation of some rare states that have accepted a regime of 'perpetual neutrality'. The prime example of a state that has such a status today is Switzerland. The feature of the regime that distinguishes it from that applying to other states is that Switzerland does not have an option to be belligerent or neutral with respect to each single conflict. The duty to remain neutral is set out in advance of the commencement of an armed conflict and concerns all armed conflicts in the future. Moreover, such a regime of perpetual neutrality implies a series of duties that exist during peacetime. Thus, Switzerland is obliged not to undertake any peacetime obligation which would compel it, in case of war, to take part in the conflict, for example an agreement of collective self-defence or a defensive alliance, particularly where the *casus foederis* is decided by majority decision. However, it must be appreciated that this duty not to enter into such agreements is perfectly consistent with the membership of the United Nations by perpetually neutral states. In effect, the UN Charter does not oblige a Member State to take part in an armed enforcement action. It merely authorises these actions, leaving the choice of participating in them to the Member States. However, economic and other peaceful sanctions must be implemented by all Member States; a duty which modern state practice and doctrine holds is not incompatible with the duties incumbent on neutral states. Thus, the traditional duties applicable to those who claimed neutrality have been modified to this extent for all members of the United Nations in their mutual relations.

3. The status of neutrality imposes *three fundamental duties* on the state that has elected to remain outside a particular armed conflict. If a state does not comply with all of these conditions, it will lose the status of neutral. It may then still be considered as 'non-belligerent', but it will not be able to claim the rights that accrue to a state that has neutral status. Thus, for example, a state which grants more favourable commercial conditions to one belligerent will not be entitled to claim the advantages of neutrality. This happened during World War II when between 1939 and their entry in the war in 1941 the United States favoured the United Kingdom. Despite the loss of neutrality, the state is not a belligerent power. The belligerent suffering from the discrimination in commercial conditions will often condemn that practice, and perhaps engage in retorsion or take peaceful counter-measures, but will refrain from attacking the 'non-belligerent' state, since such an attack would precipitate the entry into war of a further hostile state.

Furthermore, it is important to note that neutrality is limited to the context of international armed conflicts: it supposes more than one state taking part in an armed conflict. For non-international armed conflict, the rule applicable is that of non-intervention in internal affairs. If there is recognition of belligerency granted to the rebels by a third state, a position of neutrality can be taken as between the governmental and the rebel side. However, such recognition of belligerency hardly ever occurs today.

4. Let us now examine the three main conditions for being classified as neutral state:

a) *Duty of abstention*: the principle duty imposed on a neutral state is to abstain from participating in the conflict between the belligerent states, directly or indirectly, on behalf of either belligerent. In order to comply with this duty the neutral state must refrain from any acts of hostility and is prohibited from placing any part of its territory at the disposal of one belligerent, allowing passage by a belligerent through its territory or granting a belligerent the benefit of any facility for military use.[3]

b) *Duty of impartiality*: the second duty of the belligerent is to keep both belligerent sides at arm's length and not to show any preference for either.[4] This is true in, for example, commercial dealings with the belligerents. This does not mean that neutral states are obliged to cut off all commerce with the belligerents, and neither are they required to equalise all commercial dealings once the armed conflict begins when the commercial exchanges with both belligerents were not equal before the war. However, they must not discriminate by granting commercial rights to one side that they do not concede to the other. Usual state practice is to continue commerce with the belligerents on the same basis as existed prior to the commencement of hostilities. Such a stance clearly implies that some pre-existing differences can be maintained. However, war material may not be delivered, as this would potentially favour one party in the conflict over another. Changes to the pre-existing trade relationships to the detriment of one belligerent, or, in some cases, extreme imbalances in the pre-existing trading relationship being maintained without giving the other belligerent any chance to take part in trade on an equal basis, are prohibited.

The duty of impartiality mainly requires a neutral state not to discriminate against one belligerent in a way that is not justified by the very existence of the armed conflict. Thus, if it is impossible to grant equal commercial benefits to both belligerents, for example because a neutral territory is completely cut off from communication with a particular belligerent, the neutral state will not be materially able to respect a significant degree of equality. The duty of impartiality does not require a neutral state in this situation to cease all commerce with the belligerent side surrounding its territory, since that would mean economic strangulation. Switzerland found

---

[3] Hague Convention V respecting the Rights and Duties of Neutral Powers and Persons in Case of War on Land (adopted 18 October 1907, entered into force 26 January 1910) (1907) 205 CTS 299 (Hague Convention V) Art 5. The duty of abstention applies to all states as a matter of customary international law; see especially: *Horgan v An Taoiseach and others* [2003] 2 IR 468, in which the court holds that 'there is an identifiable rule of customary law in relation to the status of neutrality whereunder a neutral state may not permit the movement of large numbers of troops or munitions of one belligerent State through its territory en route to a theatre of war with another'.

[4] Hague Convention V Art 9.

itself in such a position during World War II. However, such unequal commercial streams could give rise to economic counter-measures, not amounting to hostile acts, from the other belligerent(s).

The participation in a UN peacekeeping operation, which does not have a combat mission, by the armed forces of a neutral state, is not a violation of the principle of impartiality or of neutrality. An operation of this nature may be seen as a form of good offices, which are always allowed, and the offer of which never compromises the duty of impartiality incumbent on the neutral power. The same is true for the internment on neutral territory of prisoners of war owing allegiance to one of the belligerent powers, which is provided for in a number of treaties.[5] Such a service is not contrary to the duty of impartiality and thus does not amount to a breach of neutral status.

c) *Duty of prevention*: the neutral state is obliged to defend its neutrality and the integrity of its territory against all abuses by a belligerent. It cannot tolerate such trespasses and continue to claim neutrality and all of its privileges. If the neutral state does not defend its neutrality, if necessary by force of arms, a belligerent is entitled to enter the territory of a neutral power and perform the defensive actions the neutral state should have performed itself.[6] Thus, Article 5 of Hague Convention V stipulates that, 'a neutral power must not allow any of the acts referred to in Articles 2 to 4 [violations of neutrality] to occur on its territory'.[7]

5. The duties of neutral powers do not extend to an obligation to the control of all actions of private persons on the territory of the neutral state. The traditional approach was to completely separate the public sphere of the state from the private sphere of the individual. Thus, the state had no duty to interfere with private action, even if that action was contrary to the interests of a belligerent and would have been a violation of neutrality if performed by state authorities themselves. Consequently, Article 7 of the Hague Convention V stipulates that:

> [A] neutral power is not called upon to prevent the export or transport, on behalf of one or other of the belligerents, of arms, munitions of war, or, in general, of anything which can be of use to an army or a fleet.

This old conception reflected a neat separation between the civil society and the state, based upon the conditions prevailing in the nineteenth century. Today, the civil society and the state are intertwined. The arms and ammunitions industries within neutral states are subject to state control. Therefore, states today do enact legislation preventing 'private persons' entering into commercial transactions with one belligerent for the delivery of war commodities. They do the same for commerce in general, with the objective of preventing the disturbance of the overall equilibrium of the commercial streams with the two sides of belligerency, and a potential breach of the duty of impartiality. However, it must be appreciated that the law of neutrality is directed only towards the state. Only the state has rights and duties

---

[5] See, eg: Hague Convention V Arts 11–15 and Geneva Convention III relative to the Treatment of Prisoners of War (adopted 12 August 1949, entered into force 21 October 1950) 75 UNTS 135 Art 110.

[6] See, eg: H Waldock, 'The Release of the Altmark's Prisoners' (1947) 24 *British Yearbook of International Law* 216.

[7] Hague Convention V Art 5.

under the regime of neutrality, not the individuals. If individuals are to be bound to be subject to certain rights and duties on account of neutrality considerations, it is up to the state to enact municipal legislation which imposes these duties on those within its jurisdiction.

6. Now we have seen the duties that are imposed on a neutral state, we must examine the *rights* granted to such a state by virtue of its neutral status. The most important right of the neutral state is not to be subjected to any restrictions due to the existence of an armed conflict other than those provided for in the law. The armed conflict is a factual situation that the neutral state cannot control and the existence of this state of affairs should neither advantage nor disadvantage its position: it is something done between others that cannot affect the rights accruing to the neutral state. In particular, the territory of the neutral state is inviolable, which is the most important practical application of the general right set out above. Belligerent states cannot use the territory, the land, sea or airspace, of a neutral state for passage of troops or equipment. Moreover, they cannot use any installation on the territory of neutral states for military purposes. Finally, the neutral state should remain unmolested in its commercial transactions with non-belligerent states.

Comprehension check:

a)   What are the three main duties of a neutral state?
b)   What happens if a neutral state violates one of these three duties?
c)   What is the main right of a neutral state?
d)   How can a state ensure that the duties imposed by the status of neutrality are obeyed by private actors on its territory?
e)   Is it contrary to the obligations imposed by the law of neutrality to have different levels of trade with the belligerent parties?
f)   When does neutrality cease to apply?

Answers:

a)   The three main duties are: (1) *abstention* from giving any military aid to one or the other belligerent; (2) *impartiality* between the belligerents, especially in diplomatic, commercial and political matters (but not with respect to peaceful sanctions decided by the United Nations); and (3) *prevention*, ie the duty to defend actively, if necessary by arms, the inviolability of the territory, on land, in the air and on the sea.
b)   It loses its entitlement to be treated as neutral. Thus, if it violates the rule that requires active protection of its territory, it will expose itself to belligerent action on its territory to safeguard the essential interests and rights of the aggrieved belligerent.
c)   The essential right of neutral states is the inviolability of their territory. Whereas the law of war operates to remove the peacetime obligation not to violate the territorial integrity of another state, allowing armed actions on the territory of other belligerent states, the law of neutrality maintains the full integrity of the doctrine of territorial sovereignty for the neutral state.

d) The state must legislate using the methods allowed by its municipal law in order to impose such duties on all or some persons on its territory.

e) No. A belligerent may maintain different commercial patterns, as they prevailed before the war. It is not obliged to mathematically equalise its commercial transactions with each of the belligerents as soon as an armed conflict starts. However, the neutral state should not alter its patterns of commercial transaction between the belligerents because of the war: it should maintain the previous state of affairs.

f) The general rules on the end of application of the LOAC apply to this question.[8] Thus, neutrality ceases to apply with the general close of military operations through a definitive armistice, a complete surrender or, obviously, upon the conclusion of a peace treaty.

---

[8] See generally: ch 14 above.

35

THE IMPLEMENTATION OF THE LOAC

Learning objectives: To discover the mechanisms that can be, and in many cases are, used to implement the LOAC.

1. The implementation of norms is always a difficult matter in international affairs and in international law in particular. The international situation cannot be equated to the situation within states. There is not a powerful international body that has authority over the subjects of the law; the international community does not have an international police force and a judiciary with compulsory jurisdiction; thus, coercive power exercised by the international community cannot be relied upon to enforce international obligations. The sovereignty and equality of states precludes the operation of such mechanisms, and ensures that the execution of the law is precarious and, sometimes, irregular. However, international law is often respected and implemented in fact. It may even be said that, overall, it is quantitatively better respected than municipal law. However, within international law, the LOAC is particularly likely to be breached. Supreme interests of the state are at stake. When fighting for survival, states will be reluctant to accept the constraints imposed by legal rules. Such rules may be seen as useful in the abstract, and necessary for the general welfare of states, and as such will be seen as desirable in the long term, but states may feel that these rules place excessive limits on 'necessary' military action in the particular circumstances that are present in the short term. Thus, the LOAC is often breached. Despite this, it is still essential that the LOAC exists in order that its rules form a code of conduct for belligerents and so that there is a standard of behaviour against which their behaviour can be measured and sanctions applied. Moreover, as we shall see, when telling the story of the implementation of the LOAC, we must not focus only on breaches of the law; there are many cases of proper implementation of the LOAC and of successful protection of the victims of war by actors such as the International Committee of the Red Cross (ICRC). With this in mind, one further reflection may be ventured. According to Jean Pictet, the world-renowned Vice-President of the ICRC, if one single individual is saved by the application of the LOAC, the whole exercise would have been worth the expense. In reality, the LOAC has in the past helped to protect innumerable thousands of people, combatants and non-combatants alike, and continues to do so today. It

undoubtedly saved the lives of countless numbers of people. Has the expense thus not been worthwhile?

2. Some regulation of armed conflict, as a social phenomenon, is inescapable. This is the reason we find that rules which regulate the behaviour of belligerents have existed in all civilisations and at all times. For example, armistices have to be respected; prisoners can be exchanged; some objects must be spared, such as fruit trees or places of religious importance; poisoned arms should not be employed because they lead to excessive and lasting damage; and so on. Thus, the existence of some norms regulating these activities is inevitable. The weaknesses of the mechanisms for securing the implementation of the LOAC should not push the international community to become fatalistic and inactive, nor to renounce the existence of any law regulating armed conflicts, but rather should challenge states to complete and improve the existing mechanisms through best endeavours. Hence the question arises: what are the weaknesses that we find when we examine the enforcement of the LOAC?

3. The mechanisms to ensure respect and to sanction violations of international humanitarian law (IHL) are insufficient in many ways. However, the two following inter-linked aspects are the most salient.

a)   First, the entire system of implementation is based on voluntary action, and thus on the goodwill of the parties. There are no compulsory means for the settlement of disputes over the scope of IHL protections or for the enforcement of IHL. Of course, compulsory action may be taken indirectly by the UN Security Council in the context of its Chapter VII powers.[1] However, this will be exceedingly rare, and is ill suited to the resolution of disputes regarding the implementation of the LOAC. Similarly, the current model of consent-based enforcement, shared with the whole of public international law, is inappropriate in the area of the LOAC. The relations between the belligerents are so strained that an armed conflict has erupted between them. It would be astonishing if these states accept a settlement, which implies a compromise with the enemy. The armed conflict itself proves that these states have been unable to achieve a peaceful settlement of their disputes. It is perhaps fanciful to suppose that they can reach such a settlement during or after the conflict. Moreover, as experience has shown, it may even prove difficult to organise direct contact between the parties. More often than not, one party does not recognise the other. Alternatively, as the case of the Democratic Republic of Vietnam (or North Vietnam) has shown, assertions of breaches of the LOAC are often made for propaganda purposes, and in such cases there is no interest in impartial fact finding because such fact finding would reveal the truth. As propaganda is an important tool utilised

---

[1] See, eg: UNSC Resolution 1591 (29 March 2005) UN Doc S/RES/1591, which takes into account breaches of IHL when determining that the situation in Darfur presents a threat to international peace and security. The UNSC was also responsible for setting up the ICTY and the ICTR, two bodies which are able to punish individual violations of the LOAC; see generally: UNSC Resolution 827 (25 May 1993) UN Doc S/RES/827 and UNSC Resolution 955 (8 November 1994) UN Doc S/RES/955.

by the parties, establishing the truth is particularly difficult during the strained conditions of war. The lack of willingness to cooperate also explains why there is so little case law by international tribunals concerning the LOAC.[2] Any international tribunal, to be competent, must have the consent of all of the parties to the dispute. Such consent is very rarely forthcoming for disputes arising out of an armed conflict. These questions are too sensitive for the involved states; the mistrust between them is too great.

b) Secondly, most mechanisms that are discussed under the heading of implementation are purely normative. They impose duties on states. They help to implement the law if the states comply with these duties. However, they do not impose a sanction on states if they fail to comply with their LOAC obligations. Thus, the duty to disseminate IHL and instruct members of the armed forces about its requirements is certainly a means of implementation,[3] but what happens if a state neglects to do so? If the neglect is due to absence of resources, training programs provided by the ICRC may help to bridge the gap. However, if the lack of training is due to a state not wishing to comply with these rules, for whatever reason, there is no real means of enforcement. The state may bear responsibility for the breach of duty, but the adjudication of such a dispute before international tribunals would be difficult for two reasons: first, procedurally, because dispute resolution in international law is consensual, the state that has failed to comply with the duty must agree that the case can be heard before the tribunal; and secondly, the dispute would present difficulties from a factual standpoint, as the information regarding the training given to soldiers would be in the possession of the state that is alleged to have failed to comply with the duty to instruct. The best means of implementation of IHL remains, to some extent, the incorporation of the duties imposed within the municipal law of the states. In this setting, the LOAC can take advantage of the centralised law-enforcement mechanisms that the state provides for the execution of the rules it adopts. However, again this depends on the goodwill of states.

4. Apart from the general means of enforcement known to international law, the LOAC provides for the following mechanisms. Some of these mechanisms are normative; others are institutional.

a) *Incorporation and dissemination of the LOAC in municipal law.* Rules of the LOAC accepted by a state through the ratification of, or accession to, a convention must be incorporated into the municipal law of that state in the ways provided for by its legal system.[4] Thus, the rules of the LOAC are translated into municipal law and become binding on all state authorities. For example, they will bind the military branch; they will allow a criminal court to condemn a person who has committed violations of these rules; and so on. Mere incorporation of the duties imposed by the LOAC into municipal law is

---

[2] However, Eritrea-Ethiopia Claims Commission, <http://www.pca-cpa.org/showpage.asp?pag_id=1151> accessed 20 May 2008, provides a more heartening example.

[3] Geneva Convention III relative to the Treatment of Prisoners of War (adopted 12 August 1949, entered into force 21 October 1950) 75 UNTS 135 (Geneva Convention III) Art 127.

[4] In the United Kingdom, the Geneva Conventions Act 1957.

not enough. Moreover, the state must do what is necessary to make known the rules of the LOAC. In the first place it is imperative that those who have to apply the rules of the LOAC on a day-to-day basis, such as military personnel, know the content of these rules. In reality, military forces will be given some form of military manual where the rules are expounded.[5] Moreover, some training in the LOAC will take place, the nature of which will vary according to the rank and tasks of a particular military person. Practical exercises in the field will be used to put the training into practice. However, LOAC rules should also be disseminated to the civilian population, since the LOAC contains rules that are relevant to them. The whole population should also have some basic understanding of the rules of the LOAC, even if the object of the education is only to understand that these rules apply independently from whom is right or wrong in the war. In particular, the elite of a state should have a basic knowledge of the LOAC: for example, journalists, politicians, diplomats, judges and students should be given compulsory training. Moreover, in case of a rebellion, when citizens take up arms against their own government, previous training in the LOAC will help to enhance respect for these rules by the rebels. Although the military branch of states, except very poor states, is normally well trained in the knowledge of the LOAC, the same cannot be said for the civilian population. The gap between the knowledge possessed by the military and the civilian population is still enormous, even in countries as well organised and wealthy as Switzerland or the United Kingdom. The obligation to disseminate the LOAC and to inform military personnel and civilians about LOAC rules is one that applies during peacetime, since once an armed conflict erupts it will be too late.[6]

b) *Scrutiny by the protecting power and the ICRC.* States in dispute, and particularly belligerents, normally need assistance from some neutral and independent third party to help them overcome their disagreements. The mechanism traditionally adopted within the LOAC in order to fulfil this function is the nomination of a 'protecting power'. A belligerent elects a third-party neutral state to be responsible for the protection its interests and those of its nationals with regard to the opposing belligerent. The designation of a protecting power is based on consent. When the third-party neutral state and the adverse belligerent accept the nomination, the third-party neutral state will be able to intercede in the relationship between the two belligerents in order to perform its functions as a protecting power. These functions consist mainly of: (i) channelling communications between the belligerents; and (ii) representing the state of origin, for example by visiting the prisoners of war that owe allegiance to the power which it protects who are detained in the camps of the opposing belligerent or by

---

[5] See, eg: UK Ministry of Defence, *The Manual of the Law of Armed Conflict* (Oxford, OUP, 2004).

[6] See generally: Geneva Conventions I–IV Common Articles 47/48/127/144; Protocol Additional to the Geneva Conventions of 12 August 1949, and relating to the Protection of Victims of International Armed Conflicts (adopted 8 June 1977, entered into force 7 December 1978) 1125 UNTS 3 (Additional Protocol 1) Arts 83 and 87(2); and Protocol Additional to the Geneva Conventions of 12 August 1949, and relating to the Protection of Victims of Non-International Armed Conflicts (adopted 8 June 1977, entered into force 7 December 1978) 1125 UNTS 609 (Additional Protocol II) Art 19.

being present at the trials of nationals of the protected power in the tribunals of the opposing belligerent. The two main functions of the protecting power are thus: first, to serve as a link between the two parties; and secondly, to exercise functions of protection and control.

The functions of the protecting power are regulated in Common Article 8/8/8/9 of the Geneva Conventions. This mechanism has not been used frequently in recent times; in fact, it is more or less obsolete. Since World War II, protecting powers have only been nominated in five conflicts. The reasons for the failure to nominate a protecting power were either that the parties refused to admit that they were involved in an international armed conflict (IAC); or the parties felt that agreeing to such a nomination could be interpreted as recognising the other belligerent; or that a truly neutral state was difficult to find. Alternatively, simply, the state could not afford the expenses of the protecting power, as the state that is protected has to bear these. In these situations the ICRC was called upon to act, in most cases, as a de facto substitute for the non-existent protecting power. In effect, the ICRC exercised its right of humanitarian initiatives to enhance the protection of victims. It also assisted in the implementation of the existing obligations, transmitted information between the belligerents, and controlled the application of the LOAC by the parties. If the ICRC is presented with evidence of violations of the LOAC, it normally avoids going public with it, preferring to engage in direct contact with the parties. There is no armed conflict in which the ICRC has not played, in some form or another, these multiple roles. The importance of the role played by the ICRC as a substitute for the protecting power cannot be over-emphasised.[7]

c) *The obligation to 'respect and ensure respect'*. Common Article 1 to the Geneva Conventions has the following wording, '[t]he High Contracting Parties undertake to respect and ensure respect for the present Convention in all circumstances'. This provision has been interpreted as imposing an obligation that goes beyond the duty of states parties to execute the Conventions. Common Article 1 is now seen as making clear that all states parties to the Geneva Conventions have a right and a duty to react to breaches of the Conventions. The rights and duties set out in the Geneva Conventions are thus said to be '*erga omnes*': they are rights and duties that all states parties owe to all other states parties by way of solidarity of interest. Thus, not only the state directly affected by the violation, but also all other states bound by the Conventions, can, and perhaps must, take measures.[8] Moreover, Article 1 has been interpreted as ruling out belligerent reprisals.[9] It is also clear that under Article 1 a state may not encourage or assist in violations of IHL by another state or entity.[10] A link between Common Article 1 and Article 7 of Additional Protocol I can also be established. Article 7 states that:

---

[7] See generally: ch 16 above.

[8] *Legal Consequences of the Construction of a Wall in the Occupied Palestinian Territory* (Advisory Opinion) [2004] ICJ Rep 136 paras [158]–[159]. Compare the dissenting opinion of Judge Koojimans in the same case, paras [37]–[51].

[9] *Prosecutor v Kupreskic* (Trial Judgment) IT-95-16-T (14 January 2000) para [517].

[10] *Military and Paramilitary Activities in and against Nicaragua (Nicaragua v United States of America)* (Merits) [1986] ICJ Rep 14 paras [115], [216] and [255]–[256].

The depositary of this Protocol shall convene a meeting of the High Contracting Parties, at the request of one or more of the said Parties and upon the
approval of the majority of the said Parties, to consider general problems concerning the application of the Conventions and of the Protocol.

It must be stressed that states have not yet taken their role as guardians of
the Conventions seriously. The hope that Common Article 1 could provide a
method for enforcement of the Conventions by states parties has not been
fulfilled. States are rarely willing to invest time and money and jeopardise
their relations with a belligerent in order to denounce violations and demand
redress when these violations do not affect a vital interest of that state. Sometimes a meeting of the contracting parties is asked to discuss a situation
where is appears that certain Convention obligations are being violated, such
as the situation in the Palestinian occupied territories in 1999. However,
such a discussion hardly lives up to the 'duty' to ensure respect enshrined in
Article 1. The better interpretation of the provision, based on state practice,
is that Article 1 *allows* third states to intervene, but does not *oblige* them to
do so.

d) *Fact-finding commission.* When alleged violations of IHL occur, it is often
uncertain what actually happened. Was there a violation? Or are we in fact
being confronted with propaganda? What was the precise extent of the
violation? Was a particular occurrence an accident or was it a deliberate
violation of IHL? If there was a deliberate violation, at what level of the
governmental or military hierarchy was it decided to violate the LOAC? All
of these questions are important for a correct implementation of the law. Yet,
one can easily understand why belligerent states strenuously resist the
presence of an impartial fact-finding mission on their territory during
wartime. National pride, the sensitive military nature of some information,
the importance of propaganda and many other reasons mean that this
method of dispute settlement is seen as unacceptable. Thus, it comes as no
surprise that Article 90 of Additional Protocol I, which constitutes a fact-
finding commission whose operation is based on the consent of the
belligerents, has yet to received a single application. This detailed provision is
set out below:

International Fact-Finding Commission

1. (a)   An International Fact-Finding Commission (hereinafter referred to as
'the Commission') consisting of 15 members of high moral standing and
acknowledged impartiality shall be established;

(b) When not less than 20 High Contracting Parties have agreed to accept the
competence of the Commission pursuant to paragraph 2, the depositary
shall then, and at intervals of five years thereafter, convene a meeting of
representatives of those High Contracting Parties for the purpose of elect-
ing the members of the Commission. At the meeting, the representatives
shall elect the members of the Commission by secret ballot from a list of
persons to which each of those High Contracting Parties may nominate
one person;

(c) The members of the Commission shall serve in their personal capacity and
shall hold office until the election of new members at the ensuing meeting;

(d) At the election, the High Contracting Parties shall ensure that the persons to be elected to the Commission individually possess the qualifications required and that, in the Commission as a whole, equitable geographical representation is assured;

(e) In the case of a casual vacancy, the Commission itself shall fill the vacancy, having due regard to the provisions of the preceding subparagraphs;

(f) The depositary shall make available to the Commission the necessary administrative facilities for the performance of its functions.

2. (a)   The High Contracting Parties may at the time of signing, ratifying or acceding to the Protocol, or at any other subsequent time, declare that they recognize ipso facto and without special agreement, in relation to any other High Contracting Party accepting the same obligation, the competence of the Commission to inquire into allegations by such other Party, as authorized by this Article;

(b) The declarations referred to above shall be deposited with the depositary, which shall transmit copies thereof to the High Contracting Parties;

(c) The Commission shall be competent to:

(i) inquire into any facts alleged to be a grave breach as defined in the Conventions and this Protocol or other serious violation of the Conventions or of this Protocol;

(ii) facilitate, through its good offices, the restoration of an attitude of respect for the Conventions and this Protocol;

(d) In other situations, the Commission shall institute an inquiry at the request of a Party to the conflict only with the consent of the other Party or Parties concerned;

(e) Subject to the foregoing provisions or this paragraph, the provisions of Article 52 of the First Convention, Article 53 of the Second Convention, Article 132 or the Third Convention and Article 149 of the Fourth Convention shall continue to apply to any alleged violation of the Conventions and shall extend to any alleged violation of this Protocol.

3. (a)   Unless otherwise agreed by the Parties concerned, all inquiries shall be undertaken by a Chamber consisting of seven members appointed as follows:

(i) five members of the Commission, not nationals of any Party to the conflict, appointed by the President of the Commission on the basis of equitable representation of the geographical areas, after consultation with the Parties to the conflict;

(ii) two ad hoc members, not nationals of any Party to the conflict, one to be appointed by each side;

(b) Upon receipt of the request for an inquiry, the President of the Commission shall specify an appropriate time-limit for setting up a Chamber. If any ad hoc member has not been appointed within the time-limit, the President shall immediately appoint such additional member or members of the Commission as may be necessary to complete the membership of the Chamber.

4. (a)   The Chamber set up under paragraph 3 to undertake an inquiry shall invite the Parties to the conflict to assist it and to present evidence. The

Chamber may also seek such other evidence as it deems appropriate and may carry out an investigation of the situation in loco;

(b) All evidence shall be fully disclosed to the Parties, which shall have the right to comment on it to the Commission;

(c) Each Party shall have the right to challenge such evidence.

5. (a)   The Commission shall submit to the Parties a report on the findings of fact of the Chamber, with such recommendations as it may deem appropriate;

(b) If the Chamber is unable to secure sufficient evidence for factual and impartial findings, the Commission shall state the reasons for that inability;

(c) The Commission shall not report its findings publicly, unless all the Parties to the conflict have requested the Commission to do so.

6. The Commission shall establish its own rules, including rules for the presidency or the Commission and the presidency of the Chamber. Those rules shall ensure that the functions of the President of the Commission are exercised at all times and that, in the case of an inquiry, they are exercised by a person who is not a national of a Party to the conflict.

7. The administrative expenses of the Commission shall be met by contributions from the High Contracting Parties which made declarations under paragraph 2, and by voluntary contributions. The Party or Parties to the conflict requesting an inquiry shall advance the necessary funds for expenses incurred by a Chamber and shall be reimbursed by the Party or Parties against which the allegations are made to the extent of 50 per cent of the costs of the Chamber. Where there are counter-allegations before the Chamber each side shall advance 50 per cent of the necessary funds.

e) *Criminal prosecution.* An important means of securing compliance with the LOAC is the criminal prosecution of individuals who violate the rules. Such prosecution can be performed by either the national state of the military or civilian person involved,[11] by national tribunals of third states, including the adverse belligerent, by so-called 'hybrid' tribunals, such as the Criminal Tribunal for Sierra Leone, or, finally, by international tribunals such as the Nuremberg Military Tribunal, the Tokyo Military Tribunal, the International Criminal Tribunal for the Former Yugoslavia (ICTY), the International Criminal Tribunal for Rwanda or the International Criminal Court.

On the national level, it is possible to prosecute foreign nationals for acts committed outside of the territory of the state where the prosecution takes place. This is possible because war crimes are crimes that give rise to what lawyers call 'universal jurisdiction'.[12] This means that under certain restrictive conditions, such as the presence of the accused in the territory, a state may undertake a prosecution for breaches of the LOAC that happened in a conflict anywhere else in the world. Thus, some Nazi criminals were sentenced in Canada and Australia, whereas Rwandan individuals accused of

---

[11] See, eg: *US v Calley* (1973) 1 Military Law Reporter 2488.

[12] See also: *Arrest Warrant of 11th April 2000 (Democratic Republic of Congo v Belgium)* [2002] ICJ Rep 3, Joint Separate Opinion of Judges Higgins, Kooijmans and Burgenthal, in particular paras [28]–[32] and [51].

genocidal acts have been prosecuted in Belgium and Switzerland. Imposing a criminal sanction on individuals who breach the LOAC is an indirect means of securing state compliance with IHL. It is one of the most effective means.

Not all violations of the norms of the LOAC are punishable by criminal sanctions. According to the ICTY in the *Tadic* case, in order for a violation of the LOAC to be criminally punishable, it must fulfil the following criteria:

(i) the violation must constitute an infringement of a rule of international humanitarian law;

(ii) the rule must be customary in nature or, if it belongs to treaty law, the required conditions must be met (see below, paragraph 143)[13];

(iii) the violation must be 'serious', that is to say, it must constitute a breach of a rule protecting important values, and the breach must involve grave consequences for the victim. Thus, for instance, the fact of a combatant simply appropriating a loaf of bread in an occupied village would not amount to a 'serious violation of international humanitarian law' although it may be regarded as falling foul of the basic principle laid down in Article 46, paragraph 1, of the Hague Regulations (and the corresponding rule of customary international law) whereby 'private property must be respected' by any army occupying an enemy territory;

(iv) the violation of the rule must entail, under customary or conventional law, the individual criminal responsibility of the person breaching the rule.[14]

f) *Implementation by human rights bodies.* It may be recalled that human rights monitoring mechanisms and human rights courts, such as the European Court of Human Rights and the Inter-American Court of Human Rights, are increasingly confronted with cases where alleged human rights violations have taken place during times of, usually non-international, armed conflict.[15] When these bodies adjudicate on these issues from the perspective of human rights law, they indirectly implement IHL obligations, for example with respect to physical integrity, fair trial, rights regarding detention, and so on. The number of cases concerning the violation of human rights in times of armed conflict is constantly increasing. As examples, one may merely mention the Cyprus cases, the Turkish cases and the Chechnya cases heard by the European Court of Human Rights.[16]

g) *Implementation by the UN Security Council.* The main task of the UN Security Council is not to enforce the LOAC, but to maintain the peace. The Council will be involved in determining the merits of the claims of the parties and thus be prone to distinguish the situation of the attacker and the attacked, the 'aggressor' and the 'aggressed against'. However, recent Security

---

[13] Paragraph 143 states that the breach of a treaty norm, including those imposed by special agreement, will be punishable if the treaty, '(i) was unquestionably binding on the parties at the time of the alleged offence; and (ii) was not in conflict with or derogating from peremptory norms of international law'.

[14] *Prosecutor v Tadic* (Decision on the Defence Motion for Interlocutory Appeal on Jurisdiction) IT-49-1-AR72 (2 October 1995) para [94]. See also *Prosecutor v Norman* (Decision on preliminary motion based on lack of jurisdiction (child recruitment)) SCSL-04-14-AR72(E)-131 (31 May 2004).

[15] See generally: ch 33 above.

[16] See, eg: *Isayeva v Russia* (App no 57947-49/00) (2005) 41 EHRR 39.

Council practice shows that it has often reacted to appalling IHL violations. In such cases the Security Council asks all parties to the conflict to respect the rules of IHL and threatens the parties with adverse consequences if grave violations continue.[17] Such threatened consequences can range from military operations aimed at ensuring IHL is complied with to the establishment of international criminal tribunals to prosecute persons responsible for the breaches of the LOAC. For example, during the war in the former Yugoslavia, the Security Council acted to establish the ICTY.[18] During the last 15 years, the Security Council has thus come to play an important role in ensuring the application of IHL.

Other UN organs also contribute to the implementation of IHL: for example, the General Assembly plays an important role through normative resolutions condemning breaches of the LOAC or restating the applicability of certain principles[19]; the UN High Commissioner for Refugees can assist with the implementation of norms intended to protect civilians; and so on.

h) *Role of National Red Cross or Red Crescent Societies.* The implementation of IHL is a key objective of the Red Cross Movement. National Red Cross and Red Crescent Societies make a particular contribution to the promotion of IHL within their state of origin. They cooperate with governments to this end and often take on the role of disseminating the details of the LOAC to the public at large, through a variety of methods which include running courses, visiting schools and publishing materials detailing the rights and duties embodied by IHL. The German Red Cross Society is a good example of a national society which has taken on this role. Moreover, such societies deliver medical and other aid to victims of armed conflicts.

i) *Role of non-governmental organisations in general.* Non-governmental organisations play an important role in the implementation of IHL. First, they often provide humanitarian assistance to victims of armed conflicts. Secondly, they play an important role in monitoring, reporting and mobilising public opinion concerning violations of IHL. Thus, Amnesty International prepared a detailed report which scrutinised the conduct of NATO during the armed conflict with Yugoslavia in 1999, and concluded that a series of breaches of IHL had been committed.[20] Similar reports have been prepared into the conduct of hostilities in the conflicts in Darfur, Chechnya and Lebanon in 2006.

5. The conventions provide only two mechanisms of implementation of the LOAC during *non-international armed conflicts*: (1) the obligation to disseminate the law as widely as possible[21]; and (2) the right for an impartial humanitarian body, and in particular of the ICRC, to offer humanitarian services.[22] However, the means of

---

[17] UNSC Resolution 1591, n 1.

[18] UNSC Resolution 808 (22 February 1993) UN Doc S/RES/808 and UNSC Resolution 827, n 1.

[19] See, eg: Respect for Human Rights in Armed Conflict UNGA Res 2444 (XXIII) (19 December 1968).

[20] Amnesty International, 'NATO/Federal Republic of Yugoslavia: "Collateral Damage" or Unlawful Killings? Violations of the Laws of War by NATO during Operation Allied Force' (6 June 2000) <http://asiapacific.amnesty.org/library/Index/ENGEUR700182000?open&of=ENG-SRB> accessed 20 May 2008.

[21] Additional Protocol II Art 19.

[22] Geneva Conventions I–IV Common Article 3.

implementation during IAC that have been discussed above apply analogously during NIAC. Even the fact-finding commission, the function of which is apparently limited to IAC as it is included only within Additional Protocol I, could be used in the context of a NIAC if the belligerent state and the rebels agreed. Furthermore, the duty to respect and ensure respect for the LOAC that is found in Common Article 1 to the four Geneva Conventions applies in the context of NIAC.[23] Finally, Security Council practice shows that it has not limited its actions concerning breaches of IHL to incidents taking place in the context of an IAC.[24]

Comprehension check:

a)   What is the essential weakness in the implementation of the LOAC?
b)   What are the main mechanisms for the implementation of the LOAC?
c)   Which is the most promising of these mechanisms in the present situation?
d)   What further mechanisms could be imagined to improve the situation?

Answers:

a)   The essential weakness in the implementation of the LOAC is the fact that there are no compulsory mechanisms operating independently from the consent of the belligerent states. The strained relationship between the belligerents generally impedes any agreement on a means of settlement of a dispute or on the implementation of the LOAC. The system of implementation is largely based on the goodwill of states. This is insufficient, particularly in situations of war.

b)   There are a series of specific implementation tools. Some are purely *normative*; they are simply 'duties' imposed on the states. The main normative duty is to incorporate and disseminate the rules of the LOAC within the municipal law of the state. A further normative tool is the right recognised by Common Article 1 of the Geneva Conventions for every state to intervene and seek for redress in cases of violations of IHL rules. A further set of implementation tools are *institutional*. Here, one may think of the action of 'protecting powers', which are rarely nominated today; of the ICRC; of National Red Cross and Red Crescent Societies; of non-governmental organisations; of international criminal tribunals such as the International Criminal Court; of municipal law prosecutions for war crimes; of the UN Security Council; and of human rights bodies. There is a rich array of means which, when added together, allow for a certain degree of sanction for breaches of the LOAC, albeit an insufficient one. One will notice that, apart from the ICRC, there is no international organ that is directly concerned with the implementation of the LOAC. All of the other institutional mechanisms mentioned above apply the LOAC indirectly: the Security Council in the context of the maintenance of peace, the international criminal tribunals in the context of criminal prosecution for a whole set of international crimes, and so on.

[23] *Nicaragua*, n 10, para [255].
[24] For example, the ICTR has jurisdiction to deal with war crimes committed during a NIAC, UNSC Resolution 955, n 1.

c)   It is difficult to single out one of them. The ICRC certainly has a role of paramount importance. The incorporation and dissemination of the LOAC norms is a basic and indispensable step in implementation. However, as far as sanction for IHL violations is concerned, criminal law mechanisms and to some extent the actions of the Security Council, where it chooses to become involved, have become tremendously important.

d)   This is a question that is open for reflection. Many quite different schemes and mechanisms can be imagined, and ideas for the future should not be confined too narrowly. One proposal that has been made recently is the creation of a special body in the international arena, possibly within the United Nations, that is charged with monitoring the implementation of IHL. This could be a sort of 'UN High Commissioner for IHL'. By creating such a mechanism, the international community would then close a gap that has been created because the international community does not have an international organ whose task is to monitor armed conflicts and ensure compliance with IHL. Currently, the ICRC plays an important role in this context, but its tasks are much larger than monitoring implementation. Moreover, the proper exercise of these other functions may mean that the ICRC will not be able to vigorously pursue accusations of violation, for fear of alienating the confidence of one belligerent or both, and thus jeopardising the protection of victims to which it could then be denied access. There is thus room for some new monitoring mechanism. On the other hand, any scheme for a new organ must carefully consider the value that it adds and its prospective efficacy. One should avoid piling up further, perhaps ineffective, organs, which complicate the distribution of competencies in the field of the LOAC, where there are already many complex overlaps and much competition. The question of the financial cost of the proposed new organ must also be examined, at a time where the available funds are restricted.

BIBLIOGRAPHY

This bibliography concentrates on recent publications on international humanitarian law. Older texts can be found in the *Bibliography of International Humanitarian Law*, 2nd edn, Geneva, ICRC & Henry Dunant Institute, 1987. It has been prepared by Mr Andreas Frutig, teaching assistant at the University of Berne.

1. DOCUMENTS

German

BUNDESMINISTERIUM DER VERTEIDIGUNG, *Humanitäres Völkerrecht in bewaffneten Konflikten*: *Textsammlung 1, Handbuch*, Bonn, 1992, 158 p.

French

DAVID, E, *Code de droit international humanitaire*, 2ème edn, Bruxelles, Bruylant, 2004, 860 p.

SCHINDLER, D and TOMAN, J, *Droit des conflits armés: recueil des conventions, résolutions et autres documents*, Genève, CICR/Institut Henri Dunant, 1996, 1470 p.

FRANCE, MINISTERE DES AFFAIRES ETRANGERS, *Accords de paix concernant l'ex-Yougoslavie: documents d'actualité internationale*, Paris, 1996, 71 p.

English

HUYNH, Huong T (ed), *Bibliography of International Humanitarian Law Applicable in Armed Conflicts*, 2nd edn, Geneva, ICRC & Henry Dunant Institute, 1987, 605 p.

INTERNATIONAL COMMITTEE OF THE RED CROSS, *International Law Concerning the Conduct of Hostilities: Collection of Hague Conventions and Some Other Treaties*, Geneva, ICRC Publications, 1989, 195 p.

INTERNATIONAL COMMITTEE OF THE RED CROSS, *Rules of International Humanitarian Law and other Rules relating to the Conduct of Hostilities: Collection of Treaties and other Instruments*, 2nd edn, Geneva, ICRC Publications, 2005, 266 p.

LENARCIC, DA, *Anti-personnel Land Mines: An Annotated Bibliography*, Ottawa, Department of Foreign Affairs and International Trade, 1996, 114 p.

MARTIN, FF, International Human Rights and Humanitarian Law: Treaties, Cases and Analysis, Cambridge, Cambridge University Press, 2006, 990 p.

MINISTRY OF DEFENCE OF THE FEDERAL REPUBLIC OF GERMANY, *Humanitarian Law in Armed Conflicts: Manual*, Bonn, Ministry of Defence 1992, 154 p.

REISMAN, WM (ed), *The Laws of War: A Comprehensive Collection of Primary Documents on International Governing Armed Conflict*, New York, Vintage Books, 1994, 448 p.

ROBERTS, A and GUELFF, R (eds), *Documents on the Laws of War*, 3rd edn, Oxford, Oxford University Press, 2000, 765 p.

SANAJAOBA, N (ed), *A Manual of International Humanitarian Laws*, New Delhi, Regency, 2004, 776 p.

SASSOLI, M and BOUVIER, A, *How Does Law Protect in War? Cases, Documents and Teaching Materials on Contemporary Practice in International Humanitarian Law*, 2nd edn, Geneva, International Committee of the Red Cross, 2006, 2473 p.

SCHINDLER, D and TOMAN, J, *The Laws of Armed Conflicts: A Collection of Conventions, Resolutions and Other Documents*, 3rd edn, Dordrecht, Nijhoff, 1988, 1033 p.

Italian

GREPPI, E (ed), *Codice di diritto internazionale umanitario*, Torino, Giappichelli, 2007, 468 p.

Spanish

ORIHUELA CALATAYUD, E (ed), *Derecho internacional humanitario: tratados internacionales y otros textos; estudio introductorio sobre el control del cumplimiento del derecho internacional humanitario aplicable a los conflictos aramados*, Madrid, McGraw-Hill, 1998, 901 p.

2. MONOGRAPHS

German

ADAM, S, *Kriegslisten und Perfidieverbot in der Geschichte des Kriegsaktionenrechts vor Abschluss der Haager Landkriegsordnung von 1899*, Frankfurt am Main, Peter Lang, 1992, 149 p.
BEYERLIN, U, *Abrüstung und Umweltschutz—eine völkerrechtliche Interessenkollision?* Bochum, BMV, 1994, 137 p.
von BLOCK-SCHLESIER, A, *Zur Frage der Akzeptanz des humanitären Völkerrechts am Ende des 20. Jahrhunderts*, Baden-Baden, Nomos Verlagsgesellschaft 1999, 161 p.
BÖTSCH, C, *Die Nachbefolgung des westaliierten Besatzungsrechts im Lichte des Staats- und Völkerrechts*, Frankfurt am Main, Lang, 2000, 235 p.
BUNDESMINISTERIUM DER VERTEIDIGUNG, *Humanitäres Völkerrecht in bewaffneten Konflikten*, Bonn, Bundesministerium der Verteidigung, 1999, 122 p.
BUSS, R, *Der Kombattantenstatus: die kriegsrechtliche Entstehung eines Rechtsbegriffs und seine Ausgestaltung in Verträgen des 19. und 20. Jahrhunderts*, Bochum, Brockmeyer, 1992, 245 p.
DEISEROTH, D, *Atomwaffen vor dem Internationalen Gerichtshof: Dokumentation, Analysen, Hintergründe*, Münster, Lit, 1997, 417 p.
DONNER, M, *Die neutrale Handelsschiffahrt im begrenzten militärischen Konflikt: eine völkerrechtliche Untersuchung am Beispiel des Konfliktes zwischen Irak und Iran (1980–1988)*, Kehl am Rhein, Engel, 1993, 305 p.
DÖRMANN, K, *Schutz von UN-peace-keeping-Truppen vor Landminen*, Bochum, Brockmeyer, 1995, 102 p.
EMPELL, H-M, *Nuklearwaffeneinsätze und humanitäres Völkerrecht: die Anwendung des I. Zusatzprotokolls zu den Genfer Konventionen von 1949 auf Nuklearwaffeneinsätze*, Heidelberg, FEST, 1993, 215 p.
FAVEZ, J-C, *Das internationale Rote Kreuz und das Dritte Reich: war der Holocaust aufzuhalten?* München, Bertelsmann, 1989, 592 p.
FISCHER, H (ed), *Völkerrechtliche Verbrechen vor dem Jugoslawien-Tribunal, nationalen Gerichten und dem internationalen Strafgerichtshof*, Berlin, Berlin Verlag A Spitz, 1999, 422 p.
FLECK, D (ed), *Handbuch des humanitären Völkerrechts in bewaffneten Konflikten*, München, Beck, 1994, 476 p.
FRONHÖFER, D, *Der international Menschenrechtsschutz bei inneren Konflikten*, Regensburg, Roderer, 1994, 141 p.

GANTZEL, KJ (ed), *Die Kriege nach dem Zweiten Weltkrieg 1945 bis 1992: Daten und Tendenzen, Rev und aktualisierte Neuaufl*, Münster, Lit, 1995, 323 p.

GASSER, H-P, *Humanitäres Völkerrecht: Eine Einführung*, Baden-Baden, Nomos, 2007, 253 p.

HANKE, HM, *Luftkrieg und Zivilbevölkerung: der kriegsvölkerrechtliche Schutz der Zivilbevölkerung gegen Luftbombardements von den Anfängen bis zum Ausbruch des Zweiten Weltkrieges*, Frankfurt am Main, Lang, 1991, 310 p.

HASSE, J (ed), *Humanitäres Völkerrecht: politische, rechtliche und strafgerichtliche Dimensionen*, Baden-Baden, Nomos, 2001, 597 p.

HAUG, H, *Menschlichkeit für alle: die Weltbewegung des Roten Kreuzes und des Roten Halbmonds, 3. unveränderte A*, Bern, Haupt, 1995, 715 p.

HEINSCH, R, *Die Weiterentwicklung des humanitären Völkerrechts durch die Strafgerichtshöfe für das ehemalige Jugoslawien und Ruanda*, Berlin, BWV, 2007, 413 p.

HEINTSCHEL VON HEINEGG, W, *Seekriegsrecht und Neutralität im Seekrieg*, Berlin, Duncker und Humblot, 1995, 637 p.

HELL, S, *Der Mandschurei-Konflikt: Japan, China und der Völkerbund 1931 bis 1933*, Tübingen, UVT, 1999, 3285 p.

HILLGENBERG, H, *Das Gutachten-Verfahren vor dem IGH zur völkerrechtlichen Zulässigkeit von A-Waffen*, Saarbrücken, Europa-Institut, 1996, 80 p.

KARENFORT, J, *Die Hilfsorganisation im bewaffneten Konflikt, Rolle und Status unparteiischer humanitärer Organisationen im humanitären Völkerrecht*, Frankfurt am Main, Lang, 1999, 245 p.

KÖGLER, K, *Rechtlos in Guantánamo? Folgen des US-Supreme-Court-Urteils vom 28. Juni 2004*, Marburg, Tectum, 2007, 94 p.

KUHN, M, *Die Umweltschädigung im bewaffneten Konflikt als Kriegsverbrechen*, Bochum, Brockmeyer, 1997, 40 p.

KRIST, D, *Bevölkerungsumsiedlungen nach ethnischen Kriterien—ein Instrument zur friedlichen Lösung ethnischer Konflikte?* Marburg, Tectum, 2000, 153 p.

LANGE, K, *Der Status der Aufständischen im modernen humanitären Völkerrecht*, Frankfurt am Main, Lang, 2007, 238 p.

LERCHE, C, *Militärische Abwehrbefugnisse bei Angriffen auf Handelsschiffe*, Frankfurt am Main, Lang, 1993, 226 p.

LOHS, K, *Feuer als Waffe im Umweltkrieg*, Bochum, Brockmeyer, 1997, 29 p.

MERKEL, R (ed), *Der Kosovo-Krieg und das Völkerrecht*, Frankfurt am Main, Suhrkamp, 2000, 240 p.

MEYER, G, *Menschenrechte im Bürgerkrieg: eine Untersuchung und Bestandsaufnahme der uneingeschränkt gültigen Menschenrechte unter besonderer Berücksichtigung der Einordnung des Bürgerkriegs in die Internationalen Verträge*, Dissertation, Westfälische Wilhelms-Universität Münster, 1996, 247 p.

NOLTE, G, *Eingreifen auf Einladung: zur völkerrechtlichen Zulässigkeit des Einsatzes fremder Truppen im internen Konflikt auf Einladung der Regierung*, Berlin, Springer, 1999, 699 p.

OETER, S, *Neutralität und Waffenhandel*, Berlin, Springer, 1992, 290 p.

OVERMANS, R (ed), *In der Hand des Feindes: Kriegsgefangenschaft von der Antike bis zum Zweiten Weltkrieg*, Köln, Böhlau, 1999, 551 p.

PETERKE, S, *Der völkerrechtliche Sonderstatus der internationalen Föderation der Rotkreuz- und Rothalbmondgesellschaften*, Berlin, BWV, 2006, 248 p.

RIESENBERGER, D, *Für Humanität in Krieg und Frieden: das internationale Rote Kreuz 1863–1977*, Göttingen, Vandenhoeck und Ruprecht, 1992, 304 p.

RIKLIN, A, *Die dauernde Neutralität der Schweiz*, St Gallen, Institut für Politikwiss, 1991, 73 p.

ROSIN, P, *Völkerrechtsprobleme der Verlegung von Seeminen und entsprechender Gegenmassnahmen*, Bochum, Brockmeyer, 1995, 400 p.

SALMEN, L, *Kambodscha und die UNO: der Krieg und seine Eingrenzung von 1978 bis 1993*, Berlin, dissertation.de, 1999, 207 p.

SCHÄFER, B, *Zum Verhältnis Menschenrechte und humanitäres Völkerrecht*, Potsdam, Potsdam Universitat Verlager, 2006, 104 p.

SCHALLER, C, *Humanitäres Völkerrecht und nichtstaatliche Gewaltakteure: Neue Regeln für asymmetrische Konflikte?* Berlin, SWP, 2007, 31 p.

SCHAUB, AR, *Neutralität und kollektive Sicherheit: Gegenüberstellung zweier unvereinbarer Verhaltenskonzepte in bewaffneten Konflikten und Thesen zu einem zeit- und völkerrechtsgemässen modus vivendi*, Basel, Helbing und Lichtenhahn, 1995, 138 p.

SCHÖBENER, B, *Die amerikanische Besatzungspolitik und das Völkerrecht*, Frankfurt am Main, Lang, 1991, 575 p.

von SCHORLEMER, S, *Internationaler Kulturgüterschutz: Ansätze zur Prävention im Frieden sowie im bewaffneten Konflikt*, Berlin, Duncker und Humblot, 1992, 682 p.

SCHÖTTLER, H (ed), *Die Genfer Zusatzprotokolle: Kommentare und Analysen*, Bonn, Osang-Verlager, 1993, 274 p.

SCHMIDL, EA (ed), *Freund oder Feind? Kombattanten, Nichtkombattanten und Zivilisten in Krieg und Bürgerkrieg seit dem 18. Jahrhundert*, Frankfurt am Main, Lang, 1995, 209 p.

SCHNEIDER-ENK, M, *Der völkerrechtliche Schutz humanitärer Helfer in bewaffneten Konflikten*, Hamburg, Kovac, 2008, 272 p.

SCHWAGER, E, *Ius bello durante et bello confecto: Darstellung am Beispiel von Entschädigungsansprüchen der Opfer von Antipersonenminen*, Berlin, Duncker & Humblot, 2008, 350 p.

SCHWENDIMANN, F, *Rechtsfragen des humanitären Völkerrechts bei Friedensmissionen der Vereinten Nationen*, Zürich, Schulthess, 2007, 209 p.

SPIEKER, H, *Völkergewohnheitsrechtlicher Schutz der natürlichen Umwelt im internationalen bewaffneten Konflikt*, Bochum, Brockmeyer, 1992, 462 p.

——, *Naturwissenschaftliche und völkerrechtliche Perspektiven für den Schutz der Umwelt im bewaffneten Konflikt*, Bochum, Brockmeyer, 1996, 354 p.

SPOERRI, P, *Die Fortgeltung völkerrechtlichen Besetzungsrechts während der Interimsphase palästinensischer Selbstverwaltung in der West Bank und Gaza: eine Untersuchung der Abkommen zum israelisch-palästinensischen Friedensprozess*, Frankfurt am Main, Lang, 2001, 320 p.

VOIT, W (ed), *Das humanitäre Völkerrecht im Golfkrieg und andere Rotkreuz-Fragen / 35. Tagung der Justitiare und Konventionsbeauftragten des Deutsche Roten Kreuzes vom 12–14 September 1991 in Köln*, Bochum, Brockmeyer, 1992, 186 p.

—— (ed), *Humanitäres Völkerrecht im Jugoslawienkonflikt: ausländische Flüchtlinge—andere Rotkreuzfragen*, Bochum, Brockmeyer, 1993, 250 p.

—— (ed), *Völkerrechtliche Beiträge der Tagungen der Justitiare und Konventionsbeauftragten des Deutschen Roten Kreuzes 1957–1989*, Bochum, Brockmeyer, 1995, 483 p.

—— (ed), *Vereinte Nationen und humanitäres Völkerrecht: Rechtsentwicklung und Rechtsanwendung—internationale Rotkreuz-Aktivitäten und Rotkreuz-Operationen in Osteuropa—andere aktuelle Rotkreuz-Fragen: 38. Tagung der Justitiare und Konventionsbeauftragten*, Bochum, Brockmeyer, 1997, 142 p.

—— (ed), *Völkerrecht und humanitäre Operationen in Somalia und im ehemaligen Jugoslawien—Satzungsfragen des DRK: 37. Tagung der Justitiare und Konventionsbeauftragten des Deutschen Roten Kreuzes vom 9 bis 11 September 1993 in Goslar*, Bochum, Brockmeyer, 1997, 154 p.

VOLKAN, VD, *Blutsgrenzen: die historischen Wurzeln und die psychologischen Mechanismen ethnischer Konflikte und ihre Bedeutung bei Friedensverhandlungen*, Bern, Scherz, 1999, 351 p.

VOSS, FH, *Ius belli: zum völkerrechtlichen Kriegsrecht in Europa in der sog. Spanischen Epoche der Völkerrechtsgeschichte (ca. 1500–1659)*, Baden-Baden, Nomos, 2007, 299 p.

WEISS, I, *Der völkerrechtliche Schutz von Kindern in bewaffneten Konflikten*, Dissertation, Universität Regensburg, 1992, 213 p.

WEITZ, P, *Der Begriff des Nichtkombattanten in historischen Dokumenten, Entwürfen und völkerrechtlichen Verträgen*, Berlin, Spitz, 1999, 167 p.

WIECZOREK, J, *Unrechtmässige Kombattanten und humanitäres Völkerrecht*, Berlin, Duncker und Humblot, 2005, 397 p.

WITTELER, S, *Die Regelungen der neuen Verträge des humanitären Völkerrechts und des Rechts der Rüstungsbegrenzung mit direktem Umweltbezug*, Bochum, Brockmeyer, 1993, 529 p.

ZISCHG, R, *Nicht-internationaler bewaffneter Konflikt und Völkerrecht: zur Zulässigkeit der Unterstützung der Konfliktparteien durch dritte Staaten*, Baden-Baden, Nomos, 1996, 196 p.

ZECHMEISTER, D, *Die Erosion des humanitären Völkerrechts in den bewaffneten Konflikten der Gegenwart*, Baden-Baden, 2007, Nomos, 241 p.

ZEILEISSEN, C, *Der völkerrechtliche Schutz vor militärischen Angriffen auf Kernkraftwerke*, Berlin, Duncker und Humblot, 1997, 366 p.

French

ABI-SAAB, R, *Droit humanitaire et conflits internes: origines et évolutions de la réglementation internationale*, Genève, Henri Dunant Institute, 1986, 280 p.

ARRASSEN, M, *Conduite des hostilités, droit des conflits armés et désarmement*, Bruxelles, Bruylant, 1986, 605 p.

BARDONNET, D (ed), *La Convention sur l'interdiction et l'élimination des armes chimiques: une percée dans l'entreprise multilatérale du désarmement*, Dordrecht, Martinus Nijhoff, 1995, 635 p.

BELANGER, M, *Droit international humanitaire général*, 2ème edn, Paris, Gualino, 2007, 156 p.

BIAD, A, *Droit international humanitaire*, 2ème edn, Paris, Ellipses Marketing, 2006, 139 p.

BOUSTANI, K, *Le conflit intraétatique au Liban*, Bruxelles, Bruylant, 1994, 454 p.

BUGNION, F, *Le Comité international de la Croix-Rouge et la protection des victimes de la guerre*, Genève, International Committee of the Red Cross, 1994, 1438 p.

BUIRETTE, P, *Le droit international humanitaire*, Paris, Éd. la Découverte, 1996, 123 p.

CAFLISCH, L (ed), *Permanent Court of International justice: Répertoire des décisions et des documents de la procédure écrite et orale, 5. 1. La responsabilité internationale, 2. La guerre et la neutralité*, Genève, IUHEI, 1989, 1036 p.

CAZALS, C, *La gendarmerie sous l'occupation*, Paris, Editions de la Musse, 1995, 318 p.

COHN, I, *Enfants soldats: le rôle des enfants dans les conflits armés*, Montréal, Méridien, 1995, 267 p.

CONDORELLI, L, LA ROSA, AM & SCHERRER, S (éds), *Les Nations Unies et le droit international humanitaire. Actes du colloque international à l'occasion du 50 anniversaire de l'ONU (Genève 19, 20 et 21 octobre 1995)*, Paris, Éditions Pedone, 1996, 506p.

D'ARGENT, P, *Les réparations de guerres en droit international public*, Louvain-la-Neuve, Bruylant, 2001, 895 p.

DAVID, E, *Principes de droit des conflits armés*, 4ème edn, Bruxelles, Bruylant, 2008, 1118 p.

——, *Eléments de droit pénal internationales*, Bruxelles, Bruylant, 2001–02, 473 p.

DEYRA, M, *Droit international humanitaire*, Paris, Gualino, 1998, 151 p.

EMANUELLI, C (ed), *Les casques bleus: policiers ou combattants?* Montréal, Wilson and Lafleur, 1997, 130 p.

GASSER, HP, *Le droit international humanitaire*, Genève, Henri Dunant Institute, 1993, 100 p.

GIROD, C, *Tempête sur le désert: le Comité international de la Croix-Rouge et la guerre du Golfe: 1990–1991*, Bruxelles, Bruylant, 1995, 401 p.

HAROUEL-BURELOUP, V, *Traité de droit humanitaire*, Paris, Presses Universitaires de France, 2005, 556 p.

HENZELIN, M, *Le principe de l'universalité en droit pénal international*, Bâle, Helbing & Lichtenhahn, 2000, 527 p.

KALSHOVEN, F and SANDOZ, Y (eds), *La mise en œuvre du droit international humanitaire*, Dordrecht, Martinus Nijhoff, 1989, 472 p.

KOLB, R, *Droit humanitaire et opérations de paix internationals—L'application du droit international humanitaire dans des opérations de maintien ou de rétablissement de la paix auxquelles concourt une organisation internationale*, 2ème edn, Bâle, Helbing & Lichtenhahn, 2006, 136 p.

——, *Ius in bello: Le droit international des conflits armés, Précis*, Bâle, Helbing & Lichtenhahn, 2003, 299 p.

KOLB, R, PORETTO, G et VITE, S, *L'application du droit international humanitaire et des droits de l'Homme aux organisations internationales. Forces de paix et administrations civiles transitoires*, Bruxelles, Bruylant, 2005, 504 p.

KONOPKA, J-A (ed), *La protection des biens culturels en temps de guerre et de paix d'après les conventions internationales (multilatérales): recueil de textes*, Genève, Imprimeries de Versoix, 1997, 163 p.

LAFRANCE, L, *Droit humanitaire et guerres déstructurées*, Montréal, Liber, 2006, 152 p.

LANFRANCHI, M-P et CHRISTAKIS, T, *La licéité de l'emploi d'armes nucléaires devant la Cour international de justice: analyse et documents*, Paris, Economia, 1997, 328 p.

MOREILLON, L, *Droit pénal humanitaire*, Genève, Helbing & Lichtenhahn, 2006, 378 p.

PAYE, O, *Les conflits armés de 1945 à nos jours*, Bruxelles, CERIS, 1993, 158 p.

——, *Sauve qui peut? Le droit international face aux crises humanitaires*, Bruxelles, Bruylant, 1996, 315 p.

PICTET, J, *Le droit humanitaire et la protection des victimes de la guerre*, Genève, International Committee of the Red Cross, 1973, 152 p.

—— (éd), *Commentaire des Conventions I-IV de Genève du 12 août 1949, 4 vols*, Genève, International Committee of the Red Cross, 1952–59, 542 p, 333 p, 834 p and 729 p.

ROUSSEAU, Ch, *Le droit des conflits armés*, Paris, Pedone, 1983, 629 p.

SUR, S (ed), *Le droit international des armes nucléaires*, Paris, Pedone, 1998, 206 p.

SWINARSKI, Ch (ed), *Etudes et essais sur le droit international humanitaire et sur les principes de la Croix-Rouge en l'honneur de Jean Pictet*, Genève, CICR, 1984, 1143 p.

TOMAN, J, *La protection des biens culturels en cas de conflit armé*, Paris, UNESCO, 1994, 490 p.

VONECHE CARDIA, I, *L'octobre hongrois: entre Croix Rouge et drapeau rouge: l'action du Comité international du Croix-Rouge en 1956*, Bruxelles, Bruylant, 1996, 183 p.

YUROVICS, Y, *Réflexions sur la spécificité du crime contre l'humanité*, Paris, LDGJ, 2002, 519 p.

ZEMMALI, A, *Combattants et prisonniers de guerre en droit islamique et en droit international humanitaire*, Paris, Pedone, 1997, 519 p.

English

ADAM-SMITH, P, *Prisoners of War from Gallipoli to Korea*, Harmondsworth, Viking, 1992, 599 p.

AKRAM, M, *International Humanitarian Law*, Petaling Jaya, Selangor, Malaysia, International Law Book Services, 2005, 166 p.

AKSAR, Y, *Implementing International Humanitarian Law*, London, Routledge, 2004, 314 p.

ALLAWI, AA, *The Occupation of Iraq: Winning the War, Losing the Peace*, New Haven, Yale University Press, 2007, 518 p.

AL-RAYYES, N, *The Israeli Settlements from the Perspective of International Humanitarian Law*, Ramallah, Al-Haq Institute, 2000, 139 p.

ARNOLD, R, *International Humanitarian Law and Human Rights Law*, Leiden, Martinus Nijhoff, 2008, 600 p.

——, *Law Enforcement within the Framework of Peace Support Operations*, Leiden, Martinus Nijhoff, 2008, 475 p.

—— (ed), *Practice and Policies of Modern Peace Support Operations under International Law*, Ardsley, NY, Transnational Publishers, 2006, 303 p.

—— (ed), *International Humanitarian Law and the 21st Century's Conflicts*, Lausanne, Editions Interuniversitaires Suisse, 2005, 253 p.

ASKIN, KD, *War Crimes against Women: Prosecution in International War Crimes Tribunals*, The Hague, Martinus Nijhoff, 1997, 455 p.

AUSTIN, JE (ed), *The Environmental Consequences of War*, Cambridge, Cambridge University Press, 2000, 690 p.

BABIKER, MA, *Application of the International Humanitarian and Human Rights Law to the Armed Conflicts of the Sudan*, Antwerp, Intersentia, 2007, 303 p.

BAILEY, SD, *Prohibitions and Restraints in War*, London, The Royal Institute of International Affairs, 1972, 194 p.

BARRY, NO, *War and the Red Cross: The Unspoken Mission*, Basingstoke, Macmillan, 1997, 159 p.

BASHI, S, *Disengaged Occupiers: The Legal Status of Gaza*, Tel Aviv, Gisha: Center for the Legal Protection of Freedom of Movement, 2007, 103 p.

BASSIOUNI, C, *Crimes against Humanity in International Criminal Law*, 2nd edn, Dordrecht, Martinus Nijhoff, 1992, 820 p.

BAUDENSTIEL, R, *Between Bombs and Good Intentions: The Red Cross and the Italo-Ethiopian War, 1935–1936*, New York, Berghahn Books, 2006, 342 p.

BEIGEBER, Y, *The Role and Status of International Humanitarian Volunteers and Organization: The Right and Duty to Humanitarian Assistance*, Dordrecht, Martinus Nijhoff, 1991, 414 p.

BENNETT, A, *The Geneva Convention: The Hidden Origins of the Red Cross*, Stroud, Sutton, 2005, 236 p.

BENVENISTI, E, *The International Law of Occupation*, Princeton, Princeton University Press, 1993, 241 p.

BEST, G, *War and Law since 1945*, Oxford, Clarendon, 1994, 434 p.

BLUMENTHAL, DA (ed), *The Legacy of Nuremberg*, Leiden, Martinus Nijhoff, 2008, 337 p.

BOELAERT-SUOMINEN, SAJ, *International Environmental Law and Naval War*, Newport, RI, Naval War College, 2000, 365 p.

BOISSON CHAZOURNES, L (ed), *International Law, the International Court of Justice and Nuclear Weapons*, Cambridge, Cambridge University Press, 1999, 592 p.

BOTHE M, PARTSCH, KJ and SOLF, WA, *New Rules for Victims of Armed Conflicts*, The Hague, Martinus Nijhoff, 1982, 746 p.

BOUCHET-SAULNIER, F, *The Practical Guide to Humanitarian Law*, 2nd edn, Lanham, Rowman and Littlefield, 2006, 555 p.

BOWEN, S (ed), *Human Rights, Selfdetermination and Political Change in the Occupied Palestinian Territories*, The Hague, Martinus Nijhoff, 1997, 321 p.

BREAU, S (ed), *Testing the Boundaries of International Humanitarian Law*, London, British Institute of International and Comparitive Law, 2006, 343 p.

BROWN, ME (ed), *The International Dimensions of Internal Conflict*, Cambridge, MA, MIT Press, 1996, 653 p.

BYERS, M, *War Law: International Law and Armed Conflict*, London, Atlantic, 2005, 214 pp.

BURROUGHS, J, *The Legality of Threat or Use of Nuclear Weapons: A Guide to Historic Opinion of the International Court of Justice*, Hamburg, LIT, 1997, 169 p.

BUSUTTIL, JJ, *Naval Weapons Systems and the Contemporary Law of War*, Oxford, Clarendon, 1998, 249 p.

CAHILL, KM (ed), *Clearing the Fields: Solutions to the Global Land Mines Crisis*, New York, Basic Books, 1995, 237 p.

CARPENTER, RC, *'Innocent Women and Children': Gender, Norms and the Protection of Civilians*, Aldershot, Ashgate, 2006, 217 p.

CASSESE, A (ed), *Current Problems of International Law: Essays on UN Law and the Law of Armed Conflict*, Milan, Dott. A. Giuffre, 1975, 375 p.

—— (ed), *The New Humanitarian Law of Armed Conflict*, 2 vols, Naples, Editorale Scientifica, 1979–80, 501 p and 291 p.

CHADWICK, E, *Self-determination, Terrorism and the International Humanitarian Law of Armed Conflict*, The Hague, Martinus Nijhoff, 1996, 221 p.

CLARK, RS (ed), *The Case Against the Bomb: Marshall Islands, Samoa, and Salomon Islands before the International Court of Justice in Advisory Proceedings on the Legality of the Threat or Use of Nuclear Weapons*, Camden, NJ, Rutgers University School of Law, 1996, 354 p.

COHN, I and GOODWIN-GILL, GS, *Child Soldiers: The Role of Children in Armed Conflict*, Oxford, Clarendon, 1994, 228 p.

COLL, AR (ed), *Legal and Moral Constraints on Low-intensity Conflict*, Newport, RI, Naval War College, 1995, 387 p.

COLLEGE OF EUROPE (ed), *Relevance of International Humanitarian Law to Non-state Actors: Proceedings of the Bruges Colloquium (25–26 October 2002)*, Brugge, College of Europe, 2003, 198 p.

CONWAY-LANZ, S, *Collateral Damage: Americans, Noncombatant Immunity and Atrocity after World War II*, New York, Routledge, 2006, 280 p.

CRODDY, E, *Chemical and Biological Warfare: An Annotated Bibliography*, Lanham, MD, Scarecrow Press, 1997, 429 p.

DELISSEN, AJM and TANJA, GJ (eds), *Humanitarian Law of Armed Conflict: Challenges Ahead (Essays in Honor of Frits Kalshoven)*, Dordrecht, Martinus Nijhoff, 1991, 668 p.

DETTER, I, *The Law of War*, 2nd edn, Cambridge, Cambridge University Press, 2000, 516 p.

DINSTEIN, Y (ed), *War Crimes in International Law*, The Hague, Martinus Nijhoff, 1996, 489 p.

DOEBBLER, CFJ, *Introduction to International Humanitarian Law*, Washington, DC, CD Publishing, 2005, 212 p.

DOLGOPOL, U (ed), *The Challenge of Conflict*, Leiden, Martinus Nijhoff, 2006, 628 p.

VAN DONGEN, YC, *The Protection of Civilian Populations in Time of Armed Conflict* Dissertation, Groningen University, 1991, 320 p.

DOSWALD-BECK, L, *San Remo Manual on International Law Applicable to Armed Conflicts at Sea*, Cambridge, Cambridge University Press, 1995, 257 p.

DURHAM, H (ed), *Listening to the Silences: Women and War*, Leiden, Martinus Nijhoff, 2005, 276 p.

ENGDAHL, O, *Protection of Personnel in Peace Operations*, Leiden, Martinus Nijhoff, 2007, 357 p.

EVAN WM (ed), *Nuclear Proliferation and the Legality of Nuclear Weapons*, Lanham, MD, University Press of America, 1995, 421 p.

EYFFINGER, A, *The 1899 Hague Peace Conference: 'The Parliament of Man, the Federation of the World'*, The Hague, Kluwer Law International, 1999, 480 p.

FERNANDEZ SANCHEZ, PA (ed), *The New Challenges of Humanitarian Law in Armed Conflicts*, Leiden, Martinus Nijhoff, 2005, 366 p.

FLECK, D (ed), *The Handbook of International Humanitarian Law*, 2nd edn, Oxford, Oxford University Press, 2008, 770 p.

—— (ed), *The Handbook of the Law of Visiting Forces*, Oxford, Oxford University Press, 2001, 625 p.

FORSYTHE, DP, *The International Committee of the Red Cross*, London, Routledge, 2007, 122 p.

FOX, GH, *Humanitarian Occupation*, Cambridge, Cambridge University Press, 2008, 320 p.

FOX, H and MEYERS, MA (eds), *Effecting Compliance*, London, British Institute of International and Comparative Law, 1993, 251 p.

GARDAM, JG, *Non-combatant Immunity as a Norm of International Humanitarian Law*, Dordrecht, Martinus Nijhoff, 1993, 199 p.

—— (ed), *Humanitarian Law*, Dartmouth, Ashgate, 1999, 570 p.

GARRETT, SA, *Ethics and Airpower in World War II: The British Bombing of German Cities*, New York, St. Martin's Press, 1997, 256 p.

GINGER, AF (ed), *Nuclear Weapons are Illegal: The Historic Opinion of the World Court and How it will be Enforced*, New York, The Apex Press, 1998, 561 p.

GOODWIN-GILL, G and COHN, I, *Child Soldiers: The Role of Children in Armed Conflicts*, Oxford, Clarendon, 1994, 228 p.

GOWLLAND-DEBBAS, V, (ed), *United Nations Sanctions and International Law*, The Hague, Kluwer Law International, 2001, 408 p.

GREEN, LC, *The Contemporary Law of Armed Conflict*, 3rd edn, Manchester, Manchester University Press, 2008, 434 p.

——, *Essays on the Modern Law of War*, 2nd edn, Ardsley, NY, Transnational Publishers, 1999, 604 p.

GREENBAUM, C, *Protection of Children during Armed Political Conflict: A Multidisciplinary Perspective*, Antwerp, Intersentia, 2006, 486 p.

GREENWOOD, C, *Essays on War in International Law*, London, Cameron, 2006, 700 p.

GRUNAWALT, RJ (ed), *Targeting Enemy Merchant Shipping*, Newport, RI, Naval War College, 1993, 382 p.

—— (ed), *Protection of the Environment During Armed Conflict*, Newport, RI, Naval War College, 1996, 720 p.

de GUTTRY, A (ed), *The Iran–Iraq War (1980–1988) and the Law of Naval Warfare*, Cambridge, Cambridge University Press, 1993, 573 p.

HALBROOK, SP, *Target Switzerland: Swiss Armed Neutrality in World War II*, Rockville Centre, NY, Sarpedon, 1998, 320 p.

HAUG, H and GASSER H-P (eds), *Humanity for All: The International Red Cross and Red Crescent Movement*, Berne, Haupt, 1993, 682 p.

HEINTSCHEL von HEINEGG, W (ed), *The Military Objective and the Principle of Distinction in the Law of Naval Warfare: Report, Commentaries and Proceeding of the Round-table of Experts on International Humanitarian Law Applicable to Armed Conflicts at Sea*, Bochum, Brockmeyer, 1991, 177 p.

—— (ed), *Methods and Means of Combat in Naval Warfare: Reports & Commentaries of the Round Table of Experts on International Law Applicable to Armed Conflicts at Sea, 19–23 October 1990, Université de Toulon et du Var*, Bochum, Brockmeyer, 1992, 136 p.

—— (ed), *Visit, Search, Diversion and Capture: The Effect of the United Nations Charter on Law of Naval Warfare (Reports and Commentaries of the Round Table of Experts on International Humanitarian Law Applicable to Armed Conflicts at Sea, Bergen, 20–24 September 1991)*, Bochum, Brockmeyer, 1995, 210 p.

—— (ed), *Regions of Operation of Naval Warfare: Reports and Commentaries of the Round Table of Experts on International Humanitarian Law Applicable to Armed Conflicts at Sea (Ottawa, 25–28 September 1992)*, Bochum, Brockmeyer, 1995, 150 p.

—— (ed), *International Humanitarian Law Facing New Challenges*, Berlin, Springer, 2007, 280 p.

HELM, AM (ed), *The Law of War in the 21st Century*, Newport, Naval War College, 2007, 336 p.

HENCKAERTS, J-M and DOSWALD-BECK, L, *Customary International Humanitarian Law, vol 1: Rules; vol 2: Practice*, Cambridge, Cambridge University Press, 2005, 621p and 4411p.

HENSEL, HM, *The Law of Armed Conflict: Constraints on the Contemporary Use of Military Force*, Aldershot, Ashgate, 2005, 266 pp.

——, *The Legitimate Use of Military Force: The Just War Tradition and the Customary Law of Armed Conflict*, Aldershot, Ashgate, 2008, 320 p.

HOFFMANN, T, *Dr Opinio Juris and Mr State Practice: The Strange Case of Customary International Humanitarian Law*, Budapest, Anales Universitatis Scientiarium Budapestinensis, 2006, 394 p.

HONWANA, A, *Child Soldiers in Africa*, Philadelphia, University of Philadelphia Press, 2006, 202 p.

HOYT, EP, *Inferno: The Firebombing of Japan, March 9–August 15, 1945*, Lanham, MD, Madison Books, 2000, 153 p.

HULME, K, *Wartorn Environment*, Leiden, Martinus Nijhoff, 2004, 340 p.

HUMAN RIGHTS WATCH, *Landmines: A Deadly Legacy*, New York, Human Rights Watch, 1993, 510 p.

HUTCHINSON, JF, *Champions of Charity: War and the Rise of the Red Cross*, Boulder, CO, Westview Press, 1996, 448 p.

HUTCHISON, KD, *Operation Desert Shield/Desert Storm: Chronology and Factbook*, Westport, CT, Greenwood Press, 1995, 269 p.

INTERNATIONAL COMMITTEE OF THE RED CROSS (ed), *Commentary of the Additional Protocols of 8 June 1977 to the Geneva Conventions of 12 August 1949*, Geneva, International Committee of the Red Cross, 1987, 1625 p.

—— (ed), *Report of the Expert Meeting on Multinational Peace Operations: Applicability of International Humanitarian Law and International Human Rights Law to UN Mandated Forces, Geneva*, International Committee of the Red Cross, 2004, 93 p.

INTERNATIONAL INSTITUTE OF HUMANITARIAN LAW, *Twenty Years of Humanitarian Dialogue*, San Remo, International Institute of Humanitarian Law, 1991, 94 p.

JAQUES, R (ed), *Issues in International Law and Military Operations*, Newport, Naval War College, 2006, 378 p.

JOES, AJ, *Guerilla Warfare: A Historical Biographical and Bibliographical Sourcebook*, Westport, CT, Greenwood Press, 1996, 312 p.

KÄLIN, W, *Human Rights in Times of Occupation: The Case of Kuwait*, Berne, Law Books in Europe, 1994, 156 p.

KALSHOVEN, F, *The Law of Warfare: A Summary of its Recent History and Trends in Development*, Leiden, Sijthoff, 1973, 138 p.

——, *Belligerent Reprisals*, Leiden, Martinus Nijhoff, 2005, 389 p.

——, *Reflections on the Law of War*, Leiden, Martinus Nijhoff, 2007, 1115 p.

KASTO, J, *Jus Cogens and Humanitarian law*, London, Kasto, 1994, 95 p.

KEEN, M, *The Laws of War in the Late Middle Ages*, Aldershot, Gregg Revivals, 1993, 291 p.

KHANNA, SK, *War and Human Rights*, New Dehli, Dominant Publishers, 1999, 336 p.

KLEINE-AHLBRANDT, STE, *The Protection Gap in the International Protection of Internally Displaced Persons: The Case of Rwanda*, Geneva, Universtity of Geneva, 1996, 172 p.

KOHEN, MG (ed), *Promoting Justice, Human Rights and Conflict Resolution through International Law: liber amicorum Lucius Caflisch*, Leiden, Martinus Nijhoff, 2007, 1236 p.

KOPPE, E, *The Use of Nuclear Weapons and the Protection of the Environment during International Armed Conflict*, Oxford, Hart Publishing, 2008, 447 p.

KRUMWIEDE, H-W (ed), *Civil Wars*, Baden-Baden, Nomos, 2000, 330 p.

KRUTZSCH, W and TRAPP, R, *A Commentary on the Chemical Weapons Convention*, Dordrecht, Martinus Nijhoff, 1994, 544 p.

KUPER, J, *International Law Concerning Child Civilians in Armed Conflict*, Oxford, Clarendon, 1997, 283 p.

KWAKWA, E, *The International Law of Armed Conflict: Personal and Material Fields of Application*, Dordrecht, Kluwer Academic Publishers, 1992, 208 p.

LA HAYE, E, *War Crimes in Internal Armed Conflicts*, Cambridge, Cambridge University Press, 2008, 424 p.

LEDERBERG, J (ed), *Biological Weapons: Limiting the Threat*, Cambridge, MA, MIT Press, 1999, 351 p.

LEGRO, JW, *Cooperation within Conflict: Submarines, Strategic Bombing, Chemical Warfare and Restraint in World War II*, Ann Arbor, MI, University of Michigan, 1994, 407 p.

LEVIE, HS, *The Code of International Armed Conflict, vols 1–2*, London, Oceana, 1986, 1099 p.

——, *Mine Warfare at Sea*, Dordrecht, Martinus Nijhoff, 1992, 233 p.

——, *Terrorism in War: The Law of War Crimes*, Dobbs Ferry, NY, Oceana, 1993, 721 p.

LIJINZAAD, L (ed), *Making the Voice of Humanity Heard: Essays on Humanitarian Assistance and International Humanitarian Law in Honour of HRH Princess Margriet of the Netherlands*, Leiden, Brill, 2004, 546 p.

LINNAN, DK, *Enemy Combatants, Terrorism, and Armed Conflict Law: A Guide to the Issues*, Westport, CT, Praeger Security International, 2008, 400 p.

LUNZE, S, *The Protection of Religious Personnel in Armed Conflict*, Frankfurt am Main, Lang, 2004, 219 p.

MANI, VS (ed), *Handbook of International Humanitarian Law in South Asia*, New Delhi, Oxford University Press, 2007, 262 p.

MARESCA, L (ed), *The Banning of Anti-personnel Landmines: The Legal Contribution of the International Committee of the Red Cross (1955–1995)*, Cambridge, Cambridge University Press, 2000, 670 p.

MAYBEE, L, *Custom as a Source of International Humanitarian Law: Proceedings of the Conference to Mark the Publication of the ICRC Study 'Customary International Humanitarian Law', held in New Delhi, 8–9 December 2005*, Geneva, International Committee of the Red Cross, 2006, 301 p.

McCOUBREY, H, *International Humanitarian Law: Modern Developments in the Limitation of Warfare*, 2nd edn, Aldershot, Ashgate, 1998, 326 p.

McCOUBREY, H and WHITE, ND, *International Organizations and Civil Wars*, Aldershot, Dartmouth, 1995, 294 p.

McDOUGAL, MS and FELICIANO, FP, *The International Law of War: Transnational Coercion and World Public Order*, New Haven, New Haven Press, 1994, 872 p.

MERON, T, *Human Rights and Humanitarian Norms as Customary Law*, Oxford, Clarendon, 1991, 263 p.

MERON, T, *The Humanization of International Law*, Leiden, Martinus Nijhoff, 2006, 551 p.

MEYER, MA (ed), *Aspects of the 1977 Geneva Protocols and the 1981 Weapons Convention*, London, British Institute of International and Comparative Law, 1989, 298 p.

MINEAR, L and WEISS, TG, *Humanitarian Action in Times of War: A Handbook for Practitioners*, Boulder, CO, Lynne Rienner, 1993, 107 p.

MOIR, L, *The Protection of Civilians during Non-international Armed Conflict*, Cambridge, University of Cambridge, 1997, 211 p.

MOORHEAD, C, *Dunants Dream: War, Switzerland and the History of the Red Cross*, London, HarperCollins, 1998, 780 p.

MOXLEY, CJ, *Nuclear Weapons and International Law in the Post Cold War World*, Lanham, MD, University Press of America, 2000, 813 p.

MURTHY, PA (ed), *Neutrality and Non-alignment in the 1990s*, London, Sangam, 1991, 127 p.

NABULSI, K, *Traditions of War: Occupation, Resistance and the Law*, Oxford, Oxford University Press, 1999, 293 p.

NANDA, VP, *Nuclear Weapons and the World Court*, Ardsley, NY, Transnational, 1998, 379 p.

NEFF, SC, *The Rights and Duties of Neutrals: A General History*, New York, Juris Publishing, 2000, 246 p.

NEILLANDS, R, *The Bomber War: Arthur Harris and the Allied Bomber Offensive, 1939–1945*, London, John Murray, 2001, 448 p.

NEY, JS, *Understanding International Conflicts: An Introduction to Theory and History*, New York, Longman, 2000, 244 p.

OLASOLO, H, *Unlawful Attacks in Combat Situations: From the ICTY's Case to the Rome Statute*, Leiden, Martinus Nijhoff, 2007, 320 p.

OSIEL, M, *Obeying Orders: Atrocity, Military Discipline, and the Law of War*, New Brunswick, Transaction, 1999, 398 p.

OTHMAN, MC, *Accountability for International Humanitarian Law Violations*, Berlin, Springer, 2005, 384 p.

OPPENHEIM, LF, *International Law, vol II: Disputes, War and Neutrality*, 7th edn, H Lauterpacht (ed), London, Longman, 1952, 941 p.

PAECH, N, *Memorial in Support of the Application by the General Assembly of the United Nations for an Advisory Opinion by the International Court of Justice on the Legality of the Use of Nuclear Weapons under International Law*, Bochum, Brockmeyer, 1996, 37 p.

PATRNOGIC, J, *New Issues for International Humanitarian Law Regarding Humanitarian Assistance*, Milan, Nagard, 2004, 39 p.

PAUL, TV (ed), *The Absolute Weapon Revisited: Nuclear Arms and the Emerging International Order*, Ann Arbor, MI, University of Michigan Press, 1998, 312 p.

PERNA, L, *The Formation of the Treaty Law of Non-international Armed Conflicts*, Leiden, Martinus Nijhoff, 2006, 168 p.

PETRIE, DA, *The Prize Game: Lawful Looting on the High Seas in the Days of Fighting Sail*, Annapolis, MD, Naval Insitute Press, 1999, 217 p.

PLANT, G (ed), *Environmental Protection and the Law of War*, London, Belhaven Press, 1992, 284 p.

PRICE, RM, *The Chemical Weapons Taboo*, Ithaca, NY, Cornell University Press, 1997, 233 p.

PROVOST, R, *International Human Rights and Humanitarian Law*, Cambridge, Cambridge University Press, 2002, 418 p.

QUAYE, CO, *Liberation Struggles in International Law*, Philadelphia, Temple University Press, 1991, 382 p.

RAMACHANDRAN, KS (ed), *Gulf War and Environmental Problems*, New Dehli, South Asia Books, 1991, 318 p.

RAPPERT, B, *Controlling the Weapons of War: Politics, Persuasion and the Prohibition of Inhumanity*, London, Routledge, 2006, 223 p.

RAVASI, G (ed), *The Two Additional Protocols to the Geneva Conventions: 25 Years Later, Challenges and Prospects; Current Problems of International Humanitarian Law*, Milano, Nagard, 2004, 212 p.

—— (ed), *International Humanitarian Law and Other Legal Regimes: Interplay in Situations of Violence (proceedings of the 27th round table, San Remo, 4–6 September 2003)*, Milano, Nagard, 2005, 165 p.

—— (ed), *Human Dignity Protection in Armed Conflict: Strengthening Measures for the Respect and Implementation of International Humanitarian Law and Other Rules (proceedings of the 28th round table, San Remo, 2–4 September 2004)*, Milano, Nagard, 2006, 221 p.

RONZITTI, N, *The Law of Air Warfare: Contemporary Issues*, Utrecht, Eleven International Publishing, 2006, 340 p.

ROSAS, A, *The Legal Status of Prisoners of War*, Turku, Institute for Human Rights, A°bo Akademi University, 2005, 523 p.

ROWE, P, *The Impact of Human Rights Law on Armed Forces*, Cambridge, Cambridge University Press, 2006, 259 p.

SANDVIK-NYLUND, M, *Caught in Conflicts: Civilian Victims, Humanitarian Assistance and International Law*, 2nd edn, Turku, Institute for Human Rights, Åbo Akademi University, 2003, 174 p.

SCHMITT, MN, *Blockade Law: Research Design and Sources*, Buffalo, NY, Naval War College, 1991, 63 p.

—— (ed), *The Law of Armed Conflict: Into the Next Millennium*, Newport, RI, Naval War College, 1998, 535 p.

—— (ed), *The Law of Military Operations (Liber amicorum Professor Jack Grunawalt)*, Newport, RI, Naval War College, 1998, 458 p.

—— (ed), *Levie and the Law of War*, Newport, RI, Naval War College, 1998, 515 p.

—— (ed), *International Law across the Spectrum of Conflict: Essays in Honor of Professor LC Green on the Occasion of his Eightieth Birthday*, Newport, RI, Naval War College, 2000, 607 p.

SCHMITT, MN and PEJIC, E (eds), *International Law and Armed Conflict: Exploring the Faultlines (Essays in Honour of Yoram Dinstein)*, Leiden, Martinus Nijhoff, 2007, 586 p.

SCHUMACHER, G, *A Bloody Business: America's War Zone Contractors and the Occupation of Iraq*, St Paul, Zenith Press, 2006, 304 p.

SCHWARZENBERGER, G, *The Law of Armed Conflicts*, London, Stevens, 1968, 881 p.

SHABAS, W, *Genocide in International Law: The Crime of Crimes*, Cambridge, Cambridge University Press, 2000, 624 p.

SHERRY, VN, *Persona Non Grata: The Expulsion of Lebanese Civilians from Israeli-occupied Lebanon*, New York, Human Rights Watch, 1999, 83 p.

SNOW, DM, *Uncivil Wars: International Security and the New Internal Conflicts*, Boulder, Lynne Reinner, 1996, 177 p.

SOLOMON, B, (ed), *Chemical and Biological Warfare*, New York, H W Wilson, 1999, 158 p.

STONE, J, *Legal Controls of International Conflict*, London, Stevens & Sons, 1954, 851 p.

TANCA, A, *Foreign Armed Intervention in Internal Conflict*, Dordrecht, Martinus Nijhoff, 1993, 234 p.

THOMAS, AR (ed), *Annotated Supplement to The Commander's Handbook on the Law of Naval Operations*, Newport, RI, Naval War College, 1999, 526 p.

TOMAN, J, *Protection of Cultural Property in the Event of Armed Conflict: Commentary on the Convention for the Protection of Cultural Property in the Event of Armed Conflict and its Protocols, signed on 14 May 1954 in The Hague, and on other Instruments of International Law concerning such Protection*, Dartmouth, Ashgate, 1996, 525 p.

TUCK, R, *The Rights of War and Peace: Political Thought and the International Order from Grotius to Kant*, Oxford, Oxford University Press, 1999, 243 p.

VASILESKI, V, *International Humanitarian Law in Armed Conflicts*, Skopje, Military Academy "General Mihailo Apostolski" Skopje, 2003, 538 p.

WACKERS, GL (ed), *Violation of Medical Neutrality*, Amsterdam, Thesis Publishers, 1992, 128 p.

WARNER, D (ed), *Human Rights and Humanitarian Law: The Quest for Universality*, The Hague, Martinus Nijhoff, 1997, 145, p.

WAXMAN, MC, *International Law and the Politics of Urban Air Operations*, Santa Monica, Rand, 2000, 80 p.

WEISS, TG (ed), *The United Nations and Civil Wars*, Boulder, Lynne Reinner, 1995, 235 p.

WELLS, DA, *War Crimes and Laws of War*, 2nd edn, Lanham, MD, University Press of America, 1991, 179 p.

——, *The Laws of Land Warfare: A Guide to the US Army Manuals*, Westport, CT, Greenwood Press, 1992, 201 p.

WESSELS, M, *Child Soldiers: From Violence to Protection*, Cambridge, Mass, Harvard University Press, 2006, 284 p.

WILMSHURST, E (ed), *Perspectives on the ICRC Study on Customary International Humanitarian Law*, Cambridge, Cambridge University Press, 2007, 433 p.

YAMASHITA, H, *Humanitarian Space and International Politics: The Creation of Safe Areas*, Aldershot, Ashgate, 2004, 215 p.

ZILINSKAS, RA (ed), *Biological Warfare,* Boulder, CO, Lynne Reinner, 2000, 309 p.

ZYBERI, G, *The Humanitarian Face of the International Court of Justice: Its Contribution to Interpreting and Developing International Human Rights and Humanitarian Law Rules and Principles*, Antwerp, Intersentia, 2008, 523 p.

Italian

AMIRANTE, A, *Occupazione bellica: quale ruolo per un istituto del diritto internazionale classico nel diritto internazionale moderno*, Napoli, Ed. Scientifiche Italiane, 2007, 196 p.

ARRIGO, G, *Il diritto umanitario al di là della soglia dei conflitti armati: situazioni di tensioni e disordini interni, sommosse e atti di violenza*, Roma, Casa del Libro, 1992, 190 p.

GIOFFREDI, G, *La condizione internazionale del minore nei conflitti armati*, Milano, Giuffre, 2006, 391 p.

GRADO, V, *Guerre civili e terzi Stati*, Padova, CEDAM, 1998, 416 p.

MARELLA, F, *Le opere d'arte tra cooperazione internazionale e conflitti armati*, Padova, CEDAM, 2006, 353 p.

PANZERA, AF, *La tutela internazionale dei beni culturali in tempo di guerra*, Torino, s.n., 1993, 77 p.

PAPANICOLOPULU, I (ed), *Quale diritto nei conflitti armati? Relazioni e documenti del ciclo di conferenze tenute nell'Università di Milano-Bicocca (marzo–maggio 2005)*, Milano, Giuffre, 2006, 365 p.

RONZITTI, N, *Diritto internazionale dei conflitti armati*, 2ndedn, Torino, Giappichelli, 2001, 364 p.

ZAGATO, L, *La protezione dei beni culturali in caso di conflitto armato all'alba del secondo Protocollo 1999*, Torino, Giappichelli, 2007, 314 p.

ZAMPARELLI, F, *Diritto internazionale e attività militari nello spazio extra-atmosferico:*

limitazioni giuridiche all'utilizzazione militare dello spazio extra-atmosferico e dei corpi celesti in tempo di pace, Roma, s.n., 1998, 388 p.

Spanish

ABRIL STOFFELS, R, *La protección de los niños en los conflictos armados*, Valencia, Tirant lo Blanch, 2007, 126 p.

ANGARITA, R, *Conflicto armado y derecho humanitario*, 2nd edn, Bogotà, TM- IEPRI and Comité Internacional de la Cruz Roja, 1997, 245 p.

BUONOMO BASILE, D, *Neutralidad*, Montevideo, Vinaak, 1992, 120 p.

CAMARGO, PP, *Derecho internacional humanitario*, 2 vols, Bogotà, Jurídica Radar, 1995, 526 p and 323 p.

DOMINGUEZ MATES, R, *La protección del medio ambiente en el derecho internacional humanitario*, Valencia, Tirant lo Blanch, 2005, 565 p.

ESPALIU BERDUD, C, *El estatuto jurídico de los mercenarios y de las compañias militares privadas en el derecho internacional*, Pamplona, Thomson Aranzadi, 2007, 198 p.

GARCIA RICO, EDM, *El uso de las armas nucleares y el derecho internacional: análisis sobre la legalidad de su empleo*, Madrid, Tecnos, 1999, 191 p.

JORGE URBINA, J, *Protección de las víctimas de los conflictos armados, Naciones Unidas y derecho internacional humanitario: desarrollo y aplicación del principio de distinción entre objetivos militares y bienes de carácter civil*, Valencia, Tirant lo Blanch, 2000, 439 p.

KRIEGER, CA, *Direito internacional humanitário*, Curitiba, Juruá Editora, 2004, 361 p.

LEANDRO, F DA SILVA, *As armas das vítimas: um novo prisma sobre o direito internacional humanitário e dos conflitos armados*, Lisboa, Cosmos, 2005, 372 p.

MANGAS MARTIN, A, *Conflictos armados internos y derecho internacional humanitario*, Salamanca, Universidad, 1990, 192 p.

MELLO DE ALBUQUERQUE, CD, *Direitos humanos e conflictos armados*, Rio de Janeiro, s.n, 1997, 495 p.

MOREYRA, MJ, *Conflictos armados y violencia sexual contra las mujeres*, Bueons Aires, Tirant lo Blanch, 2007, 208 p.

OJINAGA RUIZ, R, *Emergencias humanitarias y derecho internacional*, Valencia, Tirant lo Blanch, 2005, 662 p.

RODRIGUEZ-VILLASANTE Y PRIETO, JL, *El Derecho Internacional Humanitario ante los retos de los conflictos armados actuales*, Madrid, Marcial Pons, 2006, 318 p.

—— (ed), *Derecho internacional humanitario*, 2nd edn, Valencia, Tirant lo Blanch, 2007, 1006 p.

RUIZ COLOME, MA, *Guerras civiles y guerras coloniales: el problema de la responsibilidad internacional*, Madrid, Eurolex, 1996, 470 p.

SAGASTUME GEMMELL, MA, *Derecho internacional humanitario y derechos humanos*, San José, Inter-American Institute of Human Rights, 1997, 397 p.

SANTALLA VARGAS, E, *Bolivia ante el Derecho Internacional Humanitario (DIH): estudio de compatibilidad entre el ordenamiento jurídico interno y las normas de DIH*, La Paz, Plural and Comité Internacional de la Cruz Roja, 2006, 137 p.

SEGURA SERRANO, A, *El derecho internacional humanitario y las operaciones de mantenimiento de la paz de Naciones Unidas*, Madrid, Plaza y Valdés, 2007, 250 p.

SWINARSKI, C, *Principales nociones e institutos del derecho internacional humanitario como sistema de protecction de la persona humana*, 2nd edn, San José, Inter-American Institute of Human Rights, 1991, 102 p.

3. ARTICLES

German

BOTHE, M, 'Friedenssicherung und Kriegsrecht' (2004) 3 *Völkerrecht* 589–667.

——, 'Die Anwendung der Europäischen Menschenrechtskonvention in bewaffneten Konflikten—eine Überforderung?' (2005) 65(3) *Zeitschrift für ausländisches öffentliches Recht und Völkerrecht*, 615–23.

BOUVIER, A, 'Der Schutz der natürlichen Umwelt bei bewaffneten Konflikten' (1992) 43(1) *Revue internationale de la Croix-Rouge* 5–18.

——, 'Umweltschutz in bewaffneten Konflikten—Neuere Arbeiten' (1992) 43(6) *Revue internationale de la Croix-Rouge* 311–25.

BRINGMANN, O, 'Nicht-letale Waffen: Der Königsweg des humanitären Völkerrechts?' (1999) 12(4) *Humanitäres Völkerrecht* 234–40.

BRUDERLEIN, C, 'Vom Gewohnheitsrecht im humanitären Völkerrecht' (1991) 42(6) *Revue internationale de la Croix-Rouge* 331–50.

BUGNION, F, 'Das Rotkreuzrecht' (1995) 46(5) *Revue internationale de la Croix-Rouge* 243–75.

CHOPARD, J-L, 'Verbreitung der humanitärvölkerrechtlichen Bestimmungen und Zusammenarbeit mit den nationalen Rotkreuz- und Rothalbmondgesellschaften im Hinblick auf vorbeugende Massnahmen' (1995) 46(4) *Revue internationale de la Croix-Rouge* 163–83.

'Das IKRK und innerhalb ihres eigenen Landes Vertriebene' (1995) 46(3) *Revue internationale de la Croix-Rouge* 121–32.

DESCH, T, 'Der Schutz von Kulturgut bei bewaffneten Konflikten nach der Konvention von 1954' (1999) 12(4) *Humanitäres Völkerrecht* 230–4.

EICK, CN, 'Verstärkter Schutz von Kulturgut in bewaffneten Konflikten: Das Zweite Protokoll zur Haager Konvention von 1954' (1999) 12(3) *Humanitäres Völkerrecht* 143–7.

EPINEY, A, 'Zur völkerrechtlichen Verantwortlichkeit im Zusammenhang mit dem Verhalten privater Sicherheitsfirmen' (2007) 17(2) *Schweizerische Zeitschrift für internationales und europäisches Recht* 215–33.

FLECK, D, 'Probleme und Prioritäten der Implementierung des humanitären Völkerrechts' (1991) 42(2) *Revue internationale de la Croix-Rouge* 82–96.

FRONHÖFER, D, 'Das Problem der Binnenflüchtlinge im Schnittpunkt der Menschenrechte, des Humanitären Völkerrechts und internationalen Flüchtlingsrechts' (1996) 34(3) *Archiv des Völkerrechts* 276–97.

GABRIEL, JM, 'Die Gegenläufigkeit von Neutralität und humanitären Interventionen' (2000) 10(2) *Schweizerische Zeitschrift für internationales und europäisches Recht* 219–36.

GASSER, H-P, 'Gewährleistung eines ordentlichen Gerichtsverfahrens in Zeiten bewaffneter Konflikte. Die Rolle des Delegierten des IKRK' (1992) 43(3) *Revue internationale de la Croix-Rouge* 138–62.

——, 'Humanitäre Normen für innere Unruhen, Überblick über neue Entwicklungen' (1993) 44(3) *Revue internationale de la Croix-Rouge* 133–9.

——, 'Universalisierung des humanitären Völkerrechts. Der Beitrag des IKRK' (1994) 45(5) *Revue internationale de la Croix-Rouge* 194–208.

GORNIG, G, 'Die Erweiterung des Geltungsbereichs des humanitären Völkerrechts durch die Zusatzprotokolle zu den Genfer Konventionen' (1988) 27(1) *Revue de Droit Mil et de Droit de la guerre* 9–43.

GRAEFRATH, B, 'Schadenersatzansprüche wegen Verletzung humanitären Völkerrechts' (2001) 14(2) *Humanitäres Völkerrecht* 110–20.

HANKE, HM, 'Die Haager Luftkriegsregeln von 1923. Beitrag zur Entwicklung des völkerrechtlichen Schutzes der Zivilbevölkerung vor Luftangriffen' (1991) 42(3) *Revue internationale de la Croix-Rouge* 139–72.

HARROFF-TAVEL, M, 'Die Aktion des Internationalen Komitees vom Roten Kreuz bei internen Gewalttätigkeiten' (1993) 44(3) *Revue internationale de la Croix-Rouge* 103–32.

KÄMMERER, JA, 'Kriegsrepressalie oder Kriegsverbrechen? zur rechtlichen Beurteilung der Massenexekutionen von Zivilisten durch die deutsche Besatzungsmacht im Zweiten Weltkrieg' (1999) 37(3/4) *Archiv des Völkerrechts* 283–317.

KARL, W, 'Das Humanitäre Völkerrecht auf dem Weg vom Zwischenstaats- zum Weltrecht' dans W BENDEK (ed), *Development and Developing International and European Law*, Frankfurt am Main, Lang, 1999, 577–93.

KRÜGER-SPRENGEL, F, 'Non-lethal Weapons—ein Gebot des humanitären Völkerrechts' dans K IPSEN (ed), *Wehrrecht und Friedenssicherung*, Neuwied, Luchterhand, 1999, 121–35.

LAVOYER, J-P, 'Flüchtlinge und Vertriebene: humanitäres Völkerrecht und die Rolle des IKRK' (1995) 46(3) *Revue internationale de la Croix-Rouge* 99–120.

MEYROWITZ, H, 'Der Grundsatz des unnötigen Leidens oder der überflüssigen Kriegsübel. Von der St Petersburger Erklärung von 1868 zum Zusatzprotokoll I von 1997' (1994) 45(3) *Revue internationale de la Croix-Rouge* 101–27.

von MÜLINEN, F, 'Das ius in bello verstehen und voll ausschöpfen' in K IPSEN (ed), *Wehrrecht und Friedenssicherung*, Neuwied, Luchterhand, 1999, 163–74.

PAECH, N, 'Zwischen Politik und Recht: zum Gutachten des Internationalen Gerichtshofs über die Völkerrechtswidrigkeit des Einsatzes von Nuklearwaffen' (1996) 9(4) *Humanitäres Völkerrecht* 176–87.

PALWANKAR, U, 'Zur Verfügung der Staaten stehende Massnahmen, um ihrer Pflicht zur Durchsetzung des humanitären Völkerrechts nachzukommen' (1994) 45(2) *Revue internationale de la Croix-Rouge* 45–62.

PETERKE, S, ' "Headquarters Agreements" und der "quasi-diplomatische" Status des IKRK und seiner Delegierten' (2001) 14(3) *Humanitäres Völkerrecht* 179–81.

PETERS, A, 'Die Risiken von Massenvernichtungswaffen und das Völkerrecht' in T SUTTER-SOMM, F HAFNER, G SCHMID AND K SEELMANN (eds), *Risiko und Recht: Festgabe zum Schweizerischen Juristentag 2004*, Basel, Helbing & Lichtenhahn, 2004, 311–44.

PICTET, J, 'Die Entstehung des humanitären Völkerrechts' (1994) 45(6) *Revue internationale de la Croix-Rouge* 239–45.

PLATTNER, D, 'Schutz der Vertriebenen in nicht internationalen bewaffneten Konflikten' (1992) 43(6) *Revue internationale de la Croix-Rouge* 326–40.

——, 'Die Neutralität des IKRK und die Neutralität der humanitären Hilfe' (1996) 47(2) *Revue internationale de la Croix-Rouge* 77–98.

RABUS, W, 'Ist das "Söldnerverbot" des Artikels 47 des ersten Zusatzprotokolls von 1977 noch zeitgemäss?' dans G HAFNER (ed), *Liber Amicorum, Professor Ignaz Seidl-Hohenveldern in honour of his 80th birthday*, The Hague, Kluwer, 1998, 511–40.

RHINOW, RA, 'Der rote Kristall' dans S BREITENMOSER (ed), *Human Rights, Democracy and the Rule of Law, Liber Amicorum Luzius Wildhaber*, Zürich, Dike, 2007, 1513–24.

RISIUS, G and MEYER, MA, 'Der Schutz der Kriegsgefangenen vor Beleidigungen und öffentlicher Neugier' (1993) 44(4) *Revue internationale de la Croix-Rouge* 159–70.

SCHNEIDER, M, 'Der aktuelle Fall: Geiselnahme von humanitären Helfern in Somalia: der völkerrechtliche Schutz von Hilfspersonal' (2001) 14(3) *Humanitäres Völkerrecht* 153–62.

SOMMARUGA, C, 'Sind die Neutralität der Schweiz und die Neutralität des IKRK untrennbar miteinander verbunden?' (1992) 43(3) *Revue internationale de la Croix-Rouge* 127–37.

STEIN, T, 'Völkerrechtliche Aspekte von Informationsoperationen' (2000) 60 *Zeitschrift für ausländisches öffentliches Recht und Völkerrecht* 1–40.

THÜRER, D, 'Neutralität der Schweiz—Illusionen oder (humanitäre) Chance?' dans W BENDEK (ed), *Development and Developing International and European Law*, Frankfurt am Main, Lang, 1999, 741–55.

——, 'Der Kosovo-Konflikt im Lichte des Völkerrechts: Von drei—echten und scheinbaren—Dilemmata: Grundsätze des Rechts der Gewaltanwendung und des humanitären Völkerrechts' (2000) 38(1) *Archiv des Völkerrechts* 1–22.

——, 'Humanitäres Völkerrecht und amerikanisches Verfassungsrecht als Schranken im Kampf gegen den Terrorismus' (2006) 125 *Zeitschrift für schweizerisches Recht* 157–71.

——, 'Dunant's Pyramide—Gedanken zu einem "humanitären Raum"' dans S BREITENMOSER (ed), *Human Rights, Democracy and the Rule of Law, Liber Amicorum Luzius Wildhaber*, Zürich/St Gallen, Dike, 2007, 819–35.

TOMUSCHAT, C, 'Die Kapitulation: Wirkung und Nachwirkung aus völkerrechtlicher Sicht' dans R SCHRÖDER (ed), *8 Mai 1945: Befreiung oder Kapitulation?* Berlin, Spitz, 1997, 21–44.

——, 'Der 11 September und seine rechtlichen Konsequenzen' (2001) 28 *Europäische Grundrechte-Zeitung* 535–45.

WEISSBRODT, D and HICKS, PL, 'Durchsetzung des Rechts der Menschenrechte und des humanitären Völkerrechts in bewaffneten Konflikten' (1993) 44(2) *Revue internationale de la Croix-Rouge* 42–62.

ZEMMALI, A, 'Der Schutz des Wassers in Zeiten bewaffneter Konflikte' (1995) 46(6) *Revue internationale de la Croix-Rouge* 291–307.

ZIEGLER, K-H, 'Zur Entwicklung von Kriegsrecht und Kriegsverhütung im Völkerrecht des 19 und frühen 20 Jahrhunderts' (2004) 42(3) *Archiv des Völkerrechts* 271–93.

ZÖCKLER, MC, 'Laserwaffen und humanitäres Völkerrecht' dans B SIMMA (ed), *Völker- und Europarecht in der aktuellen Diskussion*, Wien, Linde, 1999, 191–212.

French

ABI-SAAB, G, 'Les mécanismes de mise en oeuvre du droit humanitaire' (1978) 82 *Revue générale de droit international public* 103–29.

——, 'Conflits armés non internationaux' dans UNESCO (ed), *Les dimensions du droit international humanitaire*, Paris, Pedone, 1986, 252–77.

ABI-SAAB, G and ABI-SAAB, R, 'Les crimes de guerre' dans H ASCENSIO, E DECAUX et A PELLET, *Droit international pénal*, Paris, Pedone, 2000, 265–89.

ABI-SAAB, R, 'Conséquences juridiques de l'édification d'un mur dans le territoire palestinien occupé: quelques réflexions préliminaires sur l'avis consultatif de la Cour internationale de Justice' (2004) 86(855) *Revue internationale de la Croix-Rouge* 633–58.

ABPLANALP, P, 'Les Conférences internationales de la Croix-Rouge, facteur de développement du droit international humanitaire et de cohésion du Mouvement international de la Croix-Rouge et du Croissant-Rouge' (1995) 77(815) *Revue internationale de la Croix-Rouge* 567–600.

ALDRICH, GH, 'Pour le respect du droit international humanitaire' (1991) 73(789) *Revue internationale de la Croix-Rouge* 312–25.

——, 'Les Protocoles additionnels de 1977: vingt ans après' (1997) 79(827) *Revue internationale de la Croix-Rouge* 543–65.

APTEL, C, 'Propos du Tribunal pénal international pour le Rwanda' (1997) 79(828) *Revue internationale de la Croix-Rouge* 721–30.

AUBERT, M, 'Le comité international de la Croix-Rouge et le problème des armes causant des maux superflus ou frappant sans discrimination' (1990) 72(786) *Revue internationale de la Croix-Rouge* 521–41.

BAUDENDISTEL, R, 'La force contre le droit: le Comité international de la Croix-Rouge et la guerre chimique dans le conflit italo-éthiopien 1935–1936' (1998) 80(829) *Revue internationale de la Croix-Rouge* 85–110.

BERNARD, V, 'Comment les mesures fiscales d'un gouvernement peuvent renforcer les sociétés nationales de la Croix-Rouge et du Croissant-Rouge' (1996) 78(820) *Revue internationale de la Croix-Rouge* 487–517.

BETTATI, M, 'L'interdiction ou la limitation d'emploi des mines: le Protocole de Genève du 3 mai 1996' (1996) 42 *Annuaire français de droit international* 187–205.

BIEDERMANN, C-C, 'Le service International de Recherches: 50 ans au service de l'humanité' (1993) 75(803) *Revue internationale de la Croix-Rouge* 473–83.

BLONDEL, J-L, 'L'humanitaire appartient-il à tout le monde?' (2000) 82(838) *Revue internationale de la Croix-Rouge* 327–37.

——, 'Rôle du CICR en matière de prévention des conflits armés: possibilités d'action et limites' (2001) 83(844) *Revue internationale de la Croix-Rouge* 923–45.

BOUSTANI, K, 'La qualification des conflits en droit international public et le maintien de la paix' (1989/1990) 6(1) *Revue québécoise de droit international* 38–58.

——, 'Souveraineté et conflits intraétatiques: quelques problèmes de droit international:

Vingt et unième congrès annuel du CCDI 1992', in Y Le BOUTHILLIER (ed), *Selected Papers in International Law*, The Hague, Kluwer Law International, 1999, 317–45.

BOUTRUCHE, T, 'Le statut de l'eau en droit international humanitaire' (2000) 82(840) *Revue internationale de la Croix-Rouge* 887–916.

BOUVIER, A, 'La protection de l'environnement naturel en période de conflit armé' (1991) 73(792) *Revue internationale de la Croix-Rouge* 599–611.

——, 'Convention sur la sécurité du personnel des Nations Unies et du personnel associé, présentation et analyse' (1995) 77(816) *Revue internationale de la Croix-Rouge* 695–725.

BOEGLI, U, 'Les relations entre organismes humanitaires et médias: quelques réflexions' (1998) 80(832) *Revue internationale de la Croix-Rouge* 677–82.

BRETT, R, 'Les organisations non gouvernementales de défense des droits de l'homme et le droit humanitaire applicable dans les conflits armés' in SOCIÉTÉ FRANÇAISE POUR LE DROIT INTERNATIONAL (ed) *La protection des droits de l'homme et l'évolution du droit international*, Paris, Pedone, 1998, 57–72.

BRUDERLEIN, C, 'De la coutume en droit international humanitaire' (1991) 73(792) *Revue internationale de la Croix-Rouge* 612–29.

BUGNION, F, 'De la fin de la Seconde Guerre mondiale à l'aube du troisième millénaire: L'action du Comité international de la Croix-Rouge sous l'empire de la guerre froide et de ses suites: 1945–1995' (1995) 77(812) *Revue internationale de la Croix-Rouge* 232–50.

——, 'La composition du Comité international de la Croix-Rouge' (1995) 77(814) *Revue internationale de la Croix-Rouge* 473–93.

——, 'Le droit de la Croix-Rouge' (1995) 77(815) *Revue internationale de la Croix-Rouge* 535–66.

——, 'Les Conventions de Genève du 12 août 1949: De la Conférence diplomatique de 1949 à la vieille du troisième millénaire' (1999) 9(4/5) *Schweizerische Zeitschrift für internationales und europäisches Recht* 371–401.

——, 'Le droit international humanitaire à l'épreuve des conflits de notre temps' (1999) 81(835) *Revue internationale de la Croix-Rouge* 487–98.

——, 'Vers une solution globale de la question de l'emblème' (2000) 82(838) *Revue internationale de la Croix-Rouge* 427–65.

——, 'Droit de Genève et Droit de la Haye' (2001) 83(844) *Revue internationale de la Croix-Rouge* 901–22.

——, 'Droit international humanitaire coutumier' (2007) 17(2) *Schweizerische Zeitschrift für internationales und europäisches Recht* 165–214.

CAFLISCH, L, 'De la réglementation à l'interdiction des mines antipersonnel' (1998) 8(1) *Schweizerische Zeitschrift für internationales und europäisches Recht* 1–50.

CAUDERAY, GC, 'Les moyens d'identification des transport sanitaires protégés' (1994) 76(807) *Revue internationale de la Croix-Rouge* 293–306.

CHOPARD, J-L, 'La diffusion des règles humanitaires et la coopération avec les Sociétés nationales de la Croix-Rouge et du Croissant-Rouge au service de la prévention' (1995) 77(813) *Revue internationale de la Croix-Rouge* 272–91.

CHRISTAKIS, T, 'De maximis non curat praetor? L'affaire de la licéité de la menace ou l'emploi d'armes nucléaires devant la CIJ' (1996) 49(2) *Revue héllénique de droit international* 355–99.

COMITE INTERNATIONAL DE LA CROIX-ROUGE, 'Rapport sur la protection des victimes de la guerre, Conférence internationale pour la protection des victimes de la guerre (Genève, 30 août-1er septembre 1993)' (1993) 75(803) *Revue internationale de la Croix-Rouge* 415–71.

——, 'La sécurité alimentaire dans les conflits armés: l'approche et l'expérience du CICR' (1996) 78(822) *Revue internationale de la Croix-Rouge* 686–96.

CONDORELLI, L, 'Le statut des forces de l'ONU et le droit international humanitaire' (1995) 78 *Rivista di diritto internazionale* 879–906.

——, 'La Cour internationale de Justice sous le poids des armes nucléaires: jura non novit curia?' (1997) 79(823) *Revue internationale de la Croix-Rouge* 9–21.

——, 'La commission internationale humanitaire d'établissement des faits: un outil obsolète ou un moyen utile de mise en œuvre du droit international humanitaire?' (2001) 83(842) *Revue internationale de la Croix-Rouge* 393–406.

DAVID, E, 'L'avis de la Cour international de Justice sur la licéité de l'emploi d'armes nucléaires' (1997) 79(823) *Revue internationale de la Croix-Rouge* 22–36.

DENIS, C, 'Le Tribunal spécial pour la Sierra Leone—Quelques observations' (2001) *Revue Belge de Droit International* 236–72.

DOMESTICI-MET, M-J, 'Cent ans après La Haye, cinquante ans après Genève: le droit international au temps de la guerre civil' (1999) 81(834) *Revue internationale de la Croix-Rouge* 277–301.

DOSWALD-BECK, L, 'Le Manuel de San Remo sur le droit international applicable aux conflits armés sur mer' (1995) 77(816) *Revue internationale de la Croix-Rouge* 635–48.

——, 'Le nouveau Protocole sur les armes à laser aveuglantes' (1996) 78(819) *Revue internationale de la Croix-Rouge* 289–321.

——, 'Le droit international humanitaire et l'avis consultatif de la Cour international de Justice sur la licéité de la menace ou l'emploi d'armes nucléaires' (1997) 79(823) *Revue internationale de la Croix-Rouge* 37–59.

DOSWALD-BECK, L et CAUDEREY, GC, 'Le développement des nouvelles armes antipersonnel' (1990) 72(786) *Revue internationale de la Croix-Rouge* 620–35.

DRAMBJAN, TS, 'Des pages méconnues de l'histoire de la Seconde Guerre mondiale: les prisonniers de guerre soviétiques en Finlande (1941–1944)' (2000) 82(839) *Revue internationale de la Croix-Rouge* 663–72.

'Droit humanitaire et droits de l'homme' (1993) 75(800) *Revue internationale de la Croix-Rouge* 93–150 (contributions par différents auteurs).

DURAND, A, 'Le Comité international de la Croix-Rouge à l'époque de la première Conférence de la Haye (1899)' (1999) 81(834) *Revue internationale de la Croix-Rouge* 353–64.

DUTLI, MT, 'Mise en œuvre du droit international humanitaire, Activités du personnel qualifié en temps de paix' (1993) 75(799) *Revue internationale de la Croix-Rouge* 5–12.

——, 'Mise en œuvre du droit international humanitaire: Mesures nationales' (1994) 76(809) *Revue internationale de la Croix-Rouge* 506–11.

DUTLI, MT et PELLANDINI, C, 'Le Comité international de la Croix-Rouge et la mise en oeuvre du système de répression des infractions aux règles du droit international humanitaire' (1994) 76(807) *Revue internationale de la Croix-Rouge* 264–79.

FENRICK, WJ, 'La Convention sur les armes classiques: un traité modeste mais utile' (1990) 72(86) *Revue internationale de la Croix-Rouge* 542–55.

FERNANDEZ FLORES, JL, 'La répression des infractions individuelle au droit de la guerre' (1991) 73(789) *Revue internationale de la Croix-Rouge* 263–311.

FUCHS, P, 'La coordination des opérations d'urgence: un problème du ressort des acteurs de l'humanitaire, ou plutôt des politiciens et des militaires?' (1995) 77(811) *Revue internationale de la Croix-Rouge* 99–106.

FUJITA, H, 'Au sujet de l'avis consultatif de la Cour internationale de Justice rendu sur la licéité des armes nucléaires' (1997) 79(823) *Revue internationale de la Croix-Rouge* 60–69.

GASSER, H-P, 'Respect des garanties judiciaires fondamentales en temps de conflit armé: Le rôle du délégué du CICR' (1992) 74(794) *Revue internationale de la Croix-Rouge* 129–52.

——, 'Les normes humanitaires pour les situations de troubles et tensions internes' (1993) 75(801) *Revue internationale de la Croix-Rouge* 238–44.

——, 'Aperçu de la Déclaration de Saint-Pétersbourg de 1869' (1993) 75(804) *Revue internationale de la Croix-Rouge* 539–44.

——, 'Universalisation du droit international humanitaire: La contribution du CICR' (1994) 76(809) *Revue internationale de la Croix-Rouge* 491–505.

——, 'Faire accepter les Protocoles par les Etats' (1997) 79(827) *Revue internationale de la Croix-Rouge* 567–75.

GAUTIER, P, 'ONG et personnalité internationale: à propos de l'accord conclu le 29 novembre 1996 entre la Suisse et la Fédération international des Sociétés de la Croix-Rouge et Croissant-Rouge' (1997) 30(1) *Revue belge du droit international* 172–89.

GOLDBLAT, J, 'La Convention sur les armes biologiques: vue générale' (1997) 79(825) *Revue internationale de la Croix-Rouge* 269–86.

GRADITZKY, T, 'La responsabilité pénale individuelle pour violation du droit international humanitaire applicable en situation de conflit armé non international' (1998) 80(829) *Revue internationale de la Croix-Rouge* 29–58.

GREENWOOD, C, 'L'avis consultatif sur les armes nucléaires et la contribution de la Cour internationale de Justice au droit international humanitaire' (1997) 79(823) *Revue internationale de la Croix-Rouge* 70–81.

GROSSRIEDER, P, 'Un avenir pour le droit international humanitaire et ses principes?' (1999) 81(833) *Revue internationale de la Croix-Rouge* 11–18.

GRUENEWALD, F, 'Avant, pendant et après l'urgence: l'expérience du CICR en perspective' (1995) 77(813) *Revue internationale de la Croix-Rouge* 292–311.

GUELLALI, A, 'Lex specialis, droit international humanitaire et droits de l'homme' (2007) 111(3) *Revue générale de droit international public* 539–74.

GUILLERMAND, J, 'Les fondements historiques de la démarche humanitaire' (1994) 76(806) *Revue internationale de la Croix-Rouge* 216–37.

GUISANDEZ GOMEZ, J, 'Le droit dans la guerre aérienne' (1998) 80(830) *Revue internationale de la Croix-Rouge* 371–88.

GUTMAN, RW, 'Les violations du droit international humanitaire sous le feu des projecteurs: le rôle des médias' (1998) 80(832) *Revue internationale de la Croix-Rouge* 667–75.

HAECK, L, 'Le droit de la guerre spatiale' (1991) 16 *Ann Air & Space Law* 307–40.

HAROUEL, V, 'Les projets genevois de révision de la Convention de Genève du 22 août 1864 (1868–1998)' (1999) 81(834) *Revue internationale de la Croix-Rouge* 365–86.

HARROFF-TAVEL, M, 'L'action du Comité international de la Croix-Rouge face aux situations de violence interne' (1993) 75(801) *Revue internationale de la Croix-Rouge* 211–37.

HAUG, H, 'La neutralité comme Principe fondamental de la Croix-Rouge' (1996) 78(822) *Revue internationale de la Croix-Rouge* 675–78.

HEINKE, HM, 'Les Règles de la Haye de 1923 concernant la guerre aérienne: Contributions au développement dans le droit international de la protection de la population civile contre les attaques aériennes' (1993) 75(799) *Revue internationale de la Croix-Rouge* 13–45.

HOFFMANN, MH, 'Les marins neutres et le droit humanitaire: un précèdent en matière de protection des neutres lors des conflits armés' (1992) 74(795) *Revue internationale de la Croix-Rouge* 285–303.

HOLLEUFER, G, 'Peut-on célébrer de 50e anniversaire des Conventions de Genève' (1999) 81(833) *Revue internationale de la Croix-Rouge* 135–48.

JIMENEZ PIERNAS, C, 'La protection des travailleurs et coopérants étrangers dans les situations de conflit interne, en particulier dans les cas de prises d'otages' (1992) 74(794) *Revue internationale de la Croix-Rouge* 153–83.

JORGE URBINA, J, 'La protection des personnes civiles au pouvoir de l'ennemi et l'établissement d'une juridiction pénale internationale' (2000) 82(840) *Revue internationale de la Croix-Rouge* 857–85.

KALSHOVEN, F, 'Les principes juridiques qui sous-tendent la Convention sur armes classiques' (1990) 72(786) *Revue internationale de la Croix-Rouge* 556–67.

KOLB, R, 'Sur l'origine du couple terminologiques *ius ad bellum* / *ius in bello*' (1997) 79(827) *Revue internationale de la Croix-Rouge* 593–602.

——, 'Aperçu de l'histoire de la Déclaration universelle des droits de l'homme et des Conventions de Genève' (1998) 80(831) *Revue internationale de la Croix-Rouge* 437–47.

——, 'Aspects historiques de la relation entre le droit international humanitaire et les droits de l'homme' (1999) 37 *Annuaire canadien de droit international* 57–97.

——, 'Le droit international public et le concept de guerre civile depuis 1945' (2001) 105 *Relations internationales* 9–29.

——, 'Etude sur l'occupation et sur l'article 47 de la IVeme Convention de Genève du 12 aout 1949 relative à la protection des personnes civiles en temps de guerre: le degré d'intangibilité des droits en territoire occupé' (2002) 10 *African Yearbook of International Law* 267–321.

——, 'De l'assistance humanitaire' (2004) 86(856) *Revue internationale de la Croix-Rouge* 853–78.

——, 'La nécessité militaire dans le droit des conflits armés: essai de clarification conceptuelle' in SOCIÉTÉ FRANÇAISE POUR LE DROIT INTERNATIONAL (ed) *La nécessité en droit international: Colloque de Grenoble*, Paris, Pedone, 2007, 151–86.

KORNBLUM, E, 'Etude comparative de différents systèmes de rapport d'auto-évaluation portant sur le respect, par les Etats, de leurs obligations internationales (1)' (1995) 77(811) *Revue internationale de la Croix-Rouge*43–78.

——, 'Etude comparative de différents systèmes de rapport d'auto-évaluation portant sur le respect, par les Etats, de leurs obligations internationales (2)' (1995) 77(812) *Revue internationale de la Croix-Rouge* 155–82.

KOSIRNIK, R, 'Les Protocoles de 1977—une étape cruciale dans le développement du droit international humanitaire' (1997) 79(827) *Revue internationale de la Croix-Rouge* 517–36.

LATTANZI, F, 'La frontière entre droit international humanitaire et droits de l'homme' dans E DECAUX (ed), *From Human Rights to International Criminal Law: Studies in Honour of an African Jurist, the Late Judge Laity Kama*, Leiden, Martinus Nijhoff, 2007, 517–70.

LAVOYER, J-P, 'Réfugiés et personnes déplacées, Droit international humanitaire et rôle du CIRC' (1995) 77(812) *Revue internationale de la Croix-Rouge* 183–202.

LAVOYER, J-P, 'Le CICR et les personnes déplacées internes' (1995) 77(812) *Revue internationale de la Croix-Rouge* 203–14.

LEVRAT, B, 'Le droit international humanitaire au Timor oriental: entre théorie et pratique' (2001) 83(841) *Revue internationale de la Croix-Rouge* 77–99.

MAHOUVE, M, 'La répression des violations du droit international humanitaire au niveau national et international' (2005) 82(3) *Revue de droit international et de droit compare* 229–73.

'Manuel de San Remo sur le droit international applicable aux conflits armés en mer préparé par des juristes internationaux et des experts navals, réunis par l'institut international de droit humanitaire: adopté en juin 1994' (1995) 77(816) *Revue internationale de la Croix-Rouge* 649–94.

MAISON, R, 'Les premiers cas d'application des dispositions pénales des Conventions de Genève par les juridictions internes' (1995) 6(2) *European Journal of International Law* 260–73.

MANGALA, J, 'Prévention des déplacements forcés de population—possibilités et limites' (2001) 83(844) *Revue internationale de la Croix-Rouge* 1076–95.

MAURICE, F, 'L'ambition humanitaire' (1992) 74(796) *Revue internationale de la Croix-Rouge* 377–87.

McCORMACK, TLH, 'Un non liquet sur les armes nucléaires: la Cour internationale de Justice élude l'application des principes généraux du droit international humanitaire' (1997) 79(823) *Revue internationale de la Croix-Rouge* 82–98.

McNEILL, JH, 'L'avis consultatif de la Cour international de Justice en l'affaire des armes nucléaires, première évaluation' (1997) 79(823) *Revue internationale de la Croix-Rouge* 110–26.

MEGEVAND, B, 'Entre insurrection et gouvernement: L'action du CICR au Mexique (janvier-août 1994)' (1995) 77(811) *Revue internationale de la Croix-Rouge* 107–21.

MEYER, MA, 'Mobilisation de l'opinion publique: pourquoi la Croix-Rouge et le Croissant-Rouge ne devraient pas s'engager les yeux fermés' (1996) 78(822) *Revue internationale de la Croix-Rouge* 660–74.

MEYROWITZ, H, 'La guerre du Golfe et le droit des conflits armés' (1992) 96(3) *Revue générale de droit international public* 551–601.

——, 'Le principe des maux superflus: De la Déclaration de Saint-Pétersbourg de 1869 au Protocole additionnel I de 1977' (1994) 76(806) *Revue internationale de la Croix-Rouge* 107–30.

MOHR, M, 'Avis consultatif de la Cour international de Justice sur la licéité de l'emploi des armes nucléaires: quelques réflexions sur les points forts et ses points faibles' (1997) 79(823) *Revue internationale de la Croix-Rouge* 99–109.

MOMTAZ, D, 'Les règles humanitaires minimales applicable en période de troubles et de tensions internes' (1998) 80(831) *Revue internationale de la Croix-Rouge* 487–95.

——, 'Le droit international humanitaire applicable aux conflits armés non internationaux' (2001) 292 *Recueil des cours, Académie de droit international de la Haye* 9–146.

MOREILLON, J, 'La promotion de la paix et de l'humanité aux XXIe siècle: Quel rôle pour la Croix-Rouge et le Croissant-Rouge?' (1994) 76(810) *Revue internationale de la Croix-Rouge* 639–55.

NUMMINEN, J, 'Violence à l'égard des femmes en situation de conflit armé: analyse effectuée selon le point de vue féminin sur la protection de la femme dans le droit international humanitaire' (1999) 9 *The Finnish Yearbook of International Law* 453–73.

O'DONNELL, D, 'Tendances dans l'application du droit international humanitaire par les mécanismes des droits de l'homme des Nations Unies' (1998) 80(831) *Revue internationale de la Croix-Rouge* 517–41.

PALWANKAR, U, 'Applicabilité du droit international humanitaire aux Forces des Nations Unies pour le maintien de la paix' (1993) 57(801) *Revue internationale de la Croix-Rouge* 245–59.

——, 'Mesures auxquelles peuvent recourir les Etats pour remplir leur obligation de faire respecter le droit international humanitaire' (1994) 76(805) *Revue internationale de la Croix-Rouge* 11–28.

PARKS, WH, 'Le protocole sur les armes incendiaires' (1990) 72(786) *Revue internationale de la Croix-Rouge* 584–604.

PATRNOGIC, J, 'Promotion et diffusion du droit international humanitaire. L'expérience de l'institut international de droit humanitaire' (1994) 8 *International Geneva Yearbook* 68–85.

PEARSON, GS, 'Interdiction des armes biologiques—Activités en cours et perspectives' (1997) 79(825) *Revue internationale de la Croix-Rouge* 287–304.

PERRET, F, 'L'action du Comité international de la Croix-Rouge à Cuba 1958–1962' (1998) 80(832) *Revue internationale de la Croix-Rouge* 707–23.

——, 'L'action du Comité international de la Croix-Rouge pendant la guerre d'Algérie (1954–1962)' (2004) 86(856) *Revue internationale de la Croix-Rouge* 917–51.

PETTITI, L-E, 'La protection des minorités en cas de conflit interne' in J AYALA LASSO (ed), *Héctor Gros Espiell amicorum liber*, Bruxelles, Bruylant, 1997, 1115–37.

PLATTNER, D, 'La Convention de 1980 sur les armes classiques et l'applicabilité des règles relative aux moyens de combat dans un conflit armé non international' (1990) 72(786) *Revue internationale de la Croix-Rouge* 605–19.

——, 'L'assistance à la population civile dans le droit international humanitaire: évolution et actualité' (1992) 74(795) *Revue internationale de la Croix-Rouge* 259–74.

——, 'La protection des personnes déplacées lors d'un conflit armé non international' (1992) 74(798) *Revue internationale de la Croix-Rouge* 592–606.

——, 'La neutralité du CICR et la neutralité de l'assistance humanitaire' (1996) 78(818) *Revue internationale de la Croix-Rouge* 169–89.

PROKOSCH, E, 'Arguments en faveur de l'introduction de restrictions concernant les armes à sous-munition: Protection humanitaire contre "nécessité militaire"' (1994) 76(806) *Revue internationale de la Croix-Rouge* 2002–215.

'Protection de l'environnement en période de conflit armé' (1992) 74(798) *Revue internationale de la Croix-Rouge* 537–91 (contributions par différents auteurs).

QUINTANA, JJ, 'Les violations du droit international humanitaire et leur répression: le Tribunal pénal international pour l'ex-Yougoslavie' (1994) 76(807) *Revue internationale de la Croix-Rouge* 247–63.

REIDY, A, 'La pratique de la Commission et de la Cour européennes des droits de l'homme en matière de droit international humanitaire' (1999) 81(835) *Revue internationale de la Croix-Rouge* 499–529.

RISIUS, G et MEYER, MA, 'La protection des prisonniers de guerre contre les insultes et la curiosité publique' (1993) 75(802) *Revue internationale de la Croix-Rouge* 310–22.

ROBERGE, M-C, 'Compétence des Tribunaux ad hoc pour l'ex-Yougoslavie et le Rwanda concernant les crimes contre l'humanité et le crime de génocide' (1997) 79(828) *Revue internationale de la Croix-Rouge* 695–710.

ROGERS, APV, 'Mines, pièges et autres dispositifs similaires' (1990) 72(786) *Revue internationale de la Croix-Rouge* 568–83.

RUSSBACH, R, 'Conflits armés, prévention et santé publique' (1999) 81(833) *Revue internationale de la Croix-Rouge* 85–102.

RYNIKER, A, 'Respect du droit international humanitaire par les forces des Nations Unies: quelques commentaires à propos de la circulaire du Secrétaire général des Nations Unies du 6 août 1999' (1999) 81(836) *Revue internationale de la Croix-Rouge* 795–817.

——, 'Position du CICR sur l'intervention humanitaire' (2001) 83(842) *Revue internationale de la Croix-Rouge* 521–26.

SAHOVIC, M, 'L'application du droit international, notamment humanitaire, dans les conflits armés auxquels prennent part des entités non-étatiques' (1998) 68(1) *Annuaire/Institut de Droit International* 251–370.

SANDOZ, Y, 'Réflexions sur la mise en œuvre du droit international humanitaire et sur le rôle du Comité international du Croix-Rouge en ex-Yougoslavie' (1993) 3(4) *Schweizerische Zeitschrift für internationales und europäisches Recht* 461–90.

——, 'Existe-t-il un "droit d'ingérence" dans le domaine de l'information? Le droit à l'information sous l'angle du droit international humanitaire' (1998) 80(832) *Revue internationale de la Croix-Rouge* 683–93.

——, 'Le demi-siècle des Conventions de Genève' (1999) 81(837) *Revue internationale de la Croix-Rouge* 49–65.

SASSOLI, M, 'La définition du terrorisme et le droit international humanitaire' in G DUFOUR (ed), *Hommage à la professeure Katia Boustany*, Montréal, Revue québécoise de droit international, 2007, 29–48.

——, 'La Cour européenne des droits de l'homme et les conflits armés' in S BREITENMOSER *Human Rights, Democracy and the Rule of Law*, Zurich, Dike, 2007, 709–31.

SCHREYER, T, 'L'action de l'Agence centrale de recherches du CIRC, dans les Balkans durant la crise des réfugiés Kosovars' (2000) 82(834) *Revue internationale de la Croix-Rouge* 209–39.

de SENARCLENS, P, 'L'humanitaire et la globalisation' (2000) 82(838) *Revue internationale de la Croix-Rouge* 311–25.

SOMMARUGA, C, 'La neutralité suisse et la neutralité du CICR sont-elles indissociables?' (1992) 74(795) *Revue internationale de la Croix-Rouge* 275–84.

——, 'Assistance aux victimes de conflits: le défi permanent du Comité international de la Croix-Rouge' (1992) 77(796) *Revue internationale de la Croix-Rouge* 388–96.

——, 'Action humanitaire et opérations de maintien de la paix' (1993) 75(801) *Revue internationale de la Croix-Rouge* 260–67.

——, 'Réflexions et convictions sur l'humanitaire d'aujourd'hui et de demain' (2000) 82(838) *Revue internationale de la Croix-Rouge* 295–310.

SWINARSKI, C, 'Aux contours des fondements du droit international humanitaire' in J MAKARCZYK (ed), *Theory of International Law at the Threshold of the 21st Century*, The Hague, Kluwer Law International, 1996, 956–78.

TAUXE, J-D, 'Faire mieux accepter le Comité international de la Croix-Rouge sur le terrain' (1999) 81(833) *Revue internationale de la Croix-Rouge* 55–61.

TICEHURST, R, 'La clause de Martens et le droit des conflits armés' (1997) 86(317) *Revue internationale de la Croix-Rouge* 133–42.

TORRELLI, M, 'Les zones de sécurité' (1995) 99(4) *Revue générale de droit international public* 787–848.

TRUNINGER, F, 'Le Comité international de la Croix-Rouge et la guerre d'indochine. De la défaite japonaise aux Accords de Genève (1945–1954)' (1994) 76(810) *Revue internationale de la Croix-Rouge* 607–38.

VIGNY, J-D, 'Standards fondamentaux d'humanité: quel avenir?' (2000) 82(840) *Revue internationale de la Croix-Rouge* 917–39.

ZEMMALI, A, 'La protection de l'eau en période de conflit armé' (1995) 77(815) *Revue internationale de la Croix-Rouge* 601–15.

ZIEGLER, AR, 'La mise en œuvre du droit international humanitaire par la Suisse' (1997) 36(3/4) *Revue de droit militaire et de droit de la guerre* 245–70.

English

ABI-SAAB, G, 'Wars of National Liberation in the Geneva Conventions and Protocols' (1979) 165 *Recueil des cours de l'Académie de droit international de La Haye* 357–445.

ABRIL STOFFELS, R, 'Legal Regulation of Humanitarian Assistance in Armed Conflict' (2004) 86(855) *Revue internationale de la Croix-Rouge* 515–46.

AESCHLIMANN, A, 'Protection of Detainees: ICRC Action behind Bars' (2005) 87(857) *Revue internationale de la Croix-Rouge* 83–122.

AKANDE, D, 'Nuclear Weapons, Unclear Law? Diciphering the Nuclear Weapons Advisory Opinion of the International Court' (1997) 68 *The British Yearbook of International Law* 165–217.

ALDRICH, GH, 'The Laws of War on Land' (2000) 94(1) *The American Journal of International Law* 42–63.

——, 'A Century of Achievement and Unfinished Work' (2000) 94(1) *The American Journal of International Law* 90–98.

——, 'Customary International Humanitarian Law' (2005) 76 *The British Yearbook of International Law* 503–24.

ALESKY, PD, 'The Yugoslav War Crimes Tribunal and International Humanitarian Law' (1998) 35(1) *International Politics* 1–30.

ALMOND, H, 'Arms Control and the Law of War: Control over Weapons and their Use' (1997) 36(3/4) *Revue de droit militaire et de droit de la guerre* 11–42.

AL-ZUHILI, SWM, 'Islam and International Law' (2005) 87(858) *Revue internationale de la Croix-Rouge* 269–83.

AMERASINGHE, CF, 'History and Sources of the Law of War' (2004) 16 *Sri Lanka Journal of International Law* 263–87.

ANNAN, K, 'Peace-keeping in Situations of Civil War' (1994) 26(4) *New York University Journal of International Law & Politics* 623–31.

ARNOLD, R, 'The Legal Implications of the Military's Humanitarisation' (2004) 43(3/4) *Revue de droit militaire et de droit de la guerre* 21–54.

ARZT, DE, 'Can Law Halt the Violence?' (2005) 11(2) *ILSA Journal of International & Comparative Law* 357–63.

BALGUY-GALLOIS, A, 'The Protection of Journalists and News Media Personnel in Armed Conflict' (2004) 86(853) *Revue internationale de la Croix-Rouge* 37–68.

BASSIOUNI, MC, 'The Normative Framework of International Humanitarian Law: Overlaps, Gaps and Ambiguities' (2998) 8(2) *Transnational Law & Contemporary Problems* 199–275.

BECKETT, JA, 'New War, Old Law: Can the Geneva Paradigm Comprehend Computers?' (2000) 13(1) *Leiden Journal of International Law* 33–51.

BEHNSEN, A, 'The Status of Mercenaries and other Illegal Combatants under International Humanitarian Law' (2003) 46 *German Yearbook of International Law* 494–536.

BELT, SW, 'Missiles over Kosovo: Emergence, Lex Lata, of a Customary Norm Requiring the Use of Precision Munitions in Urban Areas' (2000) 47 *Naval Law Review* 115–75.

BELZ, D, 'Is International Humanitarian Law Lapsing into Irrelevance in the War on International Terror?' (2006) 7(1) *Theoretical Inquiries in Law* 97–129.

BEN-NAFTALI, O, 'Missing in Legal Action: Lebanese Hostages in Israel' (2000) 41(1) *Harvard International Law Journal* 185–252.

BENVENUTI, P, 'Ensuring Observance of International Humanitarian Law: Function, Extent and Limits of the Obligations of Third States to Ensure Respect of IHL' (1989/1990) *Yearbook of the International Institute of Humanitarian Law* 27–55.

——, 'The ICTY Prosecutor and the Review of the NATO Bombing Campaign against the Federal Republic of Yugoslavia' (2001) 12(3) *European Journal of International Law* 503–29.

BERMAN, N, 'Privileging Combat? Contemporary Conflict and the legal Construction of War' (2004) 43(1) *Columbia Journal of Transnational Law* 1–71.

BHAT, PI, 'Understanding International Humanitarian Law from the Perspective of Multiculturalism' in A Jayagovind and P Waart (eds), *Reflections on Emerging International Law: Essays in Memory of Late Subrata Roy Chowdhury*, Calcutta, International Law Association and the Law Research Institute, 2004, 78–98.

BIALKE, JP, 'Al-Qaeda & Taliban: Unlawful Combatant Detainees, Unlawful Belligerency, and the International Laws of Armed Conflict' (2004) 55 *The Air Force Law Review* 1–85.

BLOKKER, N, 'The Internationalization of Domestic Conflict: the Role of the UN Security Council' (1996) 9(1) *Leiden Journal of International Law* 7–35.

BOELAERT-SUOMINEN, S, 'Grave Breaches, Universal Jurisdiction and Internal Armed Conflict: Is Customary Law moving towards a Uniform Enforcement Mechanism for all Armed Conflicts?' (2000) 5(1) *Journal of Conflict and Security Law* 63–103.

——, 'The Yugoslavia Tribunal and the Common Core of Humanitarian Law Applicable to all Armed Conflicts' (2000) 13(3) *Leiden Journal of International Law* 619–53.

——, 'Prosecuting Superiors for Crimes Committed by Subordinates: A Discussion of the First Significant Case Law since the Second World War' (2001) *Virginia Journal of International Law* 747–85.

BOLDT, N, 'Outsourcing War: Private Military Companies and International Humanitarian Law' (2004) 47 *German Yearbook of International Law* 502–44.

BOISSON DE CHAZOURNES, L, 'Common Article 1 of the Geneva Conventions Revisited: Protecting Collective Interests' (2000) 82(837) *Revue internationale de la Croix-Rouge* 67–87.

BOIVIN, A, 'Complicity and Beyond: International Law and the Transfer of Small Arms and Light Weapons' (2005) 87(859) *Revue internationale de la Croix-Rouge* 467–96.

BORDEN, A, 'The Former Yugoslavia: The War and the Peace Process' (1996) *SIPRI Yearbook* 203–50.

BORELLI, S, 'Casting Light on the Legal Black Hole: International Law and Detentions Abroad in the "War on Terror"' (2005) 87(857) *Revue internationale de la Croix-Rouge* 39–68.

BORGEN, CJ, 'The Theory and Practice of Regional Organization Intervention in Civil Wars' (1994) 26(4) *New York University Journal of International Law & Politics* 797–835.

BOTHE, M, 'International Humanitarian Law and War Crimes Tribunal: Recent Developments and Perspectives' in K WELLENS (ed), *International Law*, The Hague, Martinus Nijhoff, 1998, 581–95.

——, 'The Protection of the Civilian Population and NATO Bombing on Yugoslavia: Comments on a Report to the Prosecutor of the ICTY' (2001) 12(3) *European Journal of International Law* 531–35.

——, 'Customary International Humanitarian Law: Some Reflections on the ICRC Study' (2007) 8 *Yearbook of International Humanitarian Law* 143–78.

BRANCHE, R, 'Torture of Terrorists? Use of Torture in a "War against Terrorism": Justifications, Methods and Effects (The Case of France in Algeria, 1954–1962)' (2007) 89(867) *Revue internationale de la Croix-Rouge* 543–60.

BROWN, BS, 'Nationality and Internationality in International Humanitarian Law' (1998) 34(2) *Stanford Journal of International Law* 347–406.

BROWN, D, 'A Proposal for an International Convention to Regulate the Use of Information Systems in Armed Conflict' (2006) 47(1) *Harvard International Law Journal* 179–221.

BÜCHEL, R, 'Swiss Measures to Protect Cultural Property' (2004) 86(854) *Revue internationale de la Croix-Rouge* 325–36.

BUGNION, F, 'Jus ad Bellum, Jus in Bello and Non-international Armed Conflicts' (2003) 6 *Yearbook of International Humanitarian Law* 167–98.

——, 'The International Committee of the Red Cross and the Development of International Humanitarian Law' (2004) 5(1) *Chicago Journal of International Law* 181–215.

——, 'Legal History of the Protection of Cultural Property in the Event of Armed Conflict' (2004) 86(854) *Revue internationale de la Croix-Rouge* 313–24.

——, 'The International Committee of the Red Cross and Nuclear Weapons: From Hiroshima to the Dawn of the 21st century' (2005) 87(859) *Revue internationale de la Croix-Rouge* 511–24.

——, 'Refugees, Internally Displaced Persons, and International Humanitarian Law' (2005) 28(5) *Fordham International Law Journal* 1397–420.

BURGER, JA, 'International Humanitarian Law and the Kosovo Crisis: Lessons Learned or to be Learned' (2000) 82(837) *Revue internationale de la Croix-Rouge* 129–45.

BUSUTTIL, JJ, 'A Taste of Armageddon: The Law of Armed Conflict as Applied to Cyberwar' in GS GOODWIN-GILL (ed), *The Reality of International Law*, Oxford, Oxford University Press, 1999, 37–56.

BYRON, C, 'A Blurring of the Boundaries: The Application of International Humanitarian Law by Human Rights Bodies' (2007) 47(4) *Virginia Journal of International Law* 839–96.

CAMERON, L, 'Private Military Companies: Their Status under International Humanitarian Law and its Impact on their Regulation' (2006) 88(863) *Revue internationale de la Croix-Rouge* 573–98.

CAMPBELL, C, 'Peace and the Laws of War: The Role of International Humanitarian Law in the Post-conflict Environment' (2000) 82(839) *Revue internationale de la Croix-Rouge* 627–52.

CANNIZZARO, E, 'Contextualizing Proportionality: Jus ad Bellum and Jus in Bello in the Lebanese War' (2006) 88(864) *Revue internationale de la Croix-Rouge* 779–92.

CARILLO-SUAREZ, A, 'Hors de Logique: Contemporary Issues in International Humanitarian Law as Applied to Internal Armed Conflict' (1999) 15(1) *American University International Law Review* 1–150.

CARNAHAN, BM, 'Protecting Nuclear Facilities from Military Attack: Prospects after the Gulf War' (1992) 86(3) *American Journal of International Law* 524–41.

——, 'The Protocol on "Blinding Laser Weapons"' (1996) 90(3) *American Journal of International Law* 484–90.

——, 'Lincoln, Lieber and the Laws of War: The Origins and Limits of the Principle of Military Necessity' (1998) 92(2) *American Journal of International Law* 213–31.

CARVIN, S, 'Caught in the Cold: International Humanitarian Law and Prisoners of War during the Cold War' (2006) 11(1) *Journal of Conflict and Security Law* 67–92.

CASEY, D, 'Breaking the Chain of Violence in Israel and Palestine: Suicide Bombings and Targeted Killings under International Humanitarian Law' (2005) 32(2) *Syracuse Journal of International Law and Commerce* 311–43.

CASSESE, A, 'The Martens Clause: Half a Loaf or Simply Pie in the Sky?' (2000) 11(1) *European Journal of International Law* 187–216.

CHADWICK, E, 'The Legal Position of Prisoners, Spies and Deserters during World War I' (1997) 36(3/4) *Revue de droit militaire et de droit de la guerre* 73–113.

CHESTERMAN, S, 'The International Court of Justice, Nuclear Weapons and the Law' (1997) 44(2) *Netherlands International Law Review* 149–67.

CHETAIL, V, 'The Contribution of the International Court of Justice to International Humanitarian Law' (2003) 85(850) *Revue internationale de la Croix-Rouge* 235–69.

CHINKIN, C, 'Rape and Sexual Abuse of Women in International Law' (1994) 5(3) *European Journal of International Law* 326–41.

CHO, S, 'International Humanitarian Law and United Nations Operations in an Internal Armed Conflict' (1998) 26 *Korean Journal of International and Comparative Law* 85–111.

CHURCH, W, 'Information Warfare' (2000) 82(837) *Revue internationale de la Croix-Rouge* 205–16.

CLAPHAM, A, 'Human Rights Obligations of Non-state Actors in Conflict Situations' (2006) 88(863) *Revue internationale de la Croix-Rouge* 491–523.

COCKAYNE, J, 'The Global Reorganization of Legitimate Violence: Military Entrepreneurs and the Private Face of International Humanitarian Law' (2006) 88(863) *Revue internationale de la Croix-Rouge* 459–90.

COHEN, A, 'Administering the Territories' (2005) 38 *Israel Law Review* 24–79.

CORN, GS, 'Hamdan, Lebanon, and the Regulation of Hostilities' (2006/2007) 40(2) *Vanderbilt Journal of Transnational Law* 295–355.

COTTIER, M, 'Elements for Contracting and Regulating Private Security and Military Companies' (2006) 88(863) *Revue internationale de la Croix-Rouge* 637–63.

COUPLAND, RM, 'Review of the Legality of Weapons: The SIrUS Project' (1999) 81(835) *Revue internationale de la Croix-Rouge* 583–92.

COWLING, MG, 'The Relationship between Military Necessity and the Principle of Superflous Injury and Unnecessary Suffering in the Law of Armed Conflict' (2000) 25 *South African Yearbook of International Law* 131–60.

——, 'International Lawmaking in Action: The 2005 Customary International Humanitarian Law Study and Non-international Armed Conflicts' (2006) *African Yearbook on International Humanitarian Law* 65–87.

CRAWFORD, E, 'Unequal before the Law: The Case for the Elimination of Distinction between International and Non-international Armed Conflicts' (2007) 20(2) *Leiden Journal of International Law* 441–65.

CUADRA LACAYO, J, 'International Humanitarian Law and Irregular Warfare: Lessons learned in Latin America' (2000) 82(840) *Revue internationale de la Croix-Rouge* 941–51.

CULLEN, A, 'The Parameters of Internal Armed Conflict in International Humanitarian Law' (2004) 12 *International and Comparative Law Review* 189–229.

DAES, E-IA, 'New Types of War Crimes and Crimes against Humanity: Violations of International Humanitarian and Human Rights Law' (1993) 7 *International Geneva Yearbook* 55–78.

DALTON, JG, 'The Influence of Law on Seapower in Desert Shield/Desert Storm' (1993) 41 *Naval Law Review* 27–82.

DARCY, S, 'What Future for the Doctrine of Belligerent Reprisals' (2002) 5 *Yearbook of International Humanitarian Law* 107–30.

DAVID, E, 'The International Criminal Court: What is the Point?' in K WILLEMS (ed), *International Law: Theory and Practice (Essays in Honour of Erik Suy)*, The Hague, Martinus Nijhoff, 1998, 631–50.

——, 'Respect for the Principle of Distinction in the Kosovo War' (2000) 3 *Yearbook of International Humanitarian Law* 81–107.

DEGAGNE, R, 'The Prevention of Environmental Damage in Time of Armed Conflict: Proportionality and Precautionary Measures' (2000) *Yearbook of International Humanitarian Law* 109–29.

DELAHUNTY, RJ, 'Statehood and the Third Geneva Convention' (2005) 46(1) *Virginia Journal of International Law* 131–64.

DEMAREST, GB, 'Espionage in International Law' (1996) 24(2/3) *Denver Journal of International Law and Policy* 321–48.

DE NEVERS, R, 'The Geneva Conventions and New Wars' (2006) 121(3) *Political Science Quarterly* 369–95.

DENNIS, MJ, 'Application of Human Rights Treaties Extraterritorially in Times of Armed Conflict and Military Occupation' (2005) 99(1) *American Journal of International Law* 119–41.

DESCH, T, 'The Second Protocol to the 1954 Hague Convention for the Protection of Cultural Property in the Event of Armed Conflict' (1999) 2 *Yearbook of International Humanitarian Law* 63–90.

DETTER, I, 'The Law of War and Illegal Combatants' (2007) 75(5/6) *George Washington Law Review* 1049–104.

DIJKZEUL, D and MOKE, M, 'Public Communication Strategies of International Humanitarian Organizations' (2005) 87(860) *Revue internationale de la Croix-Rouge* 673–92.

DINGWALL, J, 'Unlawful Confinement as a War Crime' (2004) 9(2) *Journal of Conflict and Security Law* 133–79.

DINSTEIN, Y, 'Comments on War' (2004) 27(3) *Harvard Journal of Law and Public Policy* 877–92.

——, 'Article 7 of Additional Protocol I' (2005) 24 *The Australian Yearbook of International Law* 65–74.

——, 'The ICRC Customary International Humanitarian Law Study' (2006) 36 *Israel Yearbook on Human Rights* 1–15.

DOSWALD-BECK, L, 'Vessels, Aircraft and Persons Entitled to Protection During Armed Conflicts at Sea' (1994) 65 *British Yearbook of International Law* 211–301.

——, 'The San Remo Manual on International Law Applicable to Armed Conflicts at Sea' (1995) 89(1) *American Journal of International Law* 192–208.

——, 'The Protection of Medical Aircraft in International Law' (1997) 27 *Israel Yearbook on Human Rights* 151–92.

DÖRMANN, K, 'Preparatory Commission for the ICC: The Elements of War Crimes' (2001) 83(842) *Revue internationale de la Croix-Rouge* 461–87.

——, 'The Legal Situation of "Unlawful/Unprivileged Combatants"' (2003) 85(849) *Revue internationale de la Croix-Rouge* 45–74.

——, 'The International Committee of the Red Cross and its Contribution to the Development of International Humanitarian Law in Specialized Instruments' (2004) 5(1) *Chicago Journal of International Law* 217–32.

——, 'International Humanitarian Law in the Iraq Conflict' (2004) 47 *German Yearbook of International Law* 293–342.

DOSWALD-BECK, L, 'Developments in Customary International Humanitarian Law' (2005) 15(3) *Schweizerische Zeitschrift für internationales und europäisches Recht* 471–98.

——, 'The Right to Life in Armed Conflict: Does International Humanitarian Law Provide All the Answers?' (2006) 88(864) *Revue internationale de la Croix-Rouge* 881–904.

DOUGHERTY, BJ, 'Decisions of the United States Courts in regards to the Guantanamo Bay Detainees' (2005) 18(3) *Humanitäres Völkerrecht* 209–18.

DROEGE, C, 'In Truth the Leitmotiv: The Prohibition of Torture and other Forms of Ill-treatment in International Humanitarian Law' (2007) 89(867) *Revue internationale de la Croix-Rouge* 515–42.

DUTLI, MT, 'National Implementation Measures of International Humanitarian Law: Some Practical Aspects' (1998) 1 *Yearbook of International Humanitarian Law* 245–61.

DUXBURY, A, 'Drawing Lines in the Sand: Characterising Conflicst for the Purposes of Teaching International Humanitarian Law' (2007) 8(2) *Melbourne Journal of International Law* 259–72.

EDWARDS, JP, 'The Iraqi Oil "Eeapon" in the 1991 Gulf War: A Law of Armed Conflict Analysis' (1992) 40 *Naval Law Review* 105–32.

EIDE, A, ROSAS, A and MERON, T, 'Combating Lawlessness in Grey Zone Conflicts through Minimum Humanitarian Standards' (1995) 89(1) *American Journal of International Law* 215–23.

EGELAND, J, 'Arms Availability and Violations of International Humanitarian Law' (1999) 81(835) *Revue internationale de la Croix-Rouge* 673–77.

EGOROV, SA, 'The Kosovo Crisis and the Law of Armed Conflicts' (2000) 82(837) *Revue internationale de la Croix-Rouge* 183–92.

EHRENREICH BROOKS, R, 'War Everywhere: Rights, National Security Law, and the Law of Armed Conflict in the Age of Terror' (2004) 153(2) *University of Pennsylvania Law Review* 675–761.

EILDERS, C, 'Media under Fire: Fact and Fiction in Conditions of War' (2005) 87(860) *Revue internationale de la Croix-Rouge* 639–48.

EMANUELLI, C, 'The Protection Afforded to Humanitarian Assistance Personnel under the Convention on the Safety of United Nations and Associated Personnel' (1996) 9(1) *Humanitäres Völkerrecht* 4–10.

ERIKKSON, S, 'Humiliating and Degrading Treatment under International Humanitarian Law' (2004) 55 *Air Force Law Review* 269–311.

EVANS, C, 'The Double-edged Sword: Religious Influences on International Humanitarian Law' (2005) 6(1) *Melbourne Journal of International Law* 1–32.

EWUMBUE-MONONO, C, 'Respect for International Humanitarian Law by Armed Non-state Actors in Africa' (2006) 88(864) *Revue internationale de la Croix-Rouge* 905–24.

EYFFINGER, A, 'A Highly Critical Moment: Role and Record of the 1907 Hague Peace Conference' (2007) 54(2) *Netherlands International Law Review* 197–228.

FALK, RA, 'Nuclear Eeapons, International Law and the World Court: A Historic Encounter' (1997) 91(1) *American Journal of International Law* 64–75.

FALLAH, K, 'Corporate Actors: The Legal Status of Mercenaries in Armed Conflict' (2006) 88(863) *International Review of the Red Cross* 599–611.

FELICIANO, FP, 'Marine Pollution and Spoliation of Natural Resources as War Measures: A Note on some International Law Problems in the Gulf War' (1995) 39(2) *Ateneo Law Journal* 1–34.

FENRICK, WJ, 'Legal Aspects of Targeting in the Law of Naval Warfare' (1991) 29 *Canadian Yearbook of International Law* 238–82.

——, 'The Development of the Law of Armed Conflict through the Jurisprudence of the International Criminal Tribunal for the Former Yugoslavia' (1998) 3(2) *Journal of Armed Conflict Law* 197–232.

——, 'The Application of the Geneva Conventions by the International Criminal Tribunal for the Former Yugoslavia' (1999) 81(834) *Revue internationale de la Croix-Rouge* 317–29.

——, 'The Law Applicable to Targeting and Proportionality after Operation Allied Force: A View from the Outside' (2000) 3 *Yearbook of International Humanitarian Law* 53–80.

FIDLER, DP, 'The International Legal Implications of "Non-lethal" Weapons' (1999) 21(1) *Michigan Journal of International Law* 51–100.

——, '"The Meaning of Moscow: "Non-lethal" Weapons and International Law in the Early 21st Century' (2005) 87(859) *Revue internationale de la Croix-Rouge* 525–52.

FISCHER, D, 'Human Shields, Homicides, and House Fires: How a Domestic Law Analogy Can Guide International Law Regarding Human Shield Tactics in Armed Conflict' (2007) 57(2) *American University Law Review* 479–521.

FISHER, D, 'Domestic Regulation of International Humanitarian Relief in Disasters and Armed Conflict: A Comparative Analysis' (2007) 89(866) *Revue internationale de la Croix-Rouge* 345–72.

FISCHER, H, 'Limitation and Prohibition of the Use of Certain Weapons in Non-international Armed Conflicts' (1989/1990) *Yearbook of the International Institute of Humanitarian Law* 117–80.

FISCHER, T, 'The ICRC and the 1962 Cuban Missiles Crisis' (2001) 83(842) *Revue internationale de la Croix-Rouge* 287–310.

FLECK, D, 'Strategic Bombing and the Definition of Military Objectives' (1997) 27 *Israel Yearbook on Human Rights* 41–64.

——, 'International Humanitarian Law after September 11' (2003) 6 *Yearbook of International Humanitarian Law* 41–71.

——, 'International Accountability for Violations of the "Ius in Bello"' (2006) 11(2) *Journal of Conflict and Security Law* 179–99.

FLETCHER, GP, 'The Law of War and its Pathologies' (2007) 38(3) *Columbia Human Rights Law Review* 517–46.

FENRICK, WJ, 'Targeting and Proportionality During the NATO Bombing Campaign against Yugoslavia' (2001) 12(3) *European Journal of International Law* 489–502.

FORSYTHE, DP, '1949 and 1999: Making the Geneva Conventions Relevant after the Cold War' (1999) 81(834) *Revue internationale de la Croix-Rouge* 265–76.

——, 'The ICRC: A Unique Humanitarian Protagonist' (2007) 89(865) *Revue internationale de la Croix-Rouge* 63–96.

FOX, G, 'International Law and Civil Wars' (1994) 26(4) *New York University Journal of International Law & Politics* 633–54.

FRANCES, MG, 'The International Law of Blockade: New Guiding Principles in Contemporary State Practice' (1992) 1001(4) *Yale Law Journal* 893–918.

FRANKLIN, S, 'South African and International Attempts to Regulate Mercenaries and Private Military Companies' (2008) 17(1) *Transnational Law and Contemporary Problems* 239–63.

FRY, JD, 'Contextualized Legal Reviews for the Methods and Means of Warfare' (2006) 44(2) *Columbia Journal of Transnational Law* 453–519.

——, 'The UN Security Council and the Law of Armed Conflict' (2006) 38(2) *George Washington International Law Review* 327–48.

GAN, PT, 'Caught in the Crossfire: Strengthening International Protection for Internally Displaced Persons due to Internal Armed Conflict' (1994) 39(1) *Ateneo Law Journal* 1–49.

GARDAM, J, 'Protocol I to the Geneva Conventions: A Victim of Short Sighted Political Considerations?' (1989) 17(1) *Melbourne University Law Review* 107–31.

——, 'Women and the Law of Armed Conflict: Why the Silence?' (1997) 46(1) *International and Comparative Law Quarterly* 55–80.

——, 'Protection of Women in Armed Conflict' (2000) 22(1) *Human Rights Quarterly* 148–66.

GASSER, H-P, 'Law in Humanitarian Crises: Introductory Statement' in WP HEERE (ed), *International Law and The Hague's 750th Anniversary*, The Hague, TMC Asser, 1999, 349–52.

——, 'International Humanitarian Law, the Prohibition of Terrorist Acts and the Fight against Terrorism' (2001) 4 *Yearbook of International Humanitarian Law* 329–47.

GASTON, EL, 'Mercenarism 2.0? The Rise of the Modern Private Security Industry and its Implications for International Humanitarian Law Enforcement' (2008) 49(1) *Harvard International Law Journal* 221–48.

GEISS, R, 'Name, Rank, Date of Birth, Serial Number and the Right to Remain Silent' (2005) 87(860) *Revue internationale de la Croix-Rouge* 721–36.

——, 'Asymmetric Conflict Structures' (2006) 88(864) *Revue internationale de la Croix-Rouge* 757–78.

GILL, T, 'The Nuclear Weapons Advisory Opinion of the International Court of Justice and the Fundamental Distinction Between the Jus ad Bellum and the Jus in Bello' (1999) 12(3) *Leiden Journal of International Law* 613–24.

GILLARD, E-C, 'Business Goes to War: Private Military/Security Companies and International Humanitarian Law' (2006) 88(863) *Revue internationale de la Croix-Rouge* 525–72.

GOLDBLAT, J, 'Inhumane Conventional Weapons: Efforts to Strengthen the Constraints' (1995) *SIPRI Yearbook* 825–38.

——, 'The Nuclear Non-proliferation Régime: Assessment and Prospects' (1995) 256 *Recueil des cours, Académie de Droit International de la Haye* 9–191.

GRAY, C, 'Bosnia and Herzegovina: Civil War or Inter-state Conflict? Characterization and Consequences' (1997) 67 *British Yearbook of International Law* 155–97.

GREEN, LC, 'The Environment and the Law of Conventional Warfare' (1991) 29 *Canadian Yearbook of International Law* 222–82.

——, 'What is—Why is there—the Law of War?' (1994) 5 *Finnish Yearbook of International Law* 99–148.

——, 'Enforcement of the Law in Non-international Conflicts' in V GÖTZ (ed), *Liber amicorum Günther Jaenicke—zum 85. Geburtstag*, Berlin, Springer, 1998, 113–47.

——, 'Cicero and Clausewitz or Quincy Wright: The Interplay of Law and War' (1998/1999) 9 *Journal of Legal Studies* 59–98.

——, 'The International Judicial Process and the Law of Armed Conflict' (1999) 38(1) *Revue de droit militaire et de droit de la guerre* 15–89.

——, 'The Role of Discipline in the Military' (2004) 42 *Canadian Yearbook of International Law* 385–421.

GREENWOOD, C, 'Protection of Peacekeepers: The Legal Regime' (1996) 7(1) *Duke Journal of Comparative & International Law* 185–207.

——, 'The Development of International Humanitarian Law by the International Criminal Tribunal for the Former Yugoslavia' (1998) 2 *Max Planck Yearbook of United Nations Law* 97–140.

——, 'International Humanitarian Law and the United Nations Military Operations' (1998) 1 *Yearbook of International Humanitarian Law* 3–34.

Greer, JL, 'China and the Laws of War' (2006) 46(4) *Virginia Journal of International Law* 717–43.

GROSS, AM, 'The Construction of a Wall between the Hague and Jerusalem' (2006) 19(2) *Leiden Journal of International Law* 393–440.

GROSS, O, 'The Grave Breaches System and the Armed Conflict in the Former Yugoslavia' (1995) 16(3) *Michigan Journal of International Law* 783–829.

GROVER, S, 'Child Soldiers as Non-combatants: The Inapplicability of the Refugee Convention Exclusion Clause' (2008) 12 *International Journal of Human Rights* 53–65.

GUTIERREZ POSSE, HDT, 'The Relationship Between International Humanitarian Law and the International Criminal Tribunals' (2006) 88(861) *Revue internationale de la Croix-Rouge* 65–86.

HADDEN, T, 'The Law of Internal Crisis and Conflict: An Outline Prospectus for the Merger of International Human Rights Law, the Law of Armed Conflict, Refugee Law, and the Law on Humanitarian Intervention' (1999) 81(833) *Revue internationale de la Croix-Rouge* 119–33.

HAMILTON, C, 'Armed Conflict: The Protection of Children under International Law' (1997) 5(1) *International Journal of Children's Rights* 1–46.

HAMPSON, FJ, 'Mercenaires: Diagnosis before Proscription' (1991) 22 *Netherland Yearbook of International Law* 3–38.

HAPPOLD, M, 'Child Soldiers in International Law: The Legal Regulation of Children's Participation in Hostilities' (2000) 47(1) *Netherlands International Law Review* 27–52.

——, 'The Optional Protocol to the Convention on the Rights of the Child on the Involvement of Children in Armed Conflict' (2000) *Yearbook of International Humanitarian Law* 226–44.

——, 'International Humanitarian Law, War Criminality and Child Recruitment' (2005) 18(2) *Leiden Journal of International Law* 283–97.

HATFIELD-LYON, J, 'The Legality of the Zhreat or Use of Nuclear Weapons: The Impact of the International Court of Justice's Advisory Opinion on International Peace and Security, Twenty-fifth Annual CCIL Conference, 1995' in Y Le BOUTHILIER (ed), *Selected Papers in International Law*, The Hague, Kluwer, 1999, 531–51.

HEARN, WR, 'The International Legal Regime Rregulating Nuclear Deterrence and Warfare' (1990) 61 *Belgium Yearbook of International Law* 199–248.

van HEGELSOM, G-JF, 'The Law of Armed Conflict and UN Peace-keeping and Peace-enforcing Operations' (1993) 6 *Hague Yearbook of International Law* 45–58.

HEINTSCHEL VON HEINEGG, W, 'Visit, Search, Diversion and Capture in Naval Warfare: Part I, the Traditional Law' (1991) 29 *Canadian Yearbook of International Law* 283–329.

——, 'Visit, Search, Diversion and Capture in Naval Warfare: Part II, Developments since 1945' (1992) 30 *Canadian Yearbook of International Law* 89–136.

——, 'The International Law of Mine Warfare at Sea' (1993) 23 *Israel Yearbook of Human Rights* 53–76.

HEINTZE, H-J, 'On the Relationship between Human Rights Law Protection and International Humanitarian Law' (2004) 86(856) *Revue internationale de la Croix-Rouge* 789–814.

HENCKAERTS, J-M, 'New Rules for the Protection of Cultural Property in Armed Conflict: The Signification of the Second Protocol to the 1954 Hague Convention for the Protection of Cultural Property in the Event of Armed Conflict' (1999) 12(3) *Humanitäres Völkerrecht* 147–54.

——, 'Study on Customary Rules of International Humanitarian Law: Purpose, Coverage and Methodology' (1999) 81(835) *Revue internationale de la Croix-Rouge* 660–68.

——, 'Study on Customary International Humanitarian Law' (2005) 87(857) *Revue internationale de la Croix-Rouge* 175–212.

HERBY, P, 'Arms Availability and the Situation of Civilians in Armed Conflict: Summary of an ICRC Study for the 27th International Conference of the Red Cross and the Red Crescent' (1999) 81(835) *Revue internationale de la Croix-Rouge* 669–72.

HERRMANN, I and PALMIERI, D, 'A Haunting Figure: The Hostage through the Ages' (2005) 87(857) *Revue internationale de la Croix-Rouge* 135–48.

HLADIK, J, 'The 1954 Hague Convention for the Protection of Cultural Property in the Event of Armed Conflict and the Notion of Military Necessity: The Review of the 1954

Convention and the Adoption of the Second Protocol thereto (26 March 1999)' (1999) 81(835) *Revue internationale de la Croix-Rouge* 621–35.

——, 'Reporting System under the 1954 Convention for the Protection of Cultural Property in the Event of Armed Conflict' (2000) 82(840) *Revue internationale de la Croix-Rouge* 1001–16.

HOFFMAN, M, 'Peace-enforcement Actions and Humanitarian Law: Emerging Rules for "International Armed Conflict"' (2000) 82(837) *Revue internationale de la Croix-Rouge* 193–204.

van den HOLE, L, 'Towards a Test of the International Character of an Armed Conflict' (2005) 32(2) *Syracuse Journal of International Law and Commerce* 269–87.

HORTON, S, 'Kriegsraison or Military Necessity?' (2007) 30(3) *Fordham International Law Journal* 576–98.

HUGUENING-BENJAMIN, R, 'Can Public Communication Protect Victims?' (2005) 87(860) *Revue internationale de la Croix-Rouge* 661–72.

IMSEIS, A, 'Critical Reflections on the International Humanitarian Law Aspects of the ICJ Wall Advisory Opinion' (2005) 99(1) *American Journal of International Law* 102–18.

JIA, BB, 'The Doctrine of Command Responsibility: Current Problems' (2000) *Yearbook of International Humanitarian Law* 131–65.

JINKS, D, 'The Applicability of the Geneva Conventions to the "Global War on Terrorism"' (2005) 46(1) *Virginia Journal of International Law* 165–95.

JOSIPOVIAE, I, 'Responsibility for War Crimes before National Courts in Croatia' (2006) 88(861) *Revue internationale de la Croix-Rouge* 145–68.

JIVIDEN, DD 'Jus in Bello in the Twenty-first Century' (2004) 7 *Yearbook of International Humanitarian Law* 113–52.

JOCHNICK, C and NORMAND, R, 'The Legitimation of Violence: A Critical History of the Laws of War' (1994) 35(1) *Harvard International Law Journal* 49–95.

KAHN, P, 'Nuclear Weapons and the Rule of Law' (1999) 31(2/3) *New York University Journal of International Law & Politics* 349–415.

KAHN, R, 'United Nations Peace-keeping in Internal Conflicts: Problems and Perspectives' (2000) 4 *Max Planck Yearbook of United Nations Law* 543–81.

KÄLIN, W, 'Refugees and Civil Wars: Only a Matter of Interpretation?' (1991) 3(3) *International Journal of Refugee Law* 435-451.

KALSHOVEN, F, 'The Undertaking to Respect and Ensure Respect in All Circumstances: From Tiny Seed to Ripening Fruit' (1999) 2 *Yearbook of International Humanitarian Law* 3–61.

KANUCK, SP, 'Information Warfare: New Challenges for Public International Law' (1996) 37(1) *Harvard International Law Journal* 272–92.

KARIMOVA, T, 'Universal Permissive Jurisdiction for the Violation of Ccommon Article 3 of the Geneva Conventions for the Protection of the Victims of War of 12 August 1949' (2001/2002) 10 *Asian Yearbook of International Law* 125–43.

KEARNEY, M, 'The Prohibition of Propaganda for War in the International Covenant on Civil and Political Rights' (2005) 23(4) *Netherlands Quarterly of Human Rights* 551–70.

KELLENBERGER, J, 'Speaking out or Remaining Silent in Humanitarian Work' (2004) 86(855) *Revue internationale de la Croix-Rouge* 593–610.

KELLER, H and FOROWICZ, M, 'A Tightrope Walk between Legality and Legitimacy : An Analysis of the Israeli Supreme Court's Judgment on Targeted Killing' (2008) 21(1) *Leiden Journal of International Law* 165–221.

KELSEY, JTG, 'Hacking into International Humanitarian Law: The Principles of Distinction and Neutrality in the Age of Cyber Warfare' (2008) 106(7) *Michigan Law Review* 1427–51.

KLAMERT, M, 'Military Subcontractors under International Humanitarian Law' (2005) 10 *Austrian Review of International and European Law* 127–46.

KLEIN, N, 'State Responsibility for International Humanitarian Law Violations and the Work of the Eritrea Ethiopia Claims Commission so far' (2004) 47 *German Yearbook of International Law* 214–66.

KLEINBERGER, TR, 'The Iraqi Conflict: An Assessment of Possible War Crimes and the Call for Adoption of an International Criminal Code and Permanent International Criminal Tribunal' (1993) 14(1) *New York Law School Journal of International & Comparative Law* 69–106.

KLENNER, D, 'Training in International Humanitarian Law' (2000) 82(839) *Revue internationale de la Croix-Rouge* 653–62.

KOLB, R, 'Occupation in Iraq since 2003 and the Powers of the UN Security Council' (2008) 90(869) *Revue internationale de la Croix-Rouge* 29–50.

KOLB, R and GAGGIOLI, G, 'A Right to Life in Armed Conflicts? The Contribution of the European Court of Human Rights' (2007) 37 *Israel Yerbook on Human Rights* 115–63.

KRETZMER, D, 'The Advisory Opinion: The Light Treatment of International Humanitarian Law' (2005) 99(1) *American Journal of International Law* 88–102.

KÜNG, H, 'Religion, Violence and "Holy Wars"' (2005) 87(858) *Revue internationale de la Croix-Rouge* 253–68.

LANDGREN, K, 'Safety Zones and International Protection: A Dark Grey Area' (1995) 7(3) *International Journal of Refugee Law* 436–58.

LANORD, C, 'The Legal Status of National Red Cross and Red Crescent Societies' (2000) 82(840) *Revue internationale de la Croix-Rouge* 1053–77.

LA ROSA, A-M, 'Humanitarian Organizations and International Criminal Tribunals, or trying to Square the Circle' (2006) 88(861) *Revue internationale de la Croix-Rouge* 169–86.

LAVOYER, J-P, 'International Humanitarian Law: Should it be Reaffirmed, Clarified or Developed?' (2004) 34 *Israel Yearbook on Human Rights* 35–58.

LEVIE, HS, 'History of the Law of War on Land' (2000) 82(838) *Revue internationale de la Croix-Rouge* 339–50.

LEVINE, JD, 'The Doctrine of Command Responsibility and Its Application to Superior Civilian Leadership: Does the International Criminal Court Have the Correct Standard?' (2007) 193 *Military Law Review* 52–96.

LINDSEY, C, 'Women and War' (2000) 82(839) *Revue internationale de la Croix-Rouge* 561–80.

LUBELL, N, 'Challenges in Applying Human Rights Law to Armed Conflict' (2005) 87(860) *Revue internationale de la Croix-Rouge* 737–54.

LUNDIN, SJ, STOCK, T and GEISSLER, E, 'Chemical and Biological Warfare and Arms Control Developments in 1991' (1992) *SIPRI Yearbook* 147–86.

LUNZE, S, 'Serving God and Ceasar: Religious Personnel and their Protection in Armed Conflict' (2004) 86(853) *Revue internationale de la Croix-Rouge* 69–92.

MACKINTHOSH, K, 'Beyond the Red Cross: The Protection of Independent Humanitarian Organizations and their Staff in International Humanitarian Law' (2007) 89(865) *Revue internationale de la Croix-Rouge* 113–30.

MAIER, CS, 'Targeting the City: Debates and Silences about the Aerial Bombing of World War II' (2005) 87(859) *Revue internationale de la Croix-Rouge* 429–44.

MAINETTI, V, 'New Prospects for the Protection of Cultural Property in the Event of Armed Conflict: The Entry into Force of the Second Protocol to the 1954 Hague Convention' (2004) 86(854) *Revue internationale de la Croix-Rouge* 337–66.

MALANCZUK, P, 'The Kurdish Crisis and Allied Intervention in the Aftermath of the Second Gulf War' (1991) 2(2) *European Journal of International Law* 114–32.

——, 'The International Criminal Court and Landmines: What are the Consequences of Leaving the US Behind?' (2000) 11(1) *European Journal of International Law* 77–90.

MALVIYA, RA, 'International Humanitarian Law concerning Employment of Means and Methods of Combat' (2005) 5 *ISIL Yearbook of International Humanitarian Law and Refugee Law* 1–27.

MARAHUN, T, 'Environmental Damage in Times of Armed Conflict—Not "Really" a Matter of Criminal Responsibility?' (2000) 82(840) *Revue internationale de la Croix-Rouge* 1029–36.

MARESCA, L, 'A New Protocol on Explosive Remnants of War: The History and Negotiation of Protocol V to the 1980 Convention on Certain Conventional Weapons' (2004) 86(856) *Revue internationale de la Croix-Rouge* 815–35.

MATHESON, MJ, 'The Opinions of the International Court of Justice in the Threat or Use of Nuclear Weapons' (1997) 91(3) *American Journal of International Law* 417–35.

MATHEWS, RJ, 'The Influence of Humanitarian Principles in the Negotiation of Arms Control Treaties' (1999) 81(834) *Revue internationale de la Croix-Rouge* 331–52.

——, 'The 1980 Convention on Certain Conventional Weapons: A Useful Framework despite Earlier Disappointments' (2001) 83(844) *Revue internationale de la Croix-Rouge* 991–1021.

MATTLER, MJ, 'The Distinction between Civil Wars and International Wars and its Legal Implications' (1994) 26(4) *New York University Journal of International Law & Politics* 655–700.

McCOUBREY, H, 'The Nature of the Modern Doctrine of Military Necessity' (1991) 30(1–4) *Revue de droit Militaire et de Droit de la Guerre* 215–42.

——, 'International Humanitarian Law and the Kosovo Crisis' (2000) 4(3/4) *International Journal of Human Rights* 184–206.

McDONALD, A, 'The Year in Review: In National Humanitarian Law' (1999) 2 *Yearbook of International Humanitarian Law* 213–53.

McLIN, AR, 'The ICRC: An Alibi for Swiss Neutrality' (1999) 9(2) *Duke Journal of Comparative & International Law* 495–518.

McNEILL, JH, 'Protection of the Environment in Times of Armed Conflict: Environmental Protection in Military Practice' (1993) 6 *Hague Yearbook of International Law* 75–84.

MEINDERSMA, C, 'Applicability of Humanitarian Law in International and Internal Armed Conflict' (1994) 7 *Hague Yearbook of International Law* 113–40.

——, 'Legal Issues surrounding Population Transfers in Conflict Situations' (1994) 41(1) *Netherlands International Law Review* 31–83.

MEISENBERG, SM, 'Legality of Amnesties in International Humanitarian Law: The Lomé Amnesty Decision of the Special Court for Sierra Leone' (2004) 86(856) *Revue internationale de la Croix-Rouge* 837–51.

MENON, PK, Elimination of Nuclear Weapons' (1991) 30(1–4) *Revue de Droit Militaire et de Droit de la Guerre* 253–301.

MERCIER, A, 'War and Media: Constancy and Convulsion' (2005) 87(860) *Revue internationale de la Croix-Rouge* 649–60.

MERIBOUTE, Z, 'The Emblems of the 1949 Geneva Conventions: Their Content and Meaning' (2000) *Yearbook of International Humanitarian Law* 258–72.

MERON, T, 'Shakespeare's Henry V and the Law of War' (1992) 86(1) *American Journal of International Law* 1–45.

——, 'The Time has come for the United States to Ratify Geneva Protocol I' (1994) 88(1) *American Journal of International Law* 678–86.

——, 'War Crimes in Yugoslavia and the Development of International Law' (1994) 88(1) *American Journal of International Law* 78–87.

——, 'Classification of Armed Conflict in the Former Yugoslavia, Nicaragua's Fallout' (1998) 92(2) *American Journal of International Law* 236–42.

——, 'The Humanization of Humanitarian Law' (2000) 94(2) *American Journal of International Law* 239–78.

——, 'The Martens Clause, Principles of Humanity, and Dictates of Public Conscience' (2000) 94(1) *American Journal of International Law* 78–89.

——, 'Revival of Customary Humanitarian Law' (2005) 99(4) *American Journal of International Law* 817–34.

——, 'The Role of International Criminal Tribunals in the Implementation of Humanitarian Law and the Maintenance of Peace' in PA FERNANDEZ SANCHEZ (ed), *The New Challenges of Humanitarian Law in Armed Conflicts, in Honour of Professor Juan Antonio Carillo-Salcedo*, Leiden, Martinus Nijhoff, 2005, 265–8.

MEYER, M, 'The Proposed New Neutral Protective Emblem' in R BURCHILL, ND WHITE and J MORRIS (eds), *International Conflict and Security Law, Essays in Memory of Hilaire McCoubrey*, Cambridge, Cambridge University Press, 2005, 84–107.

MEYER, MA, 'The Relevance of the 50th Anniversary of the Geneva Conventions to National Red Cross and Red Crescent Societies: Reviewing the Past to Address the Future' (1999) 81(835) *Revue internationale de la Croix-Rouge* 649–59.

MILANOVIC, M, 'Lessons for Human Rights and Humanitarian Law in the War on Terror: Comparing Hamdan and the Israeli Targeted Killings Case' (2007) 89(866) *Revue internationale de la Croix-Rouge* 373–93.

MOIR, L, 'The Historical Development of the Application of Humanitarian Law in Non-international Armed Conflicts to 1949' (1998) 47 *International and Comparative Law Quarterly* 337–61.

——, 'Towards the Unification of International Humanitarian Law?' in R BURCHILL, ND WHITE and J MORRIS (eds), *International Conflict and Security Law, Essays in Memory of Hilaire McCoubrey*, Cambridge, Cambridge University Press, 2005, 108–28.

MOMTAZ, D, 'War Crimes in Non-international Armed Conflicts under the Statute of the International Criminal Court' (1999) 2 *Yearbook of International Humanitarian Law* 177–92.

——, 'Israel and the Fourth Geneva Convention: On the ICJ Advisory Opinion concerning the Separation Barrier' (2007) 8 *Yearbook of International Humanitarian Law* 344–55.

MONGELARD, E, 'Corporate Civil Liability for Violations of International Humanitarian Law' (2006) 88(863) *Revue internationale de la Croix-Rouge* 665–91.

MORRISS, DM, 'From War to Peace: A Study of Ceasefire Agreements and the Evolving Role of the United Nations' (1996) 36(4) *Virginia Journal of International Law* 801–931.

MOUSOURAKIS, G, 'Applying Humanitarian Law to Non-international Armed Conflicts' (1998) 14 *Anuario de derecho internacional* 293–319.

MUNOZ ROJAS, D, 'The Roots of Behaviour in War' (2004) 86(853) *Revue internationale de la Croix-Rouge* 189–206.

MYERS, R, 'A New Remedy for Northern Ireland: The Case for United Nations Peace-keeping Intervention in an Internal Conflict' (1990) 11(1/2) New *York Law School Journal of International & Comparative Law* 1–166.

NAQVI, Y, 'Humanitarian Assistance in Armed Conflict' (2004) 86(856) *Revue internationale de la Croix-Rouge* 879–916.

NEUMANN, N, 'Applying the Rule of Proportionality: Force Protection and Cumulative Assessment in International Law and Morality' (2006) 7 *Yearbook of International Humanitarian Law* 79–112.

NEWTON, MA, 'The Iraqi High Criminal Court: Controversy and Contributions' (2006) 88(862) *Revue internationale de la Croix-Rouge* 399–425.

OBRADOVIC, K, 'International Humanitarian Law and the Kosovo Crisis' (2000) 82(839) *Revue internationale de la Croix-Rouge* 699–731.

O'BRIEN, JC, 'The International Tribunal for Violations of International Humanitarian Law in the Former Yugoslavia' (1993) 87(4) *American Journal of International Law* 639–59.

O'DONNELL, D, 'International Treaties against Terrorism and the Use of Terrorism during Armed Conflict and by Armed Forces' (2006) 88(864) *Revue internationale de la Croix-Rouge* 853–80.

OETER, S, 'Civil War, Humanitarian Law and the United Nations' (1997) 1 *Max Planck Yearbook of United Nations Law* 195–229.

OKIMOTO, K, 'Violations of International Humanitarian Law by United Nations Forces and their Legal Consequences' (2003) 6 *Yearbook of International Humanitarian Law* 199–236.

ORAKHELASHVILI, A, 'Legal Stability and Claims of Change: The International Court's Treatment of Jus ad Bellum and Jus in Bello' (2006) 75(3/4) *Nordic Journal of International Law* 371–407.

——, 'The Interaction Between Human Rights and Humanitarian Law: Fragmentation, Conflict, Parallelism, or Convergence?' (2008) 19(1) *European Journal of International Law* 161–82.

OSWALD, BM, 'The Creation and Control of Places of Protection during United Nations Peace Operations' (2001) 83(844) *Revue internationale de la Croix-Rouge* 1013–35.

OTTO, R, 'Neighbours as Human Shields? The Israel Defense Forces' "Early Warning Procedure" and International Humanitarian Law' (2004) 86(856) *Revue internationale de la Croix-Rouge* 771–87.

PARKS, H, 'The Protection of Civilians form Air Warfare' (1997) 27 *Israel Yearbook on Human Rights* 65–111.

PASTERNACK, S, 'The Role of the Secretary-General in Helping to Prevent Civil War' (1994) 26(4) *New York University Journal of International Law & Politics* 701–59.

PEJIC, J, 'The Right to Food in Situations of Armed Conflict: The Legal Framework' (2001) 83(844) *Revue internationale de la Croix-Rouge* 1097–109.

——, 'Accountability for International Crimes: From Conjecture to Reality' (2002) 84(845) *Revue internationale de la Croix-Rouge* 13–33.

——, 'Procedural Principles and Safeguards for Internment/Administrative Detention in Armed Conflict and other Situations of Violence' (2005) 87(858) *Revue internationale de la Croix-Rouge* 375–91.

PERRIN, B, 'Promoting Compliance of Private Security and Military Companies with International Humanitarian Law' (2006) 88(863) *Revue internationale de la Croix-Rouge* 613–36.

PETRASEK, D, 'Moving Forward on the Development of Minimum Humanitarian Standards' (1998) 92(3) *American Journal of International Law* 557–63.

PFANNER, T, 'Military Uniforms and the Law of War' (2004) 86(853) *Revue internationale de la Croix-Rouge* 93–130.

——, 'Asymmetrical Warfare from the Perspective of Humanitarian Law and Humanitarian Action' (2005) 87(857) *Revue internationale de la Croix-Rouge* 149–74.

POULOS, AH, 'The 1954 Hague Convention for the Protection of Cultural Property in the Event of Armed Conflict: An Historical Analysis' (2000) 28(1) *International Journal of Legal Information* 1–44.

POWELL, CH, 'Terrorism and International Humanitarian Law' (2006) *African Yearbook on International Humanitarian Law* 118–47.

PLATTNER, D, 'International Humanitarian Law and Inalienable or Non-derogable Human Rights' in D PREMONT (ed), *Droits intangibles et Etats d'exception*, Bruxelles, Bruylant, 1996, 349–63.

PRUGH, GS, 'American Issues and Friendly Reservations regarding Protocol I, Additional to the Geneva Conventions' (1992) 31(1–4) *Revue de Droit Militaire et de Droit de la Guerre* 223–93.

QUEGINER, J-F, 'Precautions under the Law Governing the Conduct of Hostilities' (2006) 88(864) *Revue internationale de la Croix-Rouge* 793–822.

——, 'Commentary on the Protocol Additional to the Geneva Conventions of 12 August 1949, and Relating to the Adoption of an Additional Distinctive Emblem (Protocol III)' (2007) 89(865) *Revue internationale de la Croix-Rouge* 175–207.

QUIGLEY, J, 'Missiles with a Message: The Legality of United States Raid on Iraq's Intelligence Headquarters' (1994) 17(2) *Hastings International and Comparative Law Review* 241–74.

RAMEY, R, 'Armed Conflict on the Final Frontier: The Law of War in Space' (2000) 48 *Air Force Law Review* 1–157.

RANA, R, 'Contemporary Challenges in the Civil-Military Relationship: Complementarity or Incompatibility?' (2004) 86(855) *Revue internationale de la Croix-Rouge* 565–92.

REYDAMS, L, 'A la Guerre comme à la Guerre: Patterns of Armed Conflict, Humanitarian Law Responses and New Challenges' (2006) 88(864) *Revue internationale de la Croix-Rouge* 729–56

ROACH, JA, 'The Law of Naval Warfare at the Turn of Two Centuries' (2000) 94(1) *American Journal of International Law* 64–77.

ROBINSON, D, 'War Crimes in Internal Conflicts: Article 8 of the ICC Statute' (1999) 2 *Yearbook of International Humanitarian Law* 193–209.

ROBERTS, A, 'What Is A Military Occupation?' (1984) 55 *British Yearbook of International Law* 249– 305.

——, 'Prolonged Military Occupation: The Israeli Occupied Territories since 1967' (1990) 84 *American Journal of International Law* 44–103.

ROBERTSON, HB, 'The Status of Civil Aircraft in Armed Conflict' (1997) 27 *Israel Yearbook on Human Rights* 113–50.

ROBINSON, D and VON HEBEL, H, 'War Crimes in Internal Conflict: Article 8 of the ICC Statute' (1999) *Yearbook of International Humanitarian Law* 193–209.

ROGERS, APV, 'Zero-casualty Warfare' (2000) 82(837) *Revue internationale de la Croix-Rouge* 165–81.

——, 'Unequal Combat and the Law of War' (2006) 7 *Yearbook of International Humanitarian Law* 3–34.

ROLF LÜDER, S, 'The Legal Nature of the ICC and the Emergence of Supranational Elements in International Criminal Justice' (2002) 84(845) *Revue internationale de la Croix-Rouge* 79–92.

RONZITTI, N, 'The 2006 Conflict in Lebanon and International Law' (2006) 16 *Italian Yearbook of International Law* 3–19.

ROSENNE, S, 'The Nuclear Weapons Advisory Opinions of 8 July 1996' (1997) 27 *Israel Yearbook on Human Rights* 263–308.

ROSS, J, 'Black-letter Abuse: The US Legal Response to Torture since 9/11' (2007) 89(867) *Revue internationale de la Croix-Rouge* 561–90.

ROSTOW, N, 'The World Health Organization, the International Court of Justice, and Nuclear Weapons' (1995) 20(1) *Yale Journal of International Law* 151–85.

de ROVER, C, 'Police and Security Forces: A New Interest for Human Rights and Humanitarian Law' (1999) 81(835) *Revue internationale de la Croix-Rouge* 637–47.

ROWE, P, 'Kosovo 1999, the Air Campaign: Have the Provisions of Additional Protocol I Withstood the Test?' (2000) 82(837) *Revue internationale de la Croix-Rouge* 147–64.

RUDESILL, DS, 'Precision War and Responsibility' (2007) 32(2) *Yale Journal of International Law* 517–45.

RUSSO, F, 'Targeting Theory in the Law of Naval Warfare' (1992) 40 *Naval Law Review* 1–43.

SALMON, EG, 'Reflections on International Humanitarian Law and Transitional Justice: Lessons to be Learnt from the Latin American Experience' (2006) 88(862) *Revue internationale de la Croix-Rouge* 327–53.

SANDOZ, Y, 'International Humanitarian Law in the Twenty-first Century' (2003) 6 *Yearbook of International Humanitarian Law* 3–40.

——, 'Max Huber and the Red Cross' (2007) 18(1) *European Journal of International Law* 171–97.

SASSOLI, M, 'The Status of Persons Held in Guantánamo under International Humanitarian Law' (2004) 2(1) *Journal of International Criminal Justice* 96–106.

——, 'Ius ad Bellum and Ius in Bello: The Separation between the Legality of the Use of Force and Humanitarian Rules to be Respected in Warfare' (2006) 15(6) *International Humanitarian Law Series* 241–64.

——, 'Terrorism and War' (2006) 4(5) *Journal of International Criminal Justice* 959–81.

SAURA ESTAPA, J, 'Lawful Peacekeeping: Applicability of International Humanitarian Law to United Nations Peacekeeping Operations' (2007) 58(3) *Hastings Law Journal* 479–531.

SCHABAS, WA, 'Lex specialis? Belt and Suspenders? The Parallel Operation of Human Rights Law and the Law of Armed Conflict, and the Conundrum of jus ad bellum' (2007) 40(2) *Israel Law Review* 592–613.

SCHINDLER, D, 'The Different Types of Armed Conflicts According to the Geneva Conventions and Protocols' (1979-II) 163 *Receuil des cours de l'Académie de droit international de La Haye* 119–63.

——, 'Significance of the Geneva Conventions for the Contemporary World' (1999) 81(836) *Revue internationale de la Croix-Rouge* 715–29.

SCHMITT, M, 'Green War: An Assessment of the Environmental Law of International Armed Conflict' (1997) 22(1) *Yale Journal of International Law* 1–109.

——, 'The Environmental Law of War: An Invitation to Critical Reexamination' (1997) 36(1/2) *Revue de droit militaire et de droit de la guerre* 11–53.

——, 'Bellum Americanum: The US View of Twenty-first Century War and its Possible Implications for the Law of Armed Conflict' (1998) 19(4) *Michigan Journal of International Law* 1051–90.

——, 'Future War and the Principle of Discrimination' (1998) 28 *Israel Yearbook on Human Rights* 51–90.

——, 'War and the Environment: Fault Lines in the Prescriptive Landscape' (1999) 37(1) *Archiv des Völkerrechts* 25–67.

——, 'Humanitarian Law and the Environment' (2000) 28(3) *Denver Journal of International Law and Policy* 265–323.

——, 'The Conduct of Hostilities during Operation Iraqi Freedom' (2003) 6 *Yearbook of International Humanitarian Law* 73–109.

——, 'Targeting and Humanitarian Law' (2004) 34 *Israel Yearbook on Human Rights* 59–104.

——, 'Humanitarian Law and Direct Participation in Hostilities by Private Contractors or Civilian Employees' (2005) 5(2) *Chicago Journal of International Law* 511–46.

——, 'Precision Aattack and International Humanitarian Law' (2005) 87(859) *Revue internationale de la Croix-Rouge* 445–66.

——, '21st Century Conflict: Can the Law Survive?' (2007) 8(2) *Melbourne Journal of International Law* 443–76.

SCHÖNDORF, RS, 'Extra-state Armed Conflicts' (2004) 37(1) *New York University Journal of International Law & Politics* 1–78.

SCHWABACH, A, 'Environmental Damage Resulting from the NATO Military Action against Yugoslavia' (2000) 25(1) *Columbia Journal of Environmental Law* 117–40.

SCHWEBEL, SM, 'The Roles of the Security Council and the International Court of Justice in the Application of International Humanitarian Law' (1995) 27(4) *New York University Journal of International Law & Politics* 731–59.

SEYBOLT, T, 'Major Armed Conflicts' (2001) *SIPRI Yearbook* 15–58.

SHABAS, W, 'Enforcing International Humanitarian Law: Catching the Accomplices' (2001) 83(842) *Revue internationale de la Croix-Rouge* 439–60.

——, 'Was Genocide Committed in Bosnia and Herzegovina? First Judgements of the ICTY' (2001) *Fordham International Law Journal* 23–53.

SHOTWELL, CB, 'Food and the Use of Force: The Role of Humanitarian Principles in the Persian Gulf Crisis and Beyond' (1991) 30(1–4) *Revue de Droit Militaire et de Droit de la Guerre* 345–85.

SHRAGA, D, 'UN Peacekeeping Operations: Applicability of International Humanitarian Law and Responsibility for Operations-related Damage' (2000) 94(2) *American Journal of International Law* 406–12.

SIMON, D, 'The Demolition of Homes in the Israeli Occupied Territories' (1994) 19(1) *Yale Journal of International Law* 1–79.

SIMONDS, SN, 'Conventional Warfare and Environmental Protection: A Proposal for International Legal Reform' (1992) 29(1) *Stanford Journal of International Law* 165–221.

SINHA, MK, 'Hinduism and International Humanitarian Law' (2005) 87(858) *Revue Internationale de la Croix-Rouge* 285–94.

SINJELA, M, 'The United Nations and Internal/International Conflicts in Africa: A Documentary Survey' (1998) 6 *African Yearbook of International Law* 289–363.

SING, S, 'Command Responsibility of Military and Civilian Superiors' (2006) *African Yearbook on International Humanitarian Law* 42–64.

SINGER, PW, 'Talk is Cheap: Getting Serious about Preventing Child Soldiers' (2004) 37(3) *Cornell International Law Journal* 561–86.

SOCHA, E, 'International Responsibility of Individuals for Breaches of Humanitarian Law' (2002–2003) 26 *Polish Yearbook of International Law* 67–84.

SOLOMON, N, 'Judaism and the Ethics of War' (2005) 87(858) *Revue internationale de la Croix-Rouge* 295–309.

SOMER, J, 'Jungle Justice: Passing Sentence on the Equality of Belligerents in Non-international Armed Conflict' (2007) 89(867) *Revue internationale de la Croix-Rouge* 655–90.

SPIEKER, H, 'The International Criminal Court and Non-international Armed Conflicts' (2000) 13(2) *Leiden Journal of International Law* 395–425.

——, 'Twenty-five Years after the Adoption of Additional Protocol II. Breakthrough or Failure of Humanitarian Legal Protection?' (2001) 4 *Yearbook of International Humanitarian Law* 129–66.

STEINHARDT, RG, 'International Humanitarian Law in the Courts of the United States' (2004) 36(1) *George Washington International Law Review* 1–46.

STEPHENS, D, 'The Law of Armed Conflict: A Contemporary Critique' (2005) 6(1) *Melbourne Journal of International Law* 55–85.

STEPENS, DG, 'Legal Aspects of Contemporary Naval Mines Warfare' (1999) 21(4) *Loyola of Los Angeles International and Comparative Law Journal* 553–90.

von STERNBERG, MR, 'The Plight of the Non-combatant in Civil War and the New Criteria for Refugee Status' (1997) 9(2) *International Journal of Refugee Law* 169–95.

SUPERVIELLE, MEF, 'Islam, the Law of War, and the US Soldier' (2005) 21(2) *American University International Law Review* 191–219.

SZPAK, A, 'Granting Judicial Protection to the Guantanamo Detainees by the American Courts' (2004/2005) 27 *Polish Yearbook of International Law* 105–29.

TARASOFSKY, RG, 'Legal Protection of the Environment during International Armed Conflict' (1993) 24 *Netherlands Yearbook of International Law* 17–79.

TAULBEE, JL, 'Mercenaries, Private Armies and Security Companies in Contemporary Policy' (2000) 37(4) *International Politics* 433–56.

TAWIL, S, 'International Humanitarian Law and Basic Education' (2000) 82(839) *Revue internationale de la Croix-Rouge* 581–600.

TERRY, JP, 'Moscow's Corruption of the Law of Armed Conflict' (2006) 53 *Naval Law Review* 73–210.

THÜRER, D, ,International Humanitarian Law: Essence and Perspectives' (2007) 17(2) *Schweizerische Zeitschrift für internationales und europäisches Recht* 157–64.

TITTEMORE, BD, 'Belligerent in Blue Helmets: Applying International Humanitarian Law to United Nations Peace Operations' (1997) 33(1) *Stanford Journal of International Law* 61–117.

TURN, D, 'Weapons in the ICRC Study on Customary International Humanitarian Law' (2006) 11(2) *Journal of Conflict and Security Law* 201–37.

VAGTS, DF, 'The Hague Conventions and Arms Control' (2000) 94(1) *American Journal of International Law* 31–41.

VACQUEZ, CM, 'The Military Commissions Act, the Geneva Conventions, and the Courts' (2007) 101(1) *American Journal of International Law* 73–98.

VERWEY, WD, 'Observations on the Legal Protection of the Environment in Times of International Armed Conflict' (1994) 7 *Hague Yearbook of International Law* 35–52.

——, 'Protection of the Environment in Times of Armed Conflict: in Search of a New Legal Perspective' (1995) 8(1) *Leiden Journal of International Law* 7–40.

——, 'The International Court of Justice and the Legality of Nuclear Weapons: Some Observations' in K WELLENS (ed), *International Law*, The Hague, Martinus Nijhoff, 1998, 751–63.

VILJOEN, F, 'Africa's Contribution to the Development of International Human Rights and Humanitarian Law' (2001) 1 *African Human Rights Law Journal* 18–39.

VINUESA, RE, 'Interface, Correspondence and Convergence of Human Rights and International Humanitarian Law' (1998) 1 *Yearbook of International Humanitarian Law* 69–110.

VIOTTI, A, 'In Search of Symbiosis: The Security Council in the Humanitarian Domain' (2007) 89(865) *Revue internationale de la Croix-Rouge* 131–62.

VITE, S, 'Applicability of the International Law of Military Occupation to the Activities of International Organizations' (2004) 86(853) *Revue internationale de la Croix-Rouge* 9–36.

VOON, T, 'Pointing the Finger: Civilian Casualties of the NATO Bombing in the Kosovo Conflict' (2001) 16(4) *American University International Law Review* 1083–113.

WALKER, GK, 'Information Warfare and Neutrality' (2000) 33(5) *Vanderbilt Journal of Transnational Law* 1079–202.

WATKIN, K, '21-century Conflict and International Humanitarian Law' (2006) 15(6) *International Humanitarian Law Series* 265–96.

——, 'Assessing Proportionality: Moral Complexity and Legal Rules' (2007) 8 *Yearbook of International Humanitarian Law* 3–53.

WEDGWOOD, R, 'The Use of Force in Civil Disputes' (1996) 26 *Israel Yearbook on Human Rights* 239–51.

——, 'Limiting the Use of Force in Civil Disputes' in D WIPPMAN (ed), *International Law and Ethnic Conflict*, Ithaca, NY, Cornell University Press, 1998, 242–55.

WEILL, S, 'The Judicial Arm of the Occupation: the Israeli Military Courts in the Occupied Territories' (2007) 89(866) *Revue internationale de la Croix-Rouge* 395–419.

WELLS, SL, 'Crimes against Child Soldiers in Armed Conflict Situations' (2004) 12 *Tulane Journal of International and Comparative Law* 287–306.

WICKER, B, 'When is a War not a War?' in R WILLIAMSON (ed), *Some Corner of a Foreign Field*, Basingstoke, Macmillan, 1998, 38–47.

WIEBE, V, 'Footprints of Death: Cluster Bombs as Indiscriminate Weapons under International Humanitarian Law' (2000) 22(1) *Michigan Journal of International Law* 85–167.

WIGGER, A, 'Encountering Perceptions in Parts of the Muslim World and their Impact on the ICRC's Ability to be Effective' (2005) 87(858) *Revue internationale de la Croix-Rouge* 343–65.

WILBERS, MTA, 'Sexual Abuse in Times of Armed Conflict' (1994) 7(2) *Leiden Journal of International Law* 43–71.

WILLMOTT, D, 'Removing the Distinction between International and Non-international Armed Conflict in the Rome Statute of the International Criminal Court' (2004) 5(1) *Melbourne Journal of International Law* 196–219.

YUZON, EFJ, 'Deliberate Environmental Modification through the Use of Chemical and Biological Eeapons: "Greening" the International Laws of Armed Conflict to Establish an Environmentally Protective Regime' (1996) 11(5) *American University International Law Review* 793–846.

ZACHARY, S, 'Between the Geneva Conventions: Where does the Unlawful Combatant Belong?' (2005) 38(1/2) *Israel Law Review* 378–417.

ZARATE, JC, 'The Emergence of a New Dog of War: Private International Security Companies, International Law, and the New World Disorder' (1998) 34(1) *Stanford Journal of International Law* 75–162.

el ZEIDY, MM, 'Islamic Law on Prisoners of War and its Relationship with International Humanitarian Law' (2004) 14 *Italian Yearbook of International Law* 53–81.

ZIEGLER, AR, 'Domestic Prosecution and International Cooperation with regard to Violations of International Humanitarian Law: The Case of Switzerland' (1997) 7(5) *Schweizerische Zeitschrift für internationales und europäisches Recht* 561–86.

ZIMMERMANN, A, 'The Second Lebanon War' (2007) 11 *Max Planck Yearbook of United Nations Law* 99–141.

ZWANENBURG, M, 'Existentialism in Iraq: Security Council Resolution 1483 and the Law of Occupation' (2004) 86(856) *Revue internationale de la Croix-Rouge* 745–69.

ZYBERI, G, 'The Development and Interpretation of International Human Rights and Humanitarian Law Rules and Principles through the Case-law of the International Court of Justice' (2007) 25(1) *Netherlands Quarterly of Human Rights* 117–39.

Italian

CASTELLANETA, M, 'La résponsabilità internazionale degli Stati per Danni all'ambiente causati nel corso di conflitti armati' (1998) 81(3) *Rivista di diritto internazionale* 632–72.

COLANDREA, V, 'L'attribuzione allo Stato delle gravi violazioni del diritto internazionale umanitario nella giurisprudenza della Eritrea Ethiopia Claims Commission' (2006) 61(4) *La comunità internazionale* 785–800.

CONDORELLI, L, 'L'inchiesta ed il rispetto degli obblighi di diritto internazionale umanitario' in G BADIALI (ed) *Scritti degli allievi in memoria di Giuseppe Barile*, Padova, CEDAM, 1994, 225–308.

CREMASCO, M, 'Il caso Somalia' in N RONZITTI (ed), *Commando e controllo nelle forze di pace e nelle coalizioni militari*, Milano, Franco Angeli., 1999, 173–204.

FARA, V, 'Regole di ingaggio, bandi militari e costituzioni' (2006) 2 *Diritto pubblico comparato ed europeo* 525–43.

GREPPI, E, 'Diritto internazionale umanitario dei conflitti armati e diritti umani: profile di una convergenza' (1996) 51(3) *La comunità internazionale* 473–98.

MAZZA, R, 'La protezione internazionale dei beni culturali mobili in caso di conflitto armato: possibili sviluppi' in P PAONE (ed), *La protezione internazionale e la circolazione comunitaria dei beni culturali mobili*, Napoli, Editoriale Scientifica, 1998, 119–38.

MERAVIGLIA, MF, 'Il diritto internazionale umanitario e i suoi processi di formazione' (1994) 7(3) *Rivista Internazionale di Diritti dell'Uomo* 425–93.

PICONE, P, 'La "guerra del Kosovo" e il diritto internazionale generale' (2000) 83(2) *Rivista di diritto internazionale* 309–60.

RONZITTI, N, 'La Corte internazionale di giustizia e la questione della liceità della minaccia o dell'uso delle armi nucleari' (1996) 79(4) *Rivista di diritto internazionale* 861–81.

SCOTTO, G, 'I bombardamenti a tutela delle zone di interdizione al volo in Iraq' in G ARANGIO-RUIZ (ed), *Studi di diritto internazionale in onore di Gaetano Arangio-Ruiz*, vol 3, Napoli, Editoriale Scientifica, 2004, 1723–44.

TANCA, A, 'Sulla qualificazione del conflitto nell'ex Iugoslavia' (1993) 76(1) *Rivista di Diritto Internazionale* 37–51.

Spanish

COMOTTO, S, 'Derecho internacional público derecho internacional humanitario y derecho internacional de los derechos humanos' (2004) 80 *Lecciones y ensayos* 415–40.

DINSTEIN, Y, 'International humanitarian law: Hacia un nuevo orden internacional y europeo' in M PÉREZ GONZÁLEZ (ed), *Estudios en homenaje al profesor don Manuel Diez de Velasco*, Madrid, Tecnos, 1993, 245–60.

FERNANDEZ-FLORES, JL, 'Planteamiento general de las infraccdiones del Derecho de la Guerra y consideración de las atribuibles a los Estados y a las organizaciones internacionales' in M PÉREZ GONZÁLEZ (ed), *Estudios en homenaje al professor don Manuel Diez de Velasco*, Madrid, Tecnos, 1993, 319–40.

MESA, R, 'Guerra y paz en oriente medio: el drama palestino' (1993) *Cursos de dercho internacional de Vitoria-Gasteiz* 265–335.

PELAEZ MARON, JM, 'El Derecho internacional humanitario antes y desputés de la sgunda guerra mundial' (1991) *Cursos de derecho internacional de Vitoria-Gasteiz* 61–93.

PEREZ, JP y ACEVEDO, L, 'Las reparaciones en el Derecho Internacional de los Derechos Humanos, Derecho Internacional Humanitario y Derecho Penal Internacional' (2007) 23(1) *American University International Law Review* 7–49.

RODRIGUEZ MACKAY, MA, 'Las vinculaciones del derecho internacional humanitario con el derecho internacional de los derechos humanos' (2005) 55(129) *Revista peruana de derecho internacional* 138–49.

INDEX